THE CULLOM LANTERN

Most cordially yours,

W. R. Cullom,

The Cullom Lantern

A Biography of

W. R. CULLOM OF WAKE FOREST

by

JAMES H. BLACKMORE

With an Introduction by OLIN T. BINKLEY

Raleigh

Edwards & Broughton Company

1963

Library of Congress Catalogue Card No. 63-22719

PRINTED IN THE UNITED STATES OF AMERICA BY
EDWARDS & BROUGHTON COMPANY, RALEIGH, N. C.

To
Edward, Elizabeth, Sarah,
and in memory of Nancy
for sharing their father
with the rest of us
who rise up to call him
blessed.

INTRODUCTION

Religion is often studied in terms of its theologies and institutions, and these studies are valuable. However, the essence and validity of religion are discoverable in the lives of men and women who participate responsibly in God's creative and redemptive action. Yet this aspect of religion is much neglected; we have a few great biographies, but their number is altogether too few.

The announcement that a biography of Dr. W. R. Cullom was to be written brought me a special pleasure, for I was aware of his outstanding work as a teacher at Wake Forest College where he gave me and thousands of others "the habitual vision of greatness." When first I entered his classroom in the fall of 1925, almost immediately I was impressed by his friendliness and the objectivity of his mind, both of which sprang out of a sincere devotion to God. Soon I discerned his sense of mission as a Christian teacher; here was a man called to develop the minds and hearts and souls of those who studied under him. Humble, systematic, deliberate and constructive in all that he taught, he never asked that his students agree with him, but in a gentle persuasion he led them to see truth for themselves. Alert to the world-wide Christian mission enterprise, he presented an interpretation of life informed by the mind of Christ and as broad in its context as the whole human family. In this broad context he manifested a growing knowledge of God as revealed in Jesus Christ so that there was never any uncertainty about the center of his theology and the commitment of his life. Students who failed to perceive this process of thought frequently considered him a dull teacher, but he stimulated and guided the intellectual and spiritual growth of students at teachable moments in the direction of Christian maturity. Later, in 1938, when I returned to Wake Forest to succeed him as head of the Department of Religion, I was able to renew the friendship he had offered me, and again in 1952 when I came to serve as teacher at the Southeastern Baptist Theological Seminary, I was happy to renew personal relationships with him for whom I had great admiration and devotion as a spiritual father.

From the first, I realized that the writing of Dr. Cullom's biography would be exceptionally difficult. The qualities of his mind and the depth and scope of his influence were hidden from a camera and not easily accessible to a scholarly writer. It would take a real artist to capture and portray the man. Fortunately, Dr. James Blackmore decided to do the job. In addition to a creative mind and an understanding heart, he brought to the task a sense of mission and a deep loyalty to one who was to him, as to very many others, both a teacher and a friend. He had studied under Dr. Cullom and across the years their friendship had grown rich and deep, and he was determined to present a true portrait. Upon his return from Scotland in 1951 where he earned the Ph.D. degree at the University of Edinburgh, Dr. Blackmore was called to the First Baptist Church of Spring Hope where Dr. Cullom had served his last pastorate and which shared the desire to extend the ministry of his life in a biography. From time to time I received progress reports, but with the responsibilities of the pastorate and of leadership in a dynamic denomination in the midst of rapid social change Dr. Blackmore was slowed down until in 1961 he resigned the office at Spring Hope in order to complete this work.

When I had the opportunity to read the second draft of Dr. Cullom's story, I was pleased to find that Dr. Blackmore had written more than a memorial biography of a man whom he had loved and appreciated. He had presented with discrimination and integrity the Christian witness in a life which never sought prominence but which sought to serve a Living Lord. As once when Dr. Cullom was honored with testimonials of his students and associates, the aged teacher replied: "If any of this is true, then here is an example of what the Lord can do with an ordinary fellow. And if the Lord could do this in me, doubtlessly He can do more in you."

After a careful examination of the primary sources, including candid conversations with "the living human documents," with psychological insight, remarkable literary ability, and Christian devotion, Dr. Blackmore has given us here a true record and a wise appraisal of Dr. Cullom's life and work in proper historical and cultural perspectives. In my judgment this work will stir treasured memories in the minds of Dr. Cullom's wide circle of students and friends and will do great good in our troubled world.

OLIN T. BINKLEY

September 1963
Wake Forest, N. C.

FOREWORD

I almost missed him. To the youth that I was in 1936, struggling for faith and infatuated with rationalism, the Bible professor seemed prosaic and dull.

Walt Smith caused me to take a second look at "Potty" Cullom. It was at the end of the first semester of my Junior year at Wake Forest College that I was asked what work had I taken under Dr. Cullom. When I replied that I had not taken any work under him and told why, Walt looked at me fiercely: "Jim, you are judging by the appearance and mannerisms of the man, and you are wrong. This man has a lot to teach you; you will be much the poorer by not knowing him."

And Walt was right. The contact that began somewhat reluctantly with the second part of Bible One has extended through two and a half decades and has had something of "eternity" in it.

Now, I want to share that friend with others—with those abroad who often get a distorted view of Americans—with our fellow Americans who sometimes judge Southern Baptists by our worst moments and by the queerest of our ten million members—with those of the younger generation who know all the bewildering changes of the new age and who need the faith which steadied men in the old. And yet, I must confess, there is another "motive" in writing Dr. Cullom's biography. At the risk of being misunderstood, I have to put it in the ancient language of the Hebrew writers: I was "moved by God" to do so. This I have had to do—putting aside many other things—not by reason or logic but by inner compulsion and divine command.

My first expression of gratitude, therefore, must be unto God—for strength and mind to finish the task to which He called me. My second "thank-you" is to Ruth, my wife, who has shared magnificently in this—in the sacrifice of husband and father from home, in the encouragement she has given, and in the typing of the manuscripts. The third appreciation is of Dr. Cullom himself—for his cooperation in making notes and in contacting friends, for his forbearance in the searching and the probing to which, at times, I have had to subject him, and for his reading the manuscript and making corrections and suggestions. I am indebted to Dr. Cullom's children—Elizabeth, Edward, Nancy, Sarah—to his nieces (especially Mrs. Marie Cullom Porter), and to Mr. Ed Farmer (Mrs. Cullom's brother). I owe some big debts: to President Olin T. Binkley of Southeastern Baptist Theological Seminary for writing the "Introduction," to Miss Kate Matthews of the *Biblical Recorder* Staff for proofreading the manuscript, to

Mrs. Elizabeth Cullom Kelly for advice on the treatment of family matters, to Mr. T. J. Graham, Jr., of Edwards & Broughton Co. for cutting a bulky manuscript to readable length, and to Dr. A. C. Reid of Wake Forest College for general advice and help. To the librarians and staff at Wake Forest College, at Southern Baptist Theological Seminary, at Southeastern Baptist Theological Seminary; to the editors of the *Biblical Recorder* and the *Charity and Children;* to so many men and women of his classes and churches that their name must be "Legion"; to the Baptist Church of Spring Hope who shared in this work for ten years and who, at last, let me go to finish it; to the many others whose names do not appear here but who have known and loved and helped Dr. Cullom—I am profoundly grateful.

This is not all of Dr. Cullom's story. For example, incidents of pastoral counseling are omitted, and we have limited his writings, with some exceptions, to those which appeared in the *Biblical Recorder* and the *Charity and Children.* Three revisions have reduced this work to a third of its original size, which means that many interesting stories and references to many fine people have been deleted.

In this study, we have not tried to prove anything or defend anybody. We have sought to record what happened. We love Dr. Cullom, and we love him enough to tell the truth about him. Many controversies and problems are presented here; they are not all solved, but it is hoped that some light is shed on them which will lead to their solution.

At a Young People's Assembly on the eve of the Southern Baptist Convention in Wilmington, 1897, Mr. John T. Pullen of Raleigh said: "Make your life a lantern in which the Word of God burns." This story of W. R. Cullom could be likened unto such a lantern; it is of the human framework—birth, trials, dreams, love, pain, disappointments, fears, friendships, work, joys, deaths, victories, sorrows—all that make up the human drama. But the light within the lantern is more than these. (Is it not that Light which is the light of the world?) And may the Light that has burned in this life brighten you who read this story. And more—may it burn in your lantern too.

But now the human drama, and the words of the Bard of Avon will clue us into that story.

JAMES H. BLACKMORE

Warsaw, North Carolina
September 4, 1963

*"And one man in his time plays many parts,
His acts being seven ages."*
SHAKESPEARE

"First, the infant . . ."
SHAKESPEARE

FIRST AGE

CHILDHOOD IN HALIFAX COUNTY

1867-1880

Beneath a gray sky, the wind raced across white fields and shook the green pines loaded with snow. It was cold. The man who stood under the shelter of the trees puffed little clouds of vapor and pulled the coat tighter over his graying beard. With stern determination, he lowered his head into the wind and started walking through the snow to a newly built house in the white field.

The house was of sawed timbers resting on rock pillars; smoke, rising from its chimney, was a friendly sign of life in a cold white world. There was a large window near the shingle roof, and at a smaller window lower down, the face of a little boy appeared for a moment.

The man knew his arrival was being announced. As he neared the house, a door to the side opened. A man, about twenty-eight years of age with black hair and dark eyes, came out; he stood five feet, ten inches and was thin with delicate features. He was followed by a boy of eight. With a clear, cheerful voice, the father called: "Hello. Kinda cold, ain't it?"

The older man replied, "Hello," as he shook the snow off his coat and rubbed the head of the eight-year-old boy.

Opening the door behind him, the younger man said, "Come in, Mr. Johnson; nothing's happened yet."

Mr. Johnson replied, "We hadn't heard from Mary for several days, and we figured that her time was drawing near. So I came up to see about her."

Mary was sitting beside the fireplace with a baby standing by her knee; two other small children were playing in front of the fire. She was a small woman of twenty-six years of age; her manner was very gentle and quiet.

Mr. Johnson made his way to the fire and, flipping up the tail of his coat, turned to warm himself; he looked about the room. It was a large plastered room with a nine-foot ceiling. In each corner beside the fireplace, there stood a poster bed on which were pillow shams and homemade quilts. At the other end of the room a small door opened onto a stairs which led to the loft and another door to a small room where the babies slept. An odor of burning oak filled the room.

The little two-year-old had come from her mother's knee and pulled at her grandfather's leg; Mr. Johnson reached down and lifted her into the air: "Jennie, do you want a little baby brother or a baby sister?"

Little Jennie replied, "I want some honey."

Mr. Cullom spoke loudly to his father-in-law, "Whenever the children see you, they always think of the honey you bring them." Then he began coughing, and taking the tobacco out of his mouth, he threw the wad into the fire.

The older man asked, "Have you caught cold, John?"

"No more than I have had, but I'm troubled with bronchitis."

"Well, you ought to stay out of this wind as much as you can. Is there something I can do for you while I'm here?"

"No, I don't think so; we've got the fire going in the kitchen for the children, and 'Aunt Susan' knows we are expecting any time now. I believe the baby will come tonight."

- 2 -

The baby was born on the night of January fifteenth, in the year of our Lord eighteen hundred and sixty-seven. They named him Willis Richard Cullom.

"Aunt Susan" Mills had assisted as midwife in the birth of the new baby. She was a tall, thin, Negro woman with a complexion lighter than gingerbread. She wore little glasses and tied her kinky graying hair in little patches with string. She had helped in the birth of all the Cullom children and generally stayed for a few days after each birth. The older children always welcomed her and cried when she left.

As Aunt Susan finished dressing the new baby in a long white dress, the children stood around her—a little suspicious and fearful. At last, little Nan asked the inevitable question, "Aunt Susan, are you going to leave us today?"

The gentle Negro woman replied, "We'll see about it. You're near 'bout old enough to look after your little baby brother yourself, ain't you?" Then giving the infant to his mother, she reached for the box cradle and picking it up said, "Let's show de new baby de kitchen; why, he ain't never seen it in his whole life."

The kitchen was several yards away from the "great house." It was of hewn logs with a large fireplace at one end. Simpler than the main house, it was only one story and built closer to the ground; yet most of the living of the family took place in it.

Outside the snow was melting, but it was not spring yet. The air was fresh and keen. The young mother, holding her new born baby close to her, pulled her black shawl over him.

A hot fire was roaring in the big fireplace in the kitchen. Large, black, iron pots sat on the hearth, and a large kettle of water sang over the fire. Bunches of sage and red peppers added scent and color to the room. The windows were small and high so that except for the fire the room would have been dark. But now warm, bright light danced on the large wooden table and the benches; it reached to the loom and spinning wheel which had been pushed back into the corner. Aunt Susan set the box cradle down near the fire, and the young mother placed the baby snugly in it.

Dressed in a long, dark dress of coarsely made cloth and with her black hair combed tightly and knotted in the back, Mrs. Cullom scanned the room; going to the loom, she fingered the coarse thread: "I must finish this cloth soon now, for the children will soon need new clothes." Then turning back to Aunt Susan, she said, "I feel like I'm going to be all right now, but I wish you would bring in a bucket of water before you go."

Aunt Susan took a large wooden bucket from the side table and went out the open door to the well, over which hung another bucket fastened to a long pole. Pulling the bucket down into the water, she submerged it; and releasing her hold on it, the weight at the other end of the pole brought the bucket back to her reach. Coming back into the kitchen she asked, "Do you reckon, Miss Mary, dat you be strong enough to milk dem four cows?"

The young mother was already stirring the pots and without looking up replied, "Oh, yes, I'll get along all right. But if I need you I'll send for you." Glancing at the sun's ray on the floor, she murmured half aloud, "I'm late; I must cut some meat and make the cornbread to go with those peas." So the young mother hurried with the tasks which had occupied much of the time of women from the beginning of time; to her it was good to be back in her own kitchen working for those she loved.

When the sun's ray reached a certain crack on the floor, she remarked to the children, "It is time to call your father in to wash up for dinner." Going to the door, she took down from the wall a cow's horn, and placing it to her lips blew two clear blasts. Replacing the horn, she returned to the fire to turn the bread and to stir the pot. She smiled in satisfaction—dinner would be on time.

When Mr. Cullom came up, there was a Negro man with him. At one time he had been a slave, but now with his new freedom he had hired himself to work for a wage; he had been cutting wood. After washing his hands in a pan of cold water at the washbench, Mr. Cullom went to the box cradle and with his finger nudged his infant son. "How is the little Major doing?"

Little Jennie, not to be overlooked, came up beside him and peeping in at her new brother said, "He sleeps all the time."

With dinner on the table, the young family took their places around it. The mother called to the hired man outside, "Come on in to the fire, Tom; I'll fix your dinner after grace is said." And taking her place on a stool at the end of the table, she bowed her head as her husband said, "Oh, Lord, make us thankful for what we are about to receive. Amen."

- 3 -

The wind blew outside, but it was nice and warm in the "great house." In the fireplace an oak fire burned brightly, casting fantastic shadows about the room.

Charlie did not mind the shadows now, for he was eleven years old; nor did Sis who was ten. Nan sat quite independently in a chair, for a seven-year-old girl was not afraid very much. But Jennie stood close by her mother who was sewing scraps of cloth for a quilt, and Willis was nestled in his father's lap. Since his mother was busy caring for little Lucy, Willis, now three, had taken to his father.

The fire burned brightly, and the shadows—whatever they were of the past or future—seemed taken care of as long as little Willis could feel his father's arms about him. He heard his father's talking and the occasional question or comment from his brother or one of his sisters; he did not understand what they were saying, but they were all familiar, beloved voices which made him happy and content.

"Now when the thirteen colonies won their freedom," Mr. Cullom was saying, "they soon learned that independence has troubles too. Willie Jones came home from Philadelphia saying that the Continental Congress had served its purpose in coordinating the war effort, and for a time he was able to persuade the State Convention to reject the Federal Constitution. Mr. Jones never joined the Union; he even refused to welcome President Washington to Halifax, saying he would be glad to meet Mr. Washington as a gentleman and soldier—but as President of the United States, never! However, Mr. Jones shared in welcoming another distinguished guest to Halifax—General Lafayette from France; they had a grand ball for him. Everything seemed prosperous and peaceful then, but a dark storm was gathering."

Mr. Cullom shifted Willis and continued. "Some of our people had been troubled for a long time about having slaves, but the political agitation had silenced all talk in the South about freeing them. When Abraham Lincoln was elected as an Abolitionist President in 1860, most of the southern states seceded from the Union. Our state waited. When Mr. Lincoln tried to send reinforcements to Fort Sumter in the Charleston harbor of South Carolina, the Confederate forces demanded that the fort surrender. When the Union officers refused, the Confederates began bombarding the fort and, on April 12th, captured it. Mr. Lincoln called on North Carolina to furnish its quota of volunteers to put down 'the rebellion in the South,' as he called it. Virginia declared that no 'army of abolitionists under Abraham Lincoln' was going to cross its land. Within three days after the fall of Fort Sumter, thousands of men in North Carolina volunteered to defend our State. It was a sad time for many people, but they had to choose. On

May 20, 1861, a special convention in Raleigh voted North Carolina out of the Union."

Mrs. Cullom got up and put Jennie to bed. Then she sat back down, got some snuff, and took Nan in her lap. Mr. Cullom continued: "Camps appeared all over the country, and our men were called to do their part. You, Charlie, were about two and a half years old and Sis wasn't a year old. One day my brother, Jim, came and said he would go in my place so I could stay here and look after you children. He was too young to be drafted; so he volunteered to take my place. The war was terrible; the Yankees blockaded our harbors, and we didn't have the supplies we needed. But we fought on. Sometimes it looked like we might win, and then again it didn't. News was scarce and rumors were aplenty. In time we heard of Manassas, Sharpsburg, Gettysburg; then Vicksburg, Chattanooga, Atlanta. While General Lee held Grant in Virginia, Sherman marched through Georgia, looted and laid waste a path of destruction through the Carolinas. Lee fell back at Petersburg and, on April 3, 1865, abandoned Richmond. Here at home, General Baker marched his little army out of Weldon toward Raleigh to join General Johnston, when news came that Lee had surrendered; then at Earpsboro, they learned that General Johnston had surrendered to General Sherman. The war was over; the South lay in ruins and desolation. When Jim came home, he was starved and exhausted."

Mr. Cullom paused a moment, and then continued. "After Mr. Lincoln was assassinated, the Federal Congress seemed bent on taking revenge on the South; they gave the ballot to Negroes and denied it to the white people—except for the Yankee carpetbaggers who came to suck the blood out of our defeated country and the scalawags who joined in feasting on her carcass. Year before last, a former slave was sent up to represent our county at Raleigh, where many in our legislature can neither read nor write. Last year General Grant was elected president of the United States, and God only knows what is ahead of us."

Mr. Cullom looked down upon his children. Only Charlie was still awake.

"We'll drive the Yankees away," Charlie cried.

"No," replied the mother. "We've had enough of war. Now let's go to bed; tomorrow will be another day—and let's pray it will be a better one."

"Yes," said Mr. Cullom; "let's pray so." Then to his son asleep in his arms, he said, "Say, Little Major, you have not heard a word I've said. Here in Halifax County where so much has happened, you'll grow up without knowing a bit about it."

He arose and, with Willis still in his arms, went toward the small room.

- 4 -

Soft young feet touched the bare wooden floor and hurried across its wide planks. A chubby boy of five, dressed in long white flannel underclothes, came into the room where the first tint of dawn lightened the sleeping forms of his parents. But the little boy did not go to either of them; rather he went to the fireplace.

With a wooden poker, the little fellow raked the ashes off the coals and placed some fat-lightwood splinters on them. Down on his hands and knees, he blew on the coals. With his second breath, a curl of smoke arose with a fragrant pleasing odor; a thin blue flame danced into a red tongue and then flashed into a yellow fire. The little boy felt its warm glow on his face; he felt a warm pride in his heart. He had built a fire!

It was little Willis' first conscious impression to be remembered through many years. He remembers blowing on the coals and the fire dancing out; he remembers the warm glow in his heart as he put forth his hands.

Although the kindling of fires was not the ordinary task for a five-year-old boy, there were duties for Willis early in the Cullom home. He had to hold the cow's tail while his mother milked; he gathered chips from the woodpile and helped Charlie feed the mules. He shooed the flies off the freshly cut apples which had been spread out to dry and watched out for little Lucy or the new baby whom they called "Tulie." There was always something to do and plenty to learn. Just when he was beginning to know his way around the big house, the kitchen, the yard and the barn, he was introduced to a big new world outside the Cullom domain.

- 5 -

It was Sunday, and a special Sunday it was; it was preaching Sunday. Yes, it was the Sunday that they had preaching at Old Ebenezer Methodist Episcopal Church (South), and the Cullom family had been up before day getting ready for it.

Charlie and his father had fed "Old Pat" (the horse) hours ago; now she was curried and hitched to the buggy. Sis and Nan had helped Ma fix breakfast and get dinner cooked; now they were dressing themselves. Jennie, Willis and Lucy had been dressed a long time. The girls wore calico dresses, while Willis wore a pair of home-made trousers buttoned to a little white jacket; they all wore straw hats and were barefooted. Fearing to sit down lest they wrinkle their clothes, the children just stood like "Old Pat" and waited.

At last, Sis and Nan emerged from the "great house," and then

Ma with little Tulie in her arms. Ma wore a plain calico dress, dragging the ground and hiding her high-topped shoes except for the toes; she had a black bonnet on her head. The baby was covered in a long white dress.

Dressed in a black suit, tie and white shirt, Mr. Cullom assigned everyone a place; Charlie and Sis were to stand on the back axle, and Nan was to sit in the back-bottom. Next, Mrs. Cullom sat on the seat and Tulie was handed to her. Jennie and Willis sat on some old quilts on the floor board, and little Lucy took her place, standing in the middle beside her mother. Mr. Cullom squeezed into the seat, and called to the horse.

When they came to Grandpa Johnson's house, his dog, "Boston," came out to bark at them. They saw buggy-tracks leading out of the yard; so they knew Grandpa already had gone. After crossing old Quankie Creek, they approached Mr. Joe Butts's house. (Mr. Cullom was cousin to Mr. Butts; together they operated a cotton gin.) As the buggy neared his house, several children ran out of the yard and waved to them. Next, they passed Mr. Jim Dickens' log cabin. By that time Jennie's foot had started hurting Willis' hip; so Willis and Lucy changed places—except, Willis stood between his father's legs and helped drive. Somewhere on down the road between Mr. Tom Pender's and Mr. John Bert's, Willis crawled up on his father's lap and went to sleep. When he awoke, his mother had opened the "reticule" (as their lunch box was called) and was passing out biscuits. Almost before his eyes were open, he was eating his.

After a biscuit apiece, the box was put back under the seat, and the crumbs were brushed away by the time they saw the one-room, frame church building. It sat in an oak grove. Many people were already there; the yard was filled with buggies, and more were still coming. Mr. Cullom was tipping his hat this way and that way, and Mrs. Cullom was smiling all around. Charlie and Sis were looking for their friends, but the younger children just looked scared. Willis had never seen so many people before; he didn't know that in all the world there were so many.

Grandpa Johnson and another man came up to the buggy and helped them unload; Lucy cried when the man took her, and Willis was just about to do so when Charlie came beside him. They unhitched "Old Pat" and tied her to the branch of a young tree. Everybody seemed to be talking all at once: the menfolk about horses and the women about babies. Willis was bewildered; Charlie took his hand. When a crowd of bigger boys gathered around, one of them laughed at him and said he was so fat that he looked like a butterball. Willis clung tighter to Charlie's hand and tried to hide behind him. Another boy said, "Don't scare the little fellow; if you crook your finger at him now, he'll be bawling for his Ma."

Other buggies brought more excitement and more people. Then a special one turned in, and a hush came over the crowd. "It's the preacher." Willis looked up. A man, clean-shaven and dressed in black, was stopping his horse. As soon as the men stepped up to his horse's head, he stood up. He was tall. In a deep voice, he said, "Good morning." The people replied almost in chorus: "Good morning, Doctor Burton." The minister turned neither right nor left but headed straight for the church. The people followed him inside.

The church was plain; its pews were handmade as were its altar and pulpit. Behind the pulpit were three high-backed chairs. Mr. Cullom brought his family inside, but he left Mrs. Cullom and the younger children on one side, while he and Charlie sat across the aisle. Grandpa Johnson stood down at the front; suddenly he started singing, "Jesus Lover of My Soul," and everybody joined in, "Let me to Thy bosom fly." Willis was startled; he had never heard such a thing before; some babies cried. The hymn was slow and was sung with great feeling. Some older people cried too.

The preacher stood up and talked with his head thrown back and his eyes closed; then he read out of the big black book. When he finished, he drank some water from a glass which was on the table near the big book. Grandpa Johnson got up and held the tuning fork to his ear; then he started, "There is a fountain filled with blood, drawn from Immanuel's veins."

When they all sat down, two men passed plates around, and some people put money in them. Then the preacher got up, cleared his throat and started talking; this time with his eyes open. It was very quiet in the church; the sun was shining brightly through the windows; everything seemed all right. When Willis kicked his bare foot against the seat just to do something, his mother put a firm hand on his leg. He sat perfectly still for awhile; then he laid his head against his mother and went to sleep.

- 6 -

Willis might not have heard much of Dr. Burton's sermon, but he learned to preach from him. In a wooded grove about a hundred yards from the chimney of the "great house," Willis built himself a pulpit. At first he had used a stump, but at the age of six he had a better pulpit; he had driven two posts into the ground and had put a plank across the top. By now he had been to churches many times, although they didn't have preaching at Ebenezer but once a month and the Cullom family missed that quite often.

Nevertheless, Willis knew what to do; he "histed" the hymns, closed his eyes to pray and waved his arms to preach. At first, he had been ashamed for anyone to see him, but now his sisters played as if they were the mothers and fathers and brought corncobs as their babies.

Sis and Nan didn't play much because they had to help Ma with the house and the new baby, Jim; but Jennie, Lucy, Tulie and their "babies" were faithful members.

This was his favorite game—this make-believe he was a preacher. Yet at times it seemed he wasn't playing at all, but that it was very real. Sometime while he was thus re-enacting the parson of Ebenezer Methodist Church, Willis slipped through an open door unto God and knew in his heart that someday he would be a real preacher. However, now there were tasks and excitement which took him from his pulpit, as when his mother called out: "Willis, Willis, there is a chicken in the garden."

The little chubby preacher and his congregation would leave their devotions and come running out of the woods to capture the evil intruder. They rushed across the yard to the garden on the east side of the house; pushing open the gate of the rail fence, the little band of "minutemen" soon sighted the enemy who flew to the corner. When they closed in, the old hen ruffled her feathers and flew up over them and out.

"She's out, Ma," the children cried triumphantly. However, when they came back in the yard where their mother was putting dinner on a table under a mulberry tree, they saw the same old hen eating mulberries off the ground. She was sassily clucking as if to say— "Didn't catch me—didn't even touch me." Willis kicked his foot at her—"Shoo! you old chicken."

His mother put down a covered bowl on the large wooden table. "I'll have to cut her wings or she'll eat up my cabbage. Go wash up, children; your father and Charlie will be here any time now."

They ran to the water-stand by the kitchen door and dipped water with a gourd from a large oaken bucket to pour over their hands. They saw their father and Charlie at the well; so they hurried back to the table under the mulberry tree.

The mulberry tree was large and gave a nice shade; in the summer-time the Cullom family ate under it. It was a little more trouble for Mrs. Cullom and the girls, but it was nice to eat away from the big fire over which they had to cook. Maybe some day they could have a dining room, but for the present it was quite all right.

The children bowed their heads, as their father returned thanks. Then Mr. Cullom helped himself to the boiled potatoes and cabbage; he forked a piece of fat meat and broke off a large piece of corn-bread. Charlie helped himself, as Sis poured milk for all of them. Across the table Nan was waving the fly-broom, a stick with paper strips fastened to it. Mrs. Cullom was fixing the plates for the younger children; little Jim cried from the box cradle, and she sent Nan over to see about him. Willis was eating his meat like a big boy now, for his father had promised to take him to Weldon when he was a little bigger.

- 7 -

Mr. Cullom made the trip to Weldon about twice a year; as all the children could not go at one time, they took turns. Willis long remembered his first trip.

He and his father left home before day. His mother had loaded the wagon with eggs and butter, which she hoped her husband could trade for some of the necessities her hands could not supply. As they went by the Morecocks', they didn't see anyone stirring. A mile or so farther, they passed Sheriff Brickel's big house; all was quiet there too, except the dogs. At Dr. Pierce's, they saw a light in a window and some smoke rising from the kitchen chimney.

When they came to the crossroad, Mr. Cullom said, "Now that road (pointing ahead) goes to Halifax, but we'll turn here." And he turned "Old Pat" onto the road at the left. Shortly they came to Marsh Swamp which had a log bridge over the main stream. On down the road was Pierce Methodist Church on the right. Then they passed Mr. Branch's, and then to Day's crossroad. Next came the fairgrounds on the right and the railroad tracks. As they approached the railroad, Willis noticed that his father kept looking and listening and that "Old Pat's" ears were turned straight ahead. "This is the longest railroad in the world," his father declared as they bumped across the tracks; "it runs all the way from Weldon to Wilmington."

In 1874, Weldon (first called Weldon's Orchard) was a town of four or five hundred people; it was the center of four important railroads. The first of its railroads had been built in 1832 from Petersburg; the second was laid in 1834 from Norfolk; the third was completed to Wilmington in 1840, and the fourth was connected with the Raleigh-Gaston railroad in 1855. The war between the states had dealt the town quite a blow, from which it was slowly reviving. Mr. Cullom drove down its muddy street, while Willis looked in amazement from side to side. There were several general merchandise stores, a hotel or two, many saloons, a post office and down the street a little Baptist church.

Mr. Cullom turned in at Jim Gooch's general merchandise store; at the back, he unhitched his horse and tied her so she could eat the hay out of the back of the wagon. Willis helped him carry the butter and eggs in the store, and what an exciting place he found that store! It had everything—calico, white goods, meat, flour, molasses, shoes, hats, trousers, plow-points, plow-lines, matches, candy. Willis' eyes grew big. Mr. Gooch came to wait on them; he spoke to Mr. Cullom and took the eggs. After counting them, he took the butter, and wrote the amount down and gave the paper to Mr. Cullom. "If you hurry, you might show the little boy the trains as they pull out."

O, yes, thought Willis; I do want to see the trains. His father took his hand, and they hurried down the muddy street to the train shed which extended out to the tracks with the top open for the smoke from the engines.

As father and little chubby son came rushing up to it, four wood-eating engines were ready to go; they seemed like big fire-blowing monsters. Willis drew back. People were shouting and waving to each other. Suddenly someone rang a bell; four whistles blew. Children cried, and horses neighed. Willis hid behind his father, as the iron monsters began snorting and puffing out of the station. Willis was glad when they were gone; his father just laughed and released his hand. "Reckon we had just as well go now and see Brother Jim while we are down here."

"Uncle Jim" Cullom lived on the other side of the train shed; he kept a saloon. He was a very quiet and mild-mannered man. Part of the time he looked after the water tank for the railroad; he also traded horses.

After a short visit, Willis and his father went to the post office on Main or Church Street. Mr. Cullom stepped up to the window: "How-do-you-do, Mrs. Evans; does anybody out my way have any mail?" "Why, how-do-you-do, Mr. Cullom. Yes, I believe so; let me look." In a few minutes she returned. "Yes, here is your *Petersburg Messenger* and a letter for Dr. Pierce and an almanac for Captain Morecock." "Thank you, ma'am." Taking the mail and putting it carefully in his pocket, Mr. Cullom returned to Jim Gooch's store.

A group of men were sitting around a large pot-bellied stove; some were whittling; all of them were chewing tobacco. One fellow was quite angry: "I'll tell you right now if that young man comes up to my house to buggy-ride my girls, I'll tar and feather him."

Mr. Gooch came to Mr. Cullom. "Did the boy see the trains?"

"Yes, he did, but I think they scared him," replied Mr. Cullom.

"They do make a lot of noise; don't they, son? Well, now what will you be wanting for your eggs and butter, Mr. Cullom?"

As Mr. Cullom looked for the paper in his pocket, Willis heard the men around the stove laugh; then he saw one fellow hit at another. The others parted them, and Mr. Gooch told them to go outside to settle it. As the crowd of men went out, Willis looked at his father.

"No, son, that's none of our business. We'll get our rations and go home." Then turning to Mr. Gooch he said, "I need some salt, a little sugar, a can of lye, two plugs of Brown Mule, a gullet of Railroad Mill, two needles and a spool of black thread. Reckon you can put in a nickel's worth of peppermint. And do you have any coffee?"

"No, I don't; I think Ed Clark still has some. We are clean sold out," replied Mr. Gooch.

"I reckon you had better give me some new plow-lines, and a Dunn plow-point," added Mr. Cullom.

- 8 -

The years of Reconstruction in the South did not offer many opportunities for schooling. Yet here and there throughout the land there were tender souls, like "Miss Lizzie" Morecock who felt those difficulties were no excuse for coarseness and who tried to teach the young some appreciation of the better things of life. On the Sundays when they didn't have preaching, this young daughter of Captain Morecock who lived across the road from the Culloms, invited the Cullom children to come over to their log schoolhouse where she taught them to sing hymns and read them Bible stories. Willis memorized the twenty-third Psalm under her encouragement.

But this was only the beginning of lessons. Willis had to learn to read and to write. As there seemed little time for such lessons in the Cullom home, arrangements were made for Mr. Cullom's sister, Amanda, to teach Nan and Willis. This unmarried aunt lived with Grandpa and Grandma Cullom in their log cabin about four miles from Willis' home.

Early one Monday morning as Nan and Willis were walking along, Nan jumped and hollered. Willis thought he had to do the same and landed almost on top of a snake. "It's a spreading adder; look out!" cried Nan. Willis jumped again, and the snake crawled off into the cotton patch.

They were still frightened when they reached the log cabin where Grandpa and Grandma Cullom lived. This simple log cabin had a lean-to or shed-room added on the back; it also had a porch on the front. It was well constructed and built out of the best of pine logs; the top was of hand-drawn shingles. Smoke curled lazily out of one of its chimneys.

Grandpa was at the barn, hitching up a poor old horse to a wagon; the horse was bony and had sores on her shoulder. Grandpa Cullom was rather tall, clean-shaven and toothless; what showed of his hair from under his old hat was gray. He was cursing his old horse for stepping on the plow-line when the children walked up. Nan and Willis didn't know what to say; so they just stood there until he saw them and said, "Well, hello; how are you all getting along over at Joe John's?"

"We are tolerable, except Ma; it's about time for her again," replied Nan in the language of her elders.

"And Charlie's gone off to Weldon to work in the store for Uncle Jim," added Willis.

"Well, go on in the house," replied the elderly man; "you can help Manda and Mag finish the washing."

The children turned toward the house; they were not happy here. Grandma was often fussing at Aunt Manda and Aunt Mag, and from Monday until Friday was a long time to be away from home. In fact, the children were often homesick, but they were scared to say anything about it. As they approached the house, little Willis reached into his pocket and pulled out a handful of dirt.

"What have you got that in your pocket for?" asked Nan.

Tears welled up in Willis' eyes. "It's some dirt from home," he sobbed.

For a moment Nan was at a loss for words; then she replied, "Well, you had better not let Grandma see it."

When they went in through the open door, they saw their small, old grandmother squeezing water out of the clothes. Aunt Manda was dipping water from a large pot over the fire, and Aunt Mag was holding the bucket for her. "Well, look who's here," called Aunt Mag.

"Nan and Willis," exclaimed Grandma; "did your feet get wet coming across the creek? If they did, you had better come up to the fire and dry them."

The children came up to the fire. "Thank you, ma'am," replied Nan; "can I help you?"

"We are about through," replied Aunt Manda. "Do you know your spelling, Willis?"

"Yes, ma'am," replied little Willis.

"Well, we'll see about that," retorted the maiden aunt.

After a moment of silence, Nan spoke up: "Father said to tell you that he'll come after us Friday and bring some rations for what we've ate."

"Well, we can use it," replied Aunt Manda. "Run and take your coat up to the loft, Willis."

The little fellow laid down his speller on the table and moved quickly across the room to the ladder which led up to the loft where he slept.

"Nan, you sweep out the office; by that time, I'll be through dipping out this water, and Ma and Mag can hang up the clothes."

- 9 -

Aunt Manda took Willis through Webster's blue-back speller; by that time he was ready for another teacher. But as a boy of eight, he was also big enough to help with the field work. He was a good ploughboy and helped his father plow out the corn and cotton by the last of July so he could go to school before fodder-pulling time.

For a while, Willis went to Captain Brickel's school. Captain Brickel was a sick man; he had tuberculosis. Sometimes he would have an attack at school and would have to lie down on a bench while Joe Butts and some of the older boys would rub him.

Late in the summer of 1875, a Mr. Williams was hired to teach the neighborhood children in the log-office in Dr. Pierce's yard. Charlie was back home that summer; when the work was caught up, he, too, went over to the Pierce's school.

One morning Willis left home for school before Charlie was ready; he walked directly across in front of their home to join his companion, Dave Morecock. When they reached the log-office, which was about two and a half miles from their home, school already had taken in. To Willis' surprise, Charlie was there.

The class which Mr. Williams taught was composed of all ages and sizes, from nearly grown young men to little seven-year-old girls. Mr. Williams taught everything from counting to algebra, from the A.B.C.'s to Latin. At the recess period, Mr. Williams called Willis and Dave aside to inquire of their tardiness. "Willis," began Mr. Williams, "your brother tells me that you left home before he did, and yet he got here first; how did that happen?"

Willis thought that Charlie must have cut through the fields and run part of the way, but his lips tightened and he replied timidly, "I kept a steady gait, Mr. Williams."

"But how did he beat you here?" repeated the teacher.

"I don't know, sir; I kept a steady gait."

Mr. Williams replied, "Did you stop along the way?"

"No, sir, I kept a steady gait." Willis' head was low and his voice trembled.

"Well," concluded Mr. Williams, "see that you keep that steady gait." And he told the two boys they could go out to play.

- 10 -

One afternoon when he returned home from school, Willis saw a strange buggy in the yard, and there was a strange horse in the barn. Somebody had come to see them.

Under the mulberry tree, two men dressed in black suits were talking to the parents; they were preachers. They were saying that the Cullom children should be baptized. Mr. Cullom was against it.

The preachers stayed for supper. After talking about the crops, they returned to the subject of baptism for the children. Willis excused himself to get his lessons. They were still talking when he went to bed.

The next morning after breakfast, one of the preachers asked Mr. Cullom what he had decided to do about the souls of his precious children. While Mr. Cullom hesitated in answering, the other preacher said, "Brother Cullom, why don't you let us baptize them before we go; if it doesn't do any good, it won't do any harm. When they grow up, they can either confirm it or reject it."

On that basis, Mr. Cullom gave his consent. Early in the morning before Willis left for school, the preachers baptized the Cullom children.

Willis saw the preachers begin by taking his baby brother and pouring water out of a pitcher on his head. "I baptize thee, John Wesley Cullom, in the name of the Father, the Son and the Holy Ghost. Amen."

A little later that same morning, Willis hurried to meet Dave who was waiting for him by the road. "Dave, Dave," he cried out; "I've been baptized."

"You've been what?" asked his friend.

"I've been baptized," replied Willis. And pulling off his cap, he pointed to his head. "See where the water ran down."

Dave looked closely where Willis was pointing, but he did not see anything. The ceremony which meant so much to the preachers was quite vague to the boys, as they went down the road toward school. They did not understand it; nor were they encouraged to seek its meaning.

At school there was no time or place for religious instruction; reading and writing filled the day. It was not a matter of anyone's opposing religion in school; rather the attitude seems to have been that one "got religion" at church and "got larnin' " at school. So complete was this separation that Willis never heard a prayer offered in the classroom.

Nor was there any kind of regular religious teaching in his home. A prayer of gratitude was made before every meal, and his parents read the Bible as they had time and inclination. The children were taught to say their prayers before going to bed, but rarely was the whole family assembled for devotional purposes.

It would be a mistake to think that religion was lightly esteemed in the Cullom home. Rather, so precious a treasure was regarded as a personal and intimate matter. For example, the Cullom parents considered baptism something between a person and his Maker, and they had hesitated to invade that holy of holies of their children's conscience. Rather than an indifference, it was a matter of respect. Perhaps there could have been more formal religious instruction in the home, but from their parents the children seem to have caught a religious appetite which would enable them to develop spiritually on their own initiative.

Thus little Willis, who had not understood much of the baptismal service, began reading the New Testament for himself. Up by four o'clock in the morning to feed "Old Pat" and "Mule Pat," he read book after book of the Christian scriptures. When he finished, he began all over again.

- 11 -

The thirst for knowledge and religious understanding was only beginning when Willis reached the age of ten. He was still inclined to be chubby and timid. As he was getting too big to ride around on sourwood switches and as he did not care much for playing "cat," many a recess was spent in reading or talking seriously with his classmates.

One winter an Englishman, Mr. Garland, was employed by Mr.

Cullom and the neighbors to teach in a log cabin which Mr. Cullom had built about three hundred yards west of the Cullom home. It was set in a grove of oak trees out in a field. Mr. Garland was tall and slim; he was a good teacher. But he became an alcoholic, and they had to let him go.

In the meantime, Willis took up teaching himself; as a boy of eleven years old, he was hired as a teacher. That summer, a seventeen-year-old Negro boy, named Henry Fields, worked for Mr. Cullom. Henry was a bright, good-natured youth of light complexion, with "beautiful, bright sparkling eyes." One day as they worked out in the field, Henry said he wished he could read.

"Well," replied Willis, "I'll teach you."

"Yo' will? How much yo' goin' charge me?" asked Henry eagerly.

"I don't know. How much will you pay me?" replied Willis.

Henry thought a moment. He wanted so much to know how to read, but he did not have much to offer. He hesitated and then slowly ventured: "Will ten cent a month be 'nough?"

"Ten cents a month?" exclaimed Willis. "Why, yes, that will be fine, and we'll begin tonight right after supper."

The boys could hardly wait until supper was over. They stood around in the kitchen as the women finished cleaning up. At last Ma and the girls left for the "great house," leaving the kitchen to them. Willis, holding Webster's blue-back speller under his arm, took his mother's stool and sat down in front of the dying fire. Stirring the coals, he put on some chips and told Henry to bring a piece or two of wood.

After getting the fire to burn, the barefoot Negro youth went to the corner of the room and, reaching up to the rafters, pulled down a bundle of wraps and bedclothes. Returning to the fireplace he spread them out in a pallet beside Willis' stool.

"Looks like you are getting ready to go to bed, instead of learning," observed Willis.

"O, no," replied Henry as he sat down on the pallet. "I's jest makin' larnin' as easy as I's can." And his beautiful white teeth showed through his big grin.

"Well, I tell you right now, it's not easy and you've got to put your mind on it," said the teacher.

"Yas, sur; I'll put me mind on it," the Negro youth replied with serious determination.

Willis turned the book so that the light from the fire would fall on its pages; it was Webster's Elementary Spelling Book. As he opened the book, Henry moved closer so he, too, could see. "Do you know all dat's in dere?" he asked in amazement.

"Yes, I do," replied Willis with confidence. As if to prove it and to quell any doubt which might have arisen in his pupil's mind, Willis turned at random and began reading.

B-A, bay; K-E-R, cur—B-A-K-E-R, Baker. S-H-A, shay; D-Y, dee—
S-H-A-D-Y, Shady. Bakers bake bread and cakes. I like to play in the
shady grove. Good men obey the laws of God. I love to survey the
starry heavens. Never do your work in a hurry. No pleasure is equal
to a quiet conscience. The preacher is to preach the gospel. Teachers
teach their pupils, and pupils learn. Men devoted to mere amusement
misemploy their time. The drunkard's face will publish his vice and
his disgrace.

Henry looked at Willis; his eyes shone. "Do you think I can ever
learn to read like dat?" he asked.

"You sure can," assured Willis. "And now we begin at the front of
the book—not at the end." Turning back, he pointed his finger at
the alphabet. "That letter is the letter 'A'. Let's hear you say it."

Henry carefully formed his lips and repeated, "A."

"That's right," commended Willis.

Henry smiled broadly and moved closer to see the next letter.

- 12 -

Another winter Willis went to school in Weldon. He stayed at his
Uncle Jim's house; for his board and keep, he hauled wood. As soon
as he could rush home from school, he hitched the horse to a two-wheel
cart and drove to the rapids of the Roanoke for a load of wood.
Many a cold afternoon he rode along reciting his lessons or ran
beside the cart to keep warm. When he reached the clearing beside
the Roanoke's rapids, Willis paid the cutters fifty cents a cord for the
wood, loaded half of it at the time on his cart and headed home.
It would be dark when he reached Weldon. After unloading the wood
and feeding the horse, Willis came in the house to thaw out. Uncle
Jim lived alone; a Negro woman cooked dinner for him. For supper
Willis ate what was left from dinner; sometimes it was warmed over,
but often it was cold.

Up early in the morning, Willis took a lunch of biscuits and fried
meat to school which was about a mile down the railroad tracks.
Charlie Evans, a son of the postmistress, shared his desk with him. Mr.
Dowd was their teacher; although a little stern, he was pleasant and
agreeable. Willis liked him and was impressed by his forceful personality; whatever this man said, he said it "with power." When he
did not understand a problem, Willis would take his slate up to Mr.
Dowd's desk. Other students would follow. As the teacher would
work the problem or explain it, the boys would point to his fiery red
hair. Standing behind him, Willis often spread his hands over his head
as if he were warming them by a fire.

In the summer, Willis was needed back on the farm. His father's
family had continued to grow; Joe was born in 1877 and Frank in
1879. Charlie was away, working at Enfield; so Willis had to come
back to help with the crops. One day his father sent him over to

Colonel Walker's to borrow a plow-point. When he saw young Cullom, Colonel Walker invited him in.

"O no, thank you," replied the youth; "I don't have time."

"But son," answered the colonel; "you have all the time there is. Nobody has any more or any less than you have. We all have the same amount. What counts is what we do with it."

Willis early sensed life's responsibility and desired to use his time well. Late one afternoon he and a helper were plowing a field which was quite a distance from the house; they were trying to finish before dark. The helper stopped his mule and began unhitching.

"We are almost finished. Stay a little longer, and we won't lose time in coming back tomorrow," pleaded Willis.

"No," replied the other boy. "The sun has gone down, and it's time to quit. I'm going home."

When Willis' mule saw the other one go home, she neighed and pulled aside to go. But Willis tightened his lines. "We will finish." Around and around the field they went; there would be twice as much for him to do now that his helper had left. But it was foolish to quit when there was just a little more.

Nevertheless, it was getting dark; he snapped the lines on the mule's back. "Hurry, hurry—we must finish." Soon the shadows crept from the woods and covered the ground about him, but still he would not stop. "Mule Pat" could see better than he could; with her eyes and his memory they kept at their task. The shadows arose from the ground and darkened the landmarks, then brushed the vesper colors off the clouds. It was night.

In the meantime the helper had reached home and had put up his mule; he told Mr. Cullom that Willis was still plowing. Mr. Cullom walked slowly down the road in the direction of the field. With his anxiety, there was pride—that Willis shared the responsibility of the farm's work and that he didn't want to quit until the task was done. Yet he must quit; how could he be seeing at all now?

As the elder Cullom walked with these thoughts, he heard the sound of the mule's hoofs and his son's whistling. Willis had finished the field!

- 13 -

On Sundays there was time for fellowship with friends and neighbors. While their elders took afternoon naps or read or visited, the young boys would walk to each other's homes and talk or go on excursions through the woods.

Bruce Brickel, who was a little older than Willis, sometimes came with Sterling Johnson. But Willis' favorite lived right across the road from his house: Dave Morecock. These two were together more often than with anyone else. And what good times they had together! Many a Sunday afternoon was spent in just talking under the mulberry tree.

Dave had been greatly impressed by the trains at Weldon; he wanted to be an engineer. And he would tell Willis about his dream. "Some day you'll see a big engine like '49, only bigger, acoming lickety-split down the track from Wilmington," he would say with animation. "You'll have to pull your horse to a stop at the crossing, and then you'll throw up your hand to old Dave, sitting there with his eye on the track while the fireman throws in more wood. And I'll reach up and pull the whistle. Whoo-o-o, Whoo-o-o-o. I'll be going thirty miles an hour, by golly."

Willis would listen with kind admiration for his friend; he liked Dave, and he did not doubt but that someday it would happen just as he had dreamed. But Willis did not open his heart-dreams even to Dave; they were of a different kind, and Dave might not understand. He had seen her often at Ebenezer and thought she was about the prettiest thing on earth. Her name was Rosa.

While Willis could not speak of this love to Dave, there was someone to whom he did mention it, namely Erasmus Johnson, the Negro boy who had come to take Henry Fields's place on the farm.

Erasmus was about eighteen years old and quite an expert in courting, or at least he seemed so to twelve-year-old Willis. As they picked cotton, Rassus would tell of his dates. The younger white boy envied him and at last confessed that he, too, had a girl but was afraid to go to see her.

"Oh, dere ain't no need of being scared," declared Rassus with his eyes aflashing. "I's jest goes up to de house and tips my hat. 'Good evening, ma'am,' I says; 'it's sure a pretty day, ain't it?' And my girl's mother says, 'Yes, it sure is, Rassus; won't you come in de house'."

"I can't ever do that," interrupted Willis.

"Well, if yo' is a scaredy-cat, don't reckon you can; but I's atelling yo' just what to say."

Then a bright idea came to Willis. "Wait until we go to the house and you tell me what to say, and I'll write it down and memorize it. Then when I go to see Rosa, I'll recite it to her."

Erasmus was agreeable; after supper he dictated a courting speech, and Willis wrote it down. And Willis learned that speech; he memorized every word of it. He practiced it while he fed the hogs; he recited it while he cut wood. Erasmus even coached him with expression for it.

But there were two things which Willis had not told his courting-teacher. He had not thought it important to tell him that Rosa was nearly twenty years old and that his uncle, Julius, was her beau.

While he was awaiting an opportune time and the necessary courage, one Sunday afternoon at his Grandpa Cullom's, Uncle Julius asked him to go with him acalling on Miss Rosa. As he rode off with his Uncle Julius, Willis thought that he was just about as old as his uncle and that with Rassus' courting speech he could take Rosa right away from Julius.

3

Rosa was everything he had remembered. Dressed in a long blue dress with ribbons in her hair, she was beauty personified. She talked with Julius and asked Willis about his folks. She got down some old tin-type pictures and a book on the recent war. She told of the time when a horse ran away with her, and Julius told of how he once risked his life to save a lady in a run-away. But Willis never found the opportunity to say his courting speech.

Of course Erasmus would not understand, and, besides, Willis liked the way Julius talked to Rosa better than the way his teacher had taught him. Next time he would come alone or ask Dave to come with him.

But other events were to call his attention, and a new friendship was to shape his life more than Erasmus' lesson or his Uncle Julius' example.

14

Sometime during the summer of 1880, when Willis was thirteen, an itinerant Baptist preacher began coming into their community. It seemed that Colonel Walker's wife, who was a Baptist, had invited him. He began holding meetings once a month in the Morecock's school-house.

He came into the Cullom home at a time of great sorrow and left a permanent influence upon the life of the whole family, especially upon Willis. The sorrow itself dims the memory of exactly when this man of God entered Willis' life; when the family emerged from the valley, Willis found this shepherd beside him.

Perhaps the parents had heard that Charlie was not too well at Enfield, but they were unprepared for the sight of him when he was brought home about the middle of July. He was white and almost beside himself with fever. They put him in his mother's bed in the "great house." As she bent over him, Mrs. Cullom knew that he was very sick. Now a young man of twenty-one, Charlie had typhoid fever. Dr. Pierce came and left some medicine, but he said there wasn't much hope. Mrs. Cullom told the children to pray for him.

Willis went back to the place where he used to preach and buried his face in his hands. "O God, please make Charlie well; please, please, please," he sobbed over and over.

The days dragged by; they ate their bread with tears. Charlie grew worse; he threw his arms wildly and called to "Mule Pat." His mother did not leave him; day and night she was beside him; she didn't eat nor sleep. Sis and Nan cooked what was eaten and looked after the younger children, who peeped with big eyes at Big Brother. Dr. Pierce came and went; the neighbors would come and look in. The children heard them speculate whether or not "it would come tonight."

At last, on the afternoon of August 4th, it came. Mrs. Cullom broke and was led from the room. Her sobs pierced the hearts of her children; as they gathered around her, the crying mounted to alarm the Morecocks. They knew Charlie was dead.

As the women of the neighborhood gathered in the Cullom house to weep and to comfort, the menfolk had to make a coffin; the next morning they came to dig a grave in the cemetery which was in a corner of the yard. The younger children were bewildered at all the people's coming and at the older ones' crying; they cried out of fright. When they were told that they were going to put Charlie in that hole, they were horrified.

Willis understood more of death than the younger ones did, but Charlie's death shook him. He heard them hammering the nails of the coffin and watched them throw the dirt out of the grave; it was sand all the way to the bottom.

Charlie was buried the day after he died. The shock of his death left the family stunned. After the funeral, the preacher lingered and spoke softly to Mr. and Mrs. Cullom under the mulberry tree. That night—and many nights to come—little Frank asked Sis, "Will it come tonight? Will it come tonight?" She would say, "No," and assure him that everything would be all right.

Willis grieved too; his brother's death made him realize that there were some decisions he had to make. He needed somebody to help him, and he found that friend in the itinerant Baptist preacher.

"And sweet is youth . . .
AUBREY THOMAS DE VERE

SECOND AGE

A YOUTH FINDS HIMSELF

1880-1886

The Reverend Albert G. Willcox was "an Israelite" in whom there was no guile. Small of stature, he stood a little over five feet and weighed a hundred and twenty-five pounds. Yet all of those hundred and twenty-five pounds praised the Lord from the first awakening in the morning to the last thought at night.

There was a radiance about this man which time has not dimmed, for even yet when those who knew him speak of him there is a glow in their faces. His devotion to Christ and the cause of His Kingdom pulsated through his thoughts, his words, his life. When he walked alone through the woods, he praised the Creator for the trees and the wild animals which ran before him; when someone rode with him in his cart, he was anxious to introduce him to his Lord.

Sometimes this anxiety to lead others to know the Lord expressed itself abruptly. One day Mr. Willcox was riding alone when he saw a peddler bent under a heavy pack. As he drove up beside him, the preacher asked if he might give him a ride. The peddler was very grateful and, at Willcox's suggestion, put his pack on the back of the buggy and took his seat beside Mr. Willcox. And he was a Syrian. Immediately after calling to his horse, the preacher turned to the peddler; his eyes pierced into the dark eyes of his guest. "Dear brother," he asked earnestly, "are you prepared to die?"

The peddler looked down the lonesome road. "You may have the pack," he shouted, as he jumped from the buggy and took to the woods. By the time Mr. Willcox stopped the horse, the peddler was gone from sight and sound. Puzzled by this strange action, Mr. Willcox called and called, but the peddler would not come out of the woods. At the next store where he left the pack, the men roared with laughter at the bewildered preacher. "Why, Brother Willcox, that poor Syrian thought you were about to kill him when you asked if he were prepared to die." Mr. Willcox was still puzzled: "I was only asking him about the welfare of his soul."

Mr. Willcox was not as abrupt in inquiring of the welfare of young Willis' soul. Now a youth of thirteen, Willis was still shy and rather plump. Mr. Willcox seemed to have understood something of the questions and emotions of the lad whose eyes stared silently at him as he sat under the mulberry tree and talked quietly with his parents.

"You have been a great help and comfort to us through our sorrow, Brother Willcox, and yet we know very little about you. Tell us something about yourself and your people."

"Well," began the preacher, "I was born of the flesh in April, 1845, near Brinkleyville; I was born again of the spirit in 1864 and was baptized by the Reverend Doctor Thomas H. Pritchard of Raleigh.

I began serving the Lord in 1876 and was ordained last August, 1879. At our last associational meeting I was appointed an itinerant elder or missionary as my father had been before me."

"How many churches do you now have in this area?"

"In the Tar River Association which extends from Virginia down to little Washington and Greenville, we have forty Baptist churches, with over four thousand members."

"Do you look after all these churches?"

"O, no. These churches have their own pastors. I and five other itinerants or missionaries seek out new fields to build new churches."

Mr. Cullom studied a moment. "Who pays you for this work?"

Mr. Willcox replied, "The association helps us with the feeding of our horses; the people give as they are able and as we are able to serve them. I try to get my crop in early so I can go out to some 'Macedonia' and witness for the Lord."

"Are you married?"

The young preacher moved his chair. "Yes, I have just recently married Josephine Mason."

"Well," Mr. Cullom cleared his throat. "We are not ashamed to tell you that we like you and that we want you to make our home your home whenever you are in these parts. It is too late now for you to go home; so you are welcomed to spend the night with us. We don't have spacious accommodations; but there will be room, if you don't mind sleeping with Willis."

That night before going to bed, Mr. Willcox read from the Bible and prayed. As this saintly man committed that house and all who were in it to the loving care of the Heavenly Father, a special peace descended upon them.

Willis felt that it was a privilege to sleep with the preacher; he lay very quiet in the dark. "Willis," whispered the preacher, "God is good; isn't He? As you grow up, be a good man, Willis, and serve the Lord. Praise His name."

In the months that followed the two often slept together. Mr. Willcox became very fond of the youth, and Willis began to open his heart to this dear man of God. The preacher knew all kinds of things to delight the heart of a boy; he knew the way of birds and fishes; he watched the clouds and studied the stars. He played the organ and the fiddle; he made flutes of reeds and blew tunes on them. But more than all of these, this man knew God and was in on the secret of life and eternity. And Willis wanted to know this more than all the other things.

Willis went regularly to hear him preach and felt that his preaching was doing something for him that no other man's preaching had done. Yet he found himself hiding behind the door in the little schoolhouse to dodge him as far as possible. It was strange; years later (1945), he wrote:

I admired Mr. Willcox as a preacher, loved him as a man very tenderly and yet found myself in this strange way trying to hide from him when he preached to me. It is plain to me now, but it was a queer experience at the time. God was speaking to my soul, and I knew it not.

- 2 -

The Culloms looked forward to Brother Willcox's visits and preaching; they were not alone in this anticipation. Soon the Cullom's schoolhouse was crowded. When the preacher began talking of a protracted or "big" meeting, the menfolk knew that the log cabin in the Cullom yard would not be large enough.

So when the crops were laid by in the summer of 1881, the menfolk built a brush-arbor a few hundred yards from the schoolhouse. Forked posts were placed in the ground, and log rafters were laid across them; then the branches of trees and bushes were spread across them to give shade from the sun and some protection from the rain to those who gathered underneath them. This temporary shelter could be expanded indefinitely, and with the crowds that came by buggy and wagon-load, the menfolk had to keep adding on.

One afternoon Brother Willcox said the nets were so heavy with precious souls ("Praise the Lord") that he was calling in another preacher to help him. "Dr. James D. Hufham is pastor of the Baptist Church at Scotland Neck and is one of the great leaders of our time," he said; "last year at Conoconary, he led the association in pledging fifteen hundred dollars for mission work in our own area."

And the people were not disappointed in the guest minister; Dr. Hufham was an eloquent preacher, and large crowds came to hear him. He and Mr. Willcox stayed in the Cullom home, which gave Willis additional opportunities to be with them.

Dr. Hufham seemed especially kind and thoughtful of the shy fourteen-year-old boy in the Cullom family. One Tuesday afternoon under the brush-arbor, Dr. Hufham made a statement which found a ready acceptance in the youth's heart:

> Great faith is spoken of only twice in the New Testament; little faith is spoken of over and over again. It is not the quantity of one's faith that saves; it is the One in whom the faith is centered that matters. If there be one here who has little faith but that faith is centered in Jesus Christ as a personal Saviour, I want him to come and give me his hand as a token of that fact.

On this invitation, Willis stepped out and walked down to the front where the preachers were standing. Years later he would write:

> Two people in the New Testament seem to me to characterize my attitude as a Christian better than any others: (1) the publican who stood afar off smiting on his breast saying "God be merciful to me a sinner"; (2) the man who, when asked whether he believed, said "Lord, I believe; help thou mine unbelief." (W. R. Cullom, *A Summary of the Life of W. R. Cullom*, a pamphlet.)

Others came during those days; altogether, there were twelve: nine on profession of faith, requesting baptism, two "by relation," and one by letter.

- 3 -

On the first day of September, 1881, Brother Willcox led his followers about a mile from the brush-arbor to the banks of Quankie Creek. They sang such hymns as "Shall We Gather at the River" and "Am I a Soldier of the Cross," and Brother Willcox read such passages of scripture as:

> And it came to pass in those days, that Jesus came from Nazareth of Galilee, and was baptized of John in Jordan and straightway coming up out of the water, he saw the heavens opened, and the Spirit like a dove descending upon him: and there came a voice from heaven saying, Thou art my beloved Son, in whom I am well pleased. (Mark 1:9-11.)
> Know ye not, that so many of us as were baptized into Jesus Christ were baptized into his death? Therefore we are buried with him by baptism into death: that like as Christ was raised up from the dead by the glory of the Father, even so we also should walk in newness of life. (Romans 6:3-4.)

Then the minister knelt down and prayed, after which he led the nine professing believers out into the water of Quankie Creek.

Lifting his right hand upward over Willis' head, he said: "Upon your profession of faith in the Lord Jesus Christ and in obedience to His command, I baptize thee, Willis Cullom, in the name of the Father, the Son and the Holy Ghost. Amen." With his left hand back of Willis' neck, Mr. Willcox lowered him backward down into the water. The youth felt the cool water rushing over him; it was only for a second of time, and he was lifted back into the air. They changed their clothes behind blankets fastened to trees, as the others sang "Amazing Grace" and "Rock of Ages."

When they were dressed again, the new Christians returned with Brother Willcox and the others to the brush-arbor which they reverently entered. Likely Mr. Willcox told them that those who had been baptized needed to band themselves together and to covenant to live godly lives and to walk in the way of the Lord. And they voted to form a church of the twelve members, the same as the number of the Lord's first disciples.

Dr. J. D. Hufham and a young protégé of his, Bob Peele, came from Scotland Neck; these, with Mr. Willcox, formed the presbytery to establish the church there. After singing "How Firm a Foundation," "The Church's One Foundation" and "Blest Be the Tie that Binds," there was scripture and prayer. Then they covenanted themselves together in the Lord:

> Having been as we trust brought by Divine grace to embrace the Lord Jesus Christ and to give ourselves wholly to Him, we do now solemnly and joyfully covenant with each other to walk together in Him with brotherly love, to His glory as our common Lord. We do therefore in

His strength engage, that we will exercise a Christian care and watchfulness over each other and faithfully warn, exhort and admonish each other as occasion may require. That we will not forsake the assembling of ourselves together, but will uphold the public worship of God, and the ordinances of His house. That we will not omit closet and family religion at home, nor neglect the great duty of religiously training our children and those under our care for the service of Christ and the enjoyment of heaven. That as we are the light of the world and the salt of the earth, we will seek Divine aid to enable us to deny ungodliness and every worldly lust and to walk circumspectly in the world that we may win the souls of men. That we will cheerfully contribute of our prosperity according as God has prospered us for maintenance of the faithful and evangelical ministry among us, for the support of the poor, and the spread of the gospel over the earth. That we will in all conditions, even till death, strive to live to glory Him who hath called us out of darkness into His marvelous light.

And may the God of peace who brought again from the dead our Lord Jesus, that great shepherd of the sheep through the blood of the everlasting covenant make you perfect in good work, to do His will, working in us that which is well pleasing in his sight through Jesus Christ, to whom be glory for ever and ever. Amen. (Quankie Baptist Church Records.)

The members adopted eighteen articles of faith, the first of which read:

We believe that the Holy Bible was written by men divinely inspired and is the perfect treasure of heavenly instruction, that it has God for its author, salvation for its end and truth without any admixture of error for its matter, that it reveals the principles by which God will judge us, and therefore is and shall remain as the supreme standard by which all human conduct, creeds and opinions should be tried.

Trustees were appointed; deacons and a clerk were elected. The church was named "Quankie Baptist Church."

- 4 -

From the beginning Willis had been a favorite of Mr. Willcox. In this shy youth, the preacher saw wonderful abilities, and he coveted those abilities for his Lord. He had seen the boy slip behind the door of the log cabin to hear the preaching; he had seen him resist the invitation to accept Jesus as Lord until at last, upon Dr. Hufham's invitation under the brush-arbor, he came forth to profess a "little faith." But that faith would grow, and Mr. Willcox made it his business to see that it did. He asked him questions about the Bible and invited the youth to come to see him; he was delighted when at last he accepted his invitation to go with him to Reedy Creek Baptist Church.

Mr. Cullom took his son the fifteen miles over to Mr. Willcox's house. As their buggy turned off the main road, Willis caught sight of the Willcox home; it was a large, two storied, white weatherboarded house with green blinds at the windows. It had been Mr. Willcox's father's house, and his mother still made her home there.

Crape myrtles lined the road to the house; they were on both sides of the front porch and by the side porches. The walks were bordered with boxwoods. The voice of a Negro boy in the yard called out: "Here they come, Miss Josephine. Here they come, Rebben Albert." And the black boy ran toward the buggy and to the horse's bridle. From a flower garden to the east of the house came the prettiest woman that Willis had ever seen. In all loveliness of face and form, she walked more on air than on earth. Behind her came Mr. Willcox, who took her hand; and together, they came to the buggy.

"O, I am so glad you could come," welcomed Mr. Willcox, as he shook hands with Mr. Cullom. "This is my wife, Josephine; Josey, this is Mr. Cullom and my special friend, Willis." The lovely lady curtsied to the father and reached over and kissed the astonished lad on the cheek.

The Willcoxes had not been married long, and their love made the world a wonderful place. After Mr. Cullom left, they showed the youth the gardens, the chickens, the stables, the fields, the house; everything they touched shone with the magic of their love. And of course, Willis fell in love with them both. He was quiet, but all the more he drank in the radiant happiness of his pastor's home. He had heard Mr. Willcox speak often of "the glory land"; his home was surely a foretaste of it.

The next morning after a big breakfast, Willis and Mr. Willcox were ready to leave for the Reedy Creek Baptist Church. The horse and buggy were brought to the side porch, and "Miss Jo" kissed "Sweet" (as she called her husband) and Willis good-bye.

They were pleasant miles to Reedy Creek. Mr. Willcox praised God for everything in sight; he shouted friendly greetings to the folk along the road and talked earnestly with the boy beside him. Knowing that a youth of fourteen was already facing the temptations of alcoholic beverage, the preacher asked: "Willis, how do you feel about drinking?"

Willis thought of his father's taking his "health" dram every morning; he had never seen nor heard of his father's getting drunk, but he knew others who did. In Weldon there was a carpenter who drank morning, noon and night; there were other "saloon-flies" he had seen at his Uncle Jim's store. These had disgusted him; whiskey had robbed them of the best in life; what sorrows and ills it had brought them! Slowly he answered the preacher: "I am resolved to leave it out of my life."

As they approached the church, Mr. Willcox likely told Willis that the Reedy Creek Baptist Church had been founded about 1750 by Dr. Josiah Hart, a co-laborer with William Sojourner. For a time it had flourished, sending out many preachers and fostering several new churches, but there came a time when anti-missionary sentiment almost killed it. However, the church had now revived and was in good condition. About twenty people gathered at Reedy Creek for the Saturday services. After the preaching service, Brother Willcox called the church into regular conference for the transaction of business and the reception of new members. Mr. Burwell Davis called the roll and read the minutes of the last meeting. The unfinished business was discussed; after which, there was a prayer, dismissing them.

On the way home, Mr. Willcox told his friend about the associational meeting to be held at Antioch in October (1881). "Dr. T. H. Pritchard of Wake Forest College will speak on education," Mr. Willcox said. "He is one of the most eloquent speakers of our times. You should hear him."

And Willis resolved to do exactly that.

- 5 -

Willis rode a young horse to Antioch for the fifty-first session of the Tar River Association of Baptist Churches. He recalled that the colt had not been properly broken and "almost shook the ribs out" of him. Whatever discomfort he might have endured in coming, it was soon forgotten as ninety-one delegates from forty-five churches gathered for this three-day annual meeting.

When the Cullom youth walked into the Antioch Baptist Church for his first associational meeting, the Tar River Association was beginning its second half-century. In his *History of the Tar River Association 1830-1921,* Dr. Thomas J. Taylor traces the beginnings of this association to the religious refugees from England who found asylum in the woods of North Carolina as early as 1656 and who came in great numbers after 1660. At first, these dissenters (mostly Independents, Baptists and Quakers) did not have regular meetinghouses but would gather whenever and wherever they had opportunity. In 1727, Shiloh Baptist Church was organized in Camden County, Meherrin Baptist Church in Hertford County followed in 1729; these with Kehukee Baptist Church (1742) in Halifax and Reedy Creek Baptist Church (1750) in Warren made up the first four Baptist churches which sent out "colonies" in various directions until "Baptist sentiments" were preached throughout the entire state. These churches began meeting together once a year for "interview in which the conditions of the churches were carefully considered and plans were devised for forwarding the work." In 1765, they organized themselves into the Kehukee Association which included all the Baptist churches in the northeastern section of the state; in 1830, because of "the growing hostility to missionary effort on the part of the Kehukee Association," nine churches withdrew and organized themselves with five churches from the Raleigh Association into the Tar River Association.

By 1835, there were sixteen churches in the Tar River Association, but they were in such "spiritual declension" that a day of fasting and prayer was appointed. The next year the association passed a resolution declaring: "we deem it morally wrong to make, vend, and drink ardent spirits for any other than medical purposes; and that we recommend to our churches that they use every lawful means to suppress this ruinous practice in our churches." The association approved (1853) the State Convention and Wake Forest College; it contributed (1859) to the seminary located at Greenville (S.C.) and endorsed the Southern Baptist Sunday Union. It made plans for the care of aged ministers and dreamed of a Baptist College for women. However, in 1861 the association heard more pressing needs from the Confederate soldiers and in 1863, a day of fasting and prayer was held in accord with a request from President Jefferson Davis; in 1865, "the demoralized condition of the country was such that the Association did little more than take its bearings and adopt reports and resolutions looking to future activities." (At that time there were nine pastors and at least four licentiates in the association.)

Twenty-eight churches were represented at Sharon in 1869 when the "colored church" at Shiloh was unanimously received into the association. In 1874, three hundred and forty-nine baptisms were reported within the thirty-four churches, making a total membership of three thousand and seventy-two; there were nine Sunday schools.

In 1876, the association pledged five thousand dollars for the endowment of Wake Forest College. In 1876, "Home Missions" was changed to "Associational Missions," and the next year, at Pleasant Grove, the churches pledged three hundred and seventy dollars for this work.

In 1878, sixty-four delegates from thirty-six churches met at Conoconary and reported five hundred and seventy-nine baptisms for the year; Jefferson Burrell, "colored," was among the eighteen pastors who served the churches at this time. That was the year when Dr. J. D. Hufham of Scotland Neck led the association in pledging fifteen hundred dollars for preaching the gospel in "the destitute sections" of the association. The next year the executive committee reported six missionaries at work within the association; forty churches reported three hundred and seventy baptisms.

The first fifty years had been good ones; there had been depressions, war, internal strife, discouragements, but there also had been great visions, great undertakings, great advances and great victories. With faith in God and confidence in themselves, the delegates of the churches gathered in 1881 to report on another year and to make plans for greater work ahead.

- 6 -

For the youth of fourteen, that associational meeting at Antioch was a great event. T. J. Webb was elected moderator, and A. G. Willcox was re-elected clerk and treasurer; the Rev. W. P. Blake preached on Revelation 21:10-11. But the great event was Dr. T. H. Pritchard's address on higher education which he delivered from one end of

North Carolina to the other. At the time when only half of the children of school age in North Carolina attended school of any kind and when the longest school term was only nine weeks, Dr. Pritchard declared that the people must be shown the value of education so that they will be willing to be taxed to support schools, that politicians must know its value so that they will pass the necessary laws, that competent teachers must be prepared to lead the people. He said education adds greatly to the wealth of a people, increases the sources of a people's enjoyment, makes labor honorable, decreases crime and increases virtue. He thought all education should be based on the Christian religion, "for education comes from above, not from below." (*Vide,* George Washington Paschal, *History of Wake Forest College,* Wake Forest: College Press, 1943, vol. II, pp. 184-187.) After Dr. Pritchard's address, Dr. T. C. Bailey spoke on the *Biblical Recorder.* Then the delegates from the new churches were recognized; Quankie, Elm Grove, Fishing Creek and Toisnot were received into the association.

The next item on the agenda was the Executive Committee's report on Associational Missions. Sixty-six years later, Willis R. Cullom was to write:

> It was the "top" hour in the great annual meeting of the Tar River Association when Rev. George M. Duke, Dr. J. D. Hufham, Dr. T. J. Taylor, Rev. A. G. Willcox and many others began their special appeal for associational missions. As a young boy in that association I was made to feel that the work of the Kingdom of God on earth was mainly centered right there. . . . The way the brethren that I have named did lay the needs of this section on the hearts and consciences of our people in those days made them feel that the very foundations of the universe depended on the response that should be made to their appeal. As I think of all this now, it seems to me that I have never heard appeals anywhere that surpassed them in real poignancy and power. (*Charity and Children,* Thomasville, Sept. 11, 1947.)

There is no doubt that others were equally impressed, for two thousand dollars was pledged at Antioch for this work.

The associational meeting was not all sermons and appeals; there were lighter moments of laughter and meals which defied description. In the churchyard the delegates would gather around tables loaded with fried chicken, baked hams, roast beef; and the women would vie with each other in having their cakes and pies eaten before the others.

At night the houses of the community would be crowded with delegates. All the beds and couches were filled, and pallets were made on the floor. Like a group of boys on holiday, the preachers would talk and laugh late into the night. Young Cullom would enjoy all of this —even a joke on his pastor.

"Brother Willcox always knows the right thing to say for every occasion. But one time he was stumped; we were having dinner in a very poor and ill-kept home; I knew Brother Willcox couldn't commend the good woman on her house or her appearance or her children.

The surroundings were so dirty I was almost afraid to eat the food before me. I couldn't see anything about which he could brag, but I knew he would say something nice; so I waited. At last he reached over and took up the salt shaker. 'This is the nicest salt I've ever seen; how do you keep it so nice?' "

The others roared with laughter. Mr. Willcox said, "Well, it was nice salt; it was dry and not all stuck together. She said she put rice in it to keep it from getting lumpy. I told my wife about it; now we put rice in our salt shakers, and it works."

- 7 -

Young Cullom enjoyed all of this immensely and at home told and retold his experiences. It was no wonder that he was at the next association with his father, who, along with Jesse Rhea and George Branch, was appointed to represent Quankie Church.

The association that year (1882) was held in Littleton. The Culloms stopped at the home of Ezra Bowers, whose stories kept them laughing so that the younger Cullom said he "had never had a better time." At the church, he saw Mr. Willcox, who was described as "the greatest church builder in the association." Thirteen missionaries reported on their work within the seven counties of the association; six houses of worship were being built, and three new churches had been organized. For the first time Willis heard Dr. Charles E. Taylor of Wake Forest College and "intensely listened to him." The report from Quankie was good; their church had grown, and in March Mr. Willcox had preached the first sermon on Proverbs 1:23 in the new church building. It had been an eventful year for the association, for the church, for the Culloms and especially for Willis.

When the crops had been plowed out and laid by in the early summer, Willis had gone to his Uncle Ambrose Cullom who was a singing master in Warren County and who had invited Willis to come live with him a while and go to Captain John Graham's school. One day while attending this school in Fork Township, Willis had walked about two miles over to a prayer meeting which Brother George W. Coppedge was holding in Mr. Burwell Davis' home. Mr. Coppedge was a man of medium height with dark hair; at the age of thirty-six he had felt called to preach, but he could neither read nor write. He would hold the Bible in his hands and cry to read its words, but he could not. Finally he entered Wakefield school along with his children, but they soon left their father behind. At times he felt like giving up; but he was a surrendered man, and whenever he prayed "Lord, what shall I do," he always heard "Preach." So, that one thing he was determined to do. At last, light began to break, and he began reading the Bible; there would never be another book for him. He was a man of great faith, persuasion and power, especially in the backward areas. Knowing weakness, he sensed it in others and extended himself to help them.

Willis had heard all of this about Mr. Coppedge and was thus prepared for his poor grammar, but he did not realize how keenly Mr. Coppedge could sense weakness in others and how varied could be the ways of helping them. Willis was quite impressed by the Davis home; although it was not elegant, it was new and built lower to the ground than the older houses, with a long porch around the front and side. While he was looking around the front room where the group was seated, Willis heard Mr. Coppedge say, "We'll call on Brother Cullom to lead us in prayer."

Willis was dumbfounded; his throat and lips became dry. He had prayed by himself, but he had never led in public prayer. The others bowed their heads, and Willis heard his own voice saying something —the best he could, he later supposed. "I trust the Lord knew what I said, even if I didn't."

Mr. Davis took note of the youth; he needed a boy to keep books at his new cotton gin, and Willis looked as if he might do. But in all probability he first asked Brother Willcox about him; at least, Willis always thought it had been his pastor who had recommended him to Mr. Davis.

And likely it was at the associational meeting in Littleton that Mr. Davis talked with Mr. Willcox about Willis, for soon after the meeting Willis was told that Mr. Davis wanted to see him about keeping his gin-books.

- 8 -

It was still early in the morning (October, 1882) when Willis and his Uncle Ambrose arrived at the Davis store. They entered the framed log building, and Mr. Davis came toward them; he said he would pay Willis nine dollars a month and would need him until after all the cotton was ginned.

Willis went out to his uncle's buggy and got his satchel; he told his uncle goodbye and then went with Mr. Davis toward the cotton gin to begin work. As a youth of fifteen, he weighed about a hundred and twenty-five pounds; he had plenty of light sandy-colored hair. He was dressed in trousers and shirt his mother had made for him, with store-bought shoes and suspenders.

In his day, Mr. Burwell Davis was considered a rich man, but more important than his reputed wealth, he was a good man. He showed Willis the new cotton gin. Already farmers had come and were waiting on their wagons for their turn to be weighed. The cotton was to be put in large sheets (or in hampers) and weighed; then it was dumped into the farmer's stall. When a farmer had about five hundred pounds of cotton, the cotton was ginned and baled. The Cullom youth was to see the cotton weighed and mark down the amount, to report when a farmer had enough to gin, to keep the seed and to make the bales. When there was nothing to do at the gin, he was to go to the store and help out in there. Wiley H. Pridgen had charge of the general merchandise store; Willis was to share a bed with him in the back room of the store.

At noontime, Willis was introduced to the other members of the Davis family. Mrs. Davis was a plain woman but very clean and neat. She and Mr. Davis had two daughters, Sally and Mamie; like their mother, they were plain and unaffected. Wiley Pridgen already had his eye on Sally, and Mamie, at the age of thirteen, made quite an "impression" on Willis. At the table, Mr. Davis had Wiley sit to his right with Sally by his side and Willis to his left with Mamie by his side; Mrs. Davis sat at the end of the table. Thus they sat for three meals a day—with lovelight in the young men's eyes.

After the day's work, they were welcomed to sit and talk with the family until bedtime. Mr. Davis would make plans for the next day. When Wiley would speak of going across the road to their room for the night, Mr. Davis would say: "Let's have a prayer, boys, before you go." Then very honestly and simply he would pray: "Heavenly Father, we thank Thee for keeping us through the day and we pray Thee to keep us through the night. For Jesus sake. Amen."

The prayer was like him—simple, straight-forward, reverent, honest. Day in and day out, he was that way. Early each morning (except Sundays and the first Saturday of each month when the church would have its conference) he would hitch up his black mare and drive to Macon for the goods he needed in the store. His wife would fix his dinner in a dinner-bucket for him to eat on his way back. When he reached home, "the boys" would help unload the molasses, sugar, cloth, kerosene and whatever he had brought. Although he was a liberal contributor to the church, he wasted nothing; every string and nail was saved from the goods-boxes as they were opened.

- 9 -

Willis returned home a little before Christmas and laid twenty-seven dollars in his father's hand. It was the entire salary he had earned that fall at Mr. Davis'.

Mr. Joel Cullom was pleased with his son, and they both were pleased with the new church building which was in sight of their home, on land which Mr. Cullom had given. The new building was made of the best of sawed timbers and expertly constructed. It was rectangular in shape—something like forty-eight by thirty-six feet, with hand drawn shingles on its roof. At the front, there was a central door, with a large window on each side of it. Inside were homemade benches and a large iron stove; at the farther end of the room was a raised platform of about twelve-by-twelve feet with a pulpit. There were two large windows on each side of the room and two behind the pulpit.

Mrs. Cullom was also proud to show her son the cooking she had done for their Christmas. In a small building called "the dairy" (for there they kept the milk and the butter she made for trading at the store), Mrs. Cullom had stored pies and cakes of all kinds which no one—not even her son who had just returned home—could taste before that happy morning.

An air of excitement and expectancy filled the air. A hog had been killed and chickens dressed for baking. The children were beside themselves with joy; they could hardly wait until Christmas morning to find the orange, apple, gingercake and candy which Santa Claus would bring them. They hung their stockings over the fireplace.

As the children left for the big house, "Ma" reminded Willis to cover well the coals on the hearth. "We don't want to have to send one of the children for fire from a neighbor on Christmas morning." Alone, Willis sat down on the stool by the fire and opened a journal, *Biblical Recorder,* which his family had just started taking and which through the years would come to mean much to him and to his family.

As soon as Christmas was over, Willis and a Negro boy ditched "the pond field" which Mr. Cullom had bought from Captain Morecock; then they cut wood, burned off the fields and broke the land. Soon the corn and cotton were planted—and then hoed and plowed again and again until they were laid by.

Often Mr. Cullom would follow his son into the field to check on his work; he knew "thoroughness, diligence and faithful application" of what he understood to be the best of farm-methods and expected "every detail" to be done according to his instructions. Years later (1945) his son would write:

> During those early days, he drilled into me . . . that a thing worth doing at all is worth doing as it should be done. . . . Another thing that he drilled into me was that honesty is always the best policy, and that a man's word should always be better than his bond.
> My father was a man who was interested in public affairs. He taught school for a while. . . . He had a weekly newspaper come into our home in those days—*The Petersburg Messenger*— and would sit by the lightwood knot fire at night, read the paper to himself and call attention to such things as he thought worth while to my mother and the children as we sat around in silence.

In the spring of 1883, Willis was elected superintendent of the Sunday school which had about twenty students. (Mr. Willcox was still seeing that Willis had opportunity to grow.) Willis would open the hour by pitching the tune of a hymn; then he would lead in prayer or call on another to do so. Then the children would go to the back of the room for their lesson from the Bible on doctrine,

character and the good life in general; the adults would come to the
front for their lesson.

Preaching was held once a month at Quankie—on Saturday afternoon and Sunday morning. The service began with the singing of a
hymn, after which Mr. Willcox went into the pulpit and read from
the Bible. Then they would have another hymn. Many of the menfolk,
including Mr. Cullom and Mr. Branch, would wait until the concluding
of this second hymn before coming into the church; if they got to
hear Mr. Willcox take his text, they thought they had come in plenty
of time.

Mr. Willcox's manner of preaching was plain; he told many stories
in his sermons, but he was not emotional. His voice was thin, and his
spirit was humble—"as humble as ever I've known" Willis was to
say; Mr. Willcox "always apologized for himself," but he praised the
Lord for everything. He preached in a matter-of-fact attitude—plain,
logical gospel-truths. His friendliness and kindness showed and shone
through his sermons, and he was greatly loved.

- 10 -

In the fall of 1883, Willis returned to Mr. Davis who raised his
monthly salary to ten dollars. When he saw Mamie, the Cullom youth
knew she was "the prettiest thing" he had ever seen. They had their
same places at the table. Wiley Pridgen, now a man of twenty-one,
definitely was in love with Sally; and Willis, a youth of sixteen, felt
a warm thrill whenever his hand chanced to touch the hand of Mamie.

Mrs. Davis was as good a cook as he had remembered, and Mr.
Davis was just as economical, prompt and faithful as ever. "There
is no better time to do the right thing than right now," he would tell
Willis. His trips to Macon, his church attendance, his business affairs,
his prayers were just as regular as clock and calendar. Of this home,
Willis Cullom would write:

> It was here that I learned the dignity of work . . . the habit and the
> helpfulness of economy; it was here that I saw in a new and fresh
> setting the beauty and glory of a unified, affectionate, happy home life.
> It was here that I saw as never before that religion is an essential part
> of the life that now is, and not simply as a sort of preparation for the
> life to come. . . . In the eleventh chapter of Hebrews, 33rd verse, we
> note the phrase "wrought righteousness" as one of the triumphs of faith
> and one of the marks of the hero. Mr. and Mrs. Davis "wrought right-
> eousness" and made it beautiful in everyday clothes. (*Charity and
> Children*, March 18, 1943.)

On Sunday afternoons a group of young people often gathered at
the Davis home. Minnie Rodwell (White) would remember they
would go walking or would gather around the organ and sing; Willis
Cullom was especially fond of such hymns as "I Know Not What Awaits
Me," "Rock of Ages," "Work, for the Night is Coming." She would

recall, "We had some mighty good times that fall." But Willis still had his eye on Mamie. She had attended school the preceding summer with his sisters, Lucy and Tulie; so she often talked and asked about them.

The next spring, at the post office in Weldon, Willis got a letter addressed to Lucy from Mamie. He had a strange feeling that there was a message for him somewhere about it. Carefully he removed the stamp, and there on the back of the stamp was the sweetest of all messages—"I love you." How he got home, why he thought this was for him, what explanation he made of the missing stamp to his sister —he could not remember. But he treasured that stamp as the dearest letter he ever received. At last—without any coaching—he boldly wrote back to Mamie, "the sweetest thing that ever walked on earth."

- 11 -

Early in the summer of 1884 another letter came for the Cullom youth at his father's home—a letter that would take him away from that home. The letter was from Mr. Edward Rodwell of Axtell in Warren County. He was looking for a clerk, and Mr. Burwell Davis had recommended the young Mr. Cullom.

Willis was now seventeen years old—old enough to make his own way, and here was his chance. The home was crowded; there were now ten children and another one expected. He was excited at the prospects of going, but there was sadness in leaving home. Somehow he felt this would be permanent, that never again would his father's house be his home. But he couldn't stay there forever; he would have to go. His mother helped him pack his grip-sack and a box-trunk.

It was July 15th when Willis boarded the train at Weldon; every click of the wheels took him farther away from all he had known and had loved at home. When the conductor called out "Ridgeway," the train stopped, and Willis got off. There was a small crossroad station, with a few houses scattered around it; but no one was in sight. There he stood alone—a timid, frightened, homesick boy. Home was only thirty-five miles away, but to the youth it seemed he was altogether in a different world.

At last, a young Negro man (Stokes Allen) came up to him and stammeringly asked if he were Mr. Rodwell's new clerk. He helped Mister Cullom put his baggage on the wagon, and together they rode to Mr. Rodwell's store.

Mr. Edward Rodwell (about twenty-five) managed the store for his father, J. L. Rodwell, who was a brother-in-law to Mr. Burwell Davis—the two men having married sisters. The mother of Mrs. Rodwell and Mrs. Davis was "Aunt Sally" Allen who lived at the Allen homestead with her son, Walter Allen, and his wife. The Allen house was a large, two-storied frame building, with a large front porch; it was "quite a house" in those days when the young Cullom rode up to it. He would eat at the Allen table, of which he would say he had "never had better fare or company." "Aunt Sally," as Mother Allen was generally called, was a good woman; she was quick of speech, and young Cullom enjoyed talking with her. (It had been Mrs Allen's brother, Mr. John Watson, who had given the first thousand dollars for the endowment of Wake Forest College at the Tar River Associational Meeting in 1876.)

The store in which the Cullom youth was to clerk was in a corner of the Allen yard, near the Warrenton-Middleburg road. It had been built in 1872; a shed-room to the back and a porch to the front were added later. The main room was about twenty-four by twelve feet and had counters on two adjoining sides. Lamps hung from the ceiling; there was a fireplace in one corner. There was a door to the front, one on the side toward the Allen house and another on the opposite side which opened into a small room where the young clerk would sleep.

The Rodwell store was a challenge to the young clerk. He soon saw many possibilities and was eager to try his ideas. (Years later he was to comment that it seemed he had never been in a place that he felt he could really fill.) Finding some old goods pushed under the counter, he asked if he might mark the prices down to get rid of them. Mr. Rodwell was skeptical but was willing; he was surprised when they were sold quickly. Similarly on rainy days, young Cullom took out the umbrellas, opened them and hung them on nails overhead; he sold them so fast that he could hardly keep them in stock.

Often on Saturday nights when they stayed open until twelve o'clock, the store would be filled with Negroes. Once the young clerk overheard two of them talk about Grover Cleveland who was running for the presidency of the United States. "Who is yo' goin' to vote for?" he heard one ask. The other one replied, "I don't knows yet; I's waitin' to see who the white folks are fer and den I votes for de other man."

Less than a half-mile of Rodwell's store was Brown's Baptist Church (sometimes called Allen's Meeting House) which dated back to 1775. At one time an anti-missionary element had led the church to withdraw from the association, but after these anti-missionary members had been excluded in 1838, peace had been restored and the church had returned to the association. In 1855 a new building had been constructed on a beautiful location, seven miles west of Warrenton. This wooden structure (about fifty by forty feet) had large square windows and was painted white. Inside, its benches were square-boxed; its balcony was used by its Negro members.

When the Allens first took their young clerk to this church, Rev. D. A. Glenn was its pastor. As the church did not have a Sunday school, Deacon James A. Tunstall had organized one in a little school-house about a half a mile from his home. Young Cullom would walk the two or three miles from the store to the school on Sunday after-noons "to join Brother Tunstall and his little group of faithful helpers in this worthy task." (*Charity and Children,* March 27, 1947.)

- 12 -

Early in the fall of 1885, Willis Cullom received a letter from Gilbert L. Finch, a neighborhood friend in Halifax County. Knowing his desire to go to school, Gilbert invited Willis to come to Davie County to assist him by teaching the primary grades of a school of which he was principal. "You will teach during the day, and I will teach you at night and pay your expenses."

It sounded good to Mr. Cullom; he talked it over with Mr. Rodwell and recommended Knox Dickens, a cousin, for his place as clerk in the store. When Knox came, Willis went in to tell "Aunt Sally" good-bye; Mrs. Allen broke into tears. Mr. and Mrs. Walter Allen now had a son, little Sam, whom the youth caressed.

Mr. Finch met him at the station in Winston, and in a buggy they rode fifteen miles to a community called Yadkin Valley, between Farmington and the Yadkin River. The cool October night was falling about them when they reached Mr. Jim A. Sheek's house, where they would room and board. The house was a small, single-story, weather-boarded structure, with a front porch over two windows and a door; a brick chimney was at the left side. To the back, there were two rooms which opened onto a porch.

Mrs. Sheek, a small, pleasant woman, met them at the front door; her hands showed that she was accustomed to hard work. She took them into the front room where Mr. Sheek was in bed. He was a medium-size man and had "white swelling" of the bone. Mr. Cullom soon learned that he had been hit by a Minie ball at the battle of Fort Fisher. Mr. Finch told him that Mr. Sheek had been a schoolteacher himself and was a well-read man. The two daughters of the home were presented to the young schoolmaster: Lelia, a girl of nine who had "the poise and dignity of a nun," and Daisy, a tomboy of seven.

While Mrs. Sheek went to the kitchen to prepare the evening meal, Mr. Finch showed his friend their room on the back porch. It was between the Sheeks' bedroom and the kitchen; in a more prosperous time, it might have been a dining room. It had two windows and a small fireplace. The double bed in the corner had a feather mattress; there was a trundle bed under it. Mr. Finch helped Willis open his box-trunk, and they began hanging up some of his clothes when they were called to supper.

They ate in the kitchen which had a large "cookstove." The girls sat down at the table with the young men, while their mother waited on them. The supper was good; it consisted of cornbread, chicken, potatoes, collards and milk.

The school was held in the Yadkin Valley Baptist Church, which was a one-room frame building, unpainted, with a stove in the middle of the room. There were no desks, and the hand-hewn benches were not very comfortable. Mr. Finch would teach from the pulpit; Mr. Cullom would teach from the back of the church, with a dark red curtain pulled between them.

School took in at nine o'clock. By the time the boys and girls started coming in, the room was warm from a fire in the stove, and water was in the bucket in the corner. The boys were dressed in homemade pants with store-bought suspenders. The girls wore tight-waisted calico dresses with full skirts; their hair was pulled straight back and tied with ribbons, and their faces scrubbed clean and powdered white. They wore bonnets and carried book-satchels of un-bleached domestic. Both boys and girls brought lunches of biscuit or cornbread, meat or sausage, hard-boiled eggs, and sometimes an apple.

The pupils looked at the new teacher; he was young, with light sandy hair and a thin mustache. He seemed quiet and kind. After Mr. Finch divided the group, the curtain was pulled between them, and Mr. Cullom began his first class which consisted of: Floyd Hauser, Oscar Griffin, Lelia Sheek, Mattie Douthet, Conie Douthet, Sena Douthet, Dora Martin Hauser, John Cornelison, Martha Cornelison and Pearl Griffin. Some of these were in the First Home Reader, while others were finishing the Third. The young teacher kept them bent over their slates and Readers.

They had a recess in the morning, at noon and in the afternoon, during which time the children played much as they had when Mr. Cullom was one of them; sometimes the older boys tried to slip in the building with a bit of chewing tobacco in their mouths, and some of the girls would use a little snuff. School let out about four o'clock in the afternoon; children and teachers walked through muddy roads to their homes.

After supper, Mr. Finch and Mr. Cullom would sit awhile with Mr. and Mrs. Sheek, and then they would retire to their room where the younger teacher would have his lesson from the older. Thus Mr. Cullom taught in the daytime, studied his own lessons at recess time and was taught at night.

During the cold of winter, Mrs. Sheek became sick; she developed pneumonia and was very sick. A colored woman came in to do the cooking, but Mr. Cullom cared for Mrs. Sheek. He fed her, kept her temperature chart, made mustard plasters for her; only for her most personal needs would he call in Lelia. With the coming of spring,

Mrs. Sheek improved and was soon cheerfully and gratefully back at her work.

The teaching and the studying continued for Mr. Cullom. On Sundays he had a reprieve. Once a month on Saturday afternoon and Sunday morning, they had preaching which meant that the room had to be cleaned from the school and the benches arranged for the church service. The Rev. William J. Hopkins was the preacher. The Yadkin Valley Baptist Church had been organized by Elder R. W. Creeves with seven members from Eatons Church at Cana and six members from Union Hill in Forsyth County; at first it had met under a brush-arbor.

At the close of school in June of 1886, Mr. Finch resigned as principal to go to Wake Forest to study for the ministry; he recommended his associate for his position. The trustees of the school elected him, and Mr. Cullom accepted their offer.

- 13 -

Having accepted the principalship of the school, Mr. Cullom now had to get a teacher's certificate. In the summer of 1886, he returned to Warren County and to his old room at Rodwell's store. The Allens were interested in all that had happened to him in the months he had been away. He took the public school examination at Warrenton and passed without any trouble; he accepted a school near Brown's Church for six weeks, for which he would be paid thirty dollars.

Brown's Church had a new pastor, the Rev. Thomas Jerome Taylor whose eyes were crossed and whose vision was so defective that he had to hold a book right up to his face to read it. Mr. Taylor was very kind to Mr. Cullom and encouraged him in every way he could. But Mr. Taylor was kind to everyone. Once when a Negro member of his church had died, he preached her funeral at the appointed hour. However, there was some confusion about the time, for later a daughter of the woman came to Mr. Taylor in tears. The sermon had been preached and she had not been there to hear it; she wanted the preacher to have the service all over. Mr. Taylor comforted her and said, "Melissa, you come to church next Sunday, and I'll say something nice about your mother." She came and was satisfied.

Mr. Cullom kept his old room at Rodwell's store during that summer. It was small, with a low ceiling; a door opened onto the porch which extended across the front of the store. There was a small window to the side. The room was furnished with a single bed, a table and a chair; the young man's clothes were hung on nails in the wall. There was a kerosene lamp on the table.

One night, late in July, Mr. Cullom sat alone at the table. A Bible was beside him. Perhaps Mr. Finch's going into the ministry, perhaps

Mr. Taylor's encouragement, perhaps Mr. Willcox's example—all of these, perhaps—but also something more stirred within his heart and mind. Later he was to say, "I can't remember the time when I didn't feel called to preach; it seems like the call, or necessity, had always been upon me."

But that night, he arose and knelt down by his chair and told the Lord how he felt—that from his earliest thoughts, he had been led to preach and that if the Lord would take him and go with him, he would surrender his life to God's will. There were no visions or seraphims— no voice commanding him to go "preach"; there was no crisis or dramatic sequence of events. His decision came as a logical conclusion of his life, the expression of his love for the Lord.

He arose and took pen and paper. It was significant that the first person he should think of now was his beloved pastor, Mr. A. G. Willcox. The young man of nineteen who had just surrendered his life unto the service of Jesus Christ wanted to tell the dear friend who had first led him to God.

In about ten days, a letter came back from Mr. Willcox. In it there were praises to God; the pastor told that he had read Willis' letter to the church at Quankie and that the church had granted him a license to preach. As preaching was the greatest of all work, he urged his young friend to prepare himself to do it the very best he could. He wanted Willis to go to Wake Forest College; in fact, he began at once to arrange for him to do so. Of course, he knew the young man didn't have the money, but the preacher had the faith that a way would be provided. And he imparted that faith to his young friend.

"Let me but live my life from year to year
With forward face and unreluctant soul;
Not hurrying to, nor turning from, the goal"—
HENRY VAN DYKE

THIRD AGE

STUDENT YEARS AT WAKE FOREST AND LOUISVILLE

1886-1896

Having found God's will for his life, the Cullom youth sought to fulfill it. First, there was his commitment to the school in Davie County; he wrote Mr. John Griffin, chairman of the trustees, and a "beautiful" letter came back, expressing joy over his decision and wishing him well in his plans to enter Wake Forest College.

A second question was concerning his ability to preach. The church at Quankie had given him a license to preach, but was he capable to do it? Mr. Taylor soon provided him an opportunity to find out; he invited Mr. Cullom to speak at prayer meeting on the last Thursday night of August, 1886, in the church at Warrenton. Mr. Taylor opened the service with a hymn and a prayer and then presented Mr. Cullom, a sandy-headed youth of nineteen. For his text, Mr. Cullom took Matthew 11:28-30 and entitled his message "Learn of Me." There are some things we can learn from Jesus which we can't learn from anybody else, said the young man; they are: (1) who God is, (2) what life means, and (3) how we can live that life. We do not know what others thought of his ability that night, but his first sermon removed all doubts in his own mind. This one thing he must do!

The third question was not so quickly answered: how was he to finance a college education? He received thirty dollars for his summer's teaching, and Mr. Burwell Davis lent him fifteen dollars (which he later gave him). As he journeyed homeward, Willis might have wondered what help his parents could give him; however, when he reached home, he found his father sick in bed. This made him wonder if he should even try to go to college; his mother came to his rescue: "Son," she said quietly, "you go on to college; if the situation here at home gets so we have to have you, I'll send for you. Go on, if it is only for three weeks; the girls and I will do the best we can."

The youth did what he could to help out during the few days he was at home; at night he dreamed of the adventure ahead. After saying "good night" to his parents, Willis would take the pale blue catalogue of Wake Forest College (1885-1886) to his old room. In the "Introduction" was a resumé of the college's history. Prominent among the purposes of founding the Baptist State Convention of North Carolina in 1830 was the establishment of a Baptist Literary Institution in the state. In 1832, Dr. William Hooper made definite recommendations to the convention for such an institution, and a farm of six hundred and fifteen acres "in the forest of magnificent oaks of original growth in Wake County" was purchased from Dr. Calvin Jones. Under the leadership of the Rev. Dr. Samuel Wait, the institute was opened (1834) "on the manual labor principle" which was soon abandoned; four years later the name was changed to Wake Forest

College. The Rev. W. M. Wingate, the Rev. T. H. Pritchard and
others served as president until 1883 when Dr. Charles E. Taylor was
chosen. The account of admission was of special concern to the Cullom
youth:

> Candidates for admission must be able to furnish satisfactory testi-
> monials of good moral character, and if coming from other incorporated
> institutions, must present certificates of honorable dismission.
> The applicant must report to the President within twenty-four hours
> after his arrival. . . . He must give his promise in writing to abide by
> the Regulations of the college, and to demean himself at all times in
> an orderly, respectful, and gentlemanly manner.

- 2 -

In spite of the fact that early the next morning he would be leaving
for college, Willis Cullom must have slept soundly on that night of
August 31, 1886, for he knew nothing of the earthquake until his
mother told him the next morning; even then it did not impress him.

At Weldon where he boarded the train for Wake Forest, there was
talk of nothing else. A young man's going off to college was hardly
noticed; some people were still scared, while others laughed at the
funny things that happened during the quake. There were laughs
about Jim Gooch who, upon hearing the excited voices of women
outside his house, had rushed outside, clad only in his nightshirt, to
calm the frightened women. "It's only an earthquake, ladies. There's
nothing to be excited about. Let's all be calm," he kept repeating as he
darted to and fro among them. And it had been difficult to tell which
alarmed the women more—the earthquake or the sight of Mr. Gooch
in his nightshirt.

On the train Willis heard that Charleston, South Carolina, had
suffered severely from the earthquake of which there had been five
distinct shocks, the first and most violent had come about 9:35 p.m.,
and the last and longest had come at 10:28 and had lasted until 10:31.
People told of windows rattling and of dishes being thrown to the
floor. Some claimed that they had heard a roaring sound like that of a
passing train preceding and accompanying the shocks. A station or
two before Wake Forest, several students boarded the train to talk
the new men into joining one of the two rivaling literary societies, but
even these upper classmen talked of earthquake. One of the fellows
said it woke him, but he thought it was only the boys making a racket
and so went back to sleep.

When he got off the train at the new depot, September 1, 1886,
Willis Cullom looked at Wake Forest for the first time. He took a
deep breath of all that he saw. The leaves on the trees were showing
their first fall colors; goldenrods were blooming among the broom sage
and young pines in an old field between the depot and the road which
circled the campus. A Negro man was replacing the board fence

around the campus with a stone wall; this was the beloved "Doctor Tom" Jeffries, who, in his own words, had been "'lected by Dr. Taylor to take charge of de grounds, de setting of trees and cutting of walks."

The Halifax youth walked to the home of Mrs. Sidney Abernathy who had been an Allen before her marriage and had been reared in the Brown neighborhood; he was shown his room on the middle floor, and was introduced to his roommate, W. J. Matthews, a Master of Arts senior. Mr. Matthews likely showed his "newish" roommate the campus. The College Building, built in 1838 and later called Wait Hall, was a brick structure with four stories on each end for dormitories and three stories in the center for a gymnasium on the first floor and lecture-rooms above. Wingate Memorial Hall had a small chapel and classrooms on its first floor, with the big chapel on the second floor which the Baptist church used for its services. The Heck-Williams Building (1878) housed the combined libraries of the two literary societies which had their halls on the second floor—the Euzelian in the south room and the Philomathesian in the north room. The chapel, the library, and the classrooms were heated by stoves; the dormitories, by fireplaces. Each student had his own woodpile and furnished his own kerosene lamp; they got their water from an open well to the southwest corner of the College Building.

The senior student also might have told "Cullom," as the "newish" student was to be called by his classmates, that the college walks had been originally designed by Englehard and described by Professor Mills as "beautiful" because they were "mathematically correct," but that last year they had been modified "to fit the new buildings and the railroad depot." A fellow classmate of Cullom was to write: "It was always the plan of Dr. Taylor to place a walk where the trail of students' feet indicated that it was needed." (Paschal, *op. cit.,* vol. II, p. 263.) "Matthews" might well have spoken of some of the trees on the campus and told Cullom that Dr. Taylor called them his "friends." (*Vide,* Bulletin of Wake Forest College, II, p. 112.) This was only a part of this remarkable man who was to serve as college president for twenty-one years and whom Cullom was to come to know as "the wisest man I have ever known."

Although his body seemed "somewhat frail," Dr. Charles Elisha Taylor was a strong personality. His brow was large and his well-kept reddish beard was abundant; his expression was always masterful. He was a Virginian by birth (1842) and had served in the Confederate Army under both General Lee and General Jackson; he had been wounded at Kernstown. After the war, he had received the degree of Bachelor of Literature from the University of Virginia and had spent several months in Europe before coming to Wake Forest as assistant professor of languages in 1871. Two years later he had married Miss Mary Prichard, the well-educated, cultured and dedicated daughter of Rev. John L. Prichard; their beautiful Christian home radiated love and light that made it indeed blessed to all who came into it.

When W. R. Cullom became acquainted with this great and wise man, Dr. Taylor was only forty-four years old; he had the dignity of "a born gentleman" which made others be gentlemanly in his presence. He could walk with a student across the campus and converse "with the same grave courtesy he would have shown a governor, and the dross was cleared from the student's heart and he knew that he . . . could become a prince in Dr. Taylor's presence." (Paschal, *op. cit.,* vol. II, p. 250.) Dr. Taylor was recognized and respected and loved as a great leader; Dr. T. H. Pritchard would speak of "the Baptists of North Carolina, from Dr. Taylor down."

- 3 -

In the fall of 1886, Cullom felt "way down" among the Baptists of his state and among the two hundred students at Wake Forest; he was not qualified for any of the four schools or departments—Languages, Mathematics, Natural Science, Belles Letters. He had to enroll in the preparatory department, where he was assigned classes in Latin, Greek and mathematics which met five times a week in the College Building. Professor Michael was his Latin teacher, and Professor William Bailey Royall taught him Greek. Once when Professor Luther Rice Mills, his mathematics teacher, was lecturing, a student snickered at him for stuttering; the professor turned to him and said, "You - you-you—laugh be - be - cause I can't tell you what I know, and I laugh at you because you don't know what to tell."

Like many others at that time, Mr. Cullom was troubled because he had little money. As a ministerial student, he would not have to pay the thirty dollars a term for tuition; but there were other expenses —board was nine dollars a month, wood about fifty cents a month, kerosene for his lamp about a quarter a month, plus library and incidental fees and the price of textbooks and paper. Mr. Willcox had advised him to apply to the Board of Ministerial Education for assistance as soon as he arrived at Wake Forest, and he lost no time in doing so.

The Board of Ministerial Education undertook to provide its beneficiaries board, room rent and washing money; its secretary was the Rev. R. T. Vann, pastor of the Wake Forest Baptist Church. This remarkable man had lost both of his arms in an old fashioned sawmill when he was a boy of sixteen; he turned the leaves of a book with the stubs of his arms and used an attachment on his left stub to write. At times when people commented on his misfortune and bemoaned his handicap with such words as "what a pity—there is no telling what you would have been if your accident had not happened," Mr. Vann would reply: "I'll tell you exactly what I would have been if the accident had not happened—a first class sawmill hand." Mr. Vann had a beautiful tenor voice and would often sing in the midst of a sermon. He was "bright, alert and witty," and his sermons reflected these qualities.

The applicant for help from the Board had to show a license to preach from his home church; he had to be in actual need of aid and had to submit to an examination by the Board on his conversion, his call to the ministry and his views on Biblical doctrines. He also had to agree that while he was under the patronage of the Board, he would not marry or become the pastor of a church or form any business connection without the consent of the Board; if he left the ministry, he was to refund the money he had received from the Board. In 1886, the elder William Royall served on the committee for examining the applicants; Mr. Cullom was to remember that he asked each man, "Brother, do you love souls?"

The young man from Halifax County answered this and the other questions of the Board as well as he could; he agreed to the terms under which he would receive help; he reported what funds he had and what he expected to receive. After finishing, he went outside. There, Wake Forest was all about him—the buildings, the walks, the trees; he felt its spirit—the warm friendliness, the strict scholarship and pursuit after truth, the devotion to the Lord, the aspiration of bringing the best out of a man and causing him to walk with dignity and yet humbly the paths of service for humanity. The young man felt a great love swell within him for the college; he wanted to stay here. Yet he was troubled in conscience; had he been fair to the Board and told them the whole truth?

After a moment of hesitation, he turned back to the examination room and asked the privilege of making an additional statement. Then he told that when he left home, his father was sick in bed and that, as much as he wanted to go to college, he might be called home at any time and thus be unable to carry out the terms governing the grant of aid. When he left the room again, he was glad he had been honest, and Wake Forest seemed all the dearer to him.

And he stayed. His mother never wrote for him to come home; and at its next meeting at Brown's Church, the Tar River Association raised two-hundred, eighty-four dollars and fifty cents for the Ministerial Board to be used for the benefit of W. R. Cullom, M. A. Adams and L. H. Joyner, ministerial students at Wake Forest. (Taylor, *Tar River*, p. 68.)

- 4 -

From his first coming to Wake Forest, Cullom had been "courted" by the two literary societies. The catalogue described these societies as "important aids in the work of education in the preservation of wholesome sentiments among the students." They met twice a week —on Friday nights for debates and on Saturday mornings for exercise

5

in composition and elocution. After visiting both societies, Cullom decided to join the Euzelian Literary Society, into which he was duly and unforgettably initiated and where such critics as Tom Holding and Tom Hufham "jumped all over" him for his mistakes and faults in public speaking.

A snowstorm began on December 4th at eight o'clock in the morning and lasted until the night of December 6th, leaving eight inches of snow on the ground. The students dug out their wood and kept their lamps burning late into the night. Cullom was doing all right with his studies. Just before Christmas, he petitioned the faculty to take the history examination in January. When this was granted, he stayed in his room during the holidays (only two days) and "crammed" Swinson's *Outline of Universal History* into his mind. In January, he passed the examination and was permitted to enter the class on political economy. At the beginning of the second semester Cullom moved to the Euzelian dormitory on the south end of Wait Hall; his roommate was M. A. Adams of Wilson, a ministerial student.

The big day of the entire school year at Wake Forest was "Miss Annie's Day," as the students fondly called the anniversary day of the literary societies. On this day, February 11, 1887, the sun rose clear and bright. Large groups of students met the morning mail train and welcomed the Cornet Band from the "City of Oaks." At two o'clock, a large audience crowded into Memorial Hall to hear the debate, "Was the Introduction of the Negro into the United States Productive of More Good than Evil?" (The affirmative won.)

Later a special train from Raleigh brought a very large number of "legislators, friends, and blushing beauties, all as merry and as welcomed as could be." By seven o'clock in the evening the auditorium was filled; two young orators, representing their respective societies, sat on the rostrum under the beautiful silk banners with their marshals, in blue and red regalia, by their sides. (Willis R. Cullom had brought in the Euzelian banner and was seated on the rostrum.) Mr. J. B. Carlyle was presented as the orator of the Philomathesian Society. The war which had broken and impoverished the South had been ended only twenty-one years and the last federal troops of occupation had been withdrawn only ten years when Mr. Carlyle arose to address the Societies and their distinguished guests and friends on "The Lost Cause." After speaking of the causes of the war, Mr. Carlyle reviewed its events and spoke of its consequences. As paradoxical as it may seem, he said, the war had strengthened the Union; it had abolished slavery, thereby removing the stain upon the fair name of America. And, what is the duty of the South toward the Union?

> Heaven forbid that we should ever cease to cherish, to honor the memory of those who fought for the lost cause . . . but should we . . . keep alive the hate and prejudices of the war? No, never! Let these be forgotten—buried, never, never to be resurrected.

And why should we not be loyal to the union, when it is the same grand old union that Washington, Jefferson and Madison—"Southern Men all"—had helped to frame. He declared that the old feelings of prejudice and hate between the North and South were giving way to a new era of good feeling. He concluded by wishing that he could shout, like the brave Epaminondas, a command of "onward and upward!" (*The Wake Forest Student,* vol. VI, pp. 244-252.)

Mr. Carlyle sat down amid the applause of the audience, and Mr. J. L. Josey of Scotland Neck introduced the Euzelian orator, Mr. W. P. Stradley, whose subject was "The Grand Old Man." Both of these young men, according to the *Student* reporter, "did themselves credit, their subjects justice, their societies honor, and gave their appreciative audience satisfaction and pleasure."

After "a few well-chosen and clear cut remarks," Mr. Lineberry, the presiding officer, invited the audience to the literary halls for a social gathering. We are told that soon the halls and galleries in the library were filled with those who sought to make merry and to be merry.

> The band played in the Reading Room below. Cupid was evidently busy. There were quite a number of accomplished and popular young ladies present. . . . The prolonged whistle of the locomotive called the excursionists to the depot at twelve o'clock, which was many hours too soon for some to leave, and all went away with pleasant memories of Wake Forest and her boys. Others lingered in the halls until the wee small hours of a new day passed away and sealed forever the pleasures of one more Anniversary, which can safely be claimed the grandest in the history of the "twin sister" Societies of Wake Forest College.

- 5 -

The anniversary day was talked and discussed for a long time; but other matters, like studying, called for the attention of the young men, and they returned to their books. Their daily schedule began at eight o'clock with "morning prayers," which they were required to attend as they were the Sunday morning services of the local Baptist Church. These devotional services were held in the "small chapel" on the ground floor of Wingate Memorial Hall. The professors entered through a side door from a recitation room; they sat in regular seats on the platform facing the students, with the President sitting in the center chair. A bell was tapped, and the Keeper-of-the-roll called the roll of students who answered, each to his name. After a hymn, a member of the faculty read from the scriptures, sometimes making brief comments and offered prayer. The president made the announcements and dismissed the meeting. George Washington Paschal, a fellow student of W. R. Cullom, was to write of these morning services:

> It was all but impossible that these students should not have been affected as they heard President Taylor pray to God in almost all his prayers in chapel that He would help every one before him to make the very most of his life. And there was hardly a prayer in any of these

54   *The Cullom Lantern*

services in which every student was not carried back to his own home and brought into the presence of father and mother, sisters and brothers, to join with their leader in asking God's blessings upon them and His protection of their health. (Paschal, *op. cit.,* Vol. II, pp. 237-238.)

The students were reminded that they were responsible moral agents and that they would be treated as such. They were no longer boys, the President would sometimes tell them; "You are men—young men indeed, but still men—and so you must think for yourselves and act as men." In the new catalogue (1886-1887), Dr. Taylor stated the value of discipline in the development of manliness and dignity of character in young men:

> Earnest efforts are made (at Wake Forest) to develop in students sentiments of self-respect and habits of self-control. They are treated and trusted as gentlemen, and are expected to respond to this treatment by gentlemanly deportment at all times. The college is in no sense a school of reform, and the faculty very earnestly hope that young men who have formed vicious habits, or who cannot restrain themselves from mischief, will not seek to become members of the Institution. Those who do not propose to conform to the few and simple regulations of the college ought not to matriculate as students.

In 1887, some of the leading students at the college were beginning to read Charles Darwin's *Origin of the Species* and were discussing it in small groups. On Sunday evening, February 13th, Professor William Louis Poteat lectured on "The First Chapter of Genesis in the Light of Modern Knowledge." The editor of *The Student* was very pleased with what Dr. Poteat said; he reported that "the lecture completely reconciled the scientific theory of creation with that given by Moses." Others, however, were not so persuaded, and the discussions continued. Many years later Cullom was to write:

> My conception (upon entering Wake Forest) of the Bible, of religion, of church, of education and all the rest of it was very stereotyped and rigid. It had all been given to me in a lump and must be received and used in the same way. But it was not long before I began to hear some of the upper classmen speak of the new conception of how the world came into being and into its present shape and character. This new doctrine was called "evolution."
> About fifteen years after this time an old man in the country said to me one day, "Brother Cullom, what are we going to do with this 'evilution'?" The old man expressed my feeling about the matter at the time of which I am speaking in the way he pronounced the word. Occasionally I heard the word mentioned and some (to me) disturbing comment about it. If I am to be honest and frank about the matter I shall have to confess that I was thoroughly frightened, that I was about as miserable in my mental machinery as a man well could be. What was I to do? I thought I had a Bible handed directly from heaven; it seemed to me that my Bible and all my foundations were about to be swept from under me: What was I to do?
> In that trying hour I tried to do two things which seem to me now, as I look back upon them, to be as sensible things as could be done by any one under the circumstances: (1) to keep my mouth shut. There are times in one's life when that is a great achievement; it was such at that time. (2) I tried as best I could to pray. Somehow I felt that maybe God had a way for me and that in His own good time He would lead me into it. (*Charity and Children,* July 17, 1947.)

As he waited, Cullom studied his lessons and read widely. The Library Record Book of 1886-1887 shows that he checked out for that year a total of thirty-six books, of which the following are samples: *Contemporary Socialism, Universal Biography, Literary Style, History of N. C., The Theatre, Queen of Scotland, Moral Feelings, Pearson on Infidelity, The Edinburgh Review, The Life and Times of Henry Clay.*

At the commencement of 1887, an honorary degree (LL.D.) was conferred by the college upon Professor Woodrow Wilson of Bryn Mawr College. Mr. Jack Mills, the founder of the Baptist Orphanage in North Carolina, gave the alumni address; W. R. Cullom remembers this "giant both in longitude and in latitude" began his address by saying in a deep gutteral voice, "If all mistakes were fodder stacks, we'd have more fat horses." (*Charity and Children,* June 7, 1946.)

- 6 -

During the summer of 1887, W. R. Cullom sold books for B. F. Johnson and Company of Richmond, Virginia; John Robertson, a fellow student at Wake Forest, was the general agent who employed and trained him for this work. Cullom's territory was Franklin County, and the book he was to sell was entitled *Sea and Land;* also he could take orders for Bibles.

On Sunday the Cullom youth attended church services wherever he could. One morning at the close of the service at Lear's Methodist Church, near Louisburg, the pastor, Dr. Richard Whitakers, said: "Mr. Cullom has some nice Bibles to sell, which he will be glad to show you." The young man with sandy-colored thinning hair arose and spoke briefly on the Bibles and their prices; he said he was taking orders now and would deliver them in the fall, when he would collect for them. Along with many others, Mattie Lou Bolton, a young girl of seventeen, placed an order for a Bible which cost two dollars and fifty-five cents.

Seldom was there a problem of accommodation for the young ministerial student; people were very generous in welcoming him into their homes. Thus while tramping over Franklin County that summer, he came to know a great many people whose friendship he kept through the years. On one Saturday afternoon he found lodging in the home of M. R. Purnell, a few miles east of Franklinton. Mr. Purnell had been an earnest layman in whose heart the love of God burned so brightly that he was compelled to speak to others of it. As these became Christians, they grouped themselves together for worship, study and service. In time, these groups became churches—Harris Chapel, Bethany, Bethlehem, Elm Grove and others—and for their pastor they wanted the man who had led them to God, and so Brother Purnell was ordained. Although he had not been privileged to attend school, he was "educated in life and heart"; of him W. R. Cullom was to write: "I have not known a more diligent, a more earnest, a more faithful, or a more successful minister of Christ." (*Charity and Children,* May 29, 1947.)

Not only did he preach whenever the opportunity was afforded him and make friends wherever he went, but Mr. Cullom also sold Bibles and books that summer—several hundred dollars worth of them. In the fall he rented a horse and buggy and delivered his orders. With forty per cent commission of his sales, he was "in good plight" to begin his second year at Wake Forest.

At the close of his delivery, he went by his home in Halifax County and gave his father fifty dollars to help out there. (In the preceding January, his mother had lost her fourteenth and last child.) The younger children gathered around "Brother" as he told of his college experiences and the work of the summer. After this brief visit, he returned the horse and buggy and hurried back to Wake Forest, where the college already had opened.

- 7 -

In the October issue of the *Student,* J. W. Lynch wrote: "Newish! Still there's more to follow. We are coming Father Taylor, two-hundred and thirty more." And W. R. Cullom of Halifax was among them.

There were some jokes and whistles at the "newish," but the hazing of the new students was very mild. At times there were jokes on upper-classmen and even professors, for once a month on the bulletin-board tree there appeared a paper called the *Howler,* which was "published on the dark of the moon by the Sophomore class, and devoted to the interest of the Fresh, Faculty, and Fools." But the main task was the studying, and Cullom found his courses required a great deal of it. In his class on English grammar and composition, under Professor William Royall, he studied Whitney's *Essentials of English Grammar,* Kellogg's *Composition and Rhetoric,* Sweet's *Anglo-Saxon Primer* and Clark's *Practical Rhetoric.* Under Professor Mills, he completed Newcomb's *Algebra* and spent the spring term on plane, solid and spherical geometry. The principles of Latin grammar were taught in connection with the reading of Caesar's *de Bello Gallico* and Virgil's *Aeneid;* prose composition was studied in connection with original exercises which were required weekly. In his junior class of Greek, Professor W. B. Royall required the students to read Xenophon's *Anabasis* and selections from Herodus, with reviews in grammar and oral and written exercises.

A gymnasium, with "the most approved pieces of apparatus," was opened in the afternoon; but in the fall of 1887, baseball was "all the go," although the fellows still played a game they called "bullpen." And there was a new game, "football," a rude approximation of the Rugby game with much rushing and with the ball advanced only by kicking, which was played in a vacant field, north of the campus. Cullom was "not much to play ball"; other things seemed more important and took his attention. Once a week he would "work out" a little in the gymnasium and then turn to other matters. Even with the help of the Board of Ministerial Education, he found it difficult to meet expenses. Years later he was to write:

> It was necessary for me to "make every edge cut" in order to stay in college at all. D. C. Rogers and I conceived the idea of organizing a boarding club. We talked the matter over with Mrs. Baker, a widow lady, who agreed to prepare our meals for us at a nominal cost. And so we formed what was known as the Baker Club. I was the manager. I bought the groceries, made out the accounts at the end of the month, collected from each man in the club, settled with Mrs. Baker, and so forth. Each member of the club paid me a little fee—ten cents a week, I believe it was. Later there were several such houses, but ours was the first one. My recollection is that our board was about six dollars a month, and we had good food that was well prepared.
>
> Besides managing the club, I was asked through a friend of mine, Mr. Frank M. Lampkin, to serve as a sort of agent in Wake Forest for the Whiting and Horton Clothiers of Raleigh. They paid me a small fee on each suit of clothes that I sold for them. In this way I made enough to pay for my own clothes and a little more. (Biographical Notes.)

The *Student* periodical of 1887-1888 is quite revealing of the thoughts, problems and events of the campus and times. Frank B. Hendron observed that older members of the societies could identify the preachers among the new students by their "peculiar drawling, singsong style of speaking." The *Student* editors reported that President and Mrs. Grover Cleveland were well received during their tour of the southern states; they wrote of Europe:

> The crown prince of Germany is said to be suffering from Smokers Cancer. It will be remembered that the late Gen. Grant died from a like affection. The prince's recovery can scarcely be hoped for. Not only Germany but Europe at large feel a deep solicitude in his condition, as the next in succession is a young man of rash temper and boundless ambition. (Vol. VII, pp. 22, 71, 77.)

Attention was called to the "rude and ungentlemanly behaviour of some of our students" who, when a lady passes through the campus or by the college, cry out "angels on the campus!" The faculty was petitioned for a week's vacation at Christmas, and the question of studying the Bible in the college curriculum was raised. J. W. Lynch summed it all up:

> Hurrah! Christmas is coming. So are examinations. Ugh! Cheer up, boys; there are bright spots ahead—Xmas, anniversary, commencement, marriage, the millennium!

Early in the spring, revival services were held by the local Baptist Church, at the conclusion of which there was to be a baptismal service. There was quite a number of students to be baptized, but there was yet one young man who weighed heavily upon Cullom's heart and

mind—D. D. Dougherty. Dougherty had never made a profession of
faith in the Lord. On the day when Pastor Gwaltney was to have the
baptismal service, Cullom "felt inclined" to go to talk with Dougherty
about surrendering to the Lord. Dougherty roomed on the first floor
of the dormitory. As he went down the stairs to his room and as he
knocked on his door, Cullom was so uneasy that he hoped Dougherty
would not be in; but Dougherty was. Cullom walked in and told him
what was on his heart; "there is still time for you to be baptized this
very afternoon," he said. Dougherty replied: "Why, Cullom, I've been
thinking about it. I'll do it." He arose, got his clothes and, with Cullom,
hurried to the place where the others were gathering and was baptized.

- 8 -

Rev. J. W. Lynch, two years senior to W. R. Cullom, was already
an eloquent preacher when the Halifax student first heard him. Cullom
enjoyed him and often heard him at New Hope and Perry's Chapel; he
was surprised and honored when Lynch asked him to supply for him
one Sunday. Soon another surprise was to come—a letter from Rev.
T. J. Taylor stating that he had resigned the pastorate at Warren
Plains and had recommended that the church call W. R. Cullom.

In April of 1888, W. R. Cullom, now a young man of twenty-one,
rode the train to Warren Plains for a Saturday afternoon and Sunday
morning appointment. When he got off the train, a barefoot, ten-year-
old girl, with straight flaxen hair, came up to him. "Are you Mr.
Cullom?" she asked.

"Yes, I am," replied the young man.

"Papa told me to tell you that you are to have dinner at our
house." As the two walked together, the little girl said her name was
Lizzie Weldon; the preacher was to call her his "first parishioner."

Warren Plains was Mr. Cullom's first pastorate, and he always was
to have "a very tender spot" in his heart for the people there. Originally
known as Tanner's Meeting House, the church dated back before
1785; it had fostered two mission churches, but in 1851 an anti-
missionary sentiment had caused it to withdraw from the Tar River
Association. By 1875 it had declined until it had only twelve active
members. In that year, the church was moved to Warren Plains and a
small frame building was erected. In 1880, the church was received
again into the Tar River Association, and after two years of Rev.
T. J. Taylor's leadership, it was in good condition when W. R. Cullom
was called to become its pastor.

On June 23, 1888, a letter from the Warren Plains Baptist Church,
requesting the ordination of Brother W. R. Cullom, was read at the
Quankie Church. Brother Knox Dickens made a motion that the pastor
select a presbytery to examine Brother Cullom. On Saturday, July 21st,
the Rev. T. J. Taylor of Warrenton came to assist Brother Willcox in

examining the candidate. On the next day, July 22nd, Brother Willcox and Taylor reported that they had examined Brother Cullom on his views of the Bible and doctrine and had found them entirely satisfactory; they recommended that the church proceed to ordain him.

Mr. Taylor preached the ordination sermon from Second Timothy 4:2. Mr. Willcox charged his friend to be true to the word of God as revealed in the Bible. Then the young man knelt while Rev. T. J. Taylor prayed, after which the elders laid their hands upon him and blessed him. Then rising, the Rev. W. R. Cullom pronounced the benediction. The Quankie Church records show that the following letter was sent to Warren Plains:

> State of N. C.
> Halifax Co., July 22, 1888
> To the churches of Jesus Christ greetings: In accordance with a call from the Baptist Church at Quankie, the undersigned met with said church on July 22, 1888 and proceeded by prayer and imposition of hands to set apart the bearer hereof Elder W. R. Cullom to the full work of the gospel ministry, whom we hereby commend to the people of God and churches of Christ everywhere as a worthy minister of the gospel— Praying that the Great Head of the church may abundantly bless him as we subscribe ourselves your fellow laborers in the gospel.
>
> A. G. Willcox }
> T. J. Taylor   } Presbytery

To the young minister's amazement, the church at Warren Plains immediately asked him to hold an evangelistic meeting for them. Years later he wrote:

> In response to this call, I secured a set of Matthew Henry's commentary on the whole Bible. There was a little vacant log house on my father's farm which had been used as a school house. It was the same house in which Rev. A. G. Willcox began his ministry in that community seven years before. In this school house, alone with God, with my Bible and with Matthew Henry I spent a month. This was my "Arabia," so to speak. When I went to Warren Plains for the revival service, I went equipped with a good stock of humility, a little knowledge of the Bible, some fifteen or twenty sermons that I had gathered as best as I could from prayer to God, from my study of the Scriptures, and from Matthew Henry. (*Charity and Children,* August 23, 1945.)

The boy-preacher was amazed at the use the Lord made of him that summer; many were brought to know the Lord, and the whole church was strengthened.

Mr. Cullom never lived in Warren Plains; he came on the train Saturday afternoon and visited the community, mostly on foot. Mrs. Mary Hawks would recall:

> One Saturday morning we were trying to finish grading and tying up some tobacco, when Mr. Cullom came up. He joined in and helped us finish and then asked my father to go with him to visit someone who was sick.

The Nat B. Weldons had been married about three years when Mr. Cullom first came to their church; he was often in their home for dinner and to spend the night. He took "a special liking" to a niece of Mrs. Weldon, but Anna and her people belonged to another denomination; the differences of their churches discouraged them.

One Saturday night Mr. Cullom sat on the porch with Mr. Nat Weldon. After the train trip and an afternoon of visiting, the young preacher sat wearily as his friend droned on and on in a long drawn out speech. Mr. Weldon enjoyed the company of his young pastor; he would store up questions and observations for the week end when they could be together. But that Saturday night the young preacher was scarcely listening when suddenly out shot: "Brother Cullom, what do you think is the most common sin?" Mr. Cullom cleared his throat and tried to arouse himself. He was young and had not thought much on the subject; in fact, his thoughts a moment before were far away from such. But he answered: "Selfishness. I reckon selfishness is the most common sin." Many, many years later this same preacher said, "I have thought much on the question put to me that night and if I had to answer it again, I would only underscore the answer I hastily gave Nat Weldon."

The young pastor shared the conviction of the Christian's obligation to send the gospel to those who did not know Him. Tanner's Meeting House had almost died when the hearts of its people turned from the Great Commission to "go make disciples of all nations"; Warren Plains had flourished as it entered into this task. The young pastor was anxious to cultivate this missionary fervor among his members. At that time some of the Southern Baptist women were beginning to organize societies for the promotion of missions. As there was such a society at Wake Forest, the young pastor resolved to find out how it worked. He knew Dr. W. S. Simmons' daughter, Eva Belle, whom he asked permission to accompany to a meeting of the Woman's Missionary Society. Later he wrote:

> The meeting was held in the old Wait home, then occupied by Dr. and Mrs. J. B. Powers and Mrs. Powers' parents. The women met in the living room—the North room on the second floor. They gave me a big rocking chair in the middle of the room. I think my shoe is about 7½. On that occasion and in that room they seemed to me to be at least 155! My hands were correspondingly large and I had no idea at all as to where I should put them. You may be sure that I was glad to get out of that room. (Biographical Notes.)

But the young pastor had learned how to organize a missionary society; in May of 1890, the first missionary society in the Tar River Association was organized at Warren Plains.

- 9 -

In September of 1888, Mr. Cullom began his third year at Wake Forest; he took Latin, Greek, English grammar, trigonometry and political science. There was a new professor on the campus in 1888: Benjamin F. Sledd who had come to take the chair of modern languages and proceeded to take the heart of Miss Nita Purefoy, "a young woman of great charm and many accomplishments." For the week of Christmas holidays, some of the students went home; those who remained on the campus had "a pleasant time in a quiet way."

During the summer of 1889, Mr. Cullom was busy with his churches, for in addition to Warren Plains, he was serving Concord and Knap-of-Reeds in Granville County and Corinth in Franklin County. The Concord Baptist Church, organized in 1794, had about one hundred and twenty-eight members when W. R. Cullom became its "faithful pastor." In the Walter Clark home, where he often spent the night, he would open the big family Bible before bedtime and by a kerosene lamp would read to the whole family; even the four-year-old son would remember his visits through the years. In the home of Mr. Thomas D. Lyon, Mr. Cullom was considered a member of the family—so much so that the son, Sam, thought he was. Even then the young minister noted that the railroad was bringing a town into being at Creedmoor and began talking of starting a mission there.

The Knap-of-Reeds Baptist Church had been organized in 1846 by the Concord Baptist Church and by 1888 was twice the size of Concord. An extension from the main auditorium made the wooden building in the shape of the letter "L."

The Corinth Baptist Church was located in a prosperous section of Franklin County; in 1888 it had about a hundred and fifty members. In his efforts to strengthen the church, Mr. Cullom had the Rev. Walter Parker assist him in an evangelistic meeting, which reached many in that community.

- 10 -

The sensation of the opening of Wake Forest College in the fall of 1889 was "the absence of Professor Poteat's mustache." The college adopted black and gold as its official colors, and W. R. Cullom signed up for Senior Latin, Senior Greek, Senior English, Senior Math and Physics. As there were only two in the Physics class, Arthur Harris and W. R. Cullom knew that each would be called upon every time the class met, and they soon learned that Professor Lanneau "expected his pupils to know the subject in hand to the very minutest detail."

In January (1890), Mr. Cullom moved his church letter from Quankie to Wake Forest and read that a new disease, called "La-Grippe," had reached America from Europe. Soon it appeared in Wake Forest and spread rapidly among the students and faculty. One morning only ninety-eight men were present at prayers; among those who were absent was W. R. Cullom. At the beginning of the term he and his roommate, M. A. Adams, had taken a room in the home of Mr. Charles Reid, the agent at the railroad station. In her calm and gentle way, Mrs. Reid nursed Mr. Cullom as if he had been her own son; she used all of the old remedies she knew and filled him with chicken soup and hot tea. Soon he was able to return to his classes.

On February 10th, Mr. Cullom served as the secretary of an ordaining presbytery for J. W. Kenney; on February 19, 1890, the *Biblical Recorder,* the Baptist Journal of North Carolina, published his report, the first of many articles which were to appear in that periodical over his name. That spring the *Student* editors "gave a hand" to the trustees of the N. C. Baptist Female University for having decided to locate it at Raleigh; in June, they reported that "another use for the Edison phonograph had been found—to preserve the language of the Indians." But the big news of the closing months of that school year was the gas fixtures in the college library and the fine sparkling chandelier in the halls of the literary societies.

- 11 -

On September 3rd, the college opened with the news that Mr. J. A. Bostwick of New York City had offered to add one half to whatever amount, up to $50,000, which might be raised for the endowment of the college by March 1, 1891. As Dr. Taylor turned to the task of raising this money, W. R. Cullom began his study of German under Professor Sledd, who had married Miss Purefoy the preceding June. Mr. Cullom took another course in Physics under Professor Lanneau and a course in Chemistry under Professor Brewer; in addition to three hours of lectures, the chemistry course required two hours of laboratory work a week. All of these were hard courses, but the one which really scared him was Professor Poteat's Natural History. Years later, W. R. Cullom was to recall his reactions to Professor Poteat's classes:

> I went into his class in botany. He led us over the fields, through the woods, up hill and down hill, and all about the country for several miles around. This was a new method of study to me. He was leading us back very close to the real source of things. . . . Of course his method of teaching was far removed from that of the dogmatic approach to truth. He tried to bring his students into the presence of truth itself, bid them open their eyes, take careful note of what they saw, write down in their notebooks exactly what they saw and thus let each item speak for itself. These observations were made in the laboratory, discussed in the lecture room, and each man was left to see for himself and draw his own conclusions. At the time it seemed to me a rather treacherous way to teach and I confess that I was much befuddled. (*Charity and Children,* May 5, 1949.)

The problem of evolution was intensified for the young minister; as it bothered many others, J. L. Kesler, the "Eu" editor of the *Student,* came out with this advice:

> It is not an unpardonable sin to say that theology may be wrong in some particulars. . . . It is only a system of interpretation. It must always adapt itself to the wider knowledge of the time as, indeed, it has been doing through the ages. . . . Follow the Bible and it becomes to you, in your own mind's development, a growing ideal. Forms and shadows fade, but the spirit, the deeper meaning, ever new, feeds the

growing life. Follow your own faith through its transitions of doubt to a faith that is stronger and better, as it approximates nearer and nearer to the real divinity, the broader, loftier, holier, tenderer, loving humanity of the living Messiah, and you find the growing ideal nearing the reality of the perfect Unseen." (*The Student,* vol. X, p. 125.)

Of course, the "Eu" editor wrote of other things—such as the interesting game of La Crosse and the "large and glorious masquerade" which, on the night of December 18th, "went all over the Hill showing their superior ability in making fools of themselves and caused much merriment"; he reported that on January 2, 1891, a group of students had serenaded the bridal couple, Prof. and Mrs. J. B. Carlyle, from 10:00 p.m. to 5:00 a.m. in spite of the extremely cold weather. But the problems raised by the theory of evolution kept drawing the attention of the editors of the *Student* and of the world. Upon the heresy trial of the Rev. Howard MacQueay of Canton, Ohio, J. L. Kesler pleaded for "a more tolerant spirit"; in the February issue of the *Student* (1891), he wrote:

> If man seeks the truth persistently, earnestly, reverently, though clouds grow thick about him, and darkness shuts the landscape in, yet he will find it in the end. The only provision is that he shall keep on *seeking* even in the darkness, trusting to the Unseen Hand to lead him to the light.

W. R. Cullom shared the faith that he would be led to the light, and he was brought to that light by John L. Kesler himself. In February of 1891, Mr. Kesler was sick in bed; Mr. Cullom went to see his friend. At first he sat on the bed, but as they talked on, he put his head to the foot of the bed and stretched out beside Kesler. The conversation got around to the question of evolution; Cullom confessed he was troubled by it.

"Well, it doesn't trouble me anymore," replied Kesler. "The Bible says God created man, but it doesn't say how He did it. The word 'day' in the Bible is not always used for a period of twenty-four hours; it is sometimes used for a life time, as 'in the day of Abraham,' and the psalmist says a thousand years are but as a day unto the Lord. Modern science does not deny that God created the world; it only tries to understand the process of creation. God is still creating; the process of development continues. God does not change; as He works today, so He must have worked in the long ago." (W. R. Cullom; also *Student,* vol. X, pp. 125, 249.)

Cullom heard this and remembered it; as he thought upon it, light began to break through his clouds. Again and again he turned to the account of creation in Genesis; over and over it proclaims that the world and life and man are the creation of God, but nowhere does it describe the exact method God used. And peace started to come back into Cullom's mind and heart — not all at once, but gradually as the light shone through Kesler's remarks.

- 12 -

Upon the advice of President Taylor, W. R. Cullom stayed at the college another year to take his master's degree; he moved down to Mrs. Watson's boarding house and roomed with James Long of Monroe for that year of 1891-1892. In the *Student,* G. W. Paschal reported that on October 23rd Professor Mills had discussed "Recent Rainmaking Experiments" at the first meeting of the Wake Forest Scientific Society, and on November 10th, about seven hundred people witnessed "probably the best and most scientific game of foot-ball ever played in Raleigh"; Wake Forest formed a "V" on the line-up and "like a tidal wave, swept the field" to defeat the University of North Carolina.

1892 was a "leap year" and *tempus fugit*—especially for the seniors who had to prepare a thesis of two thousand words by May 1st. That spring the voice of Germany's Wilhelm II was heard as he revived talk of the divine right of kings, but the students at Wake Forest were more interested in jumping. Editor Paschal noted that at any time of day a crowd could be seen gathered around as the boys jumped. He also stated: "The campus these lovely moonshiny nights is alive with the joyous voices of happy boys who are overflowing with animal spirits."

W. R. Cullom used his "animal spirits" for something other than shouting on "lovely moonshiny nights" or jumping with the boys. Late in March of 1892 he wrote to the ministerial students with whom he had been associated at Wake Forest:

> My dear Brother,
>   I want to ask you to aid me a little in collecting some facts which I hope to make useful to the cause of Christian education, and especially to ministerial education among the Baptists of North Carolina. I want to get a little sketch of life of all the young ministers with whom I have been associated in college. I want to know something of their advantages or disadvantages at birth and in early life; something of their struggles in getting to college; some of their ups and downs while in college; whether or not they graduated and if not, why not; whether they were in debt when they left college; if they were aided by the Board of Education, if so how long, etc. . . . I . . . wish to use this information to stimulate and help other young men who need encouragement. I hope, therefore, that besides giving these things in a general way, you will mention any little incident in your life which might be helpful to the other young men struggling to get an education. I am glad that I have been associated with you in our college career. I hope to get through in June and then to meet you on the world's great battle field in the fight for our common Captain. Wishing you great success in your work, I am,
>
> Yours for the Master,
> W. R. CULLOM

The earliest reply was dated April 6th and came from Wm. Jessup Sholar in Hamilton, New York, where he was concluding eight years of college and seminary at the cost of about $3,200, of which $1,200 had been given him in scholarships; $2,000 he had gained himself, leaving about $200 which he still owed. G. L. Merrill of Sanford wrote that he came to Wake Forest when he was about thirty years old and received help from the Board of Education; four years later he left the college with a B.A. degree and "about as much money as I had when I began my course." From Newton Centre, Massachusetts, W. G. Jones wrote that he was eighteen years old before he saw a railroad and declared that "any young man with any push or energy can . . . obtain an education." L. H. Joyner, Jr., of Finch, N. C., told a different story:

> While I was at college, I had two suits of clothes, you helped me to get them. I never had any money to spend while there. I should have graduated if I had not been overcome by the limited means I had.

C. B. Williams of Winston said his indebtedness on leaving college was "about forty dollars." M. L. Kesler wrote of brushing his old clothes and of piling up the blacking on his coarse shoes to make them decent while at Wake Forest. T. C. Buchaman wrote:

> During my course at Wake Forest I had served as sexton of the literary society and of the church one year, keeping up six stoves and lamps, had sold apples and peanuts and goods, had traveled as insurance agent, had served churches, taught school in vacation and worked at the carpenter's trade. I was on the eve of leaving college once because of financial embarrassment, when Drs. Wm. Royall and C. S. Taylor (Pres.) supplied my need of $25 which I paid the next fall. I entered at 27 and finished at 32. My entire educational career was one of mental, physical and spiritual struggle, with stern penury grinning in my face.

W. M. Gilmore told of another kind of struggle:

> I suppose there comes a time in every boy's life when he is disposed to search for truth, and to doubt everything in creation. Such was my experience soon after I entered college. About the first book I read after entering college was Tolstoi's "My Religion" . . . it caused me more mental doubt. However, I did not entirely forsake the faith. I was clinging to it until I could find a more reasonable one.

(Other letters came from M. A. Adams, W. E. Crocker, J. R. Boothe, W. J. Ward, T. S. Andres, I. T. Newton, James E. Green, I. P. Hedgepeth, Albert Moses Ross, T. L. Blalock, J. R. Pace, R. R. Day, Charles V. Brooks, Junius W. Millard, John R. Moore, A. E. L. Pittman, Rufus K. Carter, M. P. Davis, Jul. E. Yates, and Jas. I. Kendrick, L. C. Horner, J. H. Ball and C. B. Johnson. All of these letters were copied by W. R. Cullom and on March 21, 1931, were presented to the Wake Forest College Library, under the title, "A Group of Ministerial Students in Wake Forest College, 1886-1892.")

- 13 -

At the class day program on Monday evening, June 6th, Mr. I. Hardesty, the class prophet, placed himself thirty years into the future and saw a new Wake Forest of "great granite buildings with electric lights and other modern improvements." On Tuesday evening, Prof. J. B. Carlyle addressed the alumni; the Baccalaureate sermon was preached on Wednesday by the Rev. Carter Helmee Jones of Tennessee. On Thursday, June 9th, W. R. Cullom and James Long had their devotional exercise together in their room before breakfast as they had done throughout the year. But this would be the last time they would read the Bible and pray together. Cullom could hardly speak; he was never given much to crying, but as he came down to breakfast that morning "mist" came into his eyes and he had difficulty in controlling himself.

In the *Recorder* of June 15, 1892, "J. C. C." reported:

> Everything conspired to make this (closing exercise) one of the most pleasant and cheering occasions. After giving, at the entrance of the hall, the "college yell," the largest class which had graduated in the State since the war, filed up the main aisle and took their places on the rostrum amid great enthusiasm from the audience.

After an invocation, the First Regiment Band of Virginia played a musical selection, and G. W. Paschal gave the salutatory address. Then, another musical number, and five seniors gave orations: C. D. Graver, "We are Drifting—Whither?"; James Long, "The Coming Man"; O. H. Dockery, Jr., "Napoleon's Greatest Marshal"; J. W. Millard, "A Meeting and a Farewell"; J. P. Spence, "A Disciple of Peace." The titles of the other theses were printed on the program; W. R. Cullom's thesis was entitled "Our Heritage." Dr. Taylor conferred the degrees: five Masters of Arts (including William [*sic*] Richard Cullom), twenty-six Bachelor of Arts and five Bachelor of Science.

In his Baccalaureate address, Dr. Taylor said the world had a right to expect three things of a college graduate: (1) scholarship, (2) common sense and practical ability, and (3) character; he urged the graduates not to disappoint the world, their parents and their God. W. W. Vass, Jr., gave the valedictory address, and the band drowned out the last sobs and shouts of the departing seniors.

- 14 -

Upon leaving Wake Forest, Mr. Cullom went to Creedmoor in Granville County where Mr. Thomas D. Lyon took him into his house as a member of his family; Mr. Cullom boarded with Mr. John Rogers. Lois Rogers Winstead would remember that even then they were beginning to think of Mr. Cullom as "the finest man of all."

All during that summer of 1892, while he was busy with the pastoral and preaching duties of four churches and the mission area of Creedmoor, Mr. Cullom's thoughts drifted dreamily to the prospect of going to the seminary at Louisville, Kentucky. Back in their room before graduation, James Long had declared that he would go to Rochester to study under the great Augustus Strong; he had decided he wanted to go to Louisville to study under the great John A. Broadus. But how could he? Upon remembering God's providence in his staying six years at Wake Forest, he was willing to trust God to provide a way at Louisville, if only he could find the means of getting there.

By the end of the summer he had saved thirty dollars. After assisting Mr. Taylor in ordaining some deacons at Warrenton, he went home where his father offered to do what he could to help him, but he knew he could do very little. At Warrenton, Dr. R. D. Fleming, a dentist and Mr. Watson's son-in-law, had told him to call upon him for a loan of a hundred dollars whenever he needed it; he remembered that kind offer and held it in reserve. The members of his churches were glad for their pastor to go to Louisville, but neither could they help. Mattie Tucker remembers:

> We were going to school at Warren Plains when you resigned to go to Louisville Seminary. I remember well how everybody hated so bad to give you up and a lot of us school girls went down to the station to see you off and how you stood in the door of the train and waved to us and we waved good-bye to you. (Letter, June 17, 1952.)

The three-car train was pulled by a wood-burning engine. At Durham, Mr. Cullom changed his little trunk and suitcase to a similar train for Greensboro, where again he had to get another train for Salisbury. At Salisbury some of the people hurried to get something to eat at the station restaurant; others bought fruit and cakes from the "hawkers" on the train, while many ate food they had brought from home. After his change at Asheville, Mr. Cullom rested his head on the upholstered seat and slept a little through the night. The next morning at the state line (Paint Rock), he took his grip and walked around a bit before getting on the train for Knoxville, Tennessee. At Knoxville, Mr. Cullom had to change trains again, this last time in the middle of the night.

It was early in the morning when Mr. Cullom stepped off the train at the Union Station in Louisville, which was quite a show place in the gay 90's; he had never seen anything like it before that early morning when he set down his bags. Its tiled floor, its large round stained-glass windows, its iron-railed balcony made it church-like; two rows of seats in the center, a barbershop, counters for candy and cigars, a restaurant, ticket-counters and telegram-stand put it into the business of this world. The country boy walked to the opposite end of the station and looked out on West Broadway Street. Louisville then was a city of 300,000, and Broadway was its main street. Some streetcars were pulled by horses; others ran on electricity. In spite of his amazement and slight fright, the young preacher was hungry; so he went back into the station, ate breakfast and inquired the way to the Southern Baptist Theological Seminary.

6

The seminary, toward which the young "Tarheel" (as North Carolinians are called) walked, was located at Fifth and Broadway. Having been founded in 1859 at Greenville, South Carolina, the seminary had been opposed by many Baptists who feared "human-learning" would hinder "spirit-teaching"; the Civil War had closed it until in 1865 it had reopened with only seven students; in 1873, it had been moved to Louisville. In 1888, the first permanent building had been erected—New York Hall, so named because it was made possible by the contributions of friends in New York. While the seminary prospered materially, it had been "sorely tried" by Dr. Crawford H. Toy who taught "the rationalistic reconstruction of the history of Israel and the relocation of the leading Old Testament documents"; he had been forced to resign. (See William W. Barnes, *The Southern Baptist Convention,* Nashville: The Broadman Press, 1954. p. 134)

Upon the death of Dr. James P. Boyce in 1888, Dr. John A. Broadus had been elected as the seminary's second president. When Mr. Cullom first came to know him in 1892, Dr. Broadus was widely known and revered; his writings reached many throughout the nation. He was "a well-proportioned man of medium stature, with unusually expressive brown eyes and countenance which expressed kindliness and sincerity." He easily won the confidence of classes and congregations—not so much by his person as by his manner of speaking; with accurate knowledge, he spoke clearly and plainly so as to make "the difficult simple" and talked with an enthusiasm which he transmitted to his listeners. (*Encyclopedia of Southern Baptists,* Nashville, Broadman Press, 1958, vol. II, pp. 1269-1270.) Under his leadership the Memorial Library had just been completed in May of 1891, and Dr. John R. Sampey had been appointed librarian.

Upon his arrival at the seminary, Mr. Cullom was assigned a room on the fourth floor of New York Hall with Joseph G. Blalock, a Wake Forest classmate. During his first night there, the fire alarms sounded. Going outside with the other students, Mr. Cullom saw blue flames streaking up through black smoke, some distance away. As he wondered what could cause such a fire, he was told it was a whiskey warehouse burning; he thought, "I don't know of anything I had rather see burn."

- 15 -

On October 1, 1892, W. R. Cullom enrolled along with approximately two hundred other young men in the Southern Baptist Theological Seminary. Thinking that one year would be the limit of his stay at the seminary, he signed up for as much work as he could. He took Biblical Introduction and Junior Greek under Dr. A. T. Robertson; and Old Testament under Dr. John R. Sampey; Dr. John A. Broadus taught him New Testament and Homiletics. In Systematic Theology, Dr. Franklin Howard Kerfoot taught him Boyce's *Abstract of System-*

atic Theology, of which he was required to memorize four or five pages for each lesson.

The classrooms were crowded. Most students spoke only when called upon to recite, but there were a few "smart alecks" whom the professors "sawed" off.

> One morning, in the New Testament English class, when the lesson was about Paul and Gamaliel, a student when reciting said that he had told his wife that morning that Broadus reminded him of Gamaliel. Quick as thought Dr. Broadus dropped his head with a quizzical smile and said: "I suppose you expect me to say that you remind me of Paul." *(Seminary Magazine,* April, 1895, p. 362.)

There could have been no mistake about W. R. Cullom in this matter. W. O. Carver remembered: "Cullom had a lot of good common sense and was a brilliant student, but he did not attract any attention to himself; among the others he was so quiet that he was hardly noticed." (Conversation at Wake Forest, Oct. 6, 1953)

Seminary life was very simple—mostly studying. There was little administrative control over the students, as they were mature men, called of God to the ministry. The dormitory rooms were furnished with beds, chairs, washstand and pitcher; each man had to fetch his own water and furnish his own kerosene lamp. There were gas lights in the halls. Everyone feared fire, but some of these serious minded students could play with this fear, especially at the expense of their unsuspecting fellow students.

Shortly after the classes had begun when the professors were really bearing down on the men, a few of the students waited until the last lamp was blown out at about two o'clock in the morning and then shouted "Fire!" Men scrambled to their feet, some grabbing up clothes; one man threw his trousers out of the window, but most of them came as they were in their night clothes. Out of their rooms they poured, down the darkened halls and stairs to the outside—to be met outside with roars of laughter. W. R. Cullom stood along with the rest of them—dressed in a long white night-shirt, with molasses holding old newspapers to his bare feet. Years later he was still angry:

> If one ever saw a lot of angry preachers, New York Hall saw them that night. I really think that we showed much of supernatural grace in that we refrained from getting guns, axes or something and mobbing those men who had perpetrated such a thing.

- 16 -

Shortly after the opening of school, Dr. A. T. Robertson asked Mr. Cullom to preach for him at a Saturday afternoon service; he would come down for the Sunday morning service, and they would return to the seminary together in the afternoon. Mr. Cullom was delighted at this opportunity to preach and to be with such a distinguished scholar. Dr. Robertson was friendly and congenial with his fellow

North Carolinian; they had studied under the same professors at Wake
Forest and had belonged to the same literary society. As they rode
back to Louisville, Mr. Cullom told him that if he had to go home
then, he would feel that the one month at the seminary had made
it well worth his while to come.

The long hours of study began telling on Mr. Cullom; late in the
winter he slept poorly and began to imagine he was not liked by his
fellow students. Unable to sleep, he often got up and walked two or
three miles up and down 2nd or 3rd Street; yet he stayed at his
books, and the professors kept on making long assignments.

Sometime during that first year at Louisville, Mr. Cullom had to
write Dr. R. D. Fleming of Warrenton for the loan of the hundred
dollars he had offered, and Dr. Fleming sent it to him. One of the
first things he did was to buy a copy of the *Parallel Authorized and
Revised Translations of the Bible;* he made this purchase from a clerk
named Henry Burnet at the Dearing Book Store. But he bought little
else; his board bill was about ten dollars a month and sometimes as
low as six dollars. A housekeeper supervised the kitchen and dining
room, made up the weekly menus (which always had pumpkin pie
on Thursday), hired help, kept accounts and divided the expenses
among the students.

The examinations were long and thorough; at nine o'clock one
night W. O. Carver, a fellow student, had to turn in his paper unfinished. But neither W. O. Carver nor W. R. Cullom had cause to
worry about passing their examinations, for they came through with
high grades; the editors of the *Wake Forest Student* reported that
W. R. Cullom stood among the first in his class. (Vol. XII, April, 1893.)

Nevertheless, in the spring of 1893, W. R. Cullom thought his
seminary opportunities were finished, when a wonderful way opened
before him. During the meeting of the Southern Baptist Convention,
the trustees of the seminary announced the inauguration of the practice
of employing tutors to assist in certain departments of the seminary;
the faculty appointed W. J. McGlothlin as tutor in Old Testament,
John S. Tanner as tutor in New Testament and W. R. Cullom as
tutor in Systematic Theology. (See the Annual Catalogue, Southern
Baptist Theological Seminary 1893-1894.) The compensation for this
work would be small—$150 a year, but the expenses at the seminary
were low. With what he could "pick up in the way of supply work,"
he thought he could continue his seminary training.

- 17 -

After a brief visit in North Carolina, Mr. Cullom returned to fill
the pulpit of J. W. Lynch, who was pastor in Danville, for the month
of July; he boarded in the home of Mr. & Mrs. Dunn on Main
Street and found the members of Danville Baptist Church "people

of wealth and culture" and very responsive. Later that summer, the Rev. George C. Cates invited him to help him in revival services at the Cox's Creek Baptist Church, where there had been some dissension in the church. Mr. Cullom preached such sermons as "What Wilt Thou Have Me to Do?" "One Thing Thou Lackest," "Jacob's Return to Bethel," and "Simon Peter: His Fall and Rise." He saw the dissension melt away and people confess their faults to each other.

During his second year (1893-1894) at Louisville, Mr. Cullom roomed with T. C. Kincannon of Virginia, "a clean, straight, able man" who was one of Dr. T. T. Eaton's assistants at the Walnut Street Baptist Church. He took Senior Greek under Dr. A. T. Robertson, Junior Hebrew under Dr. John R. Sampey, Polemic Theology and Church Government under Dr. W. H. Whitsitt and Pastoral Duties under Dr. F. H. Kerfoot. (Annual Catalogue, S.B.T.S., 1893-1894.) His duties as tutor under Dr. Kerfoot were not burdensome. He kept the records of his classes and read his students' papers; he met with "the lame ducks" two or three times a week to coach them along. He assisted the professor in every way he could, and Dr. Kerfoot must have been pleased with him for he kept him as his assistant as long as Mr. Cullom remained in the seminary.

Mr. Cullom considered Dr. Kerfoot "an eloquent man and a very able scholar." A graduate of Columbian College and Crozer Seminary, Dr. Kerfoot had travelled in Egypt and Palestine and had studied at the University of Leipzig; he had served churches in Kentucky, Maryland and New York before he came to teach at the seminary.

Mr. Cullom found Dr. Whitsitt "a very quiet, unassuming man— highly esteemed as a great historian." His approach to Baptist history was that of a scientist's trying to find the historic fact rather than to substantiate a church's dogma. His method of teaching was quite different from the memorized recitation generally used at the seminary at that time; he lectured "deliberately and quietly, with none of the tricks for stimulating attention" and often questioned students on material they were supposed to prepare. (William A. Mueller, *A History of Southern Baptist Theological Seminary*, Nashville: Broadman Press, 1959, p. 151.) To his students he would say, "Be a Baptist; don't be a half-Baptist—neither be a Baptist and a half." A native of Tennessee, Dr. Whitsitt had served as a scout and later as a chaplain in the Confederate Army; he had studied at the University of Virginia, the Southern Baptist Seminary and at the Universities of Leipzig and Berlin.

Dr. John A. Broadus, a native of Virginia, had served as pastor of the Charlottesville Baptist Church, as assistant professor of classics at the University and as chaplain to the University until 1859 when he accepted the call to become professor in the new seminary in Greenville, South Carolina. As "a prince of preachers," he aimed "to move men and to make them better." In his class he often said: "A good speech is a good thing, but the verdict is the thing. Gentlemen, when you preach, strike for a verdict." (*Seminary Magazine,* April 1895, p. 374). According to Dr. A. T. Robertson, "a favorite idea with Dr. Broadus was to let the Bible mean what it wanted to mean," which was another way of saying that one must know the historical setting and connection in order to understand a particular passage. He spoke of a "progressive conservatism" as the proper attitude towards many theological questions; "he clung to the old, if true, and accepted the new, not because it was new, but only if true." (*Ibid,* p. 360.)

Of Dr. John R. Sampey, a native of Alabama and graduate of the Southern Baptist Seminary (1885), William A. Mueller was to write:

> As he unfolded the vast sweep of God's purpose in the life of Israel, as he dramatically described the princely prophet Isaiah or the hard-pressed Jeremiah, as he unfolded the prophetic witness of the old Testament to the coming Messiah, students often sat spellbound and enraptured by his fervor and eloquence. (Mueller, *op. cit.,* pp. 211-212.)

- 18 -

Shortly after the seminary opened in 1893, the Baptist Church at Irvington, Kentucky, called W. R. Cullom as its pastor for two Sunday services a month. From Louisville he rode the train about fifty miles down the river where he was met by some of the Irvington people who took him home with them for the week end. One of these homes where he often stayed was that of the Mumford sisters, of whom he would write:

> They out-talked anyone I've ever known. They all talked at the same time. They fed me well and would often drive me around in their buggy. Miss Ellen had a lovely voice; she sang in the choir for about forty years. Miss Kittie died while I was their pastor.

Mr. and Mrs. John Wimp were also faithful members of the Irvington Baptist Church; once while riding horseback into Irvington, Mr. Wimp related to his young pastor how once he had gone into an old country church with no idea of giving himself up to the Lord when a little girl came up to him and putting her hand on his knee said, "Mr. Wimp, I am praying for you," and he surrendered to the Lord right then and there. Mr. Cullom recalls a Brother Beverly's telling him that when he and his wife were married they agreed that when one got angry the other one would stay in good humor.

About the same time he went to Irvington, Mr. Cullom was also called to the Baptist Church at Borden, Indiana, for one service a month. Borden was a small town about twenty miles north of New Albany. A physician, Dr. James Stalker, and his wife were very cordial to the young minister; he always stayed at their home. One of the Stalker family always met Mr. Cullom at the train station and accompanied him to their home where he would greet the other members of the family. After setting down his bag, he would walk around town to learn his people and their news.

At the seminary, classes began at eight o'clock in the morning, with the exception of Monday when they began at eleven-thirty; they continued throughout the day until four-thirty, except on Saturday when they concluded at twelve-thirty to enable the student pastors to get to their churches for evening services. Mr. Cullom stayed busy; yet he found time to gather his fellow North Carolinians in his room to read and discuss parts of the *Biblical Recorder;* this was the beginning of the first state groups or clubs in the seminary. Also he became sensitive to the rumbling of trouble which was beginning to beset the seminary.

It was widely believed by Baptists at that time that there had been an unbroken succession of Baptist churches from the Apostolic era. Dr. J. R. Graves, editor of the *Tennessee Baptist,* thought that those churches which held to the pattern of the "First Baptist Church" in Jerusalem were the only true churches and that the members of other churches could not be received into a true Baptist Church nor could the ministers of such churches preach in a true Baptist pulpit; in 1854, he published a book entitled, *An Old Landmark Re-Set* by Dr. J. M. Pendleton, and the movement of "Landmarkism" swept the country. In 1880 a New York magazine, *The Independent,* carried four anonymous editorials in which it was stated that the earliest English Baptists had baptized by affusion and that it was not until 1641 that immersion was "invented" as the correct mode of baptism. And it was rumored that a prominent Baptist leader had written this "betrayal" of the faith. In 1883, Dr. Whitsitt had cause to write the *Texas Baptist*: "I beg leave to say that I have never affirmed the impossibility of a succession of Baptist Churches, but I have admitted my inability to demonstrate the existence of a succession from the historical material at my command." (W. R. Cullom, *Charity and Children,* March 6, 1947. Also Barnes, *op. cit.,* p. 137.)

There were others, closer to the Seminary, who were also suspicious. Dr. T. T. Eaton, pastor of the Walnut Street Baptist Church in Louisville and editor of the *Western Recorder,* was frequently at the seminary, questioning the students on their orthodoxy and indirectly that of their professors. He offered the prize of a Walker's concordance to the one making the highest grade on an examination he gave on the subject of baptism. W. R. Cullom took this examination, along with many other students, including his friend W. O. Carver, who won the concordance. (Conversation at Wake Forest, Oct. 6, 1953.)

- 19 -

During his third year at the seminary (1894-1895), Mr. Cullom roomed on the third floor of New York Hall with John S. Tanner of

Texas, a fellow-tutor who was very interested in a young lady who had come to study music at the seminary and who attended the Walnut Street Baptist Church. In the course of the year, Tanner related to Cullom what this young lady told him of a very dear friend she had at the church—Miss Frances Farmer. This was his second hearing of Miss Farmer, for Henry Burnet, the clerk at Dearing Book Store where he bought the Parallel translations of the Bible, had spoken of his Sunday school teacher in the most appreciative terms; Tanner told more—she was fair, with brown hair and eyes, more than good-looking, with great poise and a pleasing personality. Cullom heard Tanner talk and smiled, but he stayed with his books.

His courses—Senior Hebrew, Latin Theology and Church History—required study but were not difficult. His course in Latin Theology was under Dr. Edwin Charles Dargan, who had come to the faculty in 1892. Once after Mr. Cullom had read some selections from the Bible on his class, Dr. Dargan commended him; again Mr. Cullom was grateful for the training he had received in the "Eu" Society at Wake Forest. Also that term, Mr. Cullom gave a paper on the life of Matthew T. Yates before the whole seminary at its chapel service; it was well received.

In the fall of 1894, it was generally known that Dr. Broadus was not well; upon his doctor's advice he went to Florida to spend the winter. His frequent letters to "the boys" were read in chapel by Dr. Dargan:

> Tell the students that I am doing well in this genial climate, and that my only regret is in not being able to meet my classes. Tell them to begin the new year with renewed diligence in study, to "stick" to the end, and to take good care of their health. *(Seminary Magazine,* April 1895, p. 342.)

He returned to the seminary as soon as he thought he could but it proved to be too soon, for with a weakened heart he soon developed pleurisy. A hush descended upon the halls and classrooms of the seminary; and on March 15, 1895, many eyes filled with tears when they read the headlines of the evening paper: "Dr. Broadus, our first citizen, is dying tonight." Quietly on the morning of March 16th, Dr. Broadus, surrounded by his family, fell asleep. A prominent Presbyterian minister reported:

> Everyone on the street was sad, and all spoke of the calamity that had befallen the city. . . . No one envied him his eminence. . . . He was the bond of union among the Christians of this city. *(Ibid,* p. 410.)

The funeral was set for Sunday, March 17th, at 2:30 p.m. in the Walnut Street Baptist Church. W. R. Cullom was greatly honored in being chosen as one of the pallbearers. Trustees of the seminary, "honorable citizens" of Louisville, students of the seminary and members of the Confederate Veterans Association attended in a body. The

Rev. W. D. Thomas of Richmond spoke of Dr. Broadus' influence on all classes and types of people, and Prof. W. H. Whitsitt told of first meeting Dr. Broadus in the summer of 1867.

> He had been on a visit to Lexington, Va., to preach a sermon for General Lee at the commencement of his university, and afterwards came to the University of Virginia and solicited me to attend the seminary. In the eight and twenty years that have since elapsed of almost daily intercourse, we have had many joys and sorrows together; but in all our sorrows and joys he was the greatest man I have ever known. *(Ibid.,* p. 410.)

W. R. Cullom shared in the loss of Dr. Broadus; he was also taught a lesson in humility. Years later he would say:

> When one is tempted to be proud of himself "overmuch," remember this incident: There was, of course, a very long funeral procession following Dr. Broadus' casket. A little girl noticed from her window and asked her mother who it was that was having such a long funeral procession. Her mother explained it was the funeral of the great Dr. Broadus. "Who was Dr. Broadus?" inquired the girl!!

Amid general acclaim, Dr. Whitsitt was elected to the Presidency of the seminary, and Dr. Eaton started coming more frequently to question the students' orthodoxy.

As spring approached, Mr. Tanner and his ladylove began to make plans for their wedding. Tanner wanted his roommate as his best man, and his ladylove wanted her dear friend of Walnut Street as her bridesmaid. So love set a trap for the young student-preacher from North Carolina; years later he would say—"It was in this connection that I came to going with Miss Farmer."

Miss Fanny Farmer lived with her widowed mother and brother, Ed, in a double-brick house at 520 Ward Street in Louisville. She taught piano during the week and Sunday school on Sunday. She was well balanced emotionally and could think clearly and objectively. After the Tanner wedding, she received Mr. Cullom as a caller in her home and talked with him in the huge parlor where, even in the spring, the fire had to be built hours before it would be comfortable. Mr. Cullom was quite settled and a little solemn; it always pleased him when Miss Farmer would play the piano. (Ed Farmer, conversation at Durham, April 23, 1958.)

Beside keeping company with Miss Farmer, Mr. Cullom had the work of his Master of Theology degree to occupy his attention in the spring of 1895, and then came a letter from the Baptist Church in Scotland Neck, North Carolina. Rev. R. T. Vann, their pastor, was in poor health and had been given a leave during the summer; W. R. Cullom had been recommended as a supply pastor.

That summer was a busy, happy one for Mr. Cullom. Years later he would recall that Mr. Noah Biggs often came to "the Pastorium" for a heart-to-heart talk with him; his daughter, Annie, had a little pony and buggy which Mr. Cullom used freely. During those "delightful weeks," Mr. Cullom conducted evangelistic services in the Mullin Schoolhouse and at Spring Hill; among those whom he baptized that summer was Paul Kitchin. (*Charity and Children*, Sept. 18, 1947.) As the time came for him to leave this delightful town in eastern North Carolina, the young men of the congregation presented him "a generous purse" as expression of their appreciation of what he had meant to them.

Upon leaving Scotland Neck, Mr. Cullom spent a day at Wake Forest. The college buildings, the campus and the town were familiar, but with a few exceptions the students were all strangers. He wrote:

> I have a profound conviction that our college ought to teach the Bible to every student that enters its walls. The trustees have not yet seen their way clear to introduce this. I am sure they are doing all they can with the means at their disposal. But while there is not a school of the Bible, there are a number of Bible bands, with competent leaders, which meet weekly for Bible study. (*Biblical Recorder*, Oct. 2, 1895.)

Upon his invitation, so many students came to talk with him about entering "our seminary" that he had to have a special meeting in the chapel for them.

- 20 -

It was the middle of September, 1895, when Mr. Cullom returned for his fourth and last year at Louisville. Having received his Master's degree the preceding spring, it was now his intention to work for the degree of doctor of theology. His roommate was another Texan, the Rev. Prince E. Burroughs, and he continued as tutor in Systematic Theology; he took four classes: Graduate Theology, Hebrew Seminar, Greek Seminar, History of Doctrine. On October 23rd, J. D. Robertson reported in the *Biblical Recorder* that "the N. C. boys" held a short meeting to read the latest *Recorder* and to hear Bro. Cullom's report of "the large number of the students and the interest in the study of the Bible" at Wake Forest College.

Some of the students tried to pull a joke on the new president. Mr. Cullom would write:

> My recollection is that on a day before some holiday a group of boys received cards respectfully from Dr. and Mrs. Whitsitt that they would be "at home" to these boys from 8-10 o'clock on the evening in question. At the appointed hours the boys began to come in. It took only a moment to see that Dr. and Mrs. Whitsitt were not looking for company! But a person would have to stir soon in the morning and late at night to get ahead of the Whitsitts. Dr. Whitsitt just sent around to the grocery, brought in ice cream and cake, kept the boys for the time their invitation called for, and sent them home after "a most pleasant evening"! (*Charity and Children*, March 6, 1947.)

But there was more serious trouble ahead for Dr. Whitsitt; it was being rumored that he was the author of the anonymous editorials which stated that at one time Baptists had used "sprinkling" for baptism. Mr. Cullom remembers:

> Imagine the shock and consternation amongst our people when it began to be suggested that the president of our seminary was the author of the articles in question. Many of us threw up our hands and cried "impossible!" *(Ibid.)*

In the meantime, Mr. Cullom was finding it more and more pleasant to call upon Miss Farmer at her home on Ward Street. There never was anything spectacular about his coming or unusual about his being there; his presence in the parlor or at the table in the dining room came to be taken for granted. He soon learned that Miss Farmer was an excellent reader, as well as an excellent pianist; it was difficult to tell which pleased him more—her reading or playing.

Shortly after Christmas, Mr. Cullom missed calling on Miss Farmer; then word came from the seminary that he was sick. On January 5, 1896, his illness was diagnosed by Dr. Marvin as typhoid fever— that dreaded disease that had taken Charlie's life! Miss Virginia Taylor, the regular housemother of the dormitory, cared for him until a Miss Davis came to nurse him. Miss Davis was the first trained nurse Mr. Cullom had ever seen and within a few minutes had him more comfortable than he had been. For three weeks she nursed him. Every day of those three weeks, Mr. Cartwell of Cox's Creek Baptist Church, who was visiting his daughter in Louisville, would climb three flights of stairs to inquire of the nurse how Mr. Cullom was. Another caller was Ed, Miss Farmer's brother, who brought flowers and notes from his sister. On February 5, 1896, R. G. Kendrick, Jr., wrote for the *Recorder* that Brother Cullom was gradually improving; however, "it will require time for him to regain his strength." While he was convalescing in the infirmary, Mr. Cullom prepared a list of one hundred thirteen books for the Sunday school library which he sent to the *Recorder*.

When at last Mr. Cullom could leave the infirmary, the leaves on the trees were nearly grown. He was weak and nervous and "all-to-pieces." Again he felt that all the students were against him. Dr. and Mrs. Kerfoot graciously took him into their home for a week before he returned to his classes. Although he had to leave his thesis unfinished, Mr. Cullom became able to complete his class work. He was also able to resume his visits on Ward Street, where Miss Farmer began reading Justin McCarthy's *History of our Own Times,* a work of several volumes which, G. W. Paschal was to note, could not be read in one day or one week but which required "sufficient time for mutual understanding and maturing their love one for another." Years later Mr. Paschal would write of these readings:

> Then, if not before, Cullom came to know the sustained sweetness and melody of Mrs. Cullom's voice as she read, a voice gentle and soft

yet clear with carrying power, articulate and distinct and yet expressing every shade of emphasis and emotion of the text, and yet with no trace of elocution or declamation. *(Biblical Recorder,* May 24, 1944.)

As the seminary made plans for its commencement program, it was reported that Dr. Whitsitt had been called to explain his doctrine on baptism before the Board of Trustees. Sometime prior to this, Dr. Whitsitt had written an article in which he said Roger Williams had not been immersed at his baptism. Rev. B. W. Spilman came to Dr. Whitsitt's defense:

> So far as I am concerned it makes no difference to me if Dr. Whitsitt should prove that Roger Williams never lived. If I were a Williamsite I should be very much hurt, but I do not follow Roger Williams. . . . As a matter of curious historical speculation it is a matter of much interest: as a matter affecting the orthodoxy of Dr. Whitsitt, it does not amount to a row of pins. *(Biblical Recorder,* May 13, 1896.)

Just as the seminary was closing, a telegram came to Mr. Cullom from the trustees of Wake Forest College, asking him to inaugurate the chair of the Bible at Wake Forest. This telegram and Mr. Cullom's acceptance of the position marked the close of a period of ten years of his life which had been spent in college and the seminary. That "a poor boy" could have had such an opportunity speaks favorably of the country in which he lived, of the church people who supported these schools and who helped him as a student-pastor; it also speaks highly of his own desire and efforts for an education and is gratefully remembered as a special providence of God's grace to him.

"Oh, our manhood's prime vigor!"
—BROWNING

FOURTH AGE

A YOUNG MAN BEGINS HIS WORK

1896-1904

The telegram from the Wake Forest trustees began a new epoch in Mr. Cullom's life. Although honored by the invitation to establish the Chair of Bible, he was also humbled by it. It was challenging in that its responsibility was great; it was also bewildering, for there was no pattern to follow. The doctor's dissertation was laid aside, and the young man turned his full attention to the work in which he had to pioneer. He told Miss Farmer that it was his desire "to make the Chair of the Bible at Wake Forest an influence for good, not only in the college itself, but also in reinforcing and helping the pastors and Christian leaders of the State generally." During the first part of the summer, Mr. Cullom stayed in Louisville, using the seminary library to gather what help he could for the task ahead; he wrote letters to every person in the country that he "could suspect of having any knowledge of such work."

> Only one letter that came in response to these letters was of any help whatever to me. No one seemed to know anything about the task that I was about to undertake. The one exception was a letter from Dr. James B. Shearer of Davidson College (N.C.) . . . (Who) had been doing some work in a private class and had prepared three little books for his use in this class. (Summary of the Life Story of W. R. Cullom, 1954, pp. 8-9.)

In the meantime, Josiah W. Bailey, the new editor of the *Biblical Recorder,* wrote that the College was fortunate in getting one who had taken "with credit the highest courses" at Wake Forest and the Southern Baptist Theological Seminary; he said,

> One who had known Brother Cullom as a student, remembering his quiet but persistent work, his conservative methods and solidarity of character, cannot but be sure that, while in him we have a scholarly expounder of the Bible, we have one who is sound to the core, a Baptist wrap and filling. *(BR,* June 10, 1896.)

President Charles E. Taylor wrote that the inauguration of this new School of Bible marked another milestone for the college and declared:

> If Wake Forest is a good college, it is doubtless due in part to its holding on to some old-fashioned notions, while investigating all that is new, and appropriating all that seems adapted to its needs. It is proposed to continue the same general policy. *(BR,* June 17, 1896.)

While Mr. Cullom's mind was filled with dreams and plans for the College at Wake Forest, his heart was filled with worries and fears for the seminary at Louisville. Johnson's *Universal Encyclopedia* (1896) carried an article, signed by Dr. William Heth Whitsitt, which stated that in 1641 a Baptist congregation in London sent some members to Holland to obtain immersion from a congregation of Mennonites.

Someone "had the brass to ask" Dr. Whitsitt if he had written the editorials which had appeared in *The Independent* in 1880, and Dr. Whitsitt quietly acknowledged that he was their author. *The Western Recorder* opened fire, and other Baptist journals joined in the controversy.

In the latter part of July, Mr. Cullom bade good-bye to his friends in Louisville and headed back to North Carolina. At the invitation of M. A. Adams, he stopped in Asheville for three delightful weeks of rest and relaxation. Still weak from his recent illness, Mr. Cullom welcomed this vacation with such a dear friend; those happy, relaxed days in the mountains renewed his strength and revived his spirit. They also gave him the opportunity to define the task ahead of him. In an article which appeared in the *Biblical Recorder* (August 12, 1896), Mr. Cullom stated that the school of the Bible was "in no sense a theological *adjunct* to the college"; it was no more distinctively for those looking to the ministry of the gospel than for those looking to law, to teaching, to medicine, or to any other profession. Nor was it to be "a school of polemics" where every form of unbelief and disbelief would be held up for the sake of scattering it to the four winds; he pledged to "give a positive, unequivocal, Christian stamp" to his teaching.

In a second article Mr. Cullom stated that no one who aims at a liberal well-rounded education can afford to ignore the Book which is intertwined with the history of civilized humanity; to those who believe in it as a divine revelation, the study of the Bible is of special importance.

> This has been strikingly illustrated during the last few months in connection with the controversy about Roger Williams and the English Baptists. From many things said by Baptists in this discussion, one might almost justly conclude that our very foundation as a denomination rests on the establishment of an historical occurrence of the seventeenth century. These questions of history are important and should be looked into with a sincere desire to know the truth; but when we as Baptists forget that we stand upon "the impregnable Rock of Holy Scripture" and that alone as our foundation, then we surrender our right to exist as a separate denomination and Christians. The destiny of Baptists is linked with that of the Bible. Shall not the Baptists of the State see it, that his Book shall have a worthy place in that institution which is doing more than any other one agency to shape the future of our churches throughout the State? *(BR,* August 19, 1896.)

- 2 -

When he arrived at Wake Forest in August of 1896, Mr. Cullom was twenty-nine years old. His hair had thinned considerably; he had a full reddish-brown mustache. Professor Charles E. Brewer, the young chemistry professor, met him at the train and took his grip: "You must come to my house and stay there until you can do better." Mr. Cullom replied, "Mr. Brewer, on those terms I am with you until I go to the house not made with hands." Mr. Cullom had known Mr. Brewer when he first came to the college; it was a great joy and honor to Mr. Cullom to be so cordially received by one for whom he had the highest regard. In a few days his "bags, books and paraphernalia" arrived, and Mr. Cullom took them to Purefoy Hotel, where he had rented a room on the second floor.

In September when the students began arriving, Mr. Cullom found his status had changed on the old campus; the boys tipped their hats to him and called him "Professor." He was to remark that never had he felt so much like "a fool," for it seemed to him that he was still one of them. The boys also told jokes on the new professor. One day while he was sitting at the table eating supper, one of the boys to his back asked, "Do you know why a bald-headed man is like a rabbit?" Another student replied, "No, why?" "Because he makes a little hair go a long way." And they all laughed while the young professor's bald head turned red under the few strands of hair stretched across it.

The faculty of the college was very friendly and cordial to Mr. Cullom. Dr. Lanneau referred to his former student "in a most complimentary manner," and Professor L. R. Mills still pleased him with what the Scotsman said was required of a minister:

> It takes three things to make a good min'ster: religion, education and common sense. The Lord can give you the first; schools can give the second; but if you don't have common sense, neither the Lord nor the schools can do anything for you.

The old gymnasium, which had been in the central section of the first floor in Wait Hall was now divided into two sections, with Dr. Gulley holding his law classes on the front side to the East and Professor Cullom having his Bible classes on the back side to the West. Dr. Gulley said that it was quite appropriate that the law and the gospel should go together. "Doctor Tom" was the same as when Mr. Cullom was a student: "Yassir," he would say, "me and Dr. Taylor set out mos' od de scrubbery in de campus, an' everybody gives you a big honorment on dose flowers."

In his "Wake Forest Letter" to the *Biblical Recorder* (Sept. 9, 1896), President Taylor reported the opening of the 62nd session of the college with 220 students.

> The new department for Bible study has been organized into two classes: the Junior Class, proficiency in which is required of every applicant for the degree of Bachelor of Arts, and the Senior Class which is placed among the Electic studies. The "School of the Bible" has received a warm welcome into the work of the college from the whole student body.

The *Student* (Oct. 1896) described "the success and enthusiasm in the new Bible course" as "most encouraging"; there were seventy-nine men in the Junior Class and seventy in the Senior Class, which meant that both classes had to be divided.

7

- 3 -

With great earnestness, Professor Cullom began his work. The students seemed to have expected the new course to be what they called "a snap course," but they soon found that it called for real work. George N. Cowan, a native of Jackson County and a senior ministerial student in 1896, remembers seeing a strange man with "a long flowing brown mustache" seated on the platform of the little chapel; later this man was presented as the new professor of Bible. Mr. Cowan found him "thorough in his requirements of his students."

> He would assign a certain amount of scripture for study as our lesson. The next class he would give a little test on that scripture. Then he would lecture on the passage, giving us background material and interpretation. He also would ask questions and discuss our answers. . . . His tests were as rigid as any we had in the college; he expected us to work, and we had to, if we passed. . . . I appreciated all of the professors at Wake Forest, but I don't know of any professor I had whose work I appreciated more than Doctor Cullom. (Conversation in Rocky Mount, May 17, 1961.)

R. N. Simms, another member of his first class, recalls Mr. Cullom had his material "well organized and taught with clarity."

> He talked slow enough so we could write it down in our notebooks. . . . I don't remember his having a nickname at that time; he was too dignified for that. He was a young professor, just back from the seminary—splendidly prepared and qualified; he acted the part. (Conversation in Raleigh, Sept. 10, 1958.)

In an unpublished autobiography, Charles Houston Utley of Davie County (a senior at Wake Forest College in 1896) recorded these impressions of the new Bible professor:

> A large number of students were glad of the opportunity to study the Bible under a competent, well qualified teacher; and the qualifications of Dr. Cullom were never questioned by the students. His methods were somewhat stereotyped. . . . He could prepare more outlines and have time to teach, eat, and sleep of any man ever coming into this man's life. He believed in outlines. They were thorough analyses of books, chapters, paragraphs, verses, even phrases. And he stuck to those outlines, first, last, and all the time. It is strange he never was given the nickname, 'The Outliner.' . . . But he taught his students Bible. . . . He is an excellent gentleman, a Christian; his connection with the college from the first was a decided asset.

J. Clyde Turner remembers him in 1896 as "a young man, starting his career—a perfect gentleman in his manners." He would write of being in his first class:

> I was not a Ministerial Student and my knowledge of the Bible was rather limited. For two years I was in your classes and there received, not only a more comprehensive view of the Book, but deep and lasting impressions which have lived with me through the years. . . . Your courteous and gentle manner, your godly walk day by day, and your kind words will not be forgotten. (Letter, Dec. 10, 1941.)

Quite a number of preachers visited Professor Cullom's classes.

Remembering the difficulty some of his fellow ministerial students had in going to school during his student days, Mr. Cullom welcomed them. It was not long before it was suggested that "arrangements be made for our pastors to attend Professor Cullom's Bible classes at Wake Forest for at least one month during the year." In a letter to the editor of the *Recorder* Samuel J. Porter wrote:

> The expense would be small, while the advantages to those attending would be many and varied. Many of our pastors, who have never had collegiate or seminary training, can thus receive directly some of the benefits to be derived from such training. Wake Forest is already a rallying ground for North Carolina Baptists, and such an arrangement will have a tendency to put it still nearer the hearts of the people. *(BR,* Sept. 23, 1896.)

However, what had been undertaken was not assured of continuation; on the eve of the meeting of the Baptist State Convention in Morganton, Editor Bailey wrote that unless some means be speedily raised for the support of the School of the Bible, this welcomed and popular and promising work would come to an untimely end. On Friday morning of the Convention at Morganton, Professor Cullom conducted the devotional exercises. The report on Wake Forest and the new chair of the Bible was most favorably received; a visitor from Virginia reported that "the focal point of interest of the convention was Wake Forest College." *(BR,* Dec. 23, 1896.) The Rev. C. W. Blanchard of Cary was asked "to take pledges for the chair of the Bible"; he hoped that the friends of Dr. C. Durham would "rally to the endowment of the chair of the Bible in his memory." *(BR,* Nov. 30, 1896.)

As the college was already in financial difficulty and the price of cotton was low, the trustees could not offer Mr. Cullom very much in the way of remuneration; he recalls:

> Being an experiment with the trustees and the finances of the school being very meager, they offered me a salary of six hundred dollars a year with the suggestion that I should supplement this salary with such church work as might open up. This was all quite pleasing to me, since I was anxious to preach and was anxious to see the Bible placed into the curriculum of my own beloved alma mater. *(Charity and Children,* Jan. 6, 1949.)

- 4 -

Soon after his return to Wake Forest, Mr. Cullom was called to become the pastor of the Poplar Creek Baptist Church in Vance County. This church dates back to 1850 when a few devout Baptists built a log house for their meetings; in 1859, they constructed a nicer building of sawed timbers and plastered walls. Rectangular in shape, this building had two front doors, with three large windows on each side and two behind the pulpit. Inside there were three pillars in each of the two aisles.

Rev. W. R. Cullom preached his first sermon at Poplar Creek on October 4, 1896. He tells of his travelling to this church:

> I would go to Henderson on the train and some member of the church six miles away would drive over to Henderson on his buggy, take me to church for the Saturday service, take me to his home for the night, take me to see any sick or sorrowing of the community, take me to the church Sunday morning back to his home for dinner and then to the afternoon train for Wake Forest. *(Charity and Children,* Jan. 6, 1949.)

Mr. John ("Bozy") Fleming was one of those who helped Brother Cullom in his pastorate at Poplar Creek; this man seemed "much like a brother" to him. Mr. Cullom baptized the Fleming's oldest daughter, Ola; and another daughter, Ferol, who was only two-and-a-half years old when Mr. Cullom started spending the night in their home, would recall those visits as "among the happiest memories" of her childhood days. Another home at Poplar Creek where Mr. Cullom was always welcomed was the home of Mr. and Mrs. Alec Barnes; Joseph and Alvin were little boys, and Mother Barnes and Mother Elam also made their home there. Years later the minister would recall:

> I have gone to that home at one or two in the morning and rang the door bell to be met by Alec with a cordial greeting and told to go to my room and go to bed. At breakfast time there were greetings from the youngest to the oldest that served to make the heart glad. *(Charity and Children,* Oct. 2, 1947.)

Mr. Buck Parrott had just moved into the community when Mr. Cullom first came to Poplar Creek; he was greatly impressed by the young preacher and became his life-friend. Mrs. Parrott had first heard Mr. Cullom preach a sermon on "Jesus Christ, the same yesterday, today and forever" at the Mansion Mission Station near Middleburg. A daughter of the Parrott home, Edna Mae, would write of Mr. Cullom:

> I have known and loved him all of my life. My brother, Wilson, and I used to argue about who would take up his bath water. We wanted to see him peep out of the door in his long night shirt and his little white nightcap. We would knock at the door and wait to see him. (Mrs. Edna Mae Parrott Brewer, conversation, July 16, 1953.)

There were times when the patience of the minister must have been tried as once during a service one of the ushers who was taking up the offering turned, half-way down the aisle, and asked the minister, "Brother Cullom, what's this collection for?" The minister replied calmly, "For the kingdom of God, Brother Wright." And Brother Wright proceeded with the task at hand. The Saturday business meetings each month were sometimes

> the occasion of much wrangling over the delinquencies of some members. There were certain rules of conduct by which each member was judged . . . . (1) Failure to pay church dues; (2) absence from church 3 times in succession; (3) improper behavior or conduct—and any one of these was considered grounds for dismissal from the church. (Mrs. H. B. Parrott, letter, 1953.)

In speaking of these Saturday afternoon conferences, Mr. Cullom would say later that the emphasis was negative and he tried to change it to the positive. Gradually he saw the spirit of these meetings change, and those of fiery tempers came to name their sons after the young pastor.

In the fall of 1896, Mr. Cullom also became the pastor of the Middleburg Baptist Church in Vance County. This country church had been constituted in 1885 and had "gone forward in the work of the kingdom" under the leadership of such student-pastors as J. L. White and J. W. Lynch. Of the fourteen years he was to serve this church, Mr. Cullom would write:

> The close and vital friendships formed during that time have constituted one of my richest treasures through the years. . . . The week-ends spent with them did not seem like work at all, but rather as so many pleasant outings from my routine. *(Charity and Children, Jan. 15, 1948.)*

Deacon John A. Fleming helped make those week ends at Middleburg pleasant; he was a large man (at one time he weighed 330 pounds), and his soul was even larger—"as rich and as noble a quality as it was big and comprehensive in size." His home was "a place of heart's ease" to the young preacher.

From time to time Mr. Cullom preached elsewhere; once while supplying the pulpit of "the good old First Church of Raleigh," he sat in the home of Mr. and Mrs. Carey J. Hunter and saw a boy walking with his eyes fixed on the sidewalk a few feet ahead of him.

> Mrs. Hunter sat in the room with me at the moment. She said to me as both of us looked at the boy, "That is young Clarence Poe from Chatham County. He has come to Raleigh to work for Mr. Denmark in the office of the *Progressive Farmer*. . . . I think that there must be something in this boy. He is so regular, systematic, and steady in his daily routine that one would be safe to set his clock by his passing to and fro." *(Charity and Children, March 20, 1947.)*

- 5 -

While he was busy with the work of his classes and churches, Professor Cullom was still troubled by the Whitsitt controversy. In September (1896), Dr. Whitsitt published his book, *A Question in Baptist History? Whether the Anabaptists in England Practiced Immersion Before the Year 1641,* which Dr. T. T. Eaton discussed in detail in six or more issues of the *Western Recorder,* and the opposition to Dr. Whitsitt was pressed "with utmost vigor and determination." (Mueller, *op. cit.,* p. 161.) Many were confused—even the young Bible professor was to confess:

> As one of his former students and one who had loved him very tenderly, I was much confused and greatly bewildered. . . . I was not a leader among Southern Baptists, but I really desired to support my old and much-loved teacher with what there was of me and in me. But if I may say it for myself, I wanted more to be loyal to the truth insofar

as I could find it. What was I to do? It really was quite a trying situation in which I found myself and if I, one of his former students and now a young teacher in one of our great denominational colleges was thus confused and bewildered, imagine the situation with the average Baptist who had never seen Dr. Whitsitt and . . . knew only "what he read in the papers." And what he read in the papers was a plenty! All over the South the Baptist papers as a rule were hard on the president of our Seminary. Districts, Associations, State Baptist meetings, individual churches and almost any gathering of Baptists in any place passed resolutions condemning Dr. Whitsitt and proceeded to set history straight. (*Charity and Children,* March 6, 1947.)

While this controversy continued, the heart of the young Bible professor was troubled by a more personal matter. Years later his colleague, G. W. Paschal, was to remind him:

> In that year (1896-1897) you were getting ready to marry. . . . I was your only confidant. I knew all the superior characteristics of . . . Miss Frances Farmer, even though you talked little. The course of true love did not run smooth quite all the year, and when you went (in the spring) to Louisville to make it run smoother the people at the boarding house supposed that you were gone to get your bride, and getting no denial or affirmation from me who was entrusted with your secret the students, two hundred strong, met all trains until you got back, happy and smiling because the course of true love was running regularly, but with no Mrs. Cullom. A man with a softer conscience than mine might weep for all the loss of sleep my silence caused those students.

In his column, "In and About College," G. E. Lineberry observed that the college had "three bachelor professors."

> In behalf of the Senior class we would urge the importance of their getting married before Commencement—on separate days, so that we will get a holiday on each occasion. We don't like to urge any one to enter bondage for life, but under the circumstances we think it is justifiable. And to the ladies of the Hill and elsewhere: If you ever intend to marry them, do so now.

Lineberry also reported that of the forty-one seniors their average height was five feet, ten inches; average weight was 148 pounds, with an average age of 23½ years. Seventeen and a half per cent of them smoked, and fifteen per cent chewed tobacco. Twenty-five per cent were troubled with their eyes, and sixty-one per cent were in love; English was their favorite course, with Tennyson as their poet and *Ivanhoe,* their favorite novel. He expressed pride in the advance of the Negroes in North Carolina (223,376 were in the public schools) and wished Cuba success in her efforts to gain her liberty.

Remembering the example of Dr. William Royall's meeting with some of the young preachers of the college one evening each week "to teach them a little about outlining sermons," Professor Cullom (1896) revived and broadened this work.

> It was my thought and purpose to give a young minister, during his stay in Wake Forest College, as good a general conception of his life's task as I could in the time at my disposal. Of course one must keep in mind that only a comparatively small percent of our ministers went to a Theological Seminary in those days. The group that met me in this

way was called "The Ministerial Class." . . . Occasionally, other men
were invited to come and speak to this group. It was my thought and
purpose to make use of every possible opportunity to use such men
when they came this way, not to speak of those who were with us constantly as members of our faculty, the pastor of our church, and others
in the community. (W. R. Cullom, "A Brief History of the Origin and
Development of the Cullom Ministerial Conference," being a letter
written to the Conference, April 18, 1947. Wake Forest College
Library.)

- 6 -

So great was the interest in the forthcoming Southern Baptist Convention at Wilmington, North Carolina, that it became necessary for the
Recorder to print the rules governing "the delegates and their ap-
pointments." At that time, each association was entitled to one delegate,
and for every two hundred and fifty dollars contributed within a state
to foreign and home missions an additional delegate could be appointed by that state; the Woman's Missionary Union of each state
was privileged to send five delegates. (*BR,* April 14, 1897.) On
May 5, 1897, the editor printed the names of the forty-one "state"
delegates to which North Carolina was entitled on the basis of its
mission contribution.

Although he was not chosen to represent his state, Professor Cullom
followed the newspaper accounts of the convention with great interest.
When President Jonathan Haralsen opened the convention, many
hearts were fearful of what might come of the Whitsitt controversy;
the Foreign Mission Board announced an indebtedness of $13,500,
and the convention recessed "in order that the State delegations might
meet and agree on an amount to pledge." (*BR,* May 12, 1897.)
Everyone knew that the controversy had affected the contributions
and thus, in part at least, had caused this indebtedness. Some
settlement of the controversy was essential for the progress of the
convention work. When the Convention reassembled in the afternoon,
W. E. Hatcher of Virginia "stepped to the front" and read a communication from the Seminary's Board of Trustees which reaffirmed
the adherence of the seminary to the fundamental articles of faith
adopted when the seminary was established and declared:

> We consider it our duty while demanding of those in charge of its
> departments of investigation the utmost patience in research and the
> greatest discretion in utterance, to foster rather than to repress the spirit
> of earnest and reverent investigation.

A committee had been appointed "to wait on Dr. Whitsitt," and Dr.
Whitsitt was escorted to the pulpit. Dr. Whitsitt stated that he had
long felt the articles written for the *Indpendent* were a "mistake"; he
also wished of the article in *Johnson's Encyclopedia* that he could
"honorably procure the elimination of what is offensive to any of
my brethren." Of the historical questions involved he stated:

> What I have written is the outcome of patient and honest research
> and I can do no otherwise than to reaffirm my convictions and maintain

my convictions. But if in the future it should ever be made to appear that I have erred in my conclusions I would promptly and cheerfully say so. I am a searcher after truth and will gladly hail every helper in my work. . . . I am heartily in accord with my Baptist brethren in every distinctive principle that they hold. My heart and life are bound up with Baptists, and I have no higher thought on earth than to spend my days in their fellowship and service, in the name of our Lord Jesus Christ.

Josiah W. Bailey, editor of the *Biblical Recorder,* described what followed Dr. Whitsitt's statement:

> Then was enacted, spontaneously, the scene which marked an epoch in Baptist history. The whole Convention burst forth into singing "How Firm a Foundation." Crowds on crowds gathered around Dr. Whitsitt, grasping his hand and embracing him. Strong men wept for joy. There was victory, not for Whitsitt, not for others, but for Whitsitt's Master, the Saviour of us all. The Whitsitt controversy is a thing of the past. The banner of Peace is again leading the Baptist hosts of the South. God be thanked! God be praised! (*BR,* May 12, 1897.)

In a few minutes after this joyous outburst of relief and praise, pledges to pay the debt of $13,500 had been made, with the North Carolina delegation pledging $1,125. The other services followed in a relaxed and happy spirit, until on Monday the delegates concluded "a most important . . . most encouraging . . . most gratifying convention"; at least, it seemed so to the editor of the *Recorder.*

- 7 -

At Wake Forest, Professor Cullom read all of this; he also read the letters from Louisville. Even as he copied the questions for the final examination on the blackboard, his thoughts must have been at the brick house on Ward Street.

1. Discuss the spiritual nature of man as shown in the words "image" and "likeness."
2. In what sense was the flood a salvation by water?
3. Describe the call, commission and journey of Abraham.
4. Discuss the hardening of Pharaoh's heart.
5. Draw a diagram of the tabernacle.
6. Compare the civil law of Moses with the code of Hammurabi.
7. Name and explain the sacred seasons of the Jews.
8. Describe the distribution of territory in Canaan and draw a map locating the tribes in their respective places.
9. Give a diagram of the Judges.
10. Contrast the character of Saul and David.
11. Name the two Psalms describing David's penitence and forgiveness and show the nature of each.
12. Name the principal events of David's court life.
13. Discuss the wisdom of Solomon.
14. Explain Solomon's failure as a ruler.
15. Name and characterize briefly the kings of the northern kingdom.
16. Outline the works of Elijah.
17. Describe the work of the prophet in the Old Testament.
18. Discuss the personality and work of Hosea.
19. Discuss the personality and work of Amos.

20. Discuss the personality and work of Isaiah. (Notebook for Religion One, questions for Review and Examination.)

As he waited the three hours the examination required, he dreamed of the lovely lady of his love. As soon as the papers were all in and the grades recorded, he quietly slipped out of Wake Forest and, amid the noise of the Commencement, headed for Louisville.

Early on the afternoon of June 2, 1897, the Rev. Willis R. Cullom and Miss Frances Farmer were united in marriage in the home of the bride on Ward Street; Dr. T. T. Eaton, the bride's pastor, performed the ceremony. The bride's mother, her brother, and a few close friends, including Minnie Dearing, her dear school friend, attended the service. (The Dearings had given a dinner for the bridal party.) After the ceremony, the couple took a public carriage to the train station; the old shoes which had been tied to the carriage bounced along the way and caused people to look and smile. Like her mother, the bride was "well balanced emotionally" and took her leaving home as "a matter of fact." Ed's emotions were not so perfectly controlled; he had to fight back the tears, even as he shouted out to his new brother-in-law, "Good-bye, Billie Dick." (Ed Farmer, conversation at Durham, 1953.)

The wedding ceremony had been scheduled so that the bridal couple would not have to wait long at the station. They boarded the train for Nashville, Tennessee, where they spent a day or two at the Exposition, of which the bridegroom remembers nothing. When they reached Wake Forest, the town was quiet. School was out so that there were no boys to serenade them with tin pans and horns. It pleased the young husband that it was this way; hand in hand, he walked quietly with his wife across the campus under the magnolias which perfumed the warm night air. The young couple took two rooms in the new house of Mrs. Z. V. Peed. On Wednesday night, the young professor brought his bride to prayer meeting at the church. Young Hubert Poteat (then eleven years old) thought she was "very beautiful"; she was charming, with poise and dignity and yet at times she could be very witty and clever. Everyone said that the young professor had "married wisely." (Hubert M. Poteat, conversation at Wake Forest, 1953.)

Within a few days, Mr. Cullom took his bride to visit his folks at the homeplace in Halifax County. His parents had aged some since he had left them, and the other children were all nearly grown— Mollie, the baby, was thirteen. Even the "great house" must have seemed very plain to the bride from Louisville, and the dear old kitchen must have been most primitive to her. The young husband must have fondly revisited his childhood pulpit and stood silently a moment by Charlie's grave. He learned that Dave Morecock was working with the railroad and his other friends were scattered. As they ate under the mulberry tree, his heart must have been torn between the fondness of childhood memories and a secret embarrassment as he recalled the dinner table in the Ward Street home. As they lay awake in the early night, he identified the noises of the country night for his wife, but it was the dark silence which seemed the hardest to explain. The next morning they went to the Quankie Church, of which he had once been so proud and where now they were so proud of him; but he begged off the preaching and enjoyed hearing someone else. It all must have seemed very plain and backward to the young woman from the city. On Sunday afternoon, Mr. Joel Cullom took his son and his bride to Weldon to catch the train back to Wake Forest where duties awaited the young professor.

- 8 -

The sentiment for a special class for pastors at Wake Forest had continued to develop through the fall and winter of 1896-1897. In the *Recorder* of January 13th (1897) the Rev. W. R. Gwaltney, pastor at Wake Forest, had reported that if a sufficient number of pastors should indicate their purpose to attend, "a Bible and Pastors' Institute" would be held, beginning June 20th and continuing for four weeks. On February 20, 1897, Dr. Charles E. Taylor had prophesied that the Summer School and the Pastors' Institute would mark "a turning point in the educational history of North Carolina Baptists."

Brother I. P. Hedgepeth, who as a classmate of Mr. Cullom had had to drop out of school on account of his eyes, was "one of the first to indicate his purpose to come." Others were equally enthusiastic:

"It is precisely what hundreds of pastors need." . . . "I would be glad to attend, and will if my churches will give me the time and not discount my salary." . . . "It is just what we students used to talk so much about."

On June 9, 1897, Professor Cullom stated in the *Recorder* that to lead the groups of study he had secured such men as Dr. J. W. Carter, Rev. C. A. G. Thomas, Rev. W. C. Tyree, Dr. I. T. Tichenor, Dr. E. C. Dargan, Dr. R. J. Willingham, Rev. Hight C Moore, Dr. A. M. Simms, Dr. A. C. Barron and Dr. A. E. Dickinson. He also stated that the railroads of the State had offered return tickets for one regular fare to the Institute and that a committee of arrangements was planning to meet all trains on Tuesday, June 22nd, and would help the brethren in "getting settled." (*BR,* June 16, 1897.)

Professor Cullom had made all these preparations before his departure to Louisville; after his wedding and visit to his Halifax home, he hurried back to Wake Forest to greet the first trains. Soon the preachers and scores of other people began arriving, and the Institute began. On July 7th, J. H. Lamberth reported that he had never heard better lectures and that it was "the unanimous verdict by all in attendance" that the Institute was "a gratifying success, full of hope for the future." However, in his report at the State Convention that fall, the Rev. J. B. Boone said that the Pastors' Institute had been "so thinly attended by our pastors" that the Faculty did not feel encouraged to plan for another session during the vacation of 1898. This must have hurt the young professor; he had put a great deal of himself into it and had brought in the very best men to assist him. However, he kept his disappointment to himself and turned to other duties and worked to realize other dreams.

- 9 -

In 1897, the young Bible professor was called as pastor to the Forestville Baptist Church, one and a fourth miles south of Wake Forest. This church had been organized in 1859, and its beautiful colonial building is still in use. Upon entering the front door, one comes into a vestibule, with graceful steps on one side leading upstairs. Two doors open into a rectangular auditorium; two rows of three columns down the aisles support the balconies on each side. Benches of broad oak-boards line the center section, with shorter benches on the sides next to the large clear glass windows. The church had had only two pastors prior to Professor Cullom: Doctor Brooks and Doctor Royall. Ella Gill Caddell remembers Professor Cullom's walking to Forestville for the Saturday afternoon meeting; "he would sit on the settee behind the pulpit and rest, where Dr. Royall used to lie down." "Miss Betty" Dunn was very faithful to the church, as was old mother Chapell who always sat on the back seat of the church. Mr. and Mrs. Henry Arthur Chapell had been married only a few years when Professor Cullom became their pastor; through the years he was a frequent visitor in their home and often sat on their patio, covered by a scuppernong grapevine.

In 1897, Mr. Cullom also became the pastor of the Mount Vernon Baptist Church which was the mother of four neighboring churches and of several ministers; its building was a one-room unpainted wooden structure. One of the first men Mr. Cullom met at Mount Vernon was Ransom White who had made profession of faith during a meeting Mr. Cullom had conducted at Harris Chapel; he lived across the road from the church. Another one who made herself known to the young pastor was Mrs. Beulah Allen Smith; as a girl of eight she had lived with her aunt, Mrs. William Louis Poteat, while going to the Wake Forest grammar school and had known Mr. Cullom when he was a student at the college. She was now married with four children; Mr. Cullom often spent the night in her home. On one occasion Mr. Cullom baptized an old Negro woman, named Hannah, who formerly had been a slave of Mrs. Smith's father; she often said that she wanted to die before her "ole Massa" did. (Beulah Allen Smith, conversation at Neuse, May 13, 1954.)

The young Bible professor was to become pastor of yet another church in 1897—the Youngsville Baptist Church. (This was the fifth country church he was serving; altogether they paid him five hundred dollars a year.) As a student at Wake Forest he had walked four miles from Wake Forest to teach a Sunday school class there when Dr. Royall was the pastor. Mr. James Timberlake, a very good and devout man, had been a charter member of the church and had helped in the construction of its wooden building; he was very fond of Mr. Cullom and always welcomed him in his home. Willie, their daughter, remembers as a girl of eleven seeing the two sitting by the fire talking; sometimes she was allowed to sit quietly with the baby by the fireplace and listen, but often all of the children had to stay out while "Papa talked with the Preacher." (Willie Timberlake Winstead, conversation at Youngsville, 1954.) When their pastor brought his bride to meet them, the people at Youngsville brought their dinners to the church and had an all day meeting.

- 10 -

In the fall of 1897, Professor Cullom began his second year of teaching Bible at Wake Forest College. The new college catalogue (1896-1897) listed him as a member of the Faculty; he was also listed as secretary of the college and as a member of the committee on Lectures. At that time, the few strands of hair stretched across the top of his head had disappeared, but he kept his heavy reddish mustache. His eyes were beginning to bother him and soon would require glasses. As he began his classes, he would unfasten his silver watch from the chain stretched across his expanding stomach—a habit which he also followed in the pulpit; he would call the class to order and offer a brief prayer. Then for his first class in Religion I, he would ask "What is the Bible?" and give the following answers:

    I. Negative—what it is not.
        a. It is not a treatise on science.
        b. It is not a history of mankind.
        c. It is not a history of the Jews.
        d. It is not a collection of laws and moral maxims.
    II. Positive—what it is.
        a. It is the story of God's special and progressive Revelation of
        Himself, His will and His purpose to mankind, reaching its climax
        in the person and work of Jesus of Nazareth.
            (1) It is a revelation or the story of such a Revelation.
            (2) It is a special Revelation.
            (3) Its progressiveness came step by step.
            (4) It reaches its climax in the person and work of Jesus Christ.

     b. Its main center of interest is man and his relation to God, the
Eternal Spirit.
     c. It is an Eastern book.
     d. It uses *popular* rather than scientific language.

The methodical presentation of the material, the voice and personality
of the teacher concealed the rather liberal interpretation which he
gave his classes from 1896 on through the years. The men methodically
copied down what he said; for many of them, it was years later that
they realized the value of what he had said.

For a time Professor and Mrs. Cullom continued to stay at Mrs.
Peed's; as they could not get Mrs. Cullom's piano up the stairs, it was
lifted through an upstairs window, and soon she was busy with piano
pupils. They also ate at Mrs. Peed's. Professor Paschal ate with them;
he remembered that in the fall of 1897 Joe and Winston Adams joined
their table.

     Mrs. Cullom was almost shocked at their fondness for cornbread and
molasses for closing their dinner. She was also surprised that the people
of eastern North Carolina, . . . did not know the use of cream. (Letter,
Dec. 12, 1941.)

Early in the winter Professor Cullom was looking for a house; their
two-room upstairs apartment would not be adequate when the baby
came. At last the Rev. C. W. Scarborough rented him his house, and
they moved. At the time of his marriage, Mr. Cullom had invited his
mother-in-law to make her home with him, but she had declined.
However, she accepted his invitation to come and be with her daughter
during her confinement. On the train the conductor failed to call her
until she was at Halifax, from which she telegraphed her son-in-law
about two o'clock in the morning to come and get her. When she
finally got to Wake Forest and saw her daughter and the little house
in which she was living, she remarked, "Daught (as she called her),
you are as big as your house."

Early, about three o'clock in the morning of April 5, 1898, Dr.
J. B. Powers was called to the Cullom home. A little later "Aunt
Ellen" Lewis, a Negro woman, also came to help in the delivery of a
baby boy—Edward Farmer Cullom. After several hours and as many
cups of coffee, the new father emerged from the house and was seen
walking toward the college. Shortly he was met by Professor Mills who
already had heard the news:

     I — he — hear that — that you have a baby boy at your house.
Well — let — let me con — con — congratulate you and tell you that
your life will never be the — the same again. Good day.

Edward was a nice baby, well formed and looked quite a bit like
his mother. "Aunt Ellen" stayed on to help; also Mrs. Farmer. As the

weather turned warmer and as her strength returned, Mrs. Cullom began taking her baby outside for a stroll in a baby carriage. She often strolled along with Mrs. J. H. Gorrell who also had a new baby. Often these two wives joked about their absent-minded husbands. One day Mrs. Cullom suggested that they play a trick on them: "Let's swap babies and see how long it will take them to know the difference." The young mothers picked up their babies and placed them in each other's carriages and went smilingly home. When Professor Cullom came in, he asked how the baby was; upon being told he was asleep, he picked up a book and read until supper was ready. While they were eating, Mrs. Gorrell brought in Edward; Professor Gorrell was annoyed that anyone thought him so stupid as not to know his daughter from someone else's child, especially since his baby had red hair.

As soon as Mrs. Cullom was able, Mr. Cullom took her and their infant son to his churches. Dora Eunice Greenway (Parrott) remembers when they came to Poplar Creek on a Saturday afternoon and spent the night in her parents' home; she thought Edward was the "prettiest baby" she had ever seen. After Mrs. Cullom had put him to bed, Mr. Cullom said he had brought "a good book along" and asked Mrs. Cullom to read it to the young people.

> We always had a room full of young folks when we knew Mr. Cullom was coming. He liked young folks, and they all loved him. He would shake hands with all of them and play games. One I remember was fruit basket exchange.

Mrs. Cullom was well liked in Wake Forest and had a great influence upon the women there. As the teacher of the Ladies' Sunday school class, she encouraged the women to increase the salaries of their cooks. Mrs. Charles Brewer thought she had "the best, clearest judgment" of anyone; "if I had a problem I would take it to Mrs. Cullom and she always helped me with it." Mrs. C. H. Norris, who was president of the class for many years, said,

> I can't begin to say how much we loved Mrs. Cullom; no one has been able to take the place she filled in the hearts of the people in Wake Forest. I came to Wake Forest in fear and trembling; she brought confidence and assurance to me and the other members of her class.

Mrs. Cullom's theology was very conservative; as a former member of Dr. Eaton's church, it could not have been otherwise. Her husband did not argue with her, but when he got the opportunity he spoke to her class on how we got our Bible. They were so happy together that they were hardly aware of these differences. Certainly the members of her class were not aware of them. Mrs. John Mills thought of them as a wonderful couple; "it was a great joy to be in their home." (Conversation in Wake Forest, March 7, 1952.)

- 11 -

During this time Mr. Cullom had continued to read of the Whitsitt controversy. After the Convention at Wilmington, the General Association of Kentucky had requested its representative on the Seminary's Board of Trustees "to urge and insist upon and vote for the retirement of Dr. W. H. Whitsitt," and Dr. B. H. Carroll of Texas had written an article which stirred the controversy throughout the South. State Conventions and associations began again to pass resolutions. Editor J. W. Bailey feared that the Convention would be divided if this continued; in the *Biblical Recorder* of August 11, 1897, he called upon Dr. Whitsitt to resign for "the integrity of the Southern Baptist Convention."

Reaction to this editorial was not slow; Rev. R. D. Cross of Windsor stated that Dr. Whitsitt would be sacrificed upon "the partisan spirit of some men with unholy ambition." Editor Bailey replied: "We have called upon President Whitsitt to resign for the sake of peace." (*BR,* Aug. 25, 1897.) Mr. Cross retorted: "The one who does wrong for the sake of peace, fails to gain the peace of man and loses the peace of God." Editor Bailey ended the discussion by saying that Dr. Whitsitt had lost the confidence of hundreds of brethren in every state of the Convention; any attempt to force him upon these brethren "would injure the Seminary irreparably, and would in all probability dissolve our Convention." (*BR,* Sept. 1, 1897.)

In November, the North Carolina State Convention at Oxford approved (92 to 81) Elder R. T. Vann's motion that "this convention take no action at this time upon the Whitsitt controversy." Editor Bailey reported that this was "an action of deference to the Trustees of the Seminary" and that should the vote have been on the simple question, "Should President Whitsitt resign?" it would have been "ten to one against him." Dr. A. T. Robertson of the Seminary was present for all of this; on Saturday afternoon he received pledges of six hundred and fifty dollars for the seminary which was certainly an expression of love for the seminary so sorely troubled.

In contrast to these troubles, Wake Forest was peaceful and quiet. The college had an enrollment of 238, and a new system of "underground waterworks" was being installed on the campus; on November 3rd, Rev. Thomas Dixon lectured in Memorial Hall on "The Destiny of America" for an hour and a half to a spellbound audience. Organ grinders and monkeys brought music and humor to the campus; especially did the "newishs" like the monkeys because the monkeys took off their hats to them as the students did to the professors. In the January (1898) issue of *The Student,* T. H. Lacy wrote:

> Merry Christmas
> The Bible examination is over.

At the time of the examinations, one might have thought that Wake
Forest was in the land of the midnight sun; lamps burned later as the
time until examinations grew shorter. The seller of kerosene weard the
Christmas smile during the last few weeks of the term.

That spring, John Charles McNeill "quietly and wisely smiled" at
those Spanish writers who hoped that in case of war between Spain
and the United States the southern states would take up arms against
the union.

In May, when the Southern Baptist Convention met at Norfolk,
Virginia, the country was united against Spain but the Convention
itself was divided. As soon as the convention was declared in session,
Dr. B. H. Carroll of Texas "gave notice" that next year he would
present a resolution whereby the convention would divest itself of
responsibility in the Seminary; it was moved that a committee of one
from each State be appointed to report at the next session on this
resolution.

One by one, Dr. Whitsitt's friends and supporters began to urge
him to resign until finally, on July 13th, Dr. Whitsitt submitted his
resignation, to become effective at the close of the academic session of
1898-1899. The *Recorder* greeted this as "good news" to North Carolina Baptists, "for it relieves them of a great burden." As for Dr.
Whitsitt himself, Mr. Bailey said, "We have the highest regard; he
comes out of this terrible test with a record which becomes a man
and a Christian." (*BR,* July 20, 1898.)

Mr. Cullom agreed with the *Recorder* editor and hoped for the
peace which Mr. Bailey thought this resignation would bring. Most of
the Wake Forest students were more interested in the new game of
baseball or amused at Professor Lanneau's prediction that the problems of artificial flight would someday be overcome and "the Empire
of the air will submit to man's will and be added to man's Dominion."

During the summer and fall of 1898, Dr. J. R. Sampey, Dr. E. M.
Poteat and others fought to retain Dr. Whitsitt. But on the eve of
the Convention which was meeting in Louisville in May of 1899, the
trustees (of which Dr. Charles E. Taylor was one) voted to accept
Dr. Whitsitt's resignation. When the Convention assembled, there was
"no cause to consider changing the relation of the convention and the
Seminary."

That spring (1899) Rev. J. W. Lynch of Danville, Kentucky, was
called to the Wake Forest Baptist Church; the seniors voted to graduate in "caps and gowns," and basketball, "a new thing at Wake
Forest," was being played in front of the Gore house. At their meeting
during commencement, the trustees of Wake Forest made the study
of Bible "optional." This was a blow to the young Bible professor; he
had heard the students' murmurs against his assignments and examinations, but he had reasoned his strictness was for their own good.
Although the college's new catalogue (1898-1899) listed both of his

Bible classes as "elective," he did not vary the course of study—nor the requirements.

In July of 1899, Mr. Cullom taught Bible in the summer school at Wake Forest and conducted a Sunday School Institute, which he described as "a fine success"; also he held a "most delightful meeting" at Middleburg and planned another one for Poplar Creek. In August, the editor of the *Recorder* noted that the Bible was being studied as many books instead of as one book and thought that no one would have to lose "any reverence for God's Word by making this change." (*BR,* Aug. 9, 1899.) In a long article on Christian Baptism, Sept. 13, 1899, Professor Cullom reassured those who were hesitating to be baptized that Jesus was baptized and quoted Professor Harnach as saying that in the New Testament and in ancient Christian literature, *"baptism* undoubtedly signifies immersion." Professor Cullom wrote:

> Baptism is a symbolical ordinance. When He told John at His baptism "to suffer it to be so now, for thus it becometh us to fulfill all righteousness," Jesus did not mean that "all righteousness" was fulfilled in His baptism, for that was done through His life and death and resurrection. His baptism was a symbol of that life, death, burial and resurrection. So now when the believer is baptized he gives the world, in this beautiful symbol, a picture of the plan of redemption by which he is saved. . . . Let us look back to Jesus and to His inspired apostles for our information on the subject, and when we have decided what they teach, let it be ours to obey.

- 12 -

In the fall of 1899 an observatory was being built at Wake Forest on the roof of the laboratory, and the predictions of the end of the world at the close of the century caused one Sophomore to throw his book of Lysias into the fire and to attend prayer-meeting on Monday night. As the century came to its end, Professor Cullom was thinking of his churches; on December 30th (1899), he wrote:

> Last Sunday closed my work as pastor with the churches at Youngsville and Forestville. . . . When I took charge of it (the church at Youngsville), I found a debt of about $300 resting on it. This has been wiped out, the house of worship has been improved, the church pays 25 per cent more to the pastor than ever before. . . . The Sunday School is doing better work. The Women's Mission Society is a real force in the church. And yet it must be said that the strength of the church is as yet largely potential. They ought by all means to have a man live among them, and give them at least half of his time on Sundays, and be with them in a weekly prayer meeting. . . . Forestville is one of our oldest churches and has long been known for her good works and steadfastness in the faith. In our closing service, Dr. Royall assisted . . . in the ordination of brother Phillips into the deaconship.

Years later Mr. Cullom was to confess that he had not been satisfied with his work at either of these churches. He had been "pressed with responsibilities at Wake Forest," and, as Forestville was within walking distance, he had seldom spent the night in that community. In Youngsville, he had been disappointed in the response to his appeals for

8

missions; once he gave ten dollars to start a drive, but when this was told to a man whose wealth was estimated between ten and twenty thousand dollars, the man said, "Why, that's enough already." Years later Mr. Cullom would say, "Perhaps an older man would have been more patient and would have stayed longer." Of his other churches he reported:

> Poplar Creek . . . is located in an intelligent, flourishing community, has a large number of children and young people and ought by all means to have a school in connection with it as a part of its work.
>
> Middleburg is comparatively a young church, and has quite a small membership; but a more intelligent, appreciative and progressive country church would be hard to find. They are constantly making improvements on this house of worship, are maintaining two Sunday Schools, have a good collection every time they meet for worship, and at the last appointment in this year the treasurer announced that every pledge had been paid—an experience unparalleled in my work as pastor so far.
>
> Mount Vernon is located near the Falls of Neuse in an important community. . . . This church has suffered this year in the death of several of its most useful members. . . . A large number of young men and women are growing up in the community, ready to fill the ranks of those who are passing away. . . .
>
> All these churches are maintaining evergreen Sunday Schools. Most of them have good Sunday School libraries, all of them (except Poplar Creek) have good missionary societies, all of them take a goodly number of *Biblical Recorder,* of *Charity and Children,* and of the *Foreign Mission Journal.* Every deacon in them, with one or two exceptions, is an appreciative reader of the *Recorder.*

In January of 1900, Professor Cullom began his pastorate of another rural church of fifty-three members, Brassfield, which dates back to 1823. The records of the church conferences give a picture of his work there.

> *Jan. 20, 1900.* The Church is called for conference by the new Pastor W. R. Cullom. The roll is called and minutes of last meeting read and corrected.
>
> *Mar. 17, 1900.* It is agreed to take a collection on tomorrow for Foreign Missions. It is also agreed to start the Sunday School for this year on First Sunday in April.
>
> *April 14, 1900.* Delegates are appointed to the Union Meeting at Perry's Chapel. . . . It is also agreed to take a collection on tomorrow for Home Missions.
>
> *May 19, 1900.* The church agrees to pay $100 towards supporting an orphan at Thomasville . . . also agreed to buy three dozen hymn books. It is agreed to take a collection on tomorrow for ministerial Education.
>
> *March 16, 1901.* Sister Sallie McGhee . . . is reported to be in need of help. A collection is taken for the benefit of her and others.
>
> *October 1901.* The pastor's salary is raised from $150.00 to $175.00.
>
> *Nov. 16, 1901.* The envelope system for collection is adopted.

- 13 -

Early in 1900, as he was beginning his pastorate at Brassfield, Professor Cullom went to the First International Missionary Conference in New York with Josiah W. Bailey, editor of the *Recorder,* and John

White, secretary of state missions in North Carolina. Both of these
men had studied law at Wake Forest when Mr. Cullom was a student;
as they were "pals," the Bible professor felt he was intruding upon
their friendship. A seminary acquaintance said to Mr. Cullom, "I have
a friend from South Carolina who is also alone; maybe you two can
room together."

This was the beginning of "one of the most intimate and valuable
friendships" Mr. Cullom ever had. Dr. Thomas Wiley Sloan, pastor of
the Associate Reformed Presbyterian Church in Abbeville, South Carolina, was five feet, six inches tall and "somewhat on the thin side";
he had dark hair and mustache. He and Mr. Cullom were of the
same age and "likes." At Carnegie Hall, they heard an old man from
the Fiji Islands, but it was New York City which fascinated the professor. Dr. Sloan was a graduate of Princeton and knew New York
like Mr. Cullom knew Wake Forest; he was "the personification of
kindness" and enjoyed showing the city to his new friend. He took
him to see Joe Robinson play "Rip Van Winkle"; together they saw
their first "moving picture," which Mr. Cullom was to describe later
as "not much of anything, but a marvel then."

On February 13, 1900, "the great (William Jennings) Bryan"
stopped in Wake Forest and spoke at the station for twelve minutes;
he stated the character of his campaign and appealed "to the boys for
their cooperation in making a better government to bequeath to
posterity." On March 16th, the members of the Junior Bible Class
were "the recipients of a rare treat at the hands of their esteemed
instructor and genial friend, Professor W. R. Cullom"; Mr. and Mrs.
Cullom entertained them at a reception in their home, which was
described as "a departure from the traditions of the past" and "a
good thing." (*The Student,* April, 1900.) On April 18th, the *Recorder* carried a front-page article by Professor W. R. Cullom, entitled, "Christian Service at Home and Abroad." Stating that Southern
Baptists had 150 workers in six foreign fields, Mr. Cullom asked:

> Why should we expect a different amount and a different kind of
> service from our representatives abroad from what we ourselves render
> here at home? . . . The field is the world, and the work is one. . . .
> The great law of sowing and reaping is universal, and God will not
> change it to accommodate our indifference, our lack of energy or faith-
> fulness. If the kind of sowing and cultivating that we do here would
> fail to bring forth a satisfactory result in a foreign land, we may rest
> assured that the same result will follow here.

During July and August, Mr. Cullom was busy with revival meetings
in his churches. The services at Middleburg and Brassfield were
satisfactory; but the services at Poplar Creek were held during election
week, and the pastor was disappointed. He wrote:

> Evidently many people were more concerned for the election of their
> candidates than for the election of their souls to eternal life, and for or

against the amending of the Constitution of North Carolina than for the amendment of their lives.

Poplar Creek Community has a fine crop of young people just growing into manhood and womanhood. To meet the demands of the situation, the brethren have opened a first-class school right by the church, and elected Miss Eliza Parker of Wake County, to take charge of it. They will soon improve their church house, and altogether we are hoping for a better day among them.

The Rev. J. T. Edmundson, "a master soul-winner," preached three times a day—twice at Mount Vernon and once a day at the Falls of Neuse; thirty-five joined the church.

Partly as an outgrowth of the meeting at Mount Vernon, the Falls Baptist Church was organized "on the fourth Lord's day in September, 1900," in Emory Penny's barn with the Rev. W. R. Cullom as moderator. From her childhood, Nina Woodleaf Keith remembers Mr. Cullom's taking time with the children and his great kindness toward them; "it seemed to us that Christ was shining through him." (Conversation at Neuse, May 13, 1954.) Una Allen Smith Williams recalls Mr. Cullom's baptizing her as a girl of twelve along with eight others and still treasures the New Testament her pastor gave her on that occasion; the first time she ever heard the hymn, "Ninety and Nine," was Mr. Cullom's singing it as a solo. (Conversation at Neuse, May 13, 1954.) One Sunday afternoon in the home of Mr. Jeff Roger, the young pastor lay down on a lounge in a draft and developed "a dreadful case of bronchitis"; this was the first time he was to be bothered with this illness which was to trouble him often through the years.

- 14 -

William Wright Barnes of Elm City entered Wake Forest College in the fall of 1900; in the chapel he saw Professor Cullom for the first time. The Bible teacher was five feet, seven inches tall and weighed one hundred and eighty pounds; he was bald-headed, with a mustache and "a bay window." Although the professor was "dignified," Barnes found him "approachable and friendly"; he was to take every course Mr. Cullom offered. The Bible classes were held on the second floor of Old Wait Hall, in the front central section; Professor Cullom had his desk at the farther end of the room. Books and papers cluttered up his desk. When the class assembled, Mr. Cullom would turn in his chair to face the students. W. W. Barnes remembered that he remained seated during most of the class period.

> He followed his notes very closely. In some of his classes we had formal lectures which he had in outline. Other classes were informal when he discussed a book like W. R. Harper's *The Priestly Element.*

Joe Cullom, the professor's younger brother, was a classmate and a close friend of Barnes; he was so much of the same physique as his brother that the college boys nicknamed them "Big Pot" and "Little

Pot" or "Senior Pot-bel" and "Junior Pot-bel." As a friend of Joe's, Barnes was often in the Cullom home. He found Mrs. Cullom a "beautiful, delightful person"; she was very musical and jolly, "the life of a party." She was "lively in conversation" and pleasant in every way. Joe addressed her as "Sister" with a note of admiration. Barnes was impressed then by Professor Cullom's open-mindedness. "He was always trying to learn what others were thinking and saying; he read the *British Weekly* thoroughly and attended as many different kinds of religious meetings as possible." (W. W. Barnes, at Elm City, Sept. 2, 1953.)

On November 18, 1900, another baby was born in the Cullom home; this time a girl—Elizabeth Peter, named for an "aunt" of Mrs. Cullom in Louisville. Professor Cullom would say she came with the new century. Mrs. Cullom's mother, Mrs. Farmer, was still with the Culloms and would remain with them until her death. Her presence in the home was never burdensome; she was loved and respected by her son-in-law as she was by her own daughter.

On January 14, 1901, classes were suspended so that faculty and students could attend the inauguration of Charles B. Aycock as Governor of North Carolina. On February 26th, Mr. Cullom learned of the death of Mr. Burwell Davis; the next day he wrote Mrs. Davis a letter which was to be treasured in her family for three generations.

> My heart goes out to you and your dear loved ones in this dark hour of your lives. When the sad news of Mr. Davis' death came to me yesterday, it brought back to me so much that was connected with my own early days of beginning. Indeed, I feel that I am but a boy and just beginning now, but when I stop and think of it I am brought face to face with a fact that almost twenty years have gone by since I stepped out on the threshold of the world in the cotton gin of one who had meant and always will mean so much to me. These years have been crowded to overflowing with all sorts of things, but with every one of them I have been brought to realize more and more my debt of gratitude to the good Providence that placed my young life in touch with the strong, yet beautifully simple, life of Mr. Davis.

In March, the network of underground pipes connecting the various buildings of the campus with "the handsome new water tank" was completed; Professor Shailer Matthews of the University of Chicago gave "one of the ablest and most inspiring addresses" of the year on the "Duties of Educated Men," and Professor and Mrs. Cullom again entertained the members of the Bible classes at their home. W. D. Adams, Jr., wrote:

> It is seldom that we have spent a more pleasant afternoon. Mrs. Cullom, a most charming hostess, assisted by Misses Bruce Brewer, Marie Landford, Janie Taylor, Mattie Gill, Ethel Taylor and Eva Dunn, received. Delicious refreshments, ices and cakes were served. Beautiful music was rendered by Miss Janie Taylor and Mrs. Cullom. The time of departure came but too soon, and a certain young man, who was overheard to remark that he was going to fall through on Bible this spring, just to take it again next year, voiced the sentiment of everyone present. (*Student*, April 1901.)

Edith Taylor Earnshaw remembered these "lovely parties" through the years and recalled that on one evening after Mrs. Cullom had served something, one of the neighborhood girls brought in a finger bowl with water and a piece of lemon in it. One of the young ministerial students who had never seen anything like this before took the bowl, squeezed the lemon and would have drunk it if Mrs. Cullom had not rescued him and cleverly covered up his embarrassment. (Conversation at Wake Forest, Sept. 22, 1953.)

In May "the wonder of wonders" at Wake Forest was the new gymnasium—the most popular part of it being the baths. In June, Mr. Cullom suffered another loss; Myrtle Fleming (13) whom he had baptized the summer before died in Middleburg after an illness of six weeks. Surely he had her in mind when he wrote of having seen a broken lily carved on a young man's gravestone.

> It is easy to see what it was meant to suggest, but blinding tears had doubtless caused those fond parents to misread God's meaning. The scene has often come back to me since, and has often suggested the thought that there are no unfinished lives in God's economy. . . . In light of the gospel it would have been better to have carved a bud or a small bit of the stalk. . . . Henry Drummond, at the memorial service of a young ministerial friend, said: "There are two ways in which a workman regards his work—as his own or as his master's. If it is his own, then to leave it in his prime is a catastrophe, if not a cruel and unfathomable wrong. But if it is his master's one looks not backwards, but before, putting by the well worn tools without a sign, and expecting elsewhere better work to do."

Dr. Drummond said that work is for the making of men and that God was more concerned that men be true and great than for causes to be won. When the lessons of character and grace are learned, the workers may be retired so that others may be called into the field to learn these lessons. Professor Cullom continued:

> It may be that God withdraws His workers even when their hands are fullest and their souls most ripe, to fill the vacancies with still growing men, and enrich many with the loss of one. I do not propose this, even as an explanation of the inexplicable phenomenon. . . . But when our thoughts are heavy with questions of the mysterious ways of God, it keeps reason from reeling from its throne to see even a glimpse of light. . . . The great issue for us is to make our service for God of such high order here and now that He will trust us with higher service hereafter. (*BR*, Aug. 7, 1901.)

- 15 -

On July 1st (1901), Professor Cullom was elected corresponding secretary of the Board of Education; in an article, "The Board of Education," he defined the work of the Board and appealed for its support.

> "The primary object of the Convention shall be to educate young men called of God to the ministry, and approved by the churches." This little paragraph is taken from the constitution of the North Carolina Baptist State Convention. It lays down as one of our Baptist ideals an

educated ministry. Sixty years of practical application of this principle have brought forth fruit far beyond the most sanguine hope of those who placed it in our Constitution.

Baptist churches need men of culture and training more than any other churches of the world. We have no central organization to govern and direct the policy and practice of the churches. Each church is supreme. When a Baptist pastor stands before his people he appeals to men who are absolutely their own kings and priests. The individual conscience is supreme. How essential that he should know what he is doing. Moreover, the time has come when people no longer take things for granted, but, like the noble Bereans, they are examining for themselves to see if these things be so. A system of doctrine built up on doctrinal texts without regard to their setting is a thing that will not hold in this age. As Baptists, we have nothing to lose and all to gain by a faithful interpretation of the Old Book.

. . . The decline in the number of candidates for the ministry during the past ten years in some of our most prominent denominations is most alarming. It should be a cause for profound gratitude to us here in North Carolina that already about forty applications are before the Board for the coming session, with others constantly coming in. . . . The Secretary will not be able to attend many of the Associations, but he wishes to beg that every Association will kindly give a good place on its program for the discussion of this subject, and that the churches will respond as liberally as possible. (*BR,* August 21, 1901.)

In November (1901) Professor and Mrs. Cullom gave their "annual reception" to the members of the Bible classes; the editor of the *Student* described it as "one of the most enjoyable events of the year." But the social event of the fall of 1901 was the entertainment of Principal Booker T. Washington, a Negro, at a dinner in the White House by the President of the United States. The newspapers were filled with praise and condemnation of President Theodore Roosevelt. In the midst of this discussion, Editor Bailey sent letters to a great number of prominent men of the South, "with the purpose of obtaining a clear statement of the Southern Christian's conception of his duty to the colored race." In reply, President Charles E. Taylor quoted the Golden Rule as having "no limitations arising from race, color, or previous condition of servitude"; however, he could only foresee "social disorder" coming out of the two races dining together in the South.

There is room for genuine friendship and mutual helpfulness between the races. We ought to help the colored people in their upward struggling toward home-getting, wealth-making, and better living. But we shall make a great mistake if we think that we can help them by encouraging them to hope for social equality with the white race. I think I am right about this. I want to be. (*BR,* Nov. 13, 1901.)

Dr. E. Y. Mullins, president of the Louisville seminary, thought "the question of social equality" would regulate itself and defined the white Christian's attitude as "one of sympathy, consideration and helpfulness."

We ought to do all in our power for the education and the Christianization of the Negro. We ought to be impartial toward him in our administration of the law. We ought to believe in his future and help him to realize it.

C. B. Aycock, Governor of North Carolina, wrote that all upright Southerners were willing and anxious for the Negro race to grow into the highest citizenship of which it is capable.

> . . . we are willing to give our energies and best thought to aid them in the great work necessary to make them what they are capable of, and to assist them in that elevation of character and of virtue which tends to the strengthening of the State. But to do this it is absolutely necessary that each race shall remain distinct and have a society of its own. Inside of their own race the negroes can grow as large and broad and high as God permits, with the aid, the sympathy, and the encouragement of their white neighbors.

Mr. Cullom read all of this with great interest, but his responsibility lay elsewhere. In the spring of 1902, he added a course in Hebrew to his schedule and continued to work with the ministerial students. The College Catalogue of May, 1902, stated:

> This class, organized each year by the Professor of Bible, will study the four following subjects: (1) The priniciples of sermon-making. (2) A few of the fundamental doctrines of the Christian religion. (3) The history of the New Testament Church—its organization, its functions, its ordinances, its officers. (4) A brief outline of the church's activities with special emphasis on the missionary enterprises at present. No one subject will be studied any two years in succession.
> The work done here (only one hour a week) does not count towards a degree, yet it is hoped that it will be of value in marking out the more prominent lines of a minister's work and in forming an acquaintance at first hand with some of the best literature bearing on the subjects taught, and will stimulate in the student the desire to attend a Theological Seminary.

In the summer of 1902, the editor of the *Recorder* suggested that the churches devote a month to Bible study. Mr. Cullom supported this suggestion and urged that some "intelligent, united, persistent effort" be made to meet this important matter; he made "a motion" that, on the day before the next State Convention, pastors meet together and "try to agree on some plan for concerted action." (*BR,* Sept. 3, 1902.) [Among Dr. Cullom's services to the Baptists of North Carolina, Dr. G. W. Paschal lists: "the formation of the Pastors' Conference which regularly meets every year on the eve of the meeting of the Baptist State Convention." See *BR,* Jan. 21, 1942. Was this "motion" and the meeting that followed the beginning of the North Carolina Baptist Pastors Conference?] In the *Recorder* of September 10th, which appeared in a new type and on a smaller newssheet, its editor reported that the "forward movement for Bible Study in the churches" was "fairly on foot."

There were still rumblings about President Roosevelt's dinner-party, but Editor Bailey was troubled by another matter — "the modern Baptist inquisition"; he was bold enough to make this challenge:

> No college trustee, no editor, no coterie has the right to challenge a Baptist's faith—no matter what his relation to them. Only his church

can do this. If any should make demand of us, we would show our regard for the Baptist way and the Sovereign local church by respectfully referring them to her. We commend this policy to all others. This will end the inquisition and put the would-be popes out of business. Only so can the church and the human soul be restored to the authority and the dignity with which God Almighty has invested them. (*BR*, Oct. 22, 1902.)

On the afternoon of November 12, 1902, Professor and Mrs. Cullom again entertained the Bible Classes at their home; refreshments, music and the presence of seven young ladies "added to the pleasure of the occasion, and each invited guest departed loud in their expressions of a pleasantly spent afternoon." (*Wake Forest Student,* Dec. 1902.) The editors of the *Student* reported in December that the Wake Forest Band, under the leadership of Mr. Waite Bagley, was "again in full 'blast' " and that the literary societies had announced that they would publish a college annual in the spring.

In December (1902), Professor Cullom was making plans for a school for the pastors at the college from the middle of January and continuing until the middle of February; he stated that the general purpose of this work was "(1) to broaden, deepen and enrich our own hearts in God's eternal truth and (2) to get a stronger and more intelligent grasp on our work as preachers of the gospel and shepherds of the churches of Christ." The cost would be just as light as possible; Mr. Cullom wrote: "If any pastor finds that he wishes to come but can't quite make the arrangements, let him write me, and possibly I may be able to assist him." (*BR*, Dec. 24, 1902.)

Of the "Bible Institute for Ministers," W. C. Barrett wrote in the *Recorder* (Jan. 21, 1903) that already he had been "more than paid" for his trouble and expense in attending and urged his fellow ministers "to lay down every thing and come and get . . . the rest of the studies." And H. E. Craven concluded the talk about President Roosevelt's entertaining Booker T. Washington by writing in the *Student*: "If he wants a negro to dine with him . . . that is his business."

- 16 -

At a union meeting the people of Rolesville had been crying over the resignation of their pastor when they heard Professor W. R. Cullom speak; soon they were whispering, "What do you think of Mr. Cullom?" Mrs. Fanny Rogers, a native of Virginia, said, "He's the best thing I've heard in North Carolina." And he was called to be their pastor, the third Sunday of January, 1903. The Rolesville Baptist Church had been organized in 1834 and had had such pastors as the Rev. Samuel Wait and Dr. William B. Royall. At his first Saturday afternoon conference, Mr. Cullom led the people to give five dollars for the orphanage at Thomasville and appointed Brother R. P. Hunt and

Sister Maude Freeman "to collect money to help build a church at the Falls of Neuse and also to help pay a preacher at the Royall Cotton Mill Church." (Church Records.)

In April (1903), Mr. Cullom had to borrow five hundred dollars for the beneficiaries of the Board of Education; he wrote:

> What West Point is to the Army, and what Annapolis is to the Navy, the work of the Board of Education is to the work of North Carolina Baptists. In training a man called of God into the ministry, we are helping every other object of our work.

Not only did he appeal to his brethren through the pages of the *Recorder* but Professor Cullom was "kept busy with correspondence with the pastors in all parts of the State, many of whom he knew personally." G. W. Paschal wrote of his work:

> He also found that the pastors' conferences and schools which he organized during this period were most helpful means of acquainting the pastors of the churches with the Board's work for the young ministers at the College. In order to be able to devote two Sundays a month to the work, in June, 1902, he gave up the pastorate of one of the churches he had been serving. He also gained much favor for the Board by sending out the beneficiaries, usually in pairs, in the summer vacation, to labor in the churches and with their members, helping in Sunday Schools and prayer meetings both in churches and homes, and stimulating an interest in religion among the young people. The result was that the Baptists of the State came to have a greater interest in the work and a greater desire to contribute to it . . . The salary of Dr. Cullom was . . . fixed at twenty dollars a month. (*History of Wake Forest College*, vol. II, pp. 470-471.)

Dr. Charles E. Taylor reported in the *Recorder* of August 12, 1903, that "Professor Cullom had been working hard for the Board of Education and has preached much."

In that same month (August 1903), the Saturday conference at Rolesville was taken up with "disciplinary matters." One brother's name was dropped from the roll; another was excused, and a third was to be waited upon. The next week the pastor conducted "a protracted meeting," and six "came forward for baptism" with three being "restored to full fellowship with the church." (Rolesville Church Records.)

There were a few times when Mr. Cullom walked the five miles from Wake Forest to Rolesville, but ordinarily he drove a white-faced horse, named "Molly." Maude Broughton Mitchell remembers Edward's coming with his father and playing with the calves at her father's barn. (Conversation at Wake Forest, June 25, 1953.) Occasionally Mrs. Cullom and both of the children would come. Elizabeth remembers riding in the buggy from Rolesville; to her the pine trees seemed to extend hundreds of feet into the sky. It was told that once as a very little girl she threw her father's keys out in the mud; she remembers more delightful times as when her father would bring the red ears of corn from the horse's feed and when he would tell the wonderful Uncle Remus stories. She recalls being permitted to walk slowly toward the campus after the 12:30 bell until she saw her father; then she would run into his arms and be lifted up into the air. How happily and proudly she walked, hand in hand, with him back to their home. (Elizabeth Cullom Kelly, at Wake Forest, Dec. 30, 1958.)

In 1903, Professor Cullom purchased the Edwards house on North Main Street ("Faculty Avenue") and moved his family into it. This two-story frame house, which was to be his home through the years, had a nice porch facing the street and Gore practice field, with a smaller porch on the north side. It had high, narrow windows and blinds. Inside, the hallway opened on the right to the parlor and had a stairs to the back. A large dining room and kitchen were also on the right (north) side of the house; two bedrooms were on the other side. There was a large back porch. Upstairs there were three bedrooms and a large attic-closet. The moving of his household, the work of his churches, the responsibilities he carried as secretary of the Board of Education and as professor of Bible did not take all of Mr. Cullom's time or energies; he wrote a series of articles on "The Moral Significance of Christian Baptism" which appeared in the *Biblical Recorder* from September 30th through October 14th (1903). At the Central Association, meeting at Youngsville, October 13-15, he spoke "with force and enthusiasm" on home missions and Christian education; he offered special prayer for the restoration of Dr. Royall's health and his safe return from Europe. (*BR,* Nov. 18, 1903.) In November, he "delightfully entertained" his Bible classes at his residence; in December, "the ladies at Mount Vernon" paid his expenses to the Convention at Charlotte.

In January (1904), he conducted "the winter course for pastors" at Wake Forest, where the following studies were made:

> 1. The Life of Christ—W. R. Cullom, 2. The Gospel of John—C. E. Taylor, 3. Four Great Doctrines—W. C. Tyree, 4. The Pastor Among His Flock—Livingston Johnston, 5. The Pastor and the Church at Work Together for Christ—C. J. Thompson, 6. The Pastor in His Study and in His Pulpit—H. W. Battle, 7. Special Lectures by several members of the Wake Forest Faculty, 8. A popular lecture each Thursday evening.

About twenty-five "faithful men" enrolled and heard such lectures as "The Thirty Years of the Private Life of Jesus" by Dr. W. L. Poteat and "Modern Jerusalem" by Dr. Alfred H. Moment. Dr. Taylor wrote:

> All the lectures were good. But it is freely recognized that Mr. Cullom's work alone would justify the course. It is doubtful if those who do not know him understand what a strong man we Baptists have in him. (*BR,* Feb. 10, 1904.)

The Christian Index stated that every denominational college ought to provide such a helpful course for the pastors of the State.

The success of the Pastors' Institute pleased Mr. Cullom, but as he had not moped over the disappointment of the first institute, he did not gloat over this success. Other things called his attention. He wrote of the need of correlating our educational effort and proposed the creation of a position for an "Educational Secretary of the Baptist State Convention of North Carolina," who would supervise our Sunday School work, the young people movement and our Baptist schools. (*BR,* Jan. 13, 1904.) In the *Recorder* of January 27th, he begged the brethren not to forget the struggling young ministerial students; Brother James E. Slate of Stokes County responded by giving eight hundred dollars to be used in loans to these students at Wake Forest.

- 17 -

During these busy years, Professor Cullom had not forgotten the unfinished dissertation for his doctorate. Having chosen as his topic, "The Final Fate of the Impenitent," he had done a great deal of work on it before his illness at the seminary in 1896, but there had been little time for it since then. Finally in the winter and early spring of 1904, he managed somehow to finish his manuscript.

In his introductory chapter, Mr. Cullom wrote of the importance of the "doctrine of last things" and stated:

> From a perhaps overemphasis and a far too harrowing physical conception of the torments awaiting the wicked, there has gradually come to be a general neglect of the doctrine altogether. . . . Happily for our generation these questions are now being re-opened, made more ethical, and at the same time more Biblical and reasonable.

Mr. Cullom defined the task of the theologian as that of taking the findings of physical science and of interpreting them in relation to other truths. He listed the following points from which his discussion is made: (1) permanent data—God and law. "Back of all that appears or ever has appeared is an intelligent will working ever consistently toward a definite end." (2) There is unity and diversity in the universe about us. "Every part of God's universe bears some sort of relation to every other part; but, at the same time, this does not identify individuals in the universe with each other nor with the universe itself as a whole." (3) The Bible is accepted as the word of God. "The truth in the Bible is eternal, but the vessel in which the truth is contained will not be needed when the last one of God's children shall know even as also he has been known." (4) Christ is the supreme and ultimate revelation of God to his moral creation. "To accept him unreservedly for what God means him to be to the life of a human being . . . means ultimately complete fellowship with God in all his matchless beauty and perfections."

In his second chapter, "Has Man a Conscious Existence Beyond Death?" Mr. Cullom reasoned:

God had intended death as a blessing in that it promoted a higher type of life for the race, and was probably the gateway into a fuller and richer fellowship with himself for the individual; but sin has made death the entrance into a state of permanent separation from God, and so death through sin was transformed from a blessing into a curse.

Agreeing with John Fiske that the belief in a spiritual world is beyond the range of scientific investigation, Mr. Cullom thought (1) the universality of the belief, (2) the partialness or incompleteness of man's life, (3) the revelations of the scriptures were reasons enough to believe in a "future conscious existence" and traced the development of this belief in the Bible.

In the progressive revelation of himself to the chosen people, God brought into the conscience of that people more and more a consciousness of his eternal holiness. This gave rise to the conviction of an essential moral order in the universe. But when the Hebrew saw the wicked prosper and the righteous suffer even unto death, in spite of his postulate of a moral order, he was driven to feel out for a more definite and satisfactory solution of the problem than he saw around him. It is in the midst of this struggle that we see such imprecations called down on the wicked as are recorded in the Psalms. . . . This struggle . . . is caught up and developed by the prophets from the eighth century B. C. and onwards. The "Day of Jehovah," with its double significance of grace and deliverance for the righteous and of judgment and penalty upon the wicked, is one of the most familiar conceptions in the prophets from Joel to Malachi. The climax of this growing conviction of an essential moral order in the universe is reached in Dan. 12:2, where we are told clearly and plainly that "many of them that sleep in the dust of the earth shall awake, some to everlasting life, and some to shame and everlasting contempt."

It will not be necessary to trace this doctrine through the New Testament. Jesus found it among the Jews when he came. That he added his sanction to it and made it even stronger and more definite is clear from such Scriptures as John 5:25f; Luke 16:19-31. The same is taught also by the inspired apostles after the Lord's ascension. See Acts 24:15; I Cor. 15:22; I Pet. 3:19.

In his third chapter, "The Prospect of a change after death," Mr. Cullom listed three alternatives and examined the scriptures; he concluded that "Jesus and his apostles meant to leave the impression that man is to have an everlasting existence: happy or wretched in the state in which death finds him." In the last chapter, Mr. Cullom stated that in accord with the universal reign of law, "the harvest of a man's life is gathered up in himself, and a great 'gulf' that separates people in the next world is the same that separates in this, viz.—character." After explaining the meanings of Hades, Gehenna and Tartarus, Mr. Cullom asked if descriptive passages of scripture connected with the punishment of the wicked are to be taken literally or figuratively.

They are literal in that they describe a real fact, and not a mere figment of the imagination. Our Lord spoke just as plainly and just as unequivocally of the real existence of the wicked after death as he did that of the righteous; and the same may be said of the condition of the two classes respectively. These phrases are perhaps figurative, however, in respect of their material fulfilment. . . . It would probably be better to ask whether these phrases are meant to be material or spiritual. When we speak of a "river of water of life," no one surely thinks of that river as one flowing with water made up of oxygen and hydrogen combined in the requisite proportions. It is a material figure presenting to us a great spiritual truth. The same may be said of the materialistic description of the new Jerusalem in Rev. 21. If this be true of the side of the righteous, we should naturally expect the same to be true of the side of the wicked also.

Mr. Cullom concluded that "the conditions awaiting the wicked after death are exactly suited to the inner character of each individual." He quoted Henry Drummond as saying:

> With man, it is not necessary that he should be judged from without; he will be judged from within. No witnesses need be called to give their evidence; the witnesses are himself. No gaoler need be told off to watch him; he cannot run away from himself. . . . (This court) is a vast, mysterious, self-acting organization, ramifying through the whole of nature, and without resistance or appeal, each living thing obeys its verdict.

At the appearance of Christ, men shall see themselves as they really are; they shall see the gulf and know why it cannot be crossed. As James Orr says, the scripture "leaves them divided, a universe apart in destiny." (W. R. Cullom, *The Final Fate of the Impenitent,* unpublished thesis presented to the Southern Baptist Theological Seminary, May, 1904.)

Upon finishing his thesis, Mr. Cullom sent it to a friend in Louisville who had agreed to type it, to have it bound and to submit it to the Board of Examiners. In time, the examiners notified Mr. Cullom that it was acceptable and that the degree of Doctor of Theology would be awarded him at the spring commencement.

This news brought Professor Cullom one of his happiest moments. The work which he had left undone at Louisville was now at last completed. The eight years since he left the seminary had been busy years: he had inaugurated the study of the Bible in the curriculum of Wake Forest College (1896); he had organized the ministerial conference (1896) and had begun the institutes for pastors (1897). He had suggested (1902) the meeting of pastors prior to the annual Baptist State Convention, had urged a regular concerted study of the Bible in the churches, and had recommended the employment of an "Educational Secretary" of the Convention. Quietly he had brought a new approach to Bible Study in North Carolina and without attracting much attention and without offending anyone had presented a revolutionary concept of Biblical revelation. He had worked hard for the support of the needy ministerial students and had seen the work of the Board of Education greatly increased.

Those years, 1896-1904, had been happy years. As a young man he had undertaken great things in the kingdom, and God had been pleased to bless them. He had courted and won a lovely and talented wife, and God had blessed them with two fine children. Yes, those years had been busy, happy years of beginnings. And he would go back to Louisville to receive his degree! As he would be away from home on his wedding anniversary, he purchased a copy of *An Old Sweetheart of Mine* by James Whitcomb Riley and on the fly-leaf wrote—

June 2, 1897 - June 2, 1904

Genesis 29:20

"And Jacob served seven years for Rachael, and they seemed unto him but a few days, for the love he had for her."

FIFTH AGE

THE PARSON AND PROFESSOR MELLOWS

1904-1918

The train arrived in Louisville "on time to the minute"; Ed Farmer, his wife's brother, boarded the train at First Street station. Later at Ed's room, Mr. Cullom "enjoyed a plunge into a good bath tub." On May 30, 1904, he wrote to his mother-in-law in Wake Forest:

> If we continue at Wake Forest much longer, we certainly must have such a commodity in our house. The new church is all that it has been represented to be and more if possible. . . . After church we (E. T. and myself) went to take dinner with "the folks." They asked and reasked about each of you. . . . You and Fannie may be my mother and wife at Wake Forest, but I was your son and husband yesterday at Walnut St.

On Monday, Mr. Cullom heard Dr. S. B. Messer of Detroit and had dinner at Dr. Mullins' house in the company of Dr. Messer and Dr. E. M. Poteat ("a rare treat"). On Tuesday he had dinner with the Sampeys and tea with Dr. Eaton; he wrote Mrs. Cullom:

> Can it be true that I took you away from this place seven years ago? Sunday morning as I sat in church and thought over those seven years, and thought how happy you all seem to be in your own little circle and with your larger circle of friends and loved ones, I thought it was very rude of me to come here and try to break it up. And yet, it looks like it was the Lord's goodness to me, and if He was back of it, it is all right. Aunt Amanda said Mr. McKee used to tell her that all his good luck came at one time, when he got her. I told her that mine was not that way at all, that my luck was indeed good on June 2 seven years ago, but that it had grown better all the time since. If it can be in accordance with the Lord's will, I hope we may be spared to grow old together, and may be able to accomplish a great deal of good in our lives and in the lives of our children.

That evening (May 31, 1904) in Norton Hall, he received his Doctor of Theology degree, along with Walter Oliver Lewis of Missouri. (Annual Catalogue, 1904-1905, S.B.T.S.) On June 1, 1904, he wrote to Mrs. Cullom:

> My degree was conferred last night. Quite a number of people came up to congratulate me—some of them my friends and some of them yours.

On June 1st, at McFarran, Mr. Cullom assisted in an ordination service and baptized Mrs. C. T. Ball who "said she had waited" for his coming. On June 3rd, he wrote: "Sister Ida and all are doing everything they can to make my stay here pleasant." Brother Greenwell drove him out to the abbey, where they sat at the table with the "father" and some of the "brothers." The next day he wrote:

> The lives of those poor monks are certainly very abnormal, but I told brother that maybe the Lord had a place for them as an object lesson of discipline in a time when there is so little of that in home and ordinary school. . . . Edward T. insists that I shall remain over here now until Monday and preach for Dr. Eaton Sunday night which he (Dr. E.)

has requested that I do. Edward seems so anxious for me to do so that I guess I shall remain over.

From Louisville, Dr. Cullom went to Chicago where he sought to avail himself of "the broadening influences and cultural advantages of the University." Upon his arrival (June 6th), he wrote home:

> When I went to take an elevated car to come out to the University I did not know how to do so. The young lady who sold tickets was very impatient with me, but I laughed at myself and at her too. I thought the idea of a man who had just taken his doctor's degree not knowing how to take an elevated car was ridiculous.

On June 8th, Dr. Cullom confessed he was "quite home sick"; in reply to her letter, he wrote "dear Fannie" that he was sorry she was "pinched for money" and did not wonder that she was thinking of resuming teaching piano. On June 10th he heard Dr. Edward Judson speak on his illustrious father, Adoniram Judson, and Dr. Harper lecture on "The Idea of a Future Life in the Old Testament." On June 11th, G. W. Paschal came to Chicago, and was Dr. Cullom ever happy to see him! He wrote his "dear Girl":

> I cannot tell you how glad I was to see him. He took me up into the city and showed me some of the sights. He is pretty well acquainted with the place. . . . There are so many opportunities to study and improve one's self in a large city. It really looks like we ought to be able to take a trip once a year for that purpose. If we could spend a month together each year in New York, Boston, Washington, or some such place, it would be worth a great deal to us.

At Dr. Paschal's suggestion, Dr. Cullom planned to go to St. Louis to see the Exposition; he wrote his wife about her going to Virginia Beach.

> I know it looks as if I were spending all the money, but I want you to go, and if you had rather not borrow the money from Mother, just let me know, and I will arrange to get it for you. You know we must pay Mr. Brewer $75.00 about the 9th of July. . . . I guess we will get our place paid for after a while, and pay for these trips too. Write me a business letter when you get this, that I may know what your thoughts are.

The exposition was "a great thing"; he wrote: "It looks bad that we cannot be here together, but the reason that keeps us from doing so (the children) is such a blessed one that we will think of that side, and be thankful."

Back in Chicago for more lectures (June 20th) he welcomed two letters from home, but the news of the threat of whooping cough to his children concerned him.

> "Tell it not in Gath," but there are quite a number of Negroes registering for the summer quarter. Some of them have rooms in the building in which I stay. They have not sat down at table with me, but I see them sitting in (the) same dining room. . . . Am sorry that I have given offence or grief to my friends by coming to Chicago University. Hope I may survive without contamination with what is very bad. What

would some of them say if you told them that I was trying (to) secure a seat among the Republicans in their convention to-morrow?

Later he wrote that there was little pleasure in traveling alone among strangers; to his wife he apologized:

> I reckon you think I am hard to satisfy. Last summer we went to-gether and you thought I was not enjoying it (though you were mis-taken), and this summer I am just where I have been trying to come for so long, and yet am longing so much to be at home. I really am finding all that I had expected here. . . . I think one of the greatest helps that one gets in a place of this sort is stimulus to do more work along those lines. Do you reckon the enthusiasm will withstand the many diversions that I shall have in the way of protracted meetings, Board of Education work, Associations, etc.? May be there will be a little residuum left. Hope the children will not suffer too much with their cough. I feel so sorry for them and for you too. (June 24, 1904.)

Sunday, June 26th, was a memorable day for Dr. Cullom. He wrote "dearest Fannie": "If you could attend Church where I did yesterday you would not say any thing more about my services being so long in comparison with those of Brother Burlingam." Preaching service began at 10:30; a little before twelve they had Sunday school, after which they stayed for a social chat. It was two o'clock when Dr. Cullom left the church; he wrote that the people "were very warm hearted and cordial" and many expressed "very warm appreciation" of his sermon. In the afternoon he went with the pastor to "his open-air service"; at 6:30 he was back at the church for the young people's meeting and for the evening service (7:30) when four candidates were baptized. Also on that Sunday Dr. Cullom took his first ride in an automobile: "It was the gospel automobile, but I felt that I didn't know what minute it was going to run into something and have a crash."

July 4, 1904, was quite "a noisy day" of firecrackers; at the University, he attended patriotic services. He wrote to his wife:

> Dreamed about you last night and have wanted to see you mighty bad to-day. I don't know how people get on in this world who have no one to love and no one to love them. They are certainly to be pitied. And those of us who are so richly blessed in this particular ought to appreciate our treasure. When I think of my wife and my home in this way I feel that I am indeed rich if we do have to walk by faith a good deal in the financial part of our lives. Tomorrow will be my last day in the University, and I am planning to make it a pretty full one.

On his way to the station the next evening, he fell "in the dirty mud"; he brushed off his clothes as best he could and went on to Detroit for the B.Y.P.U. (Baptist Young People Union) Convention. When he reached Detroit, he was given letters from home, in which Mrs. Cullom informed him that both of the children had been quite ill. He replied:

> Do hope that dear little Elizabeth will not get much worse. (July 7th) . . . Wish you had written me to come on home. As it is, I don't know what to do. I feel so sorry for the dear little ones, and can hardly

bear not to be there with them (July 9th) . . . Your letter of Wednesday
night telling me of Edward's fever and of how Elizabeth could not control her crying made me very anxious. Am so glad to get a more hope-
ful one to-day. (July 10th.)

As he had not received a telegram from his wife by Thursday, he
presumed that things were better and proceeded with his plans to
take a boat to Buffalo. He found Niagara Falls and everything around
it "simply overpowering"; from there, he went by train to Toronto. On
July 12th, he wrote:

Last night as I went to bed at the Grand Union Hotel I thought that
it was the first night I had every spent outside Uncle Sam's domain.
But these people are very much like . . . our southern people. . . .
To-day is the day of the Orange men.

That night on the Steamer "Kingston," Dr. Cullom wrote of the setting
sun; on the morning of July 14th, he was in Montreal:

You see I have made the rapids of the St. Lawrence all right. It
almost took my breath sometimes. . . . This morning we are going out
"to do the town." . . . I shall make some inquiries about Quebec this
morning, but hardly think I shall undertake that. If not I shall leave
here for Albany about six o'clock this evening, and ought to get to
New York about six to-morrow p.m. Am figuring on trying to run in
to Wake Forest Sunday morning about day.

- 2 -

On July 20, 1904, Dr. Cullom wrote that he had "just arrived home"
and immediately resumed his responsibilities there. He conducted revival services at Mount Vernon and Middleburg; in an article on the
Board of Education, he thanked all who had shared in the work and
asked that "one or two brethren in every association" present the work
of the Board.

With the opening of the College in September, Dr. Cullom was
soon busy with his classes and plans for the Pastors' Course. In an
article, "The Supreme Opportunity of Christ's People in This Generation," Dr. Cullom characterized his time as a truth-seeking age and
as an age of intense interest in man, the whole man. (*BR*, Nov. 30,
1904.) In a second article, he described his age further as an age
of intense interest in the Bible and in Jesus Christ and urged his
fellow-Christians to realize that "God has placed us in the midst of
unparalleled privileges and in the midst of equally unparalleled responsibilities"; he pleaded with those who occupied places of leadership in the Lord's work to realize "the necessity of getting a deep,
firm, living grasp on the fundamentals of the faith and life that they
teach and advocate." He concluded:

We all rejoice in the many ways in which laymen can and are serving
God, and making themselves active, aggressive agents in spreading His
kingdom; but the conditions set forth above would seem to open a new

day of usefulness for the minister of the gospel as such. Would not God be pleased for scores and even hundreds of our strongest, brightest and best men—men who are gifted with the power of seizing fundamentals and of leading others to see and embrace them—to turn their lives and talents into this special channel? Are you among the number? (*BR*, Dec. 21, 1904.)

In Dr. Cullom's own home, his six-year-old son was bringing in wood and coal for the fires. In the winter, Dr. Cullom was up by five or six o'clock every morning to make all the fires and to feed his horse; in the summer, he arose earlier to work in his garden. Mrs. Cullom assumed all household responsibilities; she admonished the children, and when necessary, she whipped them. Whenever her husband came home, he found everything in order; he never interfered with the house or the children.

Mrs. Cullom had resumed teaching piano and thus was able to supplement her husband's income. She kept a small black pocketbook in which she always had some money. Edward never remembers when she couldn't go to it and get some money; neither does he remember ever hearing finances discussed in the home. If there ever was any disagreement or quarrel between their father and mother, the children never heard of it. Edward remembers his Grandmother Farmer was very quiet and unobtrusive; she stayed upstairs in the south front bedroom most of the time. She did not interfere with the running of the house, which was her daughter's prerogative; she "petted" the children and in a quiet even way made a great impression on them. Nearly every Christmas "Uncle Ed" and his wife came on the train from Louisville; the whole Cullom family would be at the station to greet them. And what presents he brought the children—so many that Mrs. Cullom would scold him and put some of them away until later. For Christmas breakfast the Culloms always had fried oysters, fresh hot biscuits and strawberry preserves with milk and coffee. After "Father" read a passage of scripture, the whole family arose, pushed back their chairs and knelt down for prayer. Neither the Scripture nor the prayer seemed long to Edward; this morning devotional exercise was a part of their lives. "We grew up with it; it was just as natural as eating breakfast." When "Father" was away, "Mother" did it.

In January of 1905, Dr. Cullom thanked "the good people of Middleburg" for having sent him to the State Convention (*BR*, Jan. 4, 1905); he conducted the Pastor's Course at Wake Forest for the third year. In the first of a series of serious Bible studies in the *Biblical Recorder,* he stated: "The Bible is a product of the Spirit of God, and at the same time it is as truly a product of the several writers whose work makes up its pages." (*BR*, Jan. 4, 1905.) On January 18th his study was entitled "Adam: The End of the Physical and the Beginning of the Spiritual Creation," and on January 25th it was "Adam: The Old Testament Prodigal." On February 1st, his article had a boxed heading and was given the left front side of the second page: "Bible Studies, conducted by W. R. Cullom, Th.D., Chair of the Bible, Wake Forest College." This article was on "Some Questions in Genesis 1-3" and ran the average length of three and one-eighth columns. The fifth article appeared in the *Recorder* of February 8 in its regular place and was entitled "Adam and Physical Death." Others followed:

Feb. 15—If a Man Die Shall He Live Again?
Feb. 22—The Future Life: What Saith the Scriptures
Mar.   1—Life After Death—Climax of the Argument
Mar.   8—Cain and Abel, or External and Internal Religion
Mar. 15—Cain and His Brother
Mar. 22—Religion
Apr.   5—Noah and the Flood
Apr. 12—Noah and the Flood, No. 2
Apr. 19—Enoch: The Companion of God
May   3—Noah and His Sons
June   7—Abraham—A New Departure
June 21—Abraham and the Life of Faith

In the *Recorder* of August 2, 1905, Dr. Cullom covered the front page with "Four Essentials in Education." Education (1) must take into account Christ's view of man and (2) must consider "Christ's view of the thing to be done on this human being"; (3) it must also take into account "his view of the end or purpose of human life" and (4) consider "Christ's view of the agencies for bringing this about": (a) the Christian Home, (b) the Christian School, and (c) the Christian Church.

On October 4, 1905, the *Recorder* began another series of articles, "Exposition of the Epistle to the Romans" which Dr. W. R. Cullom had given as lectures at the "Midsummer Meeting" at Jackson Springs, June 28-30. The first of these bore the heading "Man's Great Need— the Gentiles"; the second, "Man's Great Need—the Jews" appeared on October 11th. Others followed:

Oct. 25—Guilt and Justification
Nov.   1—The Doctrine of Justification in History
Nov.   8—The Believers Security
Nov. 15—Union with Christ
Nov. 22—Man's Impotence and the Spirit's Help
Dec.   6—The Triumph of Faith—I
Dec. 20—The Triumph of Faith—II

- 3 -

While Dr. Cullom was thus busy with teaching, preaching and writing, changes were occurring at Wake Forest. Dr. Charles E. Taylor who had served as president of the college for "over a third of its long career" had resigned and the trustees had elected to succeed him Dr. William Louis Poteat, of whom the *Student* (Oct. 1905) said "a better man for the place could not have been found by looking the world over." The inauguration of President Poteat on December 7, 1905, was a great day for the Baptists in North Carolina; they came from the east and west, from the north and south to pay tribute to Wake Forest. The exercises began with the formation of the academic procession; members of the Philomathesian and Euzelian Literary Societies lined the walk to Wingate Hall. The "first division" was composed of the Alumni, headed by Major J. M. Crenshaw, the first student to matriculate at Wake Forest, and by J. C. Scarborough, a member of the first class after "the war." Next came the trustees, led by Dr. J. D. Hufham, "the Bishop of the Baptists" in North Carolina. The procession of visitors was headed by Governor Glenn and State Treasurer B. R. Lacy. The faculty followed, led by Dr. Poteat; Mr. Hubert M. Poteat eloquently played "March from Tannhauser" on the large organ. (*News and Observer,* Raleigh, N. C., Dec. 8, 1905.) After the formal services, President and Mrs. Poteat held a reception at their home that evening from nine to eleven; Mrs. W. R. Cullom, Mrs. W. B. Royall, and Mrs. John Brewer served refreshments in the dining room. About ten o'clock the student body assembled in front of the residence and made a bonfire in honor of their new president.

On December 21 (1905), Dr. George W. Paschal was married to Miss Laura Allen of Dillon, South Carolina. When they returned to Wake Forest, Dr. and Mrs. Cullom were at the station to greet them and to take them to their home. Soon the students gathered at the Cullom house from all parts "at the sound of dinner-bells, tin pans, and various other musical instruments." The editor of the *Student* reported:

> All knew the custom—a serenade was at hand. Dr. Paschal kindly responded to the call made for him and in a little speech gave a bit of advice that delighted his auditors beyond measure: "Get married," he said. But the best was to come. All were invited in to meet the bride, and this was too good for a single soul to miss. The band filed in, and more than one overcoat was buttoned tight about its wearer's neck to hide a collar, which, in the haste to join the happy throng, was left at home. But nevertheless gladness reigned and Mrs. Paschal won as many friends as there were students in the party. (*Wake Forest Student,* Jan. 1906.)

In the new college catalogue, "Bulletin of Wake Forest College," Dr. James W. Lynch was listed as "Chaplain of the College." (The year "1903" was given as the date of Dr. Cullom's doctorate; this was the beginning of an error which would be extended through the years.) All Bible courses were listed as elective; Bible One, a three-hour course for one year, was on the Old Testament, and Bible Two was on the New Testament, while Bible Three varied "from year to year according to circumstances." Professor Royall continued his class in Greek New Testament, and Dr. Cullom his in Hebrew Old Testament. The daily schedule of the college began with religious exercises from 7:58 to 8:10 each morning, but instead of meeting in the little chapel the students marched upstairs to Wingate Hall "to the softening strains of the pipe organ played by Mr. Hubert Poteat." (*Student,* Oct., 1905.)

- 4 -

In the fall of 1905, Dr. Cullom began supplying the Baptist Church at Dunn; years later he would say, "I don't believe they ever called me; I just kept on coming." This church dates back to 1885 when Elder W. R. Johnson, "a roving missionary" of the South River Association, had conducted a revival meeting in the area of the Greenwood schoolhouse, after which fourteen Baptists had banded themselves into a church. In 1887, the church moved to Dunn, a newly incorporated town, and met in a room over Mr. Allen B. Godwin's buggy repair-shop. Rev. I. T. Newton led in organizing a Sunday school and in building a church building. Before 1905, the church had had such pastors as Elder J. A. Campbell, Elder W. R. Watson, Dr. N. B. Cobb, and Luther Rice Carroll who was long remembered for his "deep piety, apostolical zeal and loving humility." (Herbert B. Taylor, *Recollections and Memories, Pertaining to the history of the First Baptist Church of Dunn,* a manuscript.)

When Dr. Cullom came to Dunn, the Baptist church had "preaching" twice a month. He traveled by train; sometimes he arrived on Friday afternoon, but most of the time he came on Saturday. Often a child would be waiting to take his black satchel and umbrella to the home in which he would be staying; if there was no one to meet him at the station, he would take his bag to Hassie McNeill's house, where he was always welcomed. When he knocked at the door, Mrs. McNeill would say, "It's Doctor Cullom," and would call to Lelia or Viola to go let him in while she put another plate at the table.

In the pulpit at Dunn, Dr. Cullom wore a black frock coat, Prince Albert style; Mr. George Pope would say, "We wouldn't have let him preach without it." Shortly after he became pastor at Dunn, Dr. Cullom invited Mr. Fred M. Day to assist him in a meeting which changed the church and town; as a business man, Mr. Day talked in a plain straight way which the people liked. They responded in a great way; nearly a hundred were baptized.

Dr. Cullom was "a good organizer." He helped organize the T.E.L. (Timothy, Eunice, Lois) Bible Class for the ladies and greatly strengthened the Woman's Missionary Society; he started (1906) the B.Y.P.U. (Baptist Young People Union) with nineteen members. At the church conference, there was "always plenty of argument," Jessie Starling would remember; "but Dr. Cullom was good at smoothing things over and calming people."

Although he was "a good preacher of sound, solid Biblical doctrine," Dr. Cullom was not esteemed for his preaching; it was the love he showed his people that caused them to love him. Herbert B. Taylor recalls that whenever Dr. Cullom stayed at his father's house, Mr. J. A. Taylor would send the boys to the neighbors to tell them "Dr. Cullom is here." In a short time a crowd of people would be gathered on the porch and yard in the summer and all over the house in the winter. Dr. Cullom would talk and teach them, and they listened as if he had been a Paul or a Peter. Dr. C. D. Bain testifies:

> All our people liked him—not so much for what he said as for his manner of life. He was not much for joking, but you could depend on what he said. His disposition was good, easy, Christian; he never offended or hurt anyone. He paid a great deal of attention to the rank and file of people and left many a New Testament in homes where it was needed or inscribed it for a child in the home. He was strong in evangelism and won a great number of people.

Eva Strickland Core recalls one Sunday morning when he was staying at their house, Dr. Cullom brought a button off his coat to her mother and said, "Sister Strickland, will you please help me get this ox out of the ditch?"

- 5 -

On June 11, 1906, a third child was born in the Cullom home, another little girl whom they named "Nancy Frances" for her Grandmother Farmer. Edward was now eight years old, and Elizabeth would soon be six. Elizabeth "favored" Dr. Cullom, but when people told her she "looked like" her father, she would cry. One night while he was playing "William Trembletoe," Dr. Cullom asked her why she cried when people said she looked like him. She said she thought they meant she had a mustache and a bald head. When he explained that people knew she had pretty long curls and that they meant her eyes were like his and her little nose was something like his, then little Elizabeth became reconciled to looking like "Papa."

In a front page article in the *Biblical Recorder* of January 23, 1907, Dr. W. R. Cullom tried to clear up "some of the misunderstanding" toward Baptists; under the title, "Foundation Principles of a Baptist Church," he declared:

> 1) The supreme and ultimate expression of God's will to men is to be found in Jesus Christ, His only begotten Son; and the source of our information as to the person, character, and work of Jesus is to be found in the Bible (Jno. 5:39) and in the eternal Spirit. Hence for Baptists, the only source of authority in matters of religion is the Bible interpreted and applied under the guide of the Spirit.
> 2) Man—made as he is in God's image and after God's likeness—is endowed with sovereignty of conscience and will that are inviolable. Even God Himself, when He makes His approach to man, says: "Behold I stand at the door and knock: if any man hear my voice and open the door, I will come in," etc.
> 3) Religion is a matter of life, and not of ritual. . . .
> 4) . . . each individual soul must make its own independent, free, sacred response to the call of God in Christ and in His Gospel. This response to the call of God we call *faith*. It may be made in childhood or in mature life; but it *must* be voluntary and independent.

5) If the above principles are true, it follows that the priesthood of all believers is a necessary fact. This means that all believers stand on the same level in Christ—justified by faith alone, and that no special place or human mediator is needed for our approach to God.

Necessary Conclusions

It is an honest effort to follow these necessary principles that Baptists are sometimes misunderstood and misinterpreted.

1) As to truth in general . . . With no creed but the Bible with no authority of State, church, or individual between a man's soul and God, Baptists are prepared to welcome truth from any source whatever. Their essential principles compel them to keep their faces always to the light. But with the conviction that all truth is consistent, Baptists must be thoroughly convinced that any proposed theory is in harmony with what has already been established as true (i.e., with the Bible) before they can accept it. We wish to try all things, and hold fast to that which is true.

2) As to specific doctrines . . . We can accept nothing that seems to us to be contrary to the teaching of that blessed book. . . .

3) Some points of differences (1) as to the church . . . (2) as to the ministry . . . (3) as to the ordinances.

We often hear it said that we should emphasize and magnify our likeness and say but little about our differences. Surely, Baptists can of all people best afford to do this. What would be the result? If all everywhere would unite to accept and practice nothing at all except what the scholarship of all denominations agrees is taught in the Bible there would probably not be a single doctrine held by Baptists left out.

We do not record these things in a spirit of boastfulness, nor with the slightest desire to reproach other people. We do it in simple justice to the Baptist position and attitude. We invite kindly criticism from any source and promise to correct, as soon as possible, anything that is shown us to be clearly contrary to the Scriptures.

In February when the students at Wake Forest were rejoicing over the new gas lights in the halls of the dormitory, Dr. Cullom wrote "The Bible and the Higher Criticism," in which he defined Higher Criticism as "the scientific investigation into the authorship, dates, sources, and composition of the books of the Bible, and into the special circumstances, if any, which called them forth." Distinguishing it from "the lower or older textual criticism, which occupies itself with the accuracy of the text," he claimed that "no one can be a real student of the Bible without doing some of the work of Higher Criticism."

Most of us are not able to follow the technical scholars in their minute analyses and fine spun theories. It is not necessary that we do so. But the time has come for us to cease calling men names because they are doing the work of Higher Critics, and to welcome every honest, devout effort to make the Bible what God has intended that it should be.

Sometime in 1907, Mrs. Farmer's sister, Amanda Fitzgerald McKee, came to Wake Forest for a visit; she brought a large rocking chair which Dr. Cullom was to use for many years. While she was in the Cullom home, she fell and broke her arm. There were many other guests in the home; once after a visit, Judge Oates sent Elizabeth some calling cards. Elizabeth also recalls once, when everyone was down on his or her knees during family prayers, seeing little Nancy

Dunn; resolutions of appreciation were adopted by the church, and Dr. Cullom welcomed the Rev. J. A. Ellis to succeed him as pastor (*BR,* June 20, 1917).

In August, Dr. Poteat announced that a new elective course in Military Science and Tactics would be offered at the College in the fall "to meet the present war-time emergency," and Dr. Livingston Johnson, the new editor of the *Recorder,* debated the government's choice of "the Y.M.C.A. as the agency through which religious (Protestant) work is to be done" at the army camps. Dr. Cullom recommended Henry C. Mabie's *From Romance to Reality* and wrote: "We have an expression of God's permanent attitude toward men" in that beautiful phrase, "good will toward men" (Lk. 2:14). After citing the apostle Paul and Phillips Brooks as examples of perpetuating God's good will toward men, he asked: "Was there ever a time in the world's history when there was such a need of men and women who can be in themselves expressions of 'good will toward men'?" (*BR,* Sept. 12, 1917.)

That fall (1917) Wake Forest College opened with a twenty-five per cent decrease in enrollment; the new uniforms for men in the training class gave "a military air to the campus." Nearly two hundred ladies of the Wake Forest chapter of the American Red Cross were busy making surgical dressings, knitting mufflers, sweaters and wristlets. The public school opened that fall in Wake Forest, and the Rev. J. W. Kincheloe began his notable pastorate at the First Baptist Church of Rocky Mount. In the *Recorder* of Sept. 19, 1917, Walter N. Johnson wrote:

> Yes, our boys are going. One traveling over North Carolina now gets the impression of soldiers rising out of the ground everywhere.
> We meet his uniform on every train; along the sandy road of the East and over the mountain trail of the West, he trudges forth to answer the call of our country and of the world.

Editor Johnson stated that "the Russian Revolution led by the Boleskeviki (*sic*), seems to have been checked by Kerensky and his army of 200,000." (*BR,* Nov. 14, 1917.)

Dr. Cullom kept his "steady gait." For his class on Christian History, he presented this introduction:

1. Proper conception of Christian History
   (1) It includes the story of the origin, progress and development of the Christian Religion and of its influence on the world.
   (2) Inner changes. Expansion is not the only thing that concerns us. As it grows it becomes more complex.
   (3) The story has been one from the beginning to the present.
2. Why study Christian History
   (1) To keep one from making a fool of himself. Learn to put things in the right place. Know the background of what you are saying.
   (2) For perspective—proportion.
   (3) For authority. Get in touch with real things.
   (4) Illustrated material.

3. The Background
    (1) Geographical—near Mediterranean Sea.
    (2) Political—Roman Empire was supreme at the time of Jesus' birth.
    (3) Cultural—Greek language, civilization, etc.
    (4) Religious:
        a. As seen in the Jewish world: Jews were found everywhere.
        b. As seen in the Gentile world.

In an article "Wide Influences from a Small Church," Dr. Cullom related a recent visit paid him by the head of an important geological survey team from Texas; this man had been a boy of thirteen in a small village church which Dr. Cullom had served while at Louisville.

> No one of us knows where our own children, the boys and girls in our classes, and the people in our little churches will be a few years hence. The parents, the teacher, the pastor and all who have the privilege of touching a young life have an opportunity to set in motion influences that may become far wider and more important than we had ever dreamed could be the case. Sometimes we may be tempted to feel that our work is in an insignificant, out-of-the-way place. But when work is done faithfully in the fear of God, and in accordance with His will, there can be nothing small or insignificant about it. Our God is a great God, and His business is a great business. There is nothing small or insignificant connected with His business. *(BR, Nov. 7, 1917.)*

At the pastors' conference in Durham (Dec. 3-4), Dr. Cullom presented Dr. W. J. McGlothin and conducted "the conference on books"; the convention which followed voted to undertake to raise a million dollars for their educational institutions. Dr. R. T. Vann said: "Current history is showing us today in Russia the baleful effects of no education, and in Germany the still more baleful effects of anti-Christian State-education." *(BR, Dec. 12, 1917.)*

In the *Recorder* of December 19th, Dr. Cullom wrote of Fred N. Day, a jeweler in Winston-Salem, who was giving half of his time to evangelistic work and all the collections to the Kingdom work. Dr. Cullom reported that Mr. Day preached "a very plain, simple gospel" and sought to bring people to a definite, whole-hearted surrender to Christ.

> Why should not many others among us be doing a work similar to that of Brother Fred N. Day? No man knows what God will do with him and through him until he gives Him an opportunity. The good Lord lead us all to know the power, the blessedness, and the fruit of a consecrated personality!

Another was busy too in seeking to enlist, encourage and develop talent; Mr. A. C. Reid, a student at Wake Forest, who had conducted a State High School Declaimers' Contest at Wake Forest the year before, was planning for the "inauguration of an essay contest for all secondary schools in North Carolina." *(Wake Forest Student,* March, 1918.)

- 22 -

Dr. R. T. Vann was elected General Manager of the Million Dollar Campaign, and Rev. C. J. Thompson was chosen as financial agent. It was proposed that of the million dollars, $300,000 would go to Wake Forest, $300,000 to Meredith, $120,000 to Chowan and $20,000 to each of the fourteen Baptist High Schools. (*BR*, Jan. 3, 1918.)

Editor Livingston Johnson wrote that the American flag in the churches savored of "a union of church and state" and declared that "the church's mission is to the whole world." (*BR*, Feb. 6, 1918.) He took note of the current discussion on the Second Coming of Christ and stated that while there is no doubt that Jesus will return in great power and glory, "the way to be prepared for Christ's second coming, is to be doing with all our might the work He had left for us to do." (*BR*, Jan. 16, 1918.)

And Dr. Cullom did exactly that; he kept at his appointed tasks, not forgetting to take time to be kind. He wrote:

> A few evenings ago I dropped into the home of the saintly Dr. William B. Royall to have a moment with him, and found him and his long-time friend and colleague, Prof. L. R. Mills, sitting and talking together. As I looked at them and thought of what they had done for the College and for the world through the College, I could almost imagine a halo of autumn glory reflected back into their faces from the lives and achievements of those whom they have touched and blessed through these years.
>
> Dr. Royall had been in continuous and active service in his special work in the Chair of Greek since the day he entered the College as a teacher just after the Civil War. During the present winter—the most trying that we have experienced for many years in this country—he has missed but very few classes. Of course, he is feeble in body, but his mind and heart are about as alert as they were twenty years ago so far as I can see. He reads the paper with the keenest interest, and when I wish to inquire how things are going in the present awful world cataclysm, I have only to step in and ask Dr. Royall. (*BR*, Feb. 20, 1918.)

Dr. Cullom was encouraged with the way the church people were "taking hold of the envelope system of regular giving"; he quoted a member of one of his country churches as saying that as important as the increased giving was, he was more impressed by "the privilege to work with God in a regular systematic fashion." (*BR*, March 10, 1918). In another article, Dr. Cullom wrote of Brown University's influence on Adoniram Judson and urged:

> (1) Let us maintain our Christian schools and make them the very best in all the land. (2) Let us maintain a strong Christian atmosphere in our Christian schools, making sure that each generation of students shall come in contact with the story of our heroes and of the noble struggles in the past. (*BR*, March 20, 1918.)

That spring when the Southern Baptist Convention met in Little Rock, Arkansas, "a deep seriousness . . . accompanied every reference to the war"; the Convention "faced the future" in adopting the goal of a million dollars for Home Missions, one and a half million for Foreign Missions and fifteen millions for education in the next five years. At the "simple and solemn" commencement exercise at Wake Forest, President William Louis Poteat told the class of 1918 that for them "the keenest challenge of this fateful hour" was a personal one and quoted the words penned by an eighteen-year-old French soldier in the grave moment before a bayonet charge:

> When this war is over and I go home, I must be a changed being. I shall have no right to be as I formerly was. Through the war mankind must be reborn, and it is our duty to be reborn first of all.

At the time when General Pershing was leading his American troops in successful assaults upon Cantigny and Belleau Wood, Dr. Cullom was being called to a task in preparing for the "new world" which should be worthy of their sacrifices.

*"The love of Christ and his Apostles twelve
He taught, but first he followed it himself."*
CHAUCER

THE SIXTH AGE

FAITHFUL IN A CHANGING WORLD

1918-1938

When Rev. C. J. Thompson resigned as financial agent for the Million Dollar Campaign, Dr. R. T. Vann turned to Dr. Cullom.

> And though the task meant his temporary release from his beloved employment as teacher of the Bible at Wake Forest and a sacrifice of his own personal feelings, we asked him to make that sacrifice, and he did so. We were sure he would if he felt that the call came from his Master. *(BR, June 2, 1918.)*

The college granted Dr. Cullom a leave of absence, and Dr. Cullom resigned his churches. As he assumed his new duties, he declared:

> (1) This is God's work. (2) I am God's servant in undertaking this work. (3) God will supply guidance and leadership in proportion to my need if I hold myself wholly committed to Him. *(BR, June 5, 1918.)*

He committed himself to raise the million dollars so that the schools might be prepared to meet "the unprecedented opportunities that are coming"; he defined his work in terms of world-reconstruction.

> (1) It is clear that a reconstruction of the whole world in the immediate future is inevitable. . . . (2) The remaking of the world will be along the line of democratic principles. . . . But are Baptists going to be prepared to do their part in the reconstruction of the earth? . . . (3) We must give special attention to the cultivation of the elementary things . . . forces which go toward the making of men and women who will be best fitted to lead us in meeting and using this fateful crisis: the Christian home, the Christian Church, the Christian school.

For the Campaign of putting "our schools on a broader, stronger and more enduring and more fruitful basis," he prayed:

> God help us to meet our task and our responsibility in a manner worthy of the task itself, worthy of ourselves as children of God and servants of the King, and worthy of the God who has graciously given to us this opportunity to cooperate with Him in the making of a new heaven and a new earth in which dwelleth righteousness. *(BR, June 19, 1918.)*

With conditions as they were, Dr. Cullom rented his house in Wake Forest and moved his family to an apartment on North Person Street in Raleigh. He was given office space in the *Recorder* Building, and Miss Lillybelle Ashworth, a very fine graduate of Meredith, became his secretary. (Later Miss Flossie Marshbanks came to help him.) He announced that on July 7th, "Christian Education" would be presented in the churches of the Central Association and that from that date the Million Dollar campaign would proceed "according to schedule."

On July 14th, the great German offensive reached Chateau-Thierry, but the American soldiers stopped it there. For those who had serious misgivings as to the timeliness of the Million Dollar Campaign, Dr. Cullom reasoned:

> The principles of Zion must become a part of a man's very life before they can become effective. The world's greatest need today is that of strong, positive Christian character. Where can such character be developed so well as in the Christian school? . . . In laying the foundations of the new society the Christian school, therefore, will necessarily be one of the most potent factors. (*BR*, Aug. 7, 1918.)

He wrote of the many calls for money in those days and suggested:

> Why should we not take our Liberty Bonds and War Savings Stamps and turn them over to this campaign? In this way we can do more than kill two birds with one rock. We can with the same money help to kill the most awful pest of a bird that ever afflicted the earth—Prussianism; and at the same time we can help to put in its place a bird that will prove the greatest blessing the world ever saw—Christian democracy. Here is an opportunity that will not come twice to the same generation. While our boys are crossing the seas and giving their lives to make the world safe for democracy, let us at home be making every reasonable sacrifice to fit our Christian schools to make a democracy that shall be safe for the world.

As the Allied forces neared the old Hindenburg Line, the Committee on the Million Dollar Endowment Fund decided to encourage the Baptists of the State to make their contributions to the fund in War Savings Stamps and Liberty Bonds rather than in cash and "to inaugurate an intensive State-wide Campaign in November to raise the entire million dollars in subscriptions by the time of the Baptist State Convention in Greensboro December 3rd"; Dr. Livingston Johnson called this "the Great Offensive" and gave Brother Gilbert Stephenson the credit for suggesting that "we make a short, red-hot campaign" (*BR*, Sept. 18, 1918).

On September 20th, the American Army commenced the Meuse-Argonne drive; the objective was Sedan, which was protected by a network of interwoven trenches averaging seven miles in width, protected by barbed wire and interspersed with concrete machine gun emplacements. Trench by trench the Germans yielded; the "doughboys" were "going over the top," and the Hindenburg Line began to crumble. In Raleigh about a hundred representative pastors, laymen and "elect ladies" met to consider ways and means of putting on the intensive campaign at once. Walter N. Gilmore reported that Dr. Cullom proved himself "a Master of Assemblies as well as a master of details in administrative work." After a series of speeches on the importance of Christian education, Mr. Joseph G. Brown, Judge Gilbert T. Stephenson and President W. L. Poteat spoke on the plan of linking the million dollar campaign with the government Liberty Bond Drive as furnishing "the supreme opportunity of doing the biggest thing ever undertaken by the Baptists of North Carolina." T. R. Pettus, the young Baptist business man who put Wilson County in first place in the War Savings Stamp campaign, "electrified the conference with a bright, crisp, optimistic talk, showing how the victory might be won by everybody 'hooking up' together and putting the job over." Dr. Livingston Johnson wrote:

> The interest grew so intense that it was difficult to hold the brethren down. The sacred ardor glowed and flamed until at some one's suggestion everybody present sprang to his feet and pledged himself wholehearted to the task of putting our great task through by Convention. Then, while still standing, a tender and moving prayer was offered for grace and guidance and victory. A few minutes afterwards another brother called for "Am I a Soldier of the Cross," and the militant notes of that old song rose and swelled from overflowing hearts, while men and women wept. As the singing was about to cease, some one suggested, "We must not close this song without that other verse:
> > Thy saints in all this glorious war
> > Shall conquer though they die."
> But here the song almost broke down because so many voices were choked with emotion. (*BR,* Oct. 2, 1918.)

The plan called for a conference to be held during the first week in October in each of the sixty associations in the State; in November "an intensive canvass" was to be made in every Baptist church in North Carolina. Editor Johnson wrote: "Our banners are in the wind, the trumpets are sounding, the hosts are mobilizing and arming, and in the strength of God we are going over!"

- 2 -

Two weeks after the Raleigh meeting, Dr. Cullom reported that "the epidemic of influenza" was making some interruptions in the work; association after association called off its annual meeting, as the epidemic grew worse. On October 23rd, he wrote:

> The whole earth is bathed in blood, and its people are under the shadow. . . . It is a time when all of us should listen to the voice of God as He speaks: "Be still, and know that I am God." . . . It is a time, surely, when people will be persuaded to cast off the superfluous, the silly, the meaningless, and give themselves wholly to the things that are worth while. . . . Is our task worth while? Is it of God and for God? If so, we need not fear. Our God will cause us to triumph gloriously. . . . In the meantime, let us . . . (get) ready to move promptly, enthusiastically, and unitedly as soon as God in his providence shall say, "Go forward."
> Associational managers who have not already done so, will please send to the central office the names of your church managers with their addresses. . . . New editions of our literature are coming from the press and will be mailed just as rapidly as we can get it. Some of the printers are sick. Let us not grow impatient in the matter. We hope also to mail blank forms for canvassers and managers, posters for churches, etc., this week.

This writing is indicative of the spirit within Dr. Cullom; while the terrible war was ending and the scourge of the influenza was killing people at home and abroad, he did not turn from the work to which he felt divinely called. The momentuous events caused him to become quiet before God, to re-examine what he was going and to be reassured it was right. And then with a good portion of common sense, he turned to what he could do under the circumstances. He did not bemoan or complain; he called for patience and faith. In the meantime he did what he could and trusted God for the time when he could do more.

Members of Dr. Cullom's family also became ill. In Wake Forest, his brother, Jim, who had stayed in his home for a time and who was clerking in a store downtown, died. News came that his brother, Frank, was ill; Marie Cullom (Porter) recalls:

> When I was in the fourth grade in the Dunn Elementary School my father had a severe case of influenza and he lingered between life and death for many days. He asked me to write "Brother" and solicit his prayers, which was a sure cure in my father's estimation. (Letters, July 28, 1952.)

Dr. William Louis Poteat reported (Oct. 23rd) that sixty per cent of the student body and eight of the professors at Wake Forest had had influenza, but "thanks to the hospital facilities . . . the three college physicians and four trained nurses . . . the college had had a remarkable escape from fatalities so far." In Raleigh, the High School building was transformed into an emergency hospital, and the ladies of the Tabernacle Baptist Church opened a soup kitchen to send food out to the homes whose inmates were sick; "automobiles have been on the go carrying food to the homes of need." Dr. Livingston Johnson said: "Nothing like this had ever visited this state within the memory of any of our citizens." Dr. Cullom reported that the advisory committee had decided "to keep the campaign in the minds and on the hearts of our people as strongly as possible while the churches are closed."

On October 30th, Dr. Livingston Johnson reported: "the German wall is crumbling . . . the end is not far distant." The Supreme War Council was in session in France; on November 5th, the Allied governments made known the terms of the Armistice. With victory in sight, the editor of *The News and Observer* shouted: "Glory to God in the highest! The whole race should go down on its knees in thanksgiving to God!" On November 8th, revolutionists gained control of Berlin; on November 10th, Kaiser Wilhelm II fled to Holland. The next morning the German envoys signed the Armistice terms. In the *Recorder* of November 13th, Editor Johnson wrote:

> We can thank God that the war is over, but a great task is ours now in straightening things up. . . . We shall be compelled to police many of the countries of Europe until things settle down. Some sort of international alliance must be worked out whereby permanent peace will be made secure. Then comes the problem of feeding a hungry world. This task will fall on America. . . . We shall be honor bound to feed the people of Germany. . . . So let us set ourselves to this great task with as much earnestness as characterized our nation in the prosecution

of the war. . . . We must also get ready to wage a war against the
spirit of militarism right here at home.

In an article, "The Call for Leadership," Dr. Cullom urged the people
to sustain "our government" in its superhuman task of following the
great ideals for which the Christian church stands and declared: "The
Christian school has before it just now its supreme opportunity." (Editor Johnson wrote of Dr. Cullom: "Perhaps no man among us during
the past two decades had wielded a wider and a better influence
over the constructive forces of righteousness among the Baptists of
North Carolina" (*BR,* Nov. 27, 1918).)

In his report on the progress of the Million Dollar Campaign,
Walter N. Gilmore reported that Scotland Neck's pledge of $20,000
was one of the largest made by an individual church and that eighteen
missionaries in China were sending "a substantial offering." But the
best news was "the munificient gift of $25,000" by the children of
the Rev. John T. Albritton, who for many years had been a faithful
and highly honored minister of the gospel in the Eastern Association.
This gift was to be used in endowing a chair of the Bible in Wake
Forest College, to be known as the "John T. Albritton Chair of the
Bible" and was to be matched by an additional $25,000 to be raised
within the bounds of the Eastern Association (*BR,* Dec. 4, 1918).
On December 11th, Dr. Cullom wrote that the next thirty days would
mark the closing up of an era of awful destruction and the beginning
of an era of construction which would be "the most wonderful and
far-reaching that the world had ever seen." He stated that if we are
to "mean anything to the all-important era upon which we are entering
. . . we must make our schools stronger and more efficient in their
God-given tasks of producing Christian leaders." Everyone was needed;
a Junior Reserve Force was organized to enlist the boys and girls in
the Million Dollar Campaign, and Dr. Cullom declared that a person
whom "education makes too proud to work had been injured by being
educated" (*BR,* Dec. 18, 1918).

- 3 -

After several postponements, the Baptist State Convention assembled
on January 14th (1919) in the First Baptist Church of Greensboro.
Like many others, Dr. J. Clyde Turner, the host pastor, was sick with
the "flu"; Dr. B. G. Gay of Durham who was to have preached the
Convention sermon, had died on the eve of the Convention. Secretary
Walter N. Johnson deeply moved the delegates when he told of having
been away from his two very sick children in a hospital room with a
man dying of the influenza; he said he heard "the sweetest music he
ever heard" and thought he was entering heaven; everything was
glorious, but he wanted to live because "there was so much to do on

earth." He awoke and found a group of Meredith girls around his bed, singing Christmas carols. He expressed the hope that soon we would have hospitals, all over our state, "built and sustained" by our Baptist churches.

On Wednesday afternoon of the Convention, Dr. Cullom reported on the campaign; at times, he said, "we have been compelled to feel our way along one day at a time, but in the end the triumph of God's grace and help will be clearer and more glorious on this account." He called upon the associational managers to report (two minutes each) what had been actually accomplished in their associations and what they could see in sight within the next thirty days. Later he wrote that, as each spoke, the effect was "cumulative" in its power to grip and to thrill; "when it was announced that these men had reported $543,979 as actually subscribed and $329,175 as being in sight the effect was little short of marvelous." After speeches by Dr. W. L. Poteat and Dr. Luther Little and several solos of "soulful music" played by Miss Charlotte Rueger on the violin, the Convention adopted a motion that the Campaign Committee use the spring in gathering up the fruits of their efforts. On Thursday afternoon as the train for Raleigh was standing under the shed at Greensboro, the announcement was made to the crowd of delegates that Nebraska had adopted the prohibition amendment; this was the thirty-sixth state to do so, and the Eighteenth Amendment thereby became a part of the federal constitution. Some one started the doxology, "Praise God from whom all blessings flow," and soon the whole depot resounded with praise (*BR,* Jan. 22, 1919).

Dr. Cullom turned to the task of concluding the Campaign. He urged his co-workers to get the pledges into "the form of Liberty Bonds, War Saving Stamps, cash or notes" and send them to Dr. R. T. Vann in Raleigh; "this is essential if we are to claim the $175,000 promised by the General Education Board of New York City." He suggested that "we try to get as many friends as possible to establish one or more scholarships in one of our colleges" and that all work together in the churches and associations in reaching their allotment.

> Hitherto the Lord has led us. During these thirty days, let us continue to look to Him for guidance and help. He often causes our little plans to miscarry in order that He may give to us something infinitely bigger and better. (*BR,* Jan. 22, 1919.)

Dr. Cullom wrote of the great responsibilities that had come upon America; in answer to the question, how shall we meet them, he said:

> God's plan is to make a man and put him right out into the midst of the conditions to be dealt with and say to him, "Subdue these things and bring them into subjection to me." This is a most glorious challenge, and it constitutes for each of us and all of us the greatest possible mission. But where are we going to get the men? What is God's plan of making men and women for strategic positions? The most cursory examination of the Christian School in this connection will more than justify

it in calling upon our people to make the most heroic sacrifices to fit it for doing its very best work in fitting men and women for the generation upon which we are entering. Hence the genuine and even pressing merits of this campaign to reinforce and equip these schools for their God-appointed task. *(BR,* Feb. 12, 1919.)

In May (1919), the Southern Baptist Convention met at Atlanta; the reports of baptisms and gifts were "unprecedentedly large." Yet bigger goals were set ahead. "Without a dissenting vote," the convention set itself to the task of raising seventy-five million dollars in five years. In a speech which was described as "the Mount Mitchell of the Convention," Dr. George W. Truett, who had just returned from France where he spent six months "preaching to our boys," declared:

It is for us to see that our lads did not die in vain. We are now world-citizens, with world-tasks beckoning us on. . . . It is a crime at any time for a man to be a little man; it is a ten-fold crime in this day.

When Dr. J. Campbell White spoke on the Interchurch World Movement, the convention heard him respectfully but coldly and flatly refused to participate. Editor Johnson explained: "Southern Baptists believe they have a distinct work to do and that they can do it better in their own way than by going into any sort of extra denominational movement" *(BR,* June 11, 1919).

- 4 -

On June 30th, Dr. Cullom and Dr. Livingston Johnson left Ridgecrest to attend a meeting in Nashville which had been called by Dr. L. R. Scarborough, the General Director of the 75 Million Dollar Campaign. They were met at the station in Nashville by Dr. and Mrs. Hight C Moore and their son, Joseph P. Moore, who had just returned from France. Dr. Johnson reported: "We were whirled to our hotel in Dr. Moore's new machine, which Joe drives like a veteran." At the meeting, November 30th to December 7th was fixed as the time for "the great drive" and every day before then was to be used in preparation for it. Dr. Truett's powerful speech in the interest of the campaign sent the workers home with "the feeling that we are undertaking a momentous task" for which "we must enlist a far greater number than we have ever reached." *(BR,* July 9, 1919.)

In July the *Recorder* began carrying full-page advertisements of the 75 Million Dollar Campaign:

Get good and ready. Create everywhere the "Will to Win." We are to Win through Unified Cooperation, Mobilized Enlistment, Enlightened Publicity, Enthused Organization, Sacrificial Giving and the Power of God. *(BR,* July 16, 1919.)

On August 10th, as State organizer of the 75 Million Campaign, Dr. Cullom conducted "devotional exercises" at "a conference of intercession" for the Campaign; he also suggested a few books, such as

Fosdick's books on prayer and faith, Patton's *World Facts and America's Responsibility,* which he thought would be helpful in preparing for "the great things ahead of us." More and more, the 75 Million Dollar Campaign filled the pages of the *Recorder*: "Inform, inspire, enthuse, enlist, arouse, mobilize, organize every Baptist Church in the South by September 1st. Service Roll in every church and a copy in Nashville Office by Sept. 15th." Soon every page had its slogans and catch-phrases. But some people were uncertain and confused; J. W. Bailey asked for more light:

> I read four Baptist weekly papers. I see much in their columns on the subject of the $75,000,000 Campaign. What is the $75,000,000 for? Is it to be endowment or is it to be distributed? What relation does it bear to the funds Baptist are now contributing?

The *Recorder* editor replied that "the 75 Million Dollar Campaign is simply putting into a budget all the benevolences of the Convention and taking pledges on them." North Carolina's part was $6,000,000, which includes "the million dollars that we are now raising for Christian education." In the *Recorder* of August 27th, Dr. L. R. Scarborough reported:

> The First Church of Anderson, South Carolina, was asked to raise $80,000. The church hilariously asked that it be put to $100,000 and the pastor says that they will make it $125,000. . . . Mr. A. E. Jennings, a great layman of Memphis, Tennessee, says he will gladly give $200,000 to the Campaign. . . . a mountain church in Arkansas which had been giving $100 a year to their pastor . . . pledged $2,500 to the Campaign. . . . Good word comes from every section. The Baptist pot is boiling. Put fuel to the fire. Create the "Will to Work and Win." Every church organized now, every church moblized now, every church informed now, every church endued with heavenly power now, is the slogan from this office.

Dr. Cullom explained that of the 75 million dollars, 20 million would go for foreign missions; 20 million for Christian education, 12 million for home missions, 11 million for state missions, and the remainder would be divided among ministerial relief, hospitals, orphanages, etc. Promising that a handbook with more information would soon be available, Dr. Cullom wrote:

> America has come into a place of leadership. . . . It is easy to see that the work of our churches must be augmented in a way somewhat commensurate with our opportunities and our responsibilities, or we shall have to take a siding while the main current of the world's life moves on without God and without hope. . . . The foundations of human life have been shaken to pieces as by a mighty earthquake. . . . For the past two years we have held everything else in abeyance in order to win the war to make the world safe for democracy. Shall we not do the same thing, and even more, in order to reconstruct on the foundations of a ruined world a democracy that is not only safe for the world, but a democracy that will prove to be nothing less than that brotherhood which was one of the most fundamental features in the teaching of Jesus? *(BR,* Oct. 1, 1919.)

In an article, "A Safe Democracy," which appeared in the *Recorder* of November 12, 1919, Dr. Cullom described democracy as being fraught with greater possibilities of good and of evil than any other form of government the world has ever tried.

> Democracy may become either a wholesome brotherhood or an irresponsible anarchy. . . . For the past century the world has been falling over itself, so to speak, in establishing democracy; whether this will mark one of the great forward steps of humanity or a drift back toward primeval chaos will depend on the type of democracy that we are to have. A safe democracy that will make the world better will be characterized by three things:

First, *Intelligence.* "The democratic ideal insists that the level of intelligence and virtue shall be so lifted as to make all mature people capable of self-government." Secondly, *A wholesome fear of God* is needed. Dr. Cullom contended for the "thought of God which regards Him as a living and present reality in every part of His universe, and as working always and everywhere in accordance with His holy nature."

> The laws of nature are laws of God, and a man can no more escape the consequences of transgressions and disobedience than he can escape his own existence. God, moreover, is personal, and man is personal, and man is responsible to God. . . . Intelligence alone may foster bigotry, tyranny, oppression; it must be tempered, sobered, controlled and directed by a personal sense of personal responsibility to God before it can be trusted with government. The conception of God, moreover, must be such as to develop a discriminating and an enforcing conscience.

To be constructive as well as safe, a democracy must include a third factor; namely, *the Spirit of Jesus,* which is characterized by "loving service." Out of this spirit of helpfulness spring hospitals, schools, churches, and every institution whose purpose it is to make the world a better place in which to live.

> No form of church government fits in quite so well with the essential principles of democracy as the congregational. Such a form of government is the most complete democracy that the world knows anything about. . . . It is the direct function of every Baptist Church in the world to generate, under God, and foster in the midst of a sinful and sinning world each of the elements set forth above—intelligence, a wholesome fear of God, the Spirit of Jesus. Our Campaign, therefore, to lift up Baptist standards, to strengthen and reinforce Baptist churches and Baptist institutions, is a campaign whose essential end it is to make a democracy that is safe for the world. . . . Everything is in the melting-pot and is being made over. In what form will our life and institutions come forth and be perpetuated in the years that be ahead? The answer to this question is locked up very largely in what we do right here right now

On November 13th, Mrs. Joel Cullom died at her home in Halifax County; she had been in declining health for some time, but she had not wanted to leave the "old home place." Dr. Cullom turned aside for her funeral and to write this tribute:

> I have heard my father say that when he was a mere boy he used to write his name on a piece of paper, gaze at it and resolve that it

should stand for something worth while. . . . The woman who came to share this name seemed to have shared likewise the noble resolution of the young husband. Their children feel grateful to them today and subscribe most heartily to the declaration of the wise man that a good name is rather to be chosen than great riches.

Hard work, rigid economy, regular habits, simple living, uncompromising morals, humble and unostentatious religion are some of the more fundamental things that characterized life in that country home. . . . Through the trying days of the Civil War, through the more trying days of the reconstruction, through the various and varying vicissitudes that naturally come with the cares and responsibilities of rearing a large family, this woman was found to be true to God, true to her husband and children, true to her neighbors and friends. After witnessing her life for fifty years it seems to me that I have never seen a woman who came nearer to filling completely the picture of the ideal woman drawn for us by the wise man (Proverbs 31) than did my mother.

Dr. Cullom did not slacken his pace one bit; in the *Recorder* of November 19th (1919), he gave instructions for reporting the Campaign canvass; each team captain was to report to the church director who was to telephone or telegraph his associational director who, in turn, was to report to Dr. Walter N. Johnson, the State Director. All of the *Recorder* of November 26th was given to "the great campaign" in which "more of our people" were to take part than were "ever before enlisted in any Kingdom enterprise." The editor urged that the canvass be made "whether it rains or shines next Sunday" and that the members of our churches "stay at home between the hours of two and five in the afternoon." Dr. Livingston Johnson, in the same issue, explained that $600,000 of notes and pledges had been received on the Million Dollar Fund, which was now merged into the 75 Million Campaign.

On December 3rd, Dr. Walter N. Johnson wrote that the reports on the pledges were pouring into his office: "We do not know where we are, but it seems now to be victory." On December 10th, he shouted: North Carolina Baptists are over the top—six million dollars and six hundred thousand! On December 17th, North Carolina's total pledges were $7,106,611.00, and the report for the whole South was $84,500,000; "this is a marvellous achievement!" (The total pledges amounted to $92,630,923.) Explaining that he had been "at the bedside of loved ones during many of the most stressful days of the campaign," Dr. Johnson said that the work at the State Headquarters had been done mostly by his comrades: T. W. Chambliss (Publicity Director), J. D. Moore (who had charge of the clerical force), and W. R. Cullom, "organizer, who moved serene and unhurried with every detail in hand, in touch with the workers on the field from the first to this good hour." Dr. Johnson stated: "Our State Campaign Headquarters is closing up its work as fast as it can. But the Campaign is still **going on**."

- 5 -

At the time when the League of Nations, without American representation, convened in Paris, Dr. Cullom was making plans for another adventure in the service of his Lord. As glorious as had been the response to the 75 Million Campaign, Dr. Cullom described it as "only the first stage" of a five-year movement.

> Most of our objectives are yet ahead of us. The money is yet to be collected and distributed; we have said that we are hoping and praying that we may win two and a half million lives into the fellowship and service of the Saviour; we have published that a great campaign of enlightenment and enlistment among our own people would be put on and pushed with determination and vigor. (*BR*, Jan. 21, 1920.)

To realize these worthy objectives, ten or twelve Mobile Schools were planned for March 8-12 and about twenty more for July 19-23. It was proposed in these schools to teach such subjects as: A Survey of World Conditions, The Pastor and His Church Facing New Conditions, The Business Side of the Church's Life, Training in Church Membership, The Church and the Child, The Church and Its Young People. Dr. Cullom wrote: "We must bring our churches to see and to seize the unique opportunity that God is giving them now or God himself will take away their candlestick." Later he stated that as Baptist leaders come from among the people they should be characterized by personal qualities of intelligence and genuine moral worth rather than by official distinctions; he understood Jesus' plan was "to put into people the spirit and the ability to do for themselves," and he saw the Mobile Schools as an instrument for carrying out that plan.

> Let a small group from each church come together in the Mobile School, pray and plan together until the fire from heaven shall catch in their souls, and then let them return to their respective churches to start the same thing among the people at home. Why should we not have these schools reproduced in two thousand churches over North Carolina? (*BR*, Feb. 18, 1920.)

In the midst of these plans and pleas, a controversy began among the Baptists of North Carolina which was to threaten all that had been done for the colleges and which was to have repercussions far into the future. In an article in *The Western Recorder*, Rev. T. T. Martin attacked an address which Dr. William Louis Poteat had made at the Baptist Congress in Richmond in 1900. In reply to this attack, Editor Livingston Johnson stated that he thought Dr. Poteat had made "a great mistake in delivering that address" but he also thought it unfair for Mr. Martin to quote a speech made twenty years ago and to ignore more recent doctrinal statements of Dr. Poteat's (*BR*, Feb. 4, 1920). Dr. Poteat appreciated Editor Johnson's defense of him and wrote the following statement of his faith for the *Recorder*.

Of course, I accept the New Testament as the law of my life and the standard of my thinking. To find its meaning and to extend its power have been the business and joy of these forty years. Jesus knows I am frail and blind, but He knows too, that my heart is set to follow Him where I cannot see, if only He will let me hear His voice. The mystery of His compassion and His redemption I do not understand, but to His sacrificial life and atoning death I look for the forgiveness of sin and the life eternal. *(BR,* Feb. 11, 1920.)

The "Committee appointed to visit the Baptist schools in the State" called upon Dr. Thurman Kitchin, dean of the Wake Forest medical department, and Dr. N. Y. Gulley, dean of the law school *(BR,* Feb. 11, 1920); likely the Committee contacted Dr. Cullom, who through all the years had been questioned concerning Dr. Poteat's teaching. (The first such inquiry had been made by one of the college's trustees when Dr. Cullom was only a student himself!) To all these inquiries Dr. Cullom stated that he had all confidence in Dr. Poteat as a gentleman, a teacher and a Christian. Years later he was to write:

I guess I was as close to him as any one in our Community and . . . I have never seen a more regular, a more faithful or a more attentive church member, a more devout or responsive worshipper, or a more cordial or a more liberal supporter of his church and its work in every respect of its life and routine. *(Charity and Children,* May 12, 1949.)

Editor Johnson told "the self-appointed guardian of Wake Forest College" to tend to his own business, that the trustees of the college were "amenable to the Baptist State Convention of North Carolina"; however, he confessed he was troubled by "our unfinished task" in collecting the pledges of the 75 Million Campaign.

Early in March (1920) the Mobile Schools had to be "called off" because of the influenza, but Dr. Cullom began making plans for a series of conferences on evangelism. He wrote that beneath "the many and multiplying signs of chaos, confusion, discontent and upheaval," there was growing, in the hearts of men, "a longing for first hand fellowship with God"; he thought that unless the people of our land and of the lands of the earth are brought into fellowship with God, "we are headed for the rocks" *(BR,* March 10, 1920). Dr. Cullom wrote that the Campaign of Evangelism aimed at making "each soul, each church, each community" a center from which would radiate influences to change others into Christians; all revivals that have changed the great currents of human life for good have worked after this fashion. *(BR,* March 17, 1920.)

But like Banquo's ghost, the question of Dr. Poteat's teachings would not be downed; Inez J. Woodall called upon Dr. Poteat to write a series of articles in simple terms on the way in which he harmonized the theory of evolution with the Book of Genesis. D. F. King declared that twice he had refused to contribute to Wake Forest College because its president was "a Higher Critic." A group of Wake Forest students at the Seminary in Louisville wrote that the teachings of Dr.

Poteat as they had known them were "in accord with the fundamentals of our faith" and that they had "unshaken faith and abiding confidence in Dr. Poteat as a Christian gentleman of unquestionable honesty." Ivan L. Bennett thought it would be unfair to ask Dr. Poteat to justify his doctrines before ordinary people who, like himself before he entered Wake Forest College, had little understanding of the relation of religion and science. Mr. Bennett said:

> When I entered Wake Forest College my inner life was a triad of faith, uncertainty, and doubt. On Dr. Poteat's Biology class, for the first time in my life, I began to lay hold upon the principles of life which later harmonized in my own thinking with the findings in Bible study and enabled me to adjust my faith so as to overcome my uncertainty and doubt. . . . He taught me to marvel at the mighty works of God, to wait and trust with my implicit faith, as we look for a fuller peace and knowledge in the infinite beyond.

All of Wake Forest College looked forward to having one of its most illustrious sons, Dr. A. C. Dixon of the great Metropolitan Tabernacle in London, to preach the Commencement sermon. What a shock it must have been when Dr. Dixon used this occasion to ridicule the doctrine of evolution and to urge the graduating class to hold on to "the old faith." Dr. W. L. Poteat and Dr. W. R. Cullom were in his audience, but they made no comment. In his newsletter to the *Recorder,* July 21, 1920, Dr. Poteat reported that at the late commencement the alumni in cooperation with the trustees had provided for an all-time Alumni Secretary and announced that Dr. Cullom would resume his work with the college on September 7th.

On June 7th, more than a hundred prospective teachers in the Mobile Schools assembled at Meredith for three days of training in their tasks; Dr. Cullom presided over the conference and directed "its many details with his usual poise and good judgment." (*BR,* June 16, 1920.) The revised plans listed twenty-eight places for the Mobile Schools with their deans, to be held simultaneously, July 19-23; there would be special classes for Bible study, for Sunday school workers, for B.Y.P.U. workers and for those responsible for "the business side" of the church. Something of the earnestness with which Dr. Cullom regarded this effort may be sensed in this plea which he made in the *Recorder* of July 7th: "Pathos in the Midst of Tragedy." He wrote that the lament over Jerusalem, "Is it nothing to you, all you that pass by?" (Lam. 1:12), was applicable to the times when "only a handful of men and women" gather at an important religious meeting in contrast to the crowds that pack our trains on Sunday going and returning from "our North Carolina watering places." He quoted a British general as saying, "Civilization has struck its tents and is again on the march"; but where are we going? asked Dr. Cullom.

> Without a revolution in thought and conduct, brought about by a rebirth of men's souls from heaven, God alone knows where we shall

13

land. . . . Is it not time for God's people to halt and take stock of
themselves? . . . I am inclined to think that about the weakest point of all
is to be found in our lukewarmness toward God and our indifference
to the things of His Kingdom. . . . Several explanations could be offered;
but no explanation explains a child's lukewarmness to his mother or his
indifference to the affairs of his father! There is only one proper course
for such a child: that is, that he come to his senses ("to himself"), as
the prodigal son did—come to his father with the most humble confession that he can make, renounce his former attitude, change his conduct,
accept whatever place the father may give him, and begin life anew in
fellowship with his father. Is it not time that judgment should begin at
the house of God, and that God's people should do just what is here
suggested?

At twenty-eight places over North Carolina our people will gather
for five days (July 19-23) to pray, to counsel, to think, to plan with
reference to these things. What will our churches do about this all-
important matter? Will they be busy with "lands," "oxen," and merchandise, domestic matters, and let this opportunity go by default? Or
will they bestir themselves as is becoming in this hour of crisis, unite
their thoughts and hearts in a serious, honest effort to find and follow
the will of God?

Others were in earnest too. Rev. J. M. Kester reported that "about
200" were committed to come to Shelby for the school; Rev. M. W.
Bucks sent out invitations to the entire constituency of the Burlington
Mobile School, and a young man from the South Yadkin Association
thanked Dr. Cullom for the benefits he already had received from
the *Prospectus,* of which several thousands of copies had been sent
out. (*BR,* July 14, 1920.) Then came July 19th, and the response
was overwhelming. The final report showed an attendance in the
schools of 1,832; 833 certificates were issued, and it was recommended
that there be "eight permanent Mobile Schools" and that each school
"concern itself to extend its work into Institutes of one day or two
days in the churches." Walter N. Johnson concluded this report: "In
many ways this has been our greatest year; but the years to come are
to be greater, because our God is leading us on." (*BR,* Nov. 17,
1920.)

When the strain of the Mobile Schools was passed and all the
reports were in, Dr. Cullom accepted Mr. N. B. Josey's offer of the
use of his cottage at Ridgecrest and took his family to the mountains
for nearly three months. Here he attended the sessions of the Board
of Education of the Southern Baptist Convention and enjoyed being
with his family in such a beautiful setting.

- 6 -

When the Cullom family returned from Ridgecrest, they moved
back into their old home on North Main Street in Wake Forest. Dr.
Cullom had enjoyed traveling over the state of North Carolina, but
with the conclusion of his work with the State Board, it seemed
"natural and right" to return to his classroom. He resumed his lectures
in his accustomed manner.

What is the Bible?
  A. Negatively
    1. It is not a treatise on science.
    2. It is not a history of mankind.
    3. It is not a history of the Jews.
    4. It is not a collection of laws and pious maxims.
  B. Positively
    1. It is the story of God's special and progressive revelation of Himself, His will and purpose for mankind, making its climax in the person and work of Jesus of Nazareth.
    2. Its main center of interest is man and man in his relation to God, the Eternal Spirit.
    3. It is an Eastern book.
    4. It uses *popular* language rather than scientific language.
The Ancient Period: Genesis 1-11
  I. General Features
    1. Length of time covered.
    2. Its relation to the balance of the Bible. Its relation is a porch or introduction. It gives the Hebrew conception as to how the world got started.
    3. Length of human life. Name of a tribe.
  II. Creation
    1. The *Fact* of creation.
    2. The method—(Bible uses popular language.)
    3. Length of day—compare this to Julius Caesar's day.
    4. The climax of creation was man.
      a. His dual makings
          (1) Body came from the dust of the Earth
          (2) He became a living Soul.
      b. The image and likeness of God. He had power to think, feel and choose.
      c. Importance
          (1) Basis of Revelation
          (2) Basis of Incarnation
          (3) Basis of Regeneration
      d. His place in the world—rulership in the earth v:26
      e. Woman—1:27; 2:18-25
      f. Echoes in other parts of the Bible, e.g. Ps. 8, Heb. 11:1ff.

It never occurred to the Bible professor that the current controversy over evolution should cause him to vary his lectures; the issue had been settled for him for a long time, and neither Mr. Martin's accusation nor Dr. Dixon's denunciation phased him. What is more surprising is that someone had not accused him of "heresy," but his mild manner made him friend of the most orthodox and his sincerity in the pursuit of truth won the respect of all.

In November, Dr. Cullom preached at Forestville and "consented to supply for the church until a pastor could be secured"; he also returned to the pulpits of Rolesville and Poplar Creek. That fall (1920) the farmers "were greatly depressed" when cotton and tobacco sold for half of their production cost; Senator Harding was elected president of the country. Editor Johnson described the public dances in Raleigh as "scandalous," and Collector J. W. Bailey reported the illicit distilling of whiskey in North Carolina as "truly appalling." In January, it was announced that the Baptist Hospital would be located in Winston, and Charles E. Maddry was chosen as the new Executive Secretary of the Baptist State Convention.

In June, Dr. Cullom reviewed his "twenty-five years with the Bible at Wake Forest." After relating his pioneering efforts in this field, he noted that nearly all colleges and universities now offered courses in Bible and presented his philosophy of Bible teaching:

> Too many people allow themselves to think of the Bible as a sort of collection of arbitrary fiats from a far-away Law-giver. . . . The principles of the Bible and the laws of nature are from the same Source. The Author of the one is the author of the other, and when a human life brings its thoughts, purposes and plans into harmony with the principles of the Bible that life is at once in harmony with the essential principles of the universe, in which it lives. It is in harmony with principles that are eternal and therefore is fitted for eternity.

He described how the scope of his work had been enlarged from two classes in the English Bible and a voluntary class for the ministerial students to classes in Beginner's Hebrew, Christian History and a course called "Religion," in which he gave: (1) an introduction to the psychology of religion, (2) "a candid facing of the principal religions of the world," (3) a brief study of Christianity as the ultimate religion of the whole human race, and (4) the philosophy of Baptist principles. He declared that teaching these six different classes was as much as any one man can do.

> Yet the work of the department should be broadened to include at least a chair of Religious Education. The new chair would bring men to study the principles, institutions and methods of Religious Education and in this way fit men to direct the Educational side of a church's work. The demand for such men is increasing rapidly and if the Christian college does not furnish them, where are they to be found?

After reviewing the Albritton gift to endow the Chair of the Bible, Dr. Cullom hinted that a chair of Religious Education could likewise be endowed and suggested that the department might be renamed the Wake Forest School of Religion.

- 7 -

In the fall of 1921, Wake Forest College opened with 475 students and a new pastor of the church, Dr. Paul Bagby. Dr. Cullom presided (Sept. 28-29) over one "of the best sessions the Central Association ever held" and to John L. Coley's appeal for help in getting a church, wrote "a most sympathetic letter" and urged him to prepare himself for that important task by coming to Wake Forest College. Years later Mr. Coley was to recall:

> The first of 1922 I landed in Wake Forest. It was Saturday night about twelve o'clock before we got our furniture arranged to get to bed. . . . Well, the day of matriculation came, and I went forth to enroll as a special student. I was absolutely ignorant that there was a fee of $22.50. I had the sum of $3.00 in cash. There I was with a wife and two children, and no job, and had come to Wake Forest College to prepare for the ministry with $3.00. One of the young preachers told me to go to Dr. Cullom. I found him at the Post Office and he so graciously shook my hand, and after telling him of my plight, he put

his arm around me and told me to let my troubles be on him. He took me to the Bursar and said, "Brother Earnshaw, you enroll brother Coley, and charge everything to me."

In March 1922, he called me into his office and told me about a church in Lee County that was without a pastor, and he was asking me to go and preach for them. I went, and they called me. . . . Dr. Robertson said in my presence one time that "Barnabas was friend of young preachers, but Barnabas was no more a friend of young preachers than Dr. Cullom has been." (Letter, Sept. 9, 1958.)

In December (1922), the college was "disgraced" by a shooting which occurred as the result of the painting of a student's shorn head with silver nitrate; the newspapers "played it big." Many friends of the college were alarmed; M. L. Kesler wrote that it was not enough for the faculty simply to announce it was opposed to hazing.

The simple announcement of regulations does not enforce them. Laws do not enforce themselves. Neither do ideals. The announcement of beautiful ideals is splendid, but they get nowhere without men behind them. *(BR,* Feb. 1, 1922.)

Editorials and articles on science, evolution, religion crowded the *Recorder* during April of 1922. More and more was written "for and against" Dr. W. L. Poteat. Dr. Poteat stated that he had been teaching biological sciences for forty years, that he had published two books on the relation of science and religion and that he had nowhere discredited the Genesis account of the origin of man.

Whenever I have referred to the creation account in Genesis I have taken pains to say two things—that the book is not a text-book in science, and the affirmation there is of the divine agency in the process without a word about the method of creation. I frankly believe that God created all things and all animals, man included, by the method of evolution. I find myself utterly unable to resist the considerations in support of that method. *(BR,* May 1922.)

Editor Johnson wrote that he had known Dr. Poteat for a quarter of a century and had been deeply impressed with his piety; "If one believes in the great fundamentals of our faith, as Dr. Poteat says he does, then his teachings cannot be dangerous, evolution or no evolution." *(BR,* May 3, 1922.) Robert H. Spiro declared that an evolutionist could not be a Christian. T. J. Taylor called upon "North Carolina Baptists who are responsible for what is taught at Wake Forest College" to be the jury on "President Poteat's Theistic Evolution." Another asked that "the discussion on evolution cease lest our faith be shaken." *(BR,* May 10, 1922.) From China, A. R. Gallimore wrote of the many missionaries in China who had come out of Wake Forest College and of their confidence in Dr. Poteat. D. F. King said the Baptists of North Carolina "will either have to endorse the teaching of the theory of evolution at Wake Forest College or demand the resignation of the president of the College." Dr. Mullins of Louisville wrote that Wake Forest College led all other Baptist Colleges in the number of men at the Seminary and that no member of the faculty had ever heard "an unsound doctrinal note" from one of them. (May 17, 1922.)

During the week of the Wake Forest Commencement, the Board of Trustees of Wake Forest College met on the campus and, "after giving careful consideration to all the facts presented," expressed "their confidence in President Poteat as a Christian and a teacher." The trustees also voted to secure a full time dean for the college and to cooperate with the Alumni Association in employing an alumni secretary. Everything looked good until on Wednesday when the trustees legalized national fraternities at Wake Forest and approved the students' Code of Customs. The reaction was not long in coming. J. K. Henderson wrote (*BR,* June 4, 1922.) that this announcement brought "a feeling of humiliation to many a Baptist in North Carolina," and Walter N. Johnson reported "a general dissatisfaction" over the matter. (Dr. Cullom missed a lot of this by spending the summer at the University of Chicago with Elizabeth and Nancy.)

- 8 -

In September of 1922, Dr. Cullom was asked to serve as "acting dean until a new one was elected." Dr. Cullom resigned some of his churches, but kept all his classes. To the parents of all the students at Wake Forest, he wrote:

> My dear Friends,
> About a week ago the Wake Forest trustees asked me to serve as Dean of the College until a permanent arrangement can be made to fill that office. The work is new to me, and it will take me a while to find myself in the new task. In speaking to the students a day or so ago I told them that I consider it the primary duty of the dean to help the students in every possible way to realize the highest ends for which they have come to college. You know, of course that the strongest influence back of any boy is his home. I am writing you therefore to urge that you join hands and hearts with me in my effort to help your boy along the line that I have indicated.
> Two things stand out conspicuously in my ideal for every student that comes to Wake Forest: (1) that by honest, faithful work he shall come to the fullest, best-rounded manhood of which he is capable; (2) that by a whole-hearted dedication of his strong rich manhood to the highest ends for which God has made him he shall make himself the greatest possible blessing to a world that is suffering unprecedented agonies today in its need for just such men.
> Whenever you have a suggestion to make to me about your boy I hope you will feel perfectly free to make it in the assurance that it will have my best attention in my effort to help him. Assuring you of my best wishes for you and for all that concerns the best interests of your boy, I am,
>
> Cordially yours,
> W. R. CULLOM, Dean

That fall Lilburn B. Moseley, of Alabama, entered Wake Forest and came into the Bible class. Dr. Cullom was to write of him:

> As I think of his first month or two in that class I must confess that he reminded me more of a young ox when he is under the yoke for the first time than of anything else I can think of. It semed to me that

almost everything I said rubbed him the wrong way. He squirmed, he twisted, he questioned, he frowned; he didn't foam at the mouth, but he must not have fallen very short of doing so. *(Charity and Children,* Aug. 28, 1947.)

Dr. Cullom was patient; the young man had great ability and was earnest in wanting to know truth.

"Dr. Cullom, Dr. Cullom," he would jump up and almost shout. Frowningly he would demand, "Do you mean you believe in evolution? How can you reconcile it with the account of creation in Genesis?"

"Mr. Moseley, read to me the account of Genesis," replied the professor, and he waited for the student to find it and read it. When he had finished, Dr. Cullom said, "Now, Mr. Moseley, tell me how Genesis relates man was created."

"It says God made man out of the dust of the ground," stormed the student.

"Yes, but does it say by what method God did it? Read it again aloud."

After several readings he had to admit that the Bible does not describe exactly how it was done but simply states the fact that God did it. (WRC, Conversation, Jan. 8, 1952.)

Years later this student was to say:

Dr. Cullom could have treated me as an ignoramus, but he was kind and gentle. When my universe was crumbling, he assured me God was still living. . . . He could say a very unusual and disturbing thing with such kindness and in such a way that it didn't seem startling at all; that's the way he sneaked up on me. . . . I took every course he offered— including Hebrew. . . . With all that was being said and written about Wake Forest College, he helped us keep our heads and see the facts clearly. There was no dodging of the issues; neither was there any alarm. There was no diffrence between the professors of Bible and Science; harmony prevailed on the campus, and the forces of religion were foremost in the defense of President Poteat.

There was no harmony away from the Wake Forest Campus. The Gaston County Baptist Association declared: "If Dr. William Louis Poteat persists in teaching the evolution of man . . . we cannot and will not give our endorsement and support." *(BR,* Oct. 25, 1922.) Other associations followed the same course, while men like Rev. R. H. Hipps stood up against such action.

"Brother Moderator," said Mr. Hipps when a similar resolution was presented in his association; "I know nothing about evolution, but I do know Dr. W. L. Poteat. I have three sons. They have all gone to Wake Forest and have taken their degrees there. All of them passed through Dr. Poteat's classroom and received instruction from him. If I had a hundred sons to educate I would send the last one of them to Wake Forest, and would urge all of them to take all the work they could with Dr. William Louis Poteat. *(Charity and Children,* June 10, 1948 and May 12, 1949.)

The effects of this controversy were felt in the offerings for the Baptist work in the state; the Raleigh office reported that it was "laboring under debt," and Editor Johnson wrote of "the deep anxiety" which many felt in facing the annual session of the State Convention.

In Winston-Salem, "the messengers" registered at the First Baptist

Church (two blocks from Union Station) and were assigned to homes
for lodging and breakfast; "jitney service" was provided to take them
to their homes and to the Salem Baptist Church where the Convention
was meeting. On Tuesday, December 12, 1922, Secretary Maddry
opened the Convention with a plea that "the messengers settle all the
questions that have disturbed us this year, so that the denomination
may get down to the real work of the Kingdom." A resolution designat-
ing Mother's Day to be observed as Hospital Day was passed, and
Messrs. Frank Vogler and Sons were thanked for "the beautiful am-
bulance" which they had given to the Baptist Hospital. On Wednesday
the Convention discussed the new location of Meredith College and,
after hours of debate, approved the Tucker farm as the new site.
At the evening session, Dr. Cullom came into the church a little early
and took a seat directly in front of the pulpit. Soon Rev. W. C. Meadows
of Pores Knob came in and, seeing Dr. Cullom, went down and sat
beside him. Dr. Cullom had come to know this "father in Israel"
during his work on the Campaigns; he also knew that Mr. Meadows
was deeply distressed because of Dr. Poteat's teachings. After the
report of the Board of Education, Dr. T. J. Taylor prayed for divine
guidance; then Dr. Vann said that there was "but one man" the Convention wanted to hear, and he was the honored president of Wake
Forest College. Editor Johnson reported:

> It was a tense moment when Dr. Poteat faced that great congregation.
> The Convention was on tip-toe of expectancy. Nobody knew what turn
> the discussion would take or what might follow Dr. Poteat's address.
> It was perfectly plain to all that Dr. Poteat felt keenly the gravity of
> the situation. (*BR*, Dec. 20, 1922.)

Dr. Cullom remembers that Dr. Poteat took a New Testament out of
his pocket and held it up for all to see. "I have here a little book
which my mother put into my hands many years ago. I dearly love
this little book and have tried to live by it." Dr. Poteat read John 16:
12-15, 33 and 18:37. He then stated that in the words, uttered on
the eve of the crucifixion, there are two great statements—one, that
the revelation of Christ is an expanding revelation; the other, that
Christ is the source, theme, and aim of all truth. In speaking of the
redemption which man and society can find in the cross, Dr. Poteat
declared:

> Christ-crucified works in the individual life a revolution so universal
> and so radical that there is no describing it save in His own immortal
> figure, the new birth. When the name of our dear brother, F. M. Jordan,
> was called this morning, you cannot guess what I thought about at once.
> I recalled a revival meeting which he held in Wake Forest College away
> back in the seventies, and but for the renovation of the building I could
> point you out the pew on the back of which I wept my heart out as I
> said to my Lord that the experience which I had at the age of twelve
> might have been genuine or not, one thing was certain now, that He
> was mine and I was His forever. I do not know what occurred in the

depths of my nature then. . . . I only know that when I yielded my heart to Him my surrender was my victory; this slavery of love these intervening years has been my emancipation.

And he will transform society by transforming its constituent units. What we require is not a new system of government, a new scheme for the distribution of wealth, a new social organization. What we need is new people. And I know of no way to make new people except Christ's way.

Dr. Poteat proceeded to state that the deeper things of life are beyond the weighing, measuring, and timing of science; "the deliverance of our moral and spiritual faculties are in their proper sphere just as legitimate and reliable as the deliverance of the reason in their proper sphere." He warned against two forms of infidelity, the first of which he listed as "the fear lest the truth be bad" and stated that we have no need of this fear as Christ declared, "I am the Truth." Therefore, Dr. Poteat urged:

Welcome Truth. Lay hold upon her. She is your life. And do not stop to calculate the adjustment and revision her fresh coming will necessitate. Welcome her, and the old truth, after the method of all life, will organize itself about the new revelation. For Truth is sovereign. She comes from God and bears His message, from whatever quarter her great eyes may look down upon you. Out of the starry deeps, illimitable and radiant, she comes to say, "The heavens declare the glory of God!" Out of the museum of the aeons, where on stony pages aspiring life records her defects and her successes, she comes to say, "In the beginning God created the heavens and the earth, the herb yielding seed, the beast of the earth after its kind, and of the dust of the ground man in His own image." Out of the far climes and dim days, through the blunders and sins and tragedies of history down to the blind jeopardies of the last wild game of war, she comes to say, "The most High ruleth in the kingdom of men, and giveth it to whomsoever He will." Out of the laboratories of the world, where keen eyes and skilled fingers pick reverently a little path of light into the mystery which envelops our life, she comes to say, "The invisible things of God are clearly seen, being perceived through the things that are made, even His everlasting power and divinity."

Dr. Poteat described the second form of infidelity as doubt of the ultimate triumph of God's purpose of redemption in Christ and proclaimed:

By the burdens He has lifted, by the doors He has opened, by the fetters he has broken, by the rising levels of life wherever He has walked among men, by the hopes which He kindled in His own dark time brightening through the centuries to this august hour, His dream is coming true.

We may hasten this glad consummation by an unwavering loyalty and devotion; by keeping Christ in the center of all our education, by stopping our piddling with this great instrument of the Kingdom—we should put into education four times the money we now propose, by— I will say it—looking to Him, not at one another. We are on a campaign to recover to our Lord a rebel world, and we talk of division. One thinks he thinks this, another remembers to have read somewhere that . . . Let us have done with our questionings, and follow where He leads. We shall be together, if we follow Him. Yonder gleams His banner above the battle line. Have done with these debates in the rear.

Up and after Him through blood and tears, after Him to victory!
(*BR*, Jan. 3, 1923.)

Dr. Cullom had listened carefully, as had Mr. Meadows and hundreds of others; later he wrote:

> When Dr. Poteat . . . sat down, Brother Meadows pulled a little
> slip of paper from his vest pocket and handed it to me . . . I think I
> can recall exactly the words on it: "Resolved by the Baptist State Con-
> vention of North Carolina that Dr. William Louis Poteat be required to
> give up his position as President of Wake Forest College on the grounds
> that he is leading the students of this institution astray in their Chris-
> tian faith." I read the paper and handed it back to Brother Meadows.
> . . . He took the little paper from my hand, tore it to pieces, leaned
> his face over close to mine and said, "I am satisfied." (*Charity and Chil-
> dren,* May 12, 1949.)

The Coronation hymn was announced, and soon every voice was
singing "All Hail the Power of Jesus' Name." As soon as the benediction was pronounced, Mr. Meadows was on the platform, "one of the
first" to express his appreciation of Dr. Poteat's address. Thursday
followed, and Friday noon ended "what many regard the greatest
session ever held by the North Carolina Baptist State Convention."
(*BR,* Dec. 20, 1922.)

Dr. Cullom had not taken an active part in this controversy, but it
should be noted that his influence had counted for Dr. Poteat. The
large number of "orthodox" ministerial students who had come from
Wake Forest College had studied under him who had steadied their
faith with the assurance that God was still in His heavens although
the work of creation might have been done in a different way than
they had first thought. Dr. Cullom had kept the friendship of the most
conservative while he opened avenues for greater revelations of truth.
Dr. Poteat did a great service for the state of North Carolina with
his great address; without it, the state might have followed other
states in prohibiting the teaching of evolution. With his devout life
and humble faith, with his keen insight and oratorical gifts, the president of Wake Forest College saved the day for liberal expression in
North Carolina; his speech received the acclaim of friend and foe. No
attention was paid to his quiet spoken dean who sat in front of him
on that memorable night. But, apparently without the conscious knowledge of either, that dean had played an important part in that victory.

- 9 -

Not many of the men on the Wake Forest campus were aware of
Dr. Cullom's contribution to the victory at Winston-Salem; to many,
his appearance and manner identified him with the conservative convention, and hence an antagonism. His strictness was resented, and
some of the students were not hesitant in showing it. Dr. Cullom
insisted on promptness in starting the chapel programs; to enforce this,

he had the doors locked promptly at the time the service was scheduled to begin. Of course, some were locked out, and these were counted absent. One morning the doors to the auditorium were missing. No mention was made of them. Early the following morning when he reached the campus, Dr. Cullom saw a large piece of cloth hanging over the front door of the chapel; in large bold letters was written: TO HELL WITH CULLOMISM. This stung Dr. Cullom. (One student remembers that he stood before it and wept.) "Doctor Tom" took down the cloth, and the doors were found; but within himself, Dr. Cullom felt defeated. He reasoned that his best service was not in the capacity of dean. Nevertheless, he kept his "steady gait"; as chairman of the Committee on Lectures, he announced that Dean Charles R. Brown of Yale would give three lectures at Wake Forest in April. Lilburn B. Moseley, who was settling down to become a first-rate student, heard Dean Brown and years later testified: "I can never get over Charles R. Brown and his words at Wake Forest." It was not long before Dr. Cullom recommended Mr. Moseley to the churches of Gardners and Vaughns in Warren County.

At the Wake Forest Commencement, the Board of Trustees elected Dr. J. W. Lynch to "a professorship in the Bible Department." Editor Johnson wrote: "There will be general rejoicing that this department is to be strengthened by bringing this cultured Christian gentleman and ripe scholar to the assistance of Dr. Cullom who, for many years, has had to teach all who took the course in Bible offered at Wake Forest." (*BR,* June 6, 1923.) What was not stated or known was that Dr. Cullom had not been consulted in this matter at all; the first he knew of it was when he read it in the newspaper. Of course, he and Dr. Lynch were friends and had great respect for each other. (Dr. Lynch bought the house next door to Dr. Cullom; he said he wanted to be in a good neighborhood.) But the circumstance of his coming must have put a strain on that friendship and was thus unfair to both of them.

That summer Dr. Cullom took some more "graduate work" in the University of Chicago under the leadership of Shailer Matthews, but he was not too busy or too far away that he could not write of the passing of Mrs. Martha Lloyd at Forestville or note the ordination of Casper C. Warren in Louisville. (*BR,* July 25, 1923.)

In the fall of 1923 Dr. Cullom spoke at the centennial celebration of the Brassfield Baptist Church, and Dr. D. B. Bryan was chosen as the new Dean of the College. Mr. Henry Belk was commended for his courses in Journalism and for superintending "the publicity work of the institution"; Professor A. C. Reid was returning "from Cornell University with his doctor's degree and from Georgia with his bride." Dr. Poteat wrote in the *Recorder*:

> The addition of Dr. J. W. Lynch to the Department of the Bible has made possible the extension of the courses in that department. He is

giving a course in Biblical literature, another in Christian ethics, a third
in Biblical Exposition. This last is designed especially to aid the young
ministers of the college, who number so far eighty-seven. It is probable
that the courses in Biblical Literature will be alternated with the courses
in Old Testament and New Testament where these are now required
for graduation, and that the course in Christian Ethics will be required
of all men another year. *(BR,* Oct. 31, 1923.)

Whatever offense Dr. Cullom suffered in having someone else take
over his prerogative in setting forth courses and requirements in his
own department he concealed by going about his own work for the
Lord. Dr. Harry Emerson Fosdick was much in the news at that time;
his case "was being discussed *pro et con*" with great feeling. In an
article, entitled "The Better Way," Dr. Cullom, perhaps unconsciously,
answered the discourtesy which had been shown him.

In talking with Dr. W. B. Royall one evening this week both of us
were lamenting the bitterness and strife that seem to be developing
among our Lord's followers at present. One of us remarked that it
would be so much better to believe the Bible down deep in our hearts
and to go forth preaching its blessed truths of life and salvation rather
than spending so much time and energy debating about it. Dr. Royall
suggested that when he was a young man he had some difficulties in
connection with his faith. For a while he read everything he could
find, such as the replies to Gibbon, replies to the *Age of Reason* and
many such things. These brought no satisfaction. He finally decided to
lay these aside and go to the Bible itself and get its message at first
hand. This experience brought assurance, strength and help that nothing
else could bring. Through the years this assurance and help, from the
Book itself, have grown sweeter, richer and ever more abiding. . . . Who
will say that is not the better way? *(BR,* Jan. 2, 1924.)

Dr. Cullom had a regular time for his visit with Dr. Royall; once a
week he went to read and discuss the *British Weekly* with this dear
teacher and friend. Mr. Moseley remembers going to Dr. Royall's
house for his Greek lesson; "Dr. Royall was blind and in bed, but he
taught us well." Mr. Moseley also remembers that Dr. Cullom spent

a lot of time with us as individuals and in our ministerial conference.
He helped us outline sermons; he discussed the elementary things of a
minister's life, and always recommended books for us to read—even
Fosdick's. "You don't have to agree with everything you read, but
Dr. Fosdick is worth reading," he would say. (Conversation, Aug. 31,
1959.)

From December 28th to January 1st, Dr. Cullom attended "the
great Student Volunteer Convention" in Indianapolis where he fellow-
shiped with Christians from "almost every country on the earth" and
heard "men of world-wide proportions" discuss "the deep things of
God." Such an experience strengthened Dr. Cullom's conviction that
"people generally are hungry for the voice of the real prophet." He
wrote:

Nor is it possible to deceive people at this point. The man who knows
God at first hand, who maintains vital fellowship with Him and who
therefore can speak with authority the life-giving word carries with
him his own credentials, and unless I am mistaken people are ready to

leave the crowded city and go out into the wilderness to hear such a
voice even as they did in the long ago.

There had been other days when "the Word of the Lord was precious,"
and he cited the example of the first apostles' giving over "the serving
of the tables" that they might have the time needed for prayer and
the ministry of the Word. "If we, preachers, are going to bring to our
people a fresh message from God, we shall have to make time for
patient, persistent waiting on God, and the churches are going to have
to look after the serving the tables." (*BR,* Jan. 30, 1924.)

Dr. Cullom was back in his classes when the news came of the
passing of "the world's first citizen"; men and women wept openly as
they learned of the death of Mr. Woodrow Wilson. Dr. Cullom shared
this grief for a lost leader, but he stayed at his task of preparing
future leaders. At Wake Forest, he lectured on "The Challenge of an
Unfinished World" and, at Brassfield, charged E. Lowell Spivey to be
a faithful minister of the Lord Jesus Christ.

- 10 -

Sometime in the spring of 1924, Dr. Cullom wrote Mr. Sherwood
Eddy about the American Seminar which Mr. Eddy was conducting
each summer in Europe. Mr. Eddy replied that he had found his own
study and travel abroad in 1920 so helpful that he had made arrangements for "a selected group of educators and lecturers" from the United
States to meet the leaders and prominent men of Europe, with the
hope that such an exchange of ideas would be "one avenue to international understanding and peace." Dr. Cullom applied and was accepted for the fourth of these seminars. On June 27, 1924, he assembled with nearly a hundred "educators and lecturers" from all over
the United States in New York for dinner. Mr. Reinhold Niebuhr, a
young pastor of Detroit, was presented as secretary and librarian of
the Seminar; he had books on the countries they would visit, and the
members of the Seminar were encouraged to read them on the boat.

On Sunday, July 6th, the group landed at Glasgow; Monday was
spent in Edinburgh. Tuesday, Dr. Cullom wrote of the York Minster:
"I have never seen a more impressive building"; on Wednesday the
Seminar toured the Rowntree Cocoa Works ("a wonderful establishment of seven thousand people who share in the management and
profit of making candy and cocoa") and dined with Mr. Arnold
Rowntree. In Manchester, July 9th, they had tea with the Lord Mayor
and inspected "another industrial plant." In London, Dr. Cullom
stayed at the Ormonds House; he rode an underground train six miles
to Toynbee Hall, where on Friday he heard Mr. J. L. Hammond
("Industrial History") and Mr. E. F. Wise ("European Situation").
Saturday the Seminar visited Westminster Abbey and heard Lord
Haldane in the House of Lords ("The Future of Democracy"); they

also visited several colleges at Oxford and attended a meeting of the
Convention of the Workers Education Movement. In a letter (July 14,
1924) home, Dr. Cullom asked Elizabeth to tell Dr. Royall that he
had heard Bishop Temple of Manchester.

> Tell him also that I heard Mr. S. K. Ratcliffe and Bishop Gore yester-
> day. . . . It is a very great privilege to be here and link yourself up
> with so much that you have heard of in the past. And the past is with
> you all the time. They are so conservative and feel that they must do
> every thing just so. They have the maid come into your room every
> evening and turn your bed down, and they do it just as if they were
> arranging a baby basket. Two maids came into my room a day or two
> ago to turn down the bed. I was very tired and had put on my night
> gown to rest. When they saw me they apologized for coming in and asked
> if [they] might turn down the bed. I told them to go ahead. I think
> they felt that the bottom would drop out that night if they did not turn
> that bed down just as it has been done from time immemorial.

On July 15th Mr. H. L. Laski reported nearly two million were un-
employed in Great Britain and prophesied that "about 1930 the labor
people will come into power." The next day the group attended a
reception "to meet members of the Russian Delegation." On Thursday
they visited the Ministry of Health and had a lunch at the Cooperative
Wholesale Society; on Friday, they heard the Rev. G. A. Studdert-
Kennedy speak of "the spiritual life trying to unify itself." Sometime
while in England, Lady Astor entertained the whole group in her
home and was delighted when Dr. Cullom informed her that he was
from North Carolina, she being Virginia-born. The week of July 21st
was filled with a visit to the British Empire Exhibition and conferences and speeches. At Lambeth Palace, the Archbishop of Canter-
bury spoke of "a common past" which ties Canada and the United
States to Great Britain. From July 28th through July 31st, there were
more speeches by Lord Robert Cecil, Mr. Graham Wallas, Mr. Norman
Angell, Mr. Sydney Pascall, Mr. George Lansbury, Mr. J. R. Clynes
and Mr. E. D. Morel. In his notebook Dr. Cullom wrote that a young
group of Oxford men who were teaching in Toynbee Hall seemed to
feel that America had lost her opportunity for moral leadership when
she failed to stand by President Wilson; he made this entry of British
humor:

> An American was riding around London on a bus. Passing St. Pauls
> he asked the driver how long it took to build it. "Five hundred years."
> "O," said the American, "We could build that in a year and a half in
> America." Passing Westminster Abbey, he asked how long it took to
> build it. "I don't know," said the driver; "it wasn't here on my last
> round."

In Holland, August 1st (1924), Dr. Cullom and his fellow travelers
visited "a cheese-making establishment" (Broek), saw "a bed built
into the wall" of a house and "foot-warmers" in the churches. From
Elam to Marken, they went by boat; a seventy-two-year-old man pulled
the boat as he walked along on the bank of the canal, while another

man pushed from the rear of the boat. Dr. Cullom described the houses as "low and squatty and high square-roofs much like the *hay ricks.*" He noted that Holland was "a small country of six million, and many of them are very poor"; they "purpose drying up the Zeiter-Zea and populate it." At Marken, Dr. Cullom saw women stacking hay and heard the church bells ring out at four o'clock.

It rained most of the way from Rotterdam to Berlin, August 2nd; they reached Berlin at 10:30 p.m. The next day, he heard Dr. A. Worlfers, a Y.M.C.A. leader, say, "With the disillusion of Wilsonian idealism . . . it looks as if each people will have to stand for itself." Dr. Hoelzsch of the University of Berlin declared that Germany had wanted its place in the sun but that other states did not wish her to have it; he said the defeat in war brought Communism into Germany. On Tuesday, Miss Gertrude Knapp of Philadelphia who was helping with the Friends' Soup Kitchens in Berlin, told the group that the Germans did not mean to be dependent on charity and that she felt "safe" walking the streets of Berlin at night. Dr. H. Delbrueck of the University said that the general impression that Germany had been preparing for the great war for years was "entirely erroneous"; to Judge Florence Allen's question, "Do you think the sinking of the "Lusitania" was right or wrong?" Dr. Delbrueck answered in a strong emphatic voice, "Wrong." Dr. Cullom took these notes as Dr. Deismann, the great New Testament scholar, spoke:

> The unfortunate war and the following revolution created a most trying situation for the German churches. . . . The days of 1918 were dark. Atheistic meetings were held in which people were exhorted to abandon the church. . . . One can see much in the new age that is disappointing. There is much that is encouraging. . . . There has been an awful demoralization. 763,000 deaths by the hunger blockade up to 1918. (Dr. Deismann fell in dead faint on the street on his way to his lectures because of the hunger blockade.) . . . The loss of missions . . . Heating and lighting the churches were forbidden . . . destruction of social service. The moral help given by other nations meant more than material help. Church of Germany seems to be receiving influxes of new power. Movements toward mysticism are widening in all directions. Prophets and leaders will arise who will lead our people into higher things. The difficulties are not yet solved but they are diminished.

On Wednesday, August 6th, Dr. Carl Munche "of the Left Wing" told of trying times when many workers had to live on bread or potatoes; he described the youth movement as "religious" but "anti-church." At a reception given the group by the Farmers' Organization, "a fine looking set" of well-dressed men and women served tea and cakes. A Professor Schückin, who had been a member of the German delegation to Versailles, told the Seminar that Germany was not alone in the war-guilt; "the basis of guilt is to be found in the international law in 1914."

On August 7th, the group visited Saarow and heard Dr. Macharlis, President of German Student Relief Work, say:

> The whole world is sick. We must try to establish truth, justice and righteousness on the earth. Take away the Ruhr disgrace and it will put the student into a frame of mind to adjust himself to the new situation. . . . Unfortunately the students feel that war is their own relief. God will bring help from a different source if we can only wait.

Pastor LeSeur, who was chaplain to Miss Cavell during the last moments of her life, said that the German Youth Movement had begun with Bible Classes for school boys, but it became "a revolt against the artifical civilization of the nineteenth century"; in 1913 more than two thousand German youths gathered near Cassal and pledged themselves "to live out self-determination and inner security." Eighty per cent of them died in the war, and the remaining ones were divided in the Revolution that followed. Pastor LeSeur concluded by saying:

> They have a deep longing and only one thing can meet this longing—the living Christ and the living Word. There is nothing more important at this hour than that they should find the right thought and the right doing. Here is the greatest hope of Germany and perhaps of a better world.

Dr. Cullom's notes on August 8th were written with a pencil; this writing is now smeared, with only bits of it readable. From several pages and perhaps several speakers, we get these bits:

> The National Socialist Party is becoming proletarian and anti-Semitic . . . In October and November of 1923 the wages would change two or three times a week; people had to sell clothes and bed-linens to purchase food . . . Nearly 100,000 miners are out of work. Some of the great industries are closing down day by day . . . The Communistic activities are very great. They get their ideas and money from Moscow.

- 11 -

On August 11th, the Seminar assembled in the Glass room of the Secretariat of the League of Nations in Geneva to hear Sir Arthur Howard report that fifty-four nations were "joined in the League" and over seven hundred men and women worked in the Secretariat "to smooth out frictions." Mr. H. R. Cummings declared: "In modern war there are no victors; in the work for peace, there are no losers!" Captain Stephen Saunders told the Seminar:

> If we are to get grievances adjusted we must allow the grievances to be stated . . . Most wars arose because the people did not have an opportunity of coming face to face with the questions involved.

Dr. Aitobe, a Japanese undersecretary, discussed education and an international language; Major General Abraham spoke on the Political Activities of the League, and Mr. Frederick Whelam lectured on the Principle of Trusteeship in Colonial Administration; that afternoon Dr. Cullom visited the church where John Calvin preached and sat in "Calvin's chair 1535." He also visited the room where the International Red Cross was founded and saw the Reformation Monument; that evening he heard Dr. Norman White tell of the League work in checking an epidemic in Russia and Poland in 1920.

On Wednesday, the Seminar heard lectures on the economic activities of the League, communication and transit in the post-war world, the problem of national minority and the international labor conference. A Mr. Hudson of Harvard University told the group:

> Men sometimes seem to think that progress will come with the suns. Not so. It must come with the intelligent application of the laws of life. Those who lived through the war ought to be able to do some little something to hand on progress. May it not be some sort of international plan for perpetuating peace?

After citing the success of the international post office work, the international work on weights and measures, Mr. Hudson stressed the need of having conferences in times of international dispute.

> When the war came on, we saw that there was no way of conference. British people say that if they could have got a conference with the Germans that there would have been no war . . . Men say when the good man meets the bad man he will fight him. When you meet the bad man you find that he is not bad after all. We need some method of bringing men together around a table. If you get the conference that we needed in 1914 you must have some permanent organization.

He described how the Corfu difficulty was resolved and said:

> In a Quaker meeting they don't take a vote. They get the sense of meeting. This is very important. What the world needs is a table around which people can sit in times of stress and at other times . . . The League of Nations is such a table.

On Thursday morning, a speaker whose name Dr. Cullom failed to write down spoke of war as "a sort of cancer on civilization"; it is anti-social, and we must organize against it. He declared that there could be no security without disarmament.

In Paris, August 16th, the Seminar group assembled in the Franklin Hotel to hear Count Fleury tell that Germany had offered to rebuild the devastation, but they had demanded houses for their workmen. (In his notebook, Dr. Cullom asked: "Was this unreasonable?") Madame Robert Fonville reported that during the war the women of France had to work and that after the war the men were not paid enough to support a family; so the women continued to work. Monsieur Fonville spoke on the colonies and protectorates of France; he said that these possessions had great wealth and that it was hoped that they would help France regain her place as one of the great world powers. The editor of *Le Martin* reviewed the five invasions France had experienced in the past one hundred and thirty years; "France is obsessed with the thought of safety first."

On Monday, Madame Claude de Nabloviller told the Seminar that in France women outnumbered the men by more than two million; children were undernourished and tubercular, and the returned soldiers

14

"are discouraged and embittered." The men cannot marry on the
salaries they make; so they turn to "the night places of pleasures" and
give up the sentiment of having a home. A Mr. Chaffer, an American
who had lived in France for seven years, spoke of the 25 Communists
who sat on the left in the House of Deputies and of the 30 million non-
communicant Roman Catholics whose only contact with religion was
their baptism, marriage and burial; he stated: "Unless revival can be
brought about in some way the nation is on the downgrade, and there
is not much evidence of spiritual revival." Dr. Cullom wrote in his
notebook:

> Madame said that the young people have no love for one another any
> more. Mr. Chaffer says they have no religion worth speaking of. No
> *love* and no *religion*. What a situation!

On Tuesday (August 19th), Monsieur M. L. Jonkoux admitted that
there should be some adjustments within the Versailles Treaty, but
Professor Nagaro of the Chamber of Deputies declared: "Without
payment from Germany, we will not be able to meet our obligations."
In his notebook, Dr. Cullom wrote of visiting Napoleon's tomb and of
"the deep questions" which came into his mind as he stood there.
Once the group was served champagne, mineral water and cake; Dr.
Cullom wrote: "Most of the crowd took water as long as it lasted and
then stood around and ate cake. I was one that simply ate cake."

On their last day in France, the group went by train to Rheims
where they heard that Mr. John D. Rockefeller had given one million
dollars for repairing the Cathedral; they rode on "a big char-a-bance"
over the Marne River and went through the region of the battle of
the Marne. The next day (Aug. 22, 1924) he wrote Mrs. Cullom:

> We went through the champagne country where another battle was
> fought, saw lots of trenches, barbed wire entanglements, went into a
> dugout 30 feet under ground . . . We saw also a number of old tanks
> that had been blown up. Saw two very interesting monuments. One
> was a monument by a Mr. Farnsworth on the spot where his son fell
> in battle in 1915. . . . The other monument was built to commemorate
> the courage and devotion of the Curiassiers who rescued the remnants
> of the lost 77th American division.

He said he would write Mr. Moseley to take his class in English
Bible through Dr. J. Patterson Smyth's *How We Got Our Bible* and
thought they had better order 50 copies of this book.

- 12 -

The Seminar group broke up on August 22nd, as a part of them
left for the Balkans. After "a good night" in Zurich, Dr. Cullom
boarded the Oriental Express and found a seat in an apartment with
a nice-looking Romanian couple. It was a rainy day, but "occasionally

the clouds would lift to let us see the beautiful scenery along the way."
Dr. Cullom made these entries in his notebook:

> We crossed the Alps through the Austrian Tyrol. From the Valley
> of the Rhine to that of the Danube. Snow caps and beautiful vales on
> all sides. Through a long tunnel. Must have been in it half an hour. . . .
> Passed Innsbruck a little after 5 p.m. It is a beautiful city. Said to
> have about 45,000 people in it. Mr. Kirby Page says it is one of the
> cheapest places in Europe to live. . . . Arrived in Vienna at 6:40 Sunday
> morning. Was met at the station by Miss Cadbury—a Quaker from
> America who is doing relief work here in Vienna. Went to the Ritz
> Hotel and took No. 3202 with Blair.

August 27, 1924, was a fine day; while going down the Danube
from Vienna to Budapest, Dr. Cullom wrote home:

> All of us were delighted with Vienna. We see signs of neglect and
> poverty on all sides. The streets are in pretty good condition, but the
> Royal palaces are in bad shape . . . I was brought to sympathize with
> the Austrian people very much. . . . On Monday afternoon we were
> invited to the home of Frau Helene Schen-Reisz to tea and to meet
> some "prominent people." We stayed until nearly 9 o'clock and there
> was not a dull moment in the time . . . Austria had been cut down to
> a very small territory and to six and one-half million inhabitants. The
> new states around here to the East seem to be very nationalistic and
> jealous of Vienna. They have put up high tariff barriers and seem to be
> doing all they can to bring Austria to destruction.

In his notebook, Dr. Cullom quoted an Austrian as saying that the
men of the older generation want no more war, but the younger ones
feel that as soon as they can get ready they must win back what had
been stolen from Austria. In his letter to Elizabeth (Aug. 29th), Dr.
Cullom described Budapest as "a perfectly beautiful city."

> A banker, helped us to see and hear several of the best men of the
> city. He took us over to his club for dinner last evening and we finished
> eating about ten o'clock. And what a dinner it was!

The next morning they visited the office of the National Hungarian
Society where everything spoke "of their purpose to get back their
lost provinces"; in the afternoon Dr. Cullom visited a Baptist pastor,
who received him "most cordially and graciously" and served him
coffee and rolls.

In Bucharest, Dr. Cullom and his group were met at the station
(August 31st) by a former student of Dr. Cullom, Mr. D. T. Hurley
and his wife, who gave Dr. Cullom letters from home; the next
morning he had breakfast with these dear friends and heard of their
missionary work in Romania. On Monday, the group toured the oil
fields as guests of the Romanian Government; "we must have gone
200 miles in automobiles . . . at 60 or 70 miles an hour." That night
the governmental officials gave them a great dinner; "I think our hosts
thought we were a queer set to leave all that liquor untouched."
Dr. Cullom found the Romanian people very "nationalistic and very

self-conscious"; he thought they would have "a great future" if they could have "able and unselfish leaders."

From Bucharest they came to Constanza on the Black Sea and took a boat for Constantinople. The sea was beautiful, but "an undertow or something gave the ship a sort of cork screw motion" and caused Dr. Cullom to miss lunch. In his letter to "My Precious Nancy" (Sept. 6th, 1924), Dr. Cullom said:

> The situation here is very tense and we could not have the conferences that we have had in the other places. Still we have had a most interesting and helpful stay here. Do you remember a Mrs. Stem who was in Youngsville a year or so ago and on whom your mother and I called one evening? She lives here and came up to the hotel to see me the first evening I was here. Her husband was away in Smyrna on business but his mother from South Carolina is with them for the winter. Both of them have been so nice to me. They have a new car and one of the best chauffeurs that I ever saw. She knows the shops, mosques, museums, etc., thoroughly, having lived here for several years.

One of the most interesting events of his stay in Constantinople was an interview with a Turkish editor, Dr. Emin, a graduate of Columbia in New York, who told them that only two of the eleven daily papers in Constantinople were "set to support the government."

At the American Bible House, some Congregational missionaries said their new medical college for women had not been allowed to open; the government would not allow any more foreign doctors to practice or to teach, because Russia had sent a lot of women doctors who turned out to be "nothing but Soviet propagandists." On a Friday evening, the Americans visited "a Charity Bazaar" in one of the leading parks of the city and heard Madame Neyieh Mohidden Hannum. Dr. Cullom wrote:

> A few Mohammedan women wore the veil over their faces but they were very few. Ten years ago when I was in Constantinople it seemed to me that most of them were veiled. . . . Men and women came in together, sat at the little tables together, drank and ate together very much as Western people do. This could not have happened ten years ago.

On Saturday, the group left Constantinople "just as the sun was going down"; the city with its many mosques and hundreds of minarets showed up "most beautifully" across the waters.

Dr. Cullom arose early Sunday morning and went out on deck to see the Dardanelles. When he looked down into the front of the ship, he saw cows and people crowded in such a condition that he declared "it was enough to turn one from eating for a week." Later that morning he heard Dr. Robinson of Johns Hopkins University speak on his work of excavation in Asia Minor. The weather that Sunday was warm and clear, and the sea was "perfectly beautiful all day"; in the late afternoon he continued his letter to Nancy:

> I can visualize things at home . . . Sister is getting off to her work . . . You are getting your ducks in a row to get out to Randolph-Macon;

Sarah is getting ready to get off to her school in the "South"; and mother is working . . . like a Trojan, whatever that may mean, to get you all off, get the school started, keep my letters answered and with a thousand other things . . . I hope you may get off to school all right, get started in good shape, and go on without trouble. Try to take just what you can do, and then stick to it faithfully and patiently. Be sure to care for your health, get plenty of sleep and keep yourself in good shape for your best all the time.

At the Palace Hotel in Athens, Dr. Cullom found letters from Mrs. Cullom and Sarah and wrote: "Bless her heart! Guess I should have cried with her when Nancy had her hair bobbed." Athens had not had rain for three months so Dr. Cullom had to be satisfied with a "sponge bath"; he and his companions "almost collapsed" under the heat. On the morning of September 8th, they visited the Acropolis, "the most glorious ruins on earth"; the next day at the office of the Commission of Education they secured a permit to remain at the Parthenon after sunset. Arriving at 6 p.m. for this second visit to the Acropolis, Dr. Cullom and his friends loitered a little while in the Museum until just before sunset when they gathered on the remains of the front steps of the Parthenon. He wrote Mrs. Cullom:

A bare rocky mountain was between us and the sun in the far away distance. As the sun began to hang just over behind this mountain it seemed to have no rays at all but was just one great red ball suspended in the heavens. Soon it began to drop behind the mountain and went out of sight a little at a time . . . Not a word was spoken by any one, but I felt very much like singing very softly the Chatauqua Hymn.

On the afternoon of September 10th, Dr. Cullom and his companions went to a reception given by Madame Paspastis in the open courtyard of her lovely home; the next day they visited a Relief-Work orphanage where a group of boys "went through a wonderful piece of drill work" and sang for the visitors. Dr. Cullom wrote Mrs. Cullom that they would leave for Belgrade that afternoon (Sept. 11th): "Hope you can hold things down until I get there, and then together we will see what we can do about getting everything in line again."

This was the last letter we have from him in Europe, but we have booklets of Milan, Florence, Venice, Bologna, which Dr. Cullom and his party visited. Among his souvenirs of this visit to Italy is a picture-card of the fourteen pastors of the North Italian Baptist Mission, grouped around "Dr. Everrette Gill, Missionary." In Rome, Dr. Cullom saw the famous sights which he had seen during his previous visits, plus some new ones. The imposing monument to Victor Emmanuel II had become something of "the sacred altar of the country," since the tomb of the Unknown Soldier was there. A new stadium bore the name of Mussolini, and the Mussolini Obelisk boldly proclaimed a new era; the guidebook which Dr. Cullom carried in his hand spoke of "the Duce's making Rome worthy of its historic mission and great destiny."

- 13 -

When Dr. Cullom arrived in Wake Forest, the college had been in session almost a month; 575 were enrolled, and the newly constructed Bostwick Hall was occupied. Dr. Cullom took charge of his classes and was back in the pulpit at Rolesville on Sunday, October 5th. In an article, "As to Revival Meetings" (*BR,* March 11, 1925), Dr. Cullom lamented "the cheap stuff that has been put into the appeal to people to surrender themselves to God" and declared: "We need preaching which the Holy Spirit can use to break up the subsoil and bring people to a realization of what life means from the standpoint of God in Christ Jesus." In a later article (*BR,* April 8, 1925), Dr. Cullom asked if we are not trying to tell people that they need only a little healing when a more careful scrutiny would reveal an alarming condition.

> Do we not need to come back to the deeper diagnosis of human nature and help man to see that sin against God is an awful reality . . . The Bible makes a great deal of the doctrine of repentance. But why should one repent when he does not feel that he is wrong? Is it not true that many people would resent the suggestion that they need to repent? . . . God had to destroy the nation that surrounded Jeremiah and take them into captivity before He could teach them. Will the same be true of His people in this generation? God forbid! At least let His prophets declare the whole counsel of God that the blood of this generation be not on our heads!

In a third article (*BR,* June 10, 1925), Dr. Cullom lamented "a tendency about us to demand popularity rather than faithfulness from the man who speaks God's message."

> In my judgment there is great need just now that God's people shall bear a testimony for Him that will touch men's consciences and make them hunger for righteousness rather than for that which is pleasing to the carnal mind.

That spring, Secretary Charles E. Maddry appealed to the Baptists of North Carolina to give through the Unified Program; he said all the Boards were in debt and faced embarrassment and possible disaster. Exactly two hundred preachers came to the Pastors School at Wake Forest which was described as "one of the most helpful denominational meetings ever held in the State." (*BR,* June 17, 1925.) During the summer, when the newspapers were filled with the Scopes "monkey-trial" which Editor Johnson described as "a kind of vaudeville performance," Dr. Cullom gave lectures on his European trip at Henderson, Rocky Mount, Mebane, Lumberton, Sylva, Warrenton, Winston-Salem, Goldsboro, Durham, Gastonia, Shelby, Wilson, Tarboro, Spring Hope, and many other places. His account book shows that he received fifty dollars from most of these places; this book also shows that the trip had cost him $1,818.75. Ralph M. Lee would write:

I remember on one occasion when he had spoken to an audience of mountain people following his trip to Europe in 1924 that a good mountaineer paid him this compliment when he said, "He is about the mostest commonest man I ever saw." I told Dr. Cullom that he meant that for a big compliment because Dr. Cullom was able to make himself at home in the most humble cottage, the smallest country church, or in the city church, or in a palatial home. (Letter, Oct. 14, 1958.)

Dr. Cullom also continued to write; he declared that amid all the appeals for more money for the denominational causes, "our greatest need" is for "spiritual-mindedness on the part of God's people." He quoted Dr. Edward C. Boynton as saying:

"The expressional endeavors of the Congregationalists have outrun the spiritual experience. The good works have gone beyond the place where they are actuated by personal experience . . . We are trying to do too much of an objective nature for the amount of subjective spiritual experience which is current in our constituency."

Dr. Cullom said we must undergird the whole structure of our denominational work with a sense of personal devotion to Jesus as Saviour and of loyalty to Him as Lord of all, in order that the wave of enthusiasm begotten in the 75 million campaign might become "an abiding and ever-growing stream of power to sustain and carry on what we had so well begun." (*BR*, Sept. 23, 1925.)

In November, Dr. Cullom wrote of "the general wrangle over religion and science" and expressed fear that Christian people were being "side-tracked from their main task" of witnessing to their faith in Jesus Christ. As an example of such side-tracking he cited the debate over the making of the cross which was going on when the Turks attacked Constantinople in 1543; if the Christians of that time had been as busy in proclaiming "the great facts of the gospel" as they were in debating whether to cross themselves with two or three fingers, history would have been different. And for our day, Dr. Cullom asked: "Which man is likely to accomplish most in neutralizing and destroying the influence of the tide of materialism which seems to be flooding us, the debater or the herald, the logician or the witness?" (*BR*, Nov. 4, 1925.)

In another article, "Real Christian Unity," Dr. Cullom told of traveling in Switzerland with people of many nationalities in one train-car; they spoke many languages, but they were all eager to see the Matterhorn.

Finally, that snow-capped monarch of the Alps appeared. Each one saw . . . that wonderful work of God. There was no need to descend to the jargon of tongues. There was a language that was infinitely above the languages, and all understood. Surely the application is apparent. Real unity will never be achieved by arguments, by votes of councils, by adoption of creeds, by edicts of popes or kings. Real unity will be achieved when we stand face to face with Jesus and, without thinking especially of one another, shall all cry spontaneously with Thomas, "My Lord and my God." (*BR*, Nov. 11, 1925.)

On December 16, 1925, in Philadelphia, Dr. Cullom addressed the newly founded Eastern Baptist Theological Seminary; he wrote:

> It seems to me there are indications that the spirit is moving in the tops of mulberry trees. Shall we not open our ears to hear the joyful sound and set our sails to be caught and moved on by this mighty spirit to greater things in this our day of opportunity?

In a review of Ben Lindsey's *The Revolt of Youth* (*BR*, Feb. 17, 1926), Dr. Cullom quoted the author as stating that many of the external restraints were gone from our young people and asked:

> When will parents, teachers, preachers and all the rest learn that God's way of life is to build from the inside and that there can be no substitute for God's way? This way requires time, thought, patience, faith and all that for success. We are willing to bestow these in growing a crop, in developing a business, in raising stock, in every sphere of life that has to do with things. When will we learn that the same law applies in the sphere of morals, in the realm of spirit? . . . Dean Charles R. Brown of Yale said that ten years ago the whole world went "to smash," not for the lack of money or energy or brains, but "because the spiritual forces of society had not been maintained at their full vigor nor of the right quality."

In a later article, "What is Man" (*BR*, April 28, 1926), Dr. Cullom wrote that it is necessary for "all of us to form some definite and workable conception as to the fundamental nature of a human being" in order that "we may know how to meet our responsibility in dealing with our own personalities" and in dealing with others. In his article, "What is a Baptist Church," Dr. Cullom said:

> When you destroy the authority and influence of the Bible you destroy the foundation on which a Baptist Church is built . . . To the extent that you increase an intelligent understanding of the Bible and a humble, sincere, honest purpose to receive and follow its teaching, to that extent you will increase the number, the power and the influence of the Baptists. (*BR*, June 2, 1926.)

Mr. Walter Lippman gave the Commencement address that spring at Wake Forest, and the Summer School for Preachers was moved to the newly constructed Meredith College. Dr. Cullom served as dean; in urging ministers to "come apart together" for this school, he declared:

> the gospel for the new day must not be a mere repetition of trite phrases gathered from Christian history . . . The only thing that is going to bring the essential help that we need in our present situation of chaos, confusion and uncertainty is the gospel of God in Christ Jesus. (*BR*, May 12, 1926.)

And nearly three hundred came! Editor Livingston Johnson visited the school one day and wrote of Dr. Cullom's lecture on "The Heart of the Gospel":

> He speaks out of a rich experience as pastor and teacher, for in addition to his work as head of the Bible department at Wake Forest, he has been pastor of churches most of the time and in that way has kept in touch with the work of the pastors and knows their difficulty. This makes it possible for him to bring to his class suggestions of a practical

nature, which help pastors in meeting difficult problems. *(BR,* June 16, 1926.)

From June 22nd through June 24th, Dr. Cullom participated in a conference on "Religious Education in America" which was held at Reynolda; he led the discussion of "Spiritual Exercises."

Sometime after this conference, the Cullom family left for Canada, with Nancy and Sarah taking turns as driving the car. At Montreal, they met Dr. Sloan whom the girls had expected to be as witty as his letters but found him to be "quite dignified and reserved." Dr. Cullom preached in the West Mount Baptist Church and in the First Baptist Church; he also had the opportunity of participating in a retreat of religious leaders conducted by Dr. Wilbert W. White of New York City. In his discussion on Church Unity, Dr. Cullom confessed that the more he watched the various efforts toward the matter of uniting the churches, the less he became interested in the end toward which they aimed. He insisted that

> we cease thinking of any such thing as uniformity in organization and try to fix our own gaze and the gaze of all who we can influence on Jesus the Christ, as Saviour and Lord as He is revealed to us in the Holy Scriptures. In my judgment, to the extent that we succeed in doing this, we shall accomplish three things: (1) We shall be brought into a blessed unity of spirit in the bonds of peace; (2) We shall be brought to a fruitfulness in Christian effort that will be possible to us in no other way; (3) We shall be brought to a strength and joy in loyalty to and in the service of a common Lord that will otherwise be impossible. *(BR,* Sept. 29, 1926.)

That fall Dr. William Louis Poteat resigned as president of Wake Forest, and Olin T. Binkley, who had entered his class the year before, returned to assist Dr. Cullom in grading papers and helping with his classes. Years later this fine student was to recall:

> On a number of occasions I was in his home to confer with him about classes and papers when he was kept in by bronchitis. I was impressed by the considerateness with which he and Mrs. Cullom treated me, even to the point of feeling that I was a member of the family. I remember with a great satisfaction his sense of reality in worship as he read the Bible and led in prayer at the family table. I was convinced also, that he considered Christian education a life-long process of learning. He read books and periodical literature, including British magazines, and in conversation with a young student he did not hesitate to open his mind and to assert what was taking place in the world in the light of the sovereignty of God and of the moral demands of Jesus Christ. (At Wake Forest, Aug. 10, 1959.)

- 14 -

In January (1927), at a conference on "Bible Study in College" in Memphis, Dr. Cullom counted eight former students who were Bible professors in various parts of the country; later in the year, he spoke at the Southern Regional B.Y.P.U. Convention and directed the Preachers' School at Meredith. In July, he conducted the funeral services of dear old "Doctor Tom" Jeffries in the Memorial Chapel of the College; a choir of white men and women sang, and the pastor of the colored church gave the principal address. Other changes occurred at Wake Forest. In September, Dr. Francis Pendleton Gaines was installed as the new president of the college, and in January of 1928, Dr. William Bailey Royall died; his mantle had long fallen on Dr. Cullom's shoulders, and yet another great teacher was in the making—Olin T. Binkley shared with Dr. Cullom the conviction that his vocation probably would be in some aspect of educational endeavor.

Again in 1928, Dr. Cullom served as dean of the Preachers School at Meredith; as Sarah, his daughter, was a student at Meredith and had a summer job there, she drove back and forth with him. Once he had a wedding in Zebulon at six o'clock in the morning, and he wanted to be back at Meredith by seven. Sarah remembers he was saying, "Drive faster, Sarah; drive faster," when a tire blew out. That was the summer when Herbert Hoover was nominated as the Republican candidate for the presidency of the United States and Al Smith was chosen as the Democratic candidate "on a wet platform." In August, Dr. Cullom taught Bible at the Sylva Baptist Encampment and wrote "The Minister and Partisan Politics," in which he said the minister *should* interest himself in politics—both as a pastor and as a citizen.

> As a pastor, (1) the minister should keep in mind that he is pastor to *all* his church . . . (2) He should do all he can to educate the consciences and hearts of his people in the attitude and spirit of Jesus. (3) He should maintain in himself and seek to cultivate in others a spirit of Christian tolerance and of undying patience . . . (4) He should be constantly trying to lift the ideals and purposes of his people to something higher than party issues.
>
> As a citizen, (1) the minister should allow no one to dictate to him what shibboleth he is to use . . . (2) He should inform himself as best he can from all angles, compare all calls for support with the eternal principles of Jesus . . . (3) He should be exceedingly cautious as to dealing in personalities. . . . Another day will come, and the minister wants to be able to hold up his head, look men in the face and summon them to better things in the name and in the spirit of his Master. (4) He should seek and grasp every opportunity to be of help to all his people, regardless of class or party.
>
> Finally . . . as pastor and as citizen, the minister should pray God to help him always to be as wise as a serpent and as harmless as a dove. (BR, Aug. 22, 1928.)

In his article, "A Study in Real Divinity," Dr. Cullom defined divinity as that which confronted Moses at the burning bush, Isaiah in the Temple, Saul on the Damascus Road. In reference to Rudolph Otto's *The Idea of Holy,* he called Dr. Otto "a mystic" and so described Paul, John, Augustine, Bernard of Clairvaux, Francis of Assisi, John Wesley, Charles H. Spurgeon, John A. Broadus; "and so must be the men who are to lead us out of our treadmill thinking and living today into a fresh, vital and vitalizing experience of God in Jesus Christ." Dr. Cullom found it encouraging that Karl Barth was "speaking out" and hoped that someone would soon give to the English readers "the benefit of what Mr. Barth is saying!"

On September 8, 1928, Dr. Cullom performed the wedding ceremony for his daughter, Elizabeth, and Mr. Fant Kelly in the living room of the Cullom home; Ed Cullom played the piano, and Nancy was the bride's attendant. In November, Editor Johnson interpreted Al Smith's defeat in the presidential election as an indication "that the people of the country are not willing to sacrifice for expediency's sake the prohibition laws which were written into our national statutes," and Dr. Cullom wrote of his rejoicing in the passing of "the old sectarian bitterness" of the past but asked if there were not "all about us today a loud, strong call for the cultivation of deeper loyalties." (*BR,* Nov. 21, 1928.) In May, Dr. Cullom presented plans for the fifth term of "our School for Ministers at Meredith," wrote of ministers' securing fields of service, and attended the meeting of the Education Commission and the Southern Baptist Convention in Memphis.

During the week of May 12th Dr. Cullom preached in the First Baptist Church of El Dorado, Arkansas, and taught two classes daily in Romans and Genesis. Rev. J. M. Gibbs wrote that he was delighted to sit again at the feet of "this mighty man of God" and that the type of work Dr. Cullom had done in El Dorado "needs to be done in all our churches throughout the land." (*BR,* June 5, 1929.) Dr. Cullom spoke in the Commencement program at Southwestern Baptist Theological Seminary at Fort Worth, Texas; Dr. William W. Barnes took great pleasure in introducing his dear teacher to the faculty and student body. In returning from Texas, Dr. Cullom spent two days in Fayetteville, "the Athens of Arkansas," where he spoke in the First Baptist Church.

- 15 -

In the spring of 1929, Dr. Cullom was asked to secure a supply preacher for the Baptist Church at Spring Hope. This church had been organized in 1889 in a store-building near the newly laid railroad. A one-room building had been erected the next year and for several years had been used for school during the week and for preaching on Sunday; the Rev. John A. Bridgers had served as teacher and preacher. The church had grown with the town, and in 1909 a new brick building had replaced the old frame building. The church had met its notes of indebtedness, had bought new furniture and had disciplined its members; it had voted to assess its members for the preacher's salary and had required all male members to attend the church conferences. It had debated building a fence around the church to keep horses and buggies off the yard; it had moved with the times in selling its old organ for a piano and in replacing the common communion cup with new individual glasses. Up to 1929, the church had been served by thirteen pastors, including such men as W. C. Nowell, A. G. Willcox, D. R. Putman, John R. Carroll and J. A. Ward. In 1929, Dr. Cullom suggested that the pulpit committee contact Rev. Olin T. Binkley who was in the Seminary. When he returned from his trip to Tennessee, Arkansas and Texas, Dr. Cullom was pleased to find Mr. Binkley in Spring Hope and to learn of his experiences at Louisville. In September, Mr. Binkley returned to Louisville and the Baptist Church at Spring Hope "voted to leave it with Dr. Cullom to supply for us until the church could secure a pastor."

Wake Forest College opened with nearly six hundred men; Jasper L. Memory, Jr., began his work with the college as a professor of education. Eleven years before, he had been a freshman himself and had been impressed by the kind, gentle and helpful spirit of Dr. Cullom. On the opening day of the college in 1929, Professor Memory was expected to sit on the platform with the other professors; this was a frightening ordeal for him. Years later he told:

> I faced the music, however, and selected Dr. Cullom as being a harmless man to sit by. As we became seated, Dr. Cullom allayed my fears by whispering, "I am glad to be sitting by a good man." That was Dr. Cullom for you, always thinking of the welfare of the other fellow.

In that same September, Dr. Cullom wrote an article on College Chapel services, in which he quoted ex-President Calvin Coolidge as saying that at Amherst they were told that the college had been founded by pious men to train students to overcome the unbelief then prevalent and that religious instruction was a part of the prescribed course for all who chose to attend the college. Dr. Cullom also cited Judge J. C. Clifford of Dunn who testified that the chapel services at Wake Forest, with the prayers of President Taylor, were "the most helpful influence" in his life. Dr. Cullom recommended that the chapel services be "entirely different" from mere assemblies; "I would insist that they should be religious, and that an earnest effort should be made through them to leave with students a definite impression as to what religion is and as to what it should mean in the life of the individual and in the life of society." (*BR,* Sept. 4, 1929.) H. M. Hocutt entered Dr. Cullom's class that fall and found such understanding that he often went to this dear teacher's office and home for counsel; he drove for him, taking him to Spring Hope and visiting friends. He was to write:

> In all these experiences I have come to see in him more and more of the likeness of Christ . . . He is a great scholar, and at the same time he is a humble servant. He lives in close contact with many great Christian leaders of this nation and of other countries, and at the same time he lives close to the humblest person about him regardless of his race or color or station in life. He is a saint among us. (Letter, Oct. 10, 1958.)

In October Dr. Charles E. Maddry reported that the receipts for the cooperative program had continued to decline; when the Convention met in November the brethren were "heavily burdened" with the indebtedness. In New York, the Stock Market crashed, with the loss of fifteen billion dollars. In an article, "A Satisfying Message for a Dissatisfied Age," Dr. Cullom said the present dissatisfaction would prove "a great blessing if it leads us to a new and richer vision of God in Christ Jesus"; he saw re-publication of John Omen's book, *Vision and Authority* as an indication that "such a vision is coming in response to a deep and growing heart hunger." (*BR*, Nov. 6, 1929.)

In March, Dr. Cullom attended a joint meeting of the Southern Baptist Educational Association and the Association of Teachers of Bible and Religious Education at Birmingham, Alabama; of this meeting he wrote:

> No religious denomination can hope to perpetuate itself to-day and at the same time function in a worthy manner in the life of its generation without schools. . . . The schools fostered by a denomination must enshrine, foster and propagate an idealism whose dominant note and purpose must be as thoroughly Christian as the very spirit and teaching of Jesus Himself. (*BR*, March 19, 1930.)

On May 5, 1930, the Spring Hope Church voted "to hold daily Vacation Bible School" and decided to have a revival meeting beginning the last Sunday in May, "to meet the convenience of Dr. Cullom who would do the preaching." The meeting began Sunday, May 25th, and lasted through Sunday, June 8th.

> Dr. W. R. Cullom led all the services being assisted by Rev. O. T. Binkley during the second week of the meeting. The Lord wonderfully blessed our community through the efforts of Dr. Cullom, his faithful servant. There were around thirty additions to the church by baptism and twelve by letter and one by statement. Brother Hocutt, student at Wake Forest College, assisted in the meeting as singer. Baptismal services in the meeting were held all along at night during the meeting, Brother Binkley doing the baptizing. (Church Records.)

Sometime that spring, Dr. Cullom went to Louisville, where he examined "the second most important New Testament document in the United States"; he visited Cave Hill Cemetery and toured the training school for women. (*BR*, June 11, 1930.) Back at Wake Forest, he heard President Gaines deliver his last address and, at the Meredith preachers' school ("the best to this date"), gave "a series of daily heart messages at seven o'clock each morning." (*BR*, June 25, 1930.)

In July, 1930, the Spring Hope Church called Dr. Cullom "to act as pastor of our church"; Dr. Cullom either "bummed" a ride with a student going that way or had someone to drive him the twenty-five miles to Spring Hope. At first, he had a room for the week end at the home of Mrs. M. H. Privette (formerly Miss Lela McNeill of Dunn), but later he roomed at Mrs. C. B. Brantley's. Always quiet and congenial, he was the choicest of guests. Never was he without a book or two in his black satchel; he would read late into the night and be up early Sunday morning to read. He ate breakfast in the home in which he was staying and, when not invited out to dinner, would eat at Mrs. Matt Saunders' boardinghouse. After the morning services and a short nap, he would start visiting both sides of a street—every house, no matter what denomination. In the evening he would stop in wherever he was asked for a little supper before returning to the church and then to Wake Forest.

After sharing in a memorial service for Rev. A. G. Willcox on August 1st, Dr. Cullom left Rev. O. T. Binkley in charge of the Spring Hope Church and took his family "into the New England States of Maine and Massachusetts, there preaching and teaching as he is ever wont to be doing his Heavenly Father's business." (Spring Hope Church minutes.) Nancy and Sarah took turns at the wheel of the car; they spent the nights in tourist homes where the people were "very kind" to them. At Northfield, they heard such men as Dr. John Hutton, Dr. G. Campbell Morgan and Dr. James Reid. Dr. Cullom visited the birthplace of Dwight L. Moody and shared some stories about him with the *Recorder* readers (August 27, 1930). From August 18th to August 30th, he participated in the School of Methods at Ocean Park, Maine, where over eight hundred religious leaders were in attendance. Dr. Cullom was impressed by "the beautiful combination of worship and fun," and "the power of a strong Christian atmosphere" which characterized the school; he was especially pleased to see two of his former students, O. P. Campbell and Lowell Q. Hayes, fill "conspicuous places in the faculty of this worthy school." The mother of Sherwood Eddy (then 82 years old) was "as eager and as interested an attendant" on Dr. Cullom's classes as any one else there; she invited Dr. and Mrs. Cullom to have a meal with her in the "Minnie's Rest" home for missionaries at Old Orchard. (*BR,* Sept. 17, 1930.) Dr. Cullom remembers, "We had a good time that summer." One thing troubled him; at Ocean Park, he noticed that Mrs. Cullom was having difficulty in climbing the stairs to their room on the second floor. After two weeks at this Baptist encampment, the Culloms went into Canada. For several Sundays Dr. Cullom supplied the pulpit of the West Mount Baptist Church of Montreal; as Sarah had to be back in school, Dr. Cullom was left in Canada to preach his last Sunday and to return home by train.

Upon reaching Wake Forest, Mrs. Cullom went to a physican and then to the hospital for a thorough examination. One day in September, Dr. Cullom called on his pastor, the Rev. J. Allen Easley, in his study at the church; he told Mr. Easley that he had "bad news" from the hospital: "The doctors tell me that Mrs. Cullom has pernicious anemia; they give her about ten years to live." Mrs. Cullom returned home and resigned as teacher of the Ladies Sunday School class at the church. There was nothing of sadness about her or her home. She continued to be jovial and bright; she read a great deal and kept her husband posted on world events.

Dr. Cullom continued in his regular work and activities. C. C. Crow was a freshman that fall; he recalls Dr. Cullom was "of the greatest help" to him.

> My wife was frail for a considerable time. It is a happy remembrance of ours to recall Dr. Cullom's many visits to our little apartment on "Sky Hill" always with a cheery smile and a "bag of fruit" for mother and the two children. (Letter, Sept. 19, 1956.)

After Christmas (1930), Dr. Cullom and Rev. Mr. Easley attended a Student-Faculty Conference on education and religion in Detroit; Reinhold Niebuhr was one of the leaders. As this conference proceeded, Dr. Cullom was impressed by the "widespread confusion in these fields" and by the determination to meet this situation realistically. Dr. Cullom thought the Sunday school lessons from the gospel of Luke could help in getting "a firm grip on the eternal verities of Christ" which would reassure us and enable us to help others; he wrote: "We having nothing to fear and much to gain. Let us do our best." (*BR,* Feb. 18, 1931.) As he left the conference on the evening of December 31st, he felt that Paul's expression about people feeling after God if haply they might find him might be said "to be quite characteristic of this day"; he wondered "whether those of us who are connected with these schools realize the tremendous importance of our own task." (*BR,* March 4, 1931.) Out of such an experience and thought, Dr. Cullom, as chairman of the Education Commission of the Southern Baptist Convention, planned a four day Faculty Retreat at Ridgecrest for August 25-28.

In an article on "Wake Forest and the Ministry," Dr. Cullom told of one of Wake Forest's oldest alumni telling that when he first began attending the sessions of our North Carolina Baptist State Convention he could count the educated ministers in the Convention on the fingers of one hand, whereas "now nearly all the ministers in the Convention are educated men, and it is practically all the outcome of the work of Wake Forest College." Dr. Cullom wrote that about twenty-five hundred ministers had received training at Wake Forest during the years since it was founded in 1834.

> In the earlier years of our history Baptists did not count much in the towns. Today our people have church buildings and church organizations which command the respect of the best people in town and cities everywhere, as well as in the countryside. It may be said also that in the earlier part of our history our people figured but slightly in the councils of State. Today many of the governors, lawmakers and leaders in civic life are members of Baptist churches and are among the most loyal, faithful and effective leaders.
>
> Nor is the mere matter of training the only thing that Wake Forest has given to its ministers. They have here caught a vision, an outlook on life as a whole, which has enabled them to take their places as real

leaders in their respective communities. . . . As we think of the task of
the minister today there was surely never a time that called more loudly
and strongly for capable, consecrated leadership than the time in which
we live. May the Old College continue to prove herself a worthy
agency in this important field. (*BR,* March 11, 1931.)

In the spring, Dr. Cullom conducted another series of meetings at
Spring Hope and read of the Southern Baptist Convention meeting in
Birmingham when its constitution was changed from representation
by "delegates" to composition "of messengers who are members of
missionary Baptist Churches cooperating with the Southern Baptist
Convention." Again he served as dean of the Preachers School at
Meredith and at the close of summer school saw his daughter, Sarah,
with Laura Helen and Catherine Paschal, receive the first degrees
awarded by Wake Forest College to women.

On August 25th, the Southern Baptist Faculty Retreat met at
Ridgecrest for three days. Mrs. Cullom told her husband that she
"hardly felt able to stand the strain of the crowd at Ridgecrest where
so many would speak to her and where she would have to do quite a
bit of climbing"; so Dr. Cullom took her to Blue Ridge nearby and
secured a room for her and Nancy where she could be quiet. Dr.
Cullom hurried back to the Baptist Assembly Grounds where, as chairman of the Education Commission, he presented such speakers as
Dr. James F. Franklin of New York, Mr. Kirby Page of New York,
Dr. Rufus W. Weaver of Washington, Dr. B. Warren Brown of
Chicago, Dr. J. W. McGlothlin of South Carolina, Dr. W. O. Carver
of Kentucky, Dr. Fred F. Brown of Tennessee. Dr. Cullom had hope
this conference would "be used of God for begetting a spirit of fellowship and even of comradeship amongst those engaged in this important task in this hour of unprecedented opportunity." (*BR,* Aug. 12,
1931.) And we do not doubt but that it was so. Dr. Cullom thought
Mrs. Cullom's experience at Blue Ridge had reinforced her, but when
she returned home, she began using a cane to help with her walking.

At the college, seventy-three ministerial students elected Ottis J.
Hagler of Charlotte as president of their Conference with S. L. Mor-
gan, Jr., as their secretary; Dr. Cullom presented Dr. H. Augustine
Smith, an authority on church music and art, and later introduced
Mr. Kirby Page who spoke on the European situation. That was the
fall when Mr. Thomas Alva Edison died and when the League of
Nations failed to halt Japan's conquest of Manchuria. Upon hearing
that Dr. Frank S. Hickman, dean of the School of Religion at Duke
University, was interested in organizing an interdenominational discussion group, Dr. Cullom wrote his endorsement of the idea and went
to its first meeting. When the question of naming the new organization
arose, Dr. Cullom told of Dr. Phillips Brooks's having sponsored a
similar group in Boston and suggested that they consider naming their

group after this distinguished Episcopal minister; the group was named "the Phillips Brooks Club."

The burden of the Baptist State Convention in Winston-Salem that November was "our bonded debt" of $942,989; new bonds at six per cent interest seemed "the only way out." Rev. J. C. Powell, missionary in Africa who was home on furlough, handed his check for the first bond to Secretary Maddry. Santford Martin of the Winston-Salem *Journal-Sentinel* delighted the sober Convention with this story of a man campaigning for Congress.

> "The isms are about to destroy our country; send me to Congress and I will destroy pessimism, atheism, socialism, communism, bolshevism," he declared. At that point an old man, leaning upon his staff managed to raise up and said, "Include rheumatism, and I'll vote for you." *(BR,* Nov. 18, 1931.)

Dr. Cullom did what he could to help those less fortunate than himself. Dr. Gulley gave him milk which Mrs. Cullom dipped and distributed from her front porch. The church at Spring Hope had "a White Christmas" program, at which time the people brought gifts for the needy; this service began at five o'clock with a song service, and the church was filled "to capacity."

- 16 -

Financial disaster was widespread at the beginning of 1932. Mr. J. S. Farmer, editor of the *Biblical Recorder,* argued for laws requiring banks to guarantee every deposit and pleaded for the Special Emergency Mission Relief offering to save the work of the Home and Foreign Mission Boards. Dr. Cullom taught in the Wake Forest summer school and, in the chapel exercise of July 4th, said: "The Christian is under obligation to think, to reach intelligent conclusions for himself on the deep things of God; he must not let others do his thinking for him." Editor Farmer thought if all preachers would take this idea to themselves they would have "no need to borrow ritualism to make their services interesting." *(BR,* July 27, 1932.) In August, Editor Farmer quoted Dr. Cullom as saying that the centralization of our denominational organizations had robbed our churches and associations of a sense of responsibility for their work and as calling upon every association to assert its importance and to make a complete survey of its own territory with a view of its complete evangelization.

Sometime in 1932, Dr. Cullom went to New York to hear the report of an inquiry on the effectiveness of the missionary effort of seven leading Protestant denominations. Dr. Cullom recalls that as Mr. John D. Rockefeller, Jr., was to be present, everyone had been careful to dress formally. At the appointed hour Mr. Rockefeller and one of his sons appeared; they were in business suits. Mr. Rockefeller apologized: "Gentlemen, we beg to be excused for our dress; you see, my son and I are working men." Dr. Cullom also recalls that Dr. Rufus Jones was "an important member" of this Laymen's Missionary Committee and that Dr. Jones made a most favorable impression. (*Charity and Children*, Dec. 23, 1948.)

In September (1932), Governor O. Max Gardner addressed more than eight hundred students at the opening of Wake Forest College; at Spring Hope, Dr. Cullom conducted "a week of preaching on the Book of Acts." In urging his fellow Baptists to rally behind whoever might be chosen as the new secretary and treasurer of the Baptist State Convention, Dr. Cullom referred to an article in one of America's most influential religious papers which stated that the western nations were experiencing fundamental upheavals which would have repercussions in social and political readjustments for decades and quoted from the *Layman's Appraisment of the Work of Christian Churches among the Non-Christian Peoples of the Earth*, that it was no longer a case of which prophet or book or church but "the case that must now be stated is the case for any religion at all." (*BR*, Nov. 9, 1932.) In November, Professor M. A. Huggins was elected the new secretary, and 850 delegates pledged themselves "to cooperate heartily" with him in his "arduous duties."

Dr. and Mrs. Cullom continued helping students and townpeople as they could. More than one student stayed in Wake Forest by their kindness; others found meaning and purpose for their lives by the interest and love of their Bible teacher. Millard Brown would testify:

> When I was in the first semester of my sophomore year at Wake Forest, I felt called to the Gospel ministry, but I had had aspirations to become a lawyer. I sought Dr. Cullom's advice and help. He met with me one day in private conference in his classroom in the old administration building. . . . After kindly and fatherly pointing out some of the requisites and qualifications necessary for both the preaching ministry and the legal profession, then he said: "Let's have a word of prayer about what you ought to do." He got down on his knees, disregarding the oily floor, and prayed for me, asking God to give me a clear cut decision and to direct my life. His prayer was answered just a few weeks after that when I fully surrendered to enter the ministry. I consider his prayer to have been the turning point. (Letter, April 20, 1953.)

Before the Christmas holidays, Dr. Cullom gave to each of his students a small copy of Raphael's Sistine Madonna, which Dr. Cullom described as "the greatest painting in the world." (*BR*, Feb. 15, 1933.) The day after Christmas (1932), he performed the wedding ceremony for Nancy, his second daughter, and Lawrence Harris, a recent law-graduate and athlete of Wake Forest; the service took place in the Cullom home, with the family and a few close friends present.

On March 4, 1933, Dr. and Mrs. Cullom sat together before their radio and heard President Franklin D. Roosevelt make his inaugural address; immediately the new president led Congress in passing the new banking act, the farm relief bill, and the reforestation program. But shadows fell across Europe; on March 23rd, the German Reichstag voted (441 to 91) dictatorial powers to Adolf Hitler who promised to stamp out the enemies of the nation with "ruthless barbarity." The *Recorder* editor wondered how "the great German people" could submit to such a one; at an assembly of 75,000 people in Madison Square Garden, Bishop W. T. Manning (Episcopal), Bishop Francis J. McConnell (Methodist) and Mr. Al Smith (Roman Catholic) denounced the German persecution of the Jews.

On May 5th, 1933, about three o'clock in the morning, the town of Wake Forest was aroused by fire. The ninety-eight-year-old Wait Hall was aflame! The students who roomed in the dormitory wings of the building escaped uninjured, but all equipment and furnishings were destroyed; only the college records in a fireproof vault were preserved. The next morning Dr. Cullom was informed of the fire and told that "the boys" were saying when the fire reached his barrel of old sermons there was an explosion—so dry were they! Dr. Cullom laughed at their "little joke," but he grieved for the dear old college building and was concerned about his lectures. Arrangements were made for classes to be held in the halls of the literary societies and in the library. Mr. R. N. Simms of Raleigh came to Dr. Cullom's rescue; he sent his notebooks of Dr. Cullom's lectures. We might well believe that Dr. Cullom carried out President Kitchin's request for classes to be resumed "with no undue disruption," for his students were soon back to section VII, paragraph Capital B, item 4.

That spring Dr. Cullom preached the baccalaureate sermon at the Wake Forest public school and was given another opportunity to help Rev. C. C. Crow:

> During the trying days of "33" money was at a premium. Banks were closed. I had to have a little more money than I had to graduate. I met Dr. Cullom one morning and asked him if he could tell me where I might borrow . . . $25.00. He graciously consented to make me the loan. More than a year passed after I graduated before I was located in the active pastorate. Among the first moneys I received I sent him the twenty-five dollars and asked him to send me the amount of interest due. I received this statement from him "I am sending you the Dutchman's receipt 'I ish satisfied'." (Letter, Sept. 19, 1956.)

On May 12th, Dr. Cullom was in Cincinnati for a meeting of the College Committee of the Association Church Boards of Education, at which there was much discussion of the question, "Are our colleges side-stepping religion?" Dr. Robert L. Kelly, Executive Secretary of the Association, was asked to collect such data as he could on this subject; he, in turn, asked Dr. Cullom to assist him. Dr. Cullom wrote teachers of religion, college trustees and presidents, pastors and alumni of Baptist colleges for their answers to the question. In Spring Hope, the church voted to dispense with the evening services during the summer "to allow our pastor to go home on Sunday afternoon"; also the church clerk noted in his records that Dr. Cullom was to spend the latter part of August in "western North Carolina, Louisville and Chicago." Dr. Cullom took his family to Louisville, where Brother Ed had rented a furnished apartment for them; Dr. Cullom went on alone to the University of Chicago for "some courses."

Of the eight hundred and seventy-three students who enrolled for the fall term at Wake Forest, six hundred and ten were Baptist and seventy-four were ministerial students. J. Winston Pearce was president of the Ministerial Class; "under the leadership and guidance of Dr. W. R. Cullom," who had been "in direct charge of the class for thirty-seven years, the class studied the challenge of the present hour to the ministers of Religion" and other kindred topics. (Wake Forest College *Howler,* 1934.)

- 17 -

From the many answers he received to the question, "Are our colleges side-stepping religion?" Dr. Cullom wrote that there is much evidence that "the fruit of our college training is good" and cited several examples of Christian influence of teachers upon their students. (*BR,* Aug. 23, 1933.) However, one professor wrote: "There has been a strong disposition in some denominational colleges to assume no official and little personal responsibility for the religion of students." A trustee replied that before a faculty member was engaged inquiry was made of "his church relationship," but another wrote that he was forced to say the colleges were "side-stepping genuine Christian work." A pastor wrote that for several years he had felt "our Baptist Colleges were more interested in coming up to the standard and in producing a winning football team than in the religious life of the students." Another pastor stated:

> So many of our young people are returning from college with a wholly indifferent attitude toward religion. . . . It would be unfair to lay this blame altogether to our colleges when I see the growing and alarming tendency of a great host of fathers and mothers at home to neglect the work of the Kingdom. (*BR,* Aug. 30, 1933.)

One college president assured Dr. Cullom that by precept and example his college was trying "to make every student become loyal to Christ and to His teaching." Another said, "We have Bible courses for which college credit is given, and our chapel is an instrument for reaching the whole student body." A third one wrote:

> We hold a religious week each year with an outstanding minister as leader. . . . This comes in the middle of the year after the football season is over and before the baseball season begins. During that week we try to major upon religion and to get the whole college group to give religion the right of way, and to think and act accordingly. (*BR,* Sept. 6, 1933.)

In the fall (1933) Dr. Cullom performed the wedding ceremony for

Sarah, his youngest daughter, and Dr. C. Chilton Pearson; the service was conducted in the Cullom home with only the bride's family and a few friends present.

Dr. Cullom continued to evaluate the information he had received on the subject "Are our colleges side-stepping religion" and condensed it into these impressions, which he shared with the *Recorder* readers:

1. A marked change in the matter of atmosphere, in the matter of emphasis, and in the matter of standards of success has come into our Christian Colleges during the past fifty years. . . . In some respects life in college is much richer now than it was then, but it seems to be a fact, nevertheless, that there has come to pass in these institutions a marked loss of interest in what we used to think were cultural studies, in the matter of serious application to duty, and in the spirit of hard work.

2. A second observation is that these colleges are in their essential spirit and work a true and representative part of their own age. How could they be otherwise? Five years ago last March Dr. Rufus M. Jones of Harvard College read a paper before the World Missionary Conference. . . . [in which] he expressed the conviction that the greatest foe of both real and organized religion . . . at this time was . . . secularism. The conference agreed with Dr. Jones most heartily. A father in North Carolina some time ago entered a rather vigorous protest against the Christian Colleges of the State because they allow their students to smoke cigarettes. I asked this father whether his own sons smoked cigarettes at home. He admitted that they did! Our colleges are not monasteries shut off by high walls from the rest of the world. They are a part and parcel of the essential life of their age. . . .

3. A third observation is that there has come to pass amongst us a marked change in people's conception of the essential nature and purpose of religion itself. . . . A generation ago religion was largely a protest against some form of error; it was a matter of denominational loyalty; it was an effort to help people to escape the flames of hell and to prepare them to live in a future world; it was made up all too largely perhaps of taboos; it was more or less . . . of a negative character; it was rigid, crystallized, and (except on special occasions) quite dry and void of personal interest. . . . Over against all this, it seems to me that religion today is very much more of an experience of God as a present reality; salvation is an increasingly happy process; heaven is a present possession to a degree and a happy assurance of infinitely more of the same sort awaiting our attainments. . . . In my judgment we have a much more wholesome conception of religion than our fathers had fifty and a hundred years ago.

4. When we think of our colleges and of religion from the standpoint of former days we shall probably have to conclude that our colleges, in company with our homes and even with our churches, are side-stepping religion. When we bring ourselves, however, to think of religion as I have tried to describe it above, and bring ourselves to hope (and may we not say to believe?) that we are in the happy process of changing from the old to the new, and that we are beginning a new chapter in the matter of appropriating God's present love and grace, may we not assure ourselves that our colleges are trying to adapt their new point of view to the spirit and ideals of Jesus? One cannot but think here of the contrast that our Lord made on one occasion between Himself and John the Baptist. . . .

5. My last observation is that our colleges are really trying to lead a movement in home, in church, in business, in politics, in social life, in all life that shall make Jesus King of kings and Lord of lords. One may say that the wish is father to thought, and I am free to admit that much could be said for that view of the matter. Before any such conclusion is reached, however, it should be borne in mind that the most pessimistic

piece of evidence that I have gathered and furnished asserts that a change
for the better has been observed. My final word, then, shall be that I
will take my stand among those who "hope all things" and "believe
all things."

In concluding, Dr. Cullom exhorted the Colleges to realize their real
purpose and ultimate aims; to "our constituency," he urged that we all

"try to improve our own spiritual lives to the end that our homes may
send to our colleges boys and girls in whom a strong and wholesome
foundation of character has been laid," and that we make our churches
"generators of spiritual power." *(BR,* Jan. 24, 1934.)

Early in the morning of February 14, 1934, Wingate Memorial
Hall at Wake Forest was destroyed by fire; the priceless old oil portraits
which covered the chapel walls were irreplaceable. However, Dr. Cullom presented another treasure to the college library—a note-book,
"Toiling Up the Heights," which was made up of copies of the letters
which he had received from his fellow ministerial students in 1892;
in the preface, he wrote: "The students of today do not have the
disadvantages of those forty years ago; but if they are to succeed,
they need courage like theirs."

In May (1934), Wake Forest College celebrated its centennial
anniversary. The *Biblical Recorder* had a special issue, in which Dr.
Cullom wrote of the Department of Religion; four hundred and forty-
six men were enrolled in this department at that time. On May 30th,
the governor of North Carolina, representatives of all the colleges in
the state and many other distinguished guests assembled for the dedication of the new Wait Hall and for the Commencement; the college
was pleased to have seventy-eight of its alumni listed in the *Who's
Who in America,* and Dr. Cullom was one of them. *(BR,* June 6, 1934.)

That summer, Douglas M. Branch was doing odd jobs around Wake
Forest to enable him to continue his education; he often drove for
Dr. Cullom. On a hot Saturday afternoon, they were returning from
Spring Hope when one of the tires on Dr. Cullom's new Dodge went
flat. Mr. Branch pulled over to the side of the dirt road, got out, pulled
off his coat, rolled up his sleeves and changed the tire. Years later
he wrote:

Before re-entering the car I took my pocket handkerchief from my
pocket and wiped the dirt from my hands. You can imagine what this
did to the pocket handkerchief. I thought no more about the incident
and we drove on back to Wake Forest without further difficulty. A few
days later . . . I found at our front door a small package with my name
on it and taking the package inside my wife and I opened it to find
that it contained a new and very nice white linen pocket handkerchief.
(Letter, March 15, 1962.)

In an article, "Is Education a Blessing or a Curse?" *(BR,* Aug. 29,
1934), Dr. Cullom warned against the danger of knowledge without
Christ and told of a room of mirrors which distort a man's image until
he finds a particular spot which is in a cross; so it is in education—

only in the cross of Christ can man see himself as he really is and find the education that holds his ultimate future.

- 18 -

In the fall of 1934, the enrollment at Wake Forest College exceeded a thousand; Howard Ford, who was rooming in the Cullom home at that time, remembers that Mrs. Cullom was an invalid.

> She was greatly interested in the ministerial students of the college. She believed that a Baptist minister should be a student and show some evidence of culture. She would encourage the young minister to listen to good music. She would use any opportunity that presented itself to help him cultivate gracious manners and good table etiquette.

For two years, Mr. Ford drove Dr. Cullom to Spring Hope three Sundays in each month; during this time, he came to know Dr. Cullom "as the highest type Christian gentleman" he has ever known.

> He was also very prompt and regular in habit. We started our journey to Spring Hope on the minute. . . . We drove exactly fifty miles per hour except on curves and at intersections. If the speedometer reached fifty-two miles per hour he seemed to sense it without looking. Immediately there would be some gentle reminder such as this: "Ford, you are in a hurry this morning; are you not?" I would let it drop back to exactly fifty and he would relax.

In January of 1935, Dr. Cullom recommended Emil Brunner's *The Mediator* as "the most important contribution to Christian Theology in 1934" and at Nashville, Tennessee, shared in a conference on the New Training Course of the Baptist Sunday School Board. He also attended the annual meeting of the Council of Church Boards of Education in Atlanta, Georgia. In an article, "Uniting for attack on Secularism" (*BR,* Feb. 6, 1935), Dr. Cullom urged the church-related colleges to prove that they are "competent to educate our youth of today in a manner that will stem the tide of moral disaster."

> The only education that is really full and complete is the education that seeks to discover, to develop, and to link up the whole man with the essential tasks of the world. And the wise man of Hebrew literature makes very clear to us who the whole man is—it is the man who takes God into consideration and obeys Him. (Eccleciastes 12:13.)

Nor did he overlook the importance of the home in religious education. In another article he wrote: "I appreciate all that we are doing in our schools, but the great school of religion is the home and the chief teacher in this school is the mother." (*BR,* Feb. 6, 1935.) In a third article, he urged preachers to proclaim "the great facts and assurances of the Gospels" in the language of everyday life; let them "link up" these truths with "the homely problems and difficulties of daily living," if they really want to help people. He recognized that this type of preaching can come only as "the result of vital fellowship with God in

Christ and of intelligent, sympathetic fellowship with folks in their daily grind."

> If a man wants to preach to people in such a way as to help them, I would say, "Love the people and say what you please to them." Paul's pregnant saying about "speaking the truth in love" should hang as a perpetual motto over every minister's desk. *(BR,* March 20, 1935.)

Dr. Cullom described E. Stanley Jones's *Christ's Alternative to Communism* as "a singing call to God's people to let the world see who Christ is and what He proposes to do"; in Spring Hope, he taught Dr. P. E. Burrough's *Our Baptist People* to about fifteen or twenty men and women who met with him each Sunday evening, while B.Y.P.U. was in session, and recommended that other pastors try "this experiment in adult education." *(BR,* June 19, 1935.) In June, he represented Wake Forest College in the dedication of the Duke Chapel; in July, he wrote of the need of a new chapel at Wake Forest and envisioned "a beautiful building, in thorough keeping with the best traditions and with the present spirit of Wake Forest."

At the time when Italy invaded Ethiopia, Dr. Cullom gave the charge to George Griffin at his ordination in Pittsboro and, at the centennial celebration of the Wake Forest Baptist Church, reviewed the pastorates of five of her ministers. At the request of the General Board, he attended a meeting at Guilford College, on October 14th, at which a provisional constitution for the North Carolina Council of Churches was adopted. In the *Biblical Recorder* of November 6, 1935, Dr. Cullom stated that at the next Baptist State Convention a recommendation would be presented that "our people take the necessary steps of sharing in the councils and the work of this body"; he included the constitution for study and discussion. However, the Convention, meeting in Asheville that year, voted that neither the General Board nor the Convention would have any official connection with the North Carolina Council of Churches.

In the *Recorder* of February 19, 1936, Dr. Cullom (at 69) was described as "still in the vigor of his manhood"; "no one can estimate the service he has rendered as professor of Bible at Wake Forest College." In March, Dr. Cullom quoted from Dr. James Reid's *Why Be Good?*

> If goodness is to be rightly understood and to become the guiding principle of life, it must be seen in its true place, as the way of life that follows from a right relationship between us and God. What we call goodness cannot be separated from the view of life as fellowship with God in an eternal order into which he brings us in Christ. Only as we come into our place in that fellowship can we find the principles which guide our lives, the authority which binds because it is what our souls see to be good, and what is not least important, the power to be and do what we see to be right.

That was the March when Hitler sent German soldiers into the Rhineland, calling all agreements "scraps of paper." In an editorial on Negro

Education in North Carolina, the *Biblical Recorder* reported that in the hundred and twenty accredited high schools for Negroes in North Carolina, there were six thousand, five hundred Negro teachers and over twenty-five thousand Negro students; there were over five thousand Negro students in the Negro colleges of the State. (*BR,* March 25, 1936.) That spring the Wake Forest baseball team won the state championship, and refrigerators were displayed in Raleigh. At Spring Hope the church added three women to the board of Deacons, and Dr. Kyle Yates of Louisville assisted Dr. Cullom in conducting "the best revival" the church had had in several years. But there was another issue which was to overshadow all these—at least, at that time for most Baptists in North Carolina and for Dr. Cullom in particular.

- 19 -

In June of 1936, Wake Forest College concluded another year of progress; a new gymnasium was in use, and plans were made to build a new dormitory on the old Simmons corner. Upon a petition of the student body, the trustees authorized the use of the gymnasium by the students for faculty-supervised dances for one year. Editor Farmer of the *Recorder* was quick to say that the trustees had made a serious mistake; "many Baptists will think that faith has not been kept with those who with prayers and tears and sacrifices founded the college and have supported it through the years." (June 10, 1936.) He further declared (June 24th) that the action of the trustees "vitally concerns every interest of the Baptists of North Carolina," as Wake Forest College "sets the social standards for the Baptists of the State." Reaction was not slow in coming. L. L. Johnson declared, "Dancing stands among a company of evil things." E. G. Willis wrote, "The time has come for the Baptists of North Carolina to cry and cry aloud against this most ungodly practice." (*BR,* June 24, 1936.)

Al Martin, president of the student body, wrote that he was a ministerial student and did not dance, but he felt that the morals of the student body would be lifted if it were given clean and organized dances. (*BR,* July 15, 1936.) Editor Farmer asked for the names of the ministerial students, the sons of ministers and missionaries who voted for the dance. C. C. Jones noted that the school is "evidently quite different from what it was years ago"; then he added, "of course the daddies and mommies of these boys are different too." Protests and resolutions followed.

President Kitchin of Wake Forest was deeply troubled by all of this; he turned to Dr. Cullom who said:

> Dr. Kitchin, it is not a question of *whether or not* the men are going to dance; it is a question of *where* they are going to dance. It would seem to me much better to have a dance once or twice a month in the gymnasium from eight to one o'clock under the supervision of our

faculty than for the men to go over to Raleigh to have their dances in any kind of place for all kinds of hours.

Dr. Kitchin thanked Dr. Cullom and went home. The next morning he telephoned Dr. Cullom and asked if he might use what he had said for publication. Dr. Cullom replied, "Dr. Kitchin, I don't say a thing to which I would not sign my name; I'll prepare a statement at once." Dr. Kitchin showed Dr. Cullom's statement to Dr. Gulley, Dr. Gorrell, and Dr. Lynch who, of their own accord, added similar statements. On July 29, 1936, the *Biblical Recorder* was headlined with the caption "Four of the Old Guard Surrender" and gave the statements of the four professors. Eighty-one-year-old Dean Emeritus of Wake Forest College Law School, Dr. Needham Y. Gulley, said: "The majority of the Trustees thought it better to control the situation than to ignore it. I think they acted wisely." Dr. J. H. Gorrell, for forty-two years professor at Wake Forest College, stated:

> Dancing has become more or less common in every social community in North Carolina. The churches by and large do not and cannot prohibit dancing today. Wake Forest College cannot prohibit dancing. But Wake Forest College can and should control dancing.

Dr. J. W. Lynch, seventy-one-year-old professor of Religion at Wake Forest College whose pastorates include ten years at the Wake Forest Baptist Church, said he would infinitely prefer his two daughters' dancing in the presence of loved ones, friends and members of the faculty to their being out late at night in distant places among strangers. Dr. Cullom's statement was prefaced by the statement that in forty years of teaching Religion at Wake Forest College he had taught the majority of ministers who were pastors of Baptist churches in North Carolina. Dr. Cullom said:

> 1. It has been my thought and desire during my forty years teaching at the college to see an institution develop here that would foster and maintain such ideals and such a spirit as would tend to lead the students into a personal fellowship with Christ and into lives of rich usefulness in Kingdom service. I think our people should know that there has been and is still going on on our campus a movement toward the cultivation of these deeper and richer things.
>
> 2. The specific question of dancing is only one of such questions which are confronting us in all sorts of ways. With respect to the particular problem at hand, the trustees were not confronted with the question of dancing or not dancing. It was rather the question of dancing in all sorts of places and in all sorts of crowds or dancing in our own gymnasium in the midst of such people as would be acceptable to the mothers and fathers of those engaging in the dance. Under these circumstances, I am inclined to think that the trustees did the best thing.
>
> 3. Until homes, churches, and schools shall bring themselves to deal more adequately with the problem of begetting and fostering a deeper, richer, and stronger spiritual life in our people, we will not be in position to treat questions and issues that simply touch the surface.

Editor Farmer declared that the trustees and faculty of Wake Forest College needed prayer: "The Baptists of North Carolina want Christian ideals taught and practiced by the trustees, faculty and students in our colleges. They demand no less." (*BR,* July 29, 1936.)

The *Recorder* was filled with denunciation and protests: "Shocked." (J. Louis Price) . . . "I left a dance hall convinced of sin; now I am really disheartened . . . to see the people I had confidence in advocating the dance." (J. Andrew Morgan.) . . . "Wake Forest College will suffer unless the action is rescinded." (Alfred L. Chaplin.) . . . "betrayed." (Mrs. C. L. Westor.) . . . "Wake Forest College should no more permit dancing within her sacred walls than the 2,346 Baptist churches in North Carolina should permit it in theirs." (A. D. Kinnett.) . . . "If those who in their classrooms cannot conscientiously subscribe to the historical position of the denomination sponsoring them, then they should . . . resign." (John C. Cowell, Jr.) . . . "Now the students not only govern themselves but likewise the trustees and the faculty. And they would even have the Baptist denomination subject to their desires." (Theo. B. Davis.) . . . "Resolved that we, the Yadkin Association, go on record as protesting." (G. R. Renegan.) . . . "North Carolina Baptists will never stand for this thing." (T. L. Cashwell.) . . . "ashamed." (E. J. Harrell.) . . . "If they go far enough to have the first dance, it's goodbye, Wake Forest." (J. M. Fleming.) . . . "My head hangs in shame." (H. M. Stroup.) . . . "greatly humiliated" (I. L. Yearby.) . . . "Out of harmony with the life of an effective Christian witness." (R. A. Kelly.) . . . "Now, won't these dear saintly doctors look funny teaching the young ministerial students how to execute the various two-steps, the Charleston, and a lot of other shifts and slides?" (S. V. T. Chamblee.) . . . "There are hundreds of parents just now asking themselves why they should send their boys to Wake Forest." (D. B. Humphrey.)

D. M. Branch, president of the Ministerial Conference at Wake Forest, reported that the number of ministerial students favoring dancing could be "numbered on one's fingers"; another ministerial student declared: "It was quite a shock to us to see the men who taught us God's Word . . . come out in favor of worldly practices just because 'everybody else is doing it'." Mrs. J. L. Gillespie exclaimed "O, Dr. Cullom, why did you do it? Why?" (*BR,* Aug. 12, 1936.) Others joined the chorus: "I Thes. 5:22" (Kenneth Clark.) . . . "It is impossible to supervise without placing sanction upon the dance." (H. M. Hocutt.) . . . "I am grieved at the meat they are eating. Rom. 14:15" (W. C. Wescott.) . . . "Our churches have let down the bars for anything that the devil wants to put in . . . we have not obeyed God's word." (C. J. Ward.) . . . "Every Baptist Church . . . is vitally affected." (E. J. Harrell.) . . . "The attitude assumed by the teachers of the Bible at Wake Forest toward dancing . . . is more far reaching than it first appears." (M. A. Adams.) . . . "The college let in the 'Trojan Horse' when they let Greek letter fraternities in." (R. G. Kendrick.) . . . "resolved that we, the representatives of the churches of the Carolina Baptist Association, express our disapproval." (A. I. Justice.) . . . "Be it resolved by the Red Oak Baptist Church . . . that we protest." (Geo. May.) . . . "We, the Western Avenue Baptist Church of Statesville, do most earnestly express our disapproval." (C. J. Allen.) . . . "Be it resolved by all the pastors of the Eastern Baptist Association . . . that we . . . petition the Board of Trustees of Wake Forest College to rescind its action." (R. C. Foster.)

Dr. W. L. Poteat, who had been out of the state when the controversy began, tried to join the "four old guards," but his letter never appeared in the *Recorder*. However, Editor Farmer did print two letters in their favor. Mrs. Robert E. Royall stated that she had known "these wise, cultured, consecrated Christian gentlemen for fifty years as neighbors and friends" and confessed that it was beyond her comprehension why the religious paper of her denomination should insult them. Irving S. Carlyle said he could not stand by silently and see these four distinguished Christian gentlemen in their old age subjected to such unjust criticism.

> I have known each of these four gentlemen since the days of my early youth. They were teachers and my friends, and I say unhesitantly that there is nothing cowardly in the make-up of either of them. They are as fine, as true, as Christian men as ever ministered to their fellow men on this earth. When you say that these men have surrendered, you are mistaken. Sympathetic understanding, tolerance of the opinions of others, and a charitable attitude toward others are not the marks of a coward. I think you have done a grave injustice to these four noble men, and I hope that you will take steps to correct it. *(BR, Aug. 12, 1936.)*

During all of this, Dr. Cullom kept his "steady gait." It has been told that when he got his mail at the post office he would throw the *Biblical Recorder* in the wastebasket or run his walking stick through it; but he was not using a walking stick at that time, and such action would have been out of character. It is more likely that the sermon he preached in the Wake Forest Baptist Church on September 1, 1936, came the nearest of revealing his thoughts on the matter as anything he said or did. Pastor Easley was conducting a series of "Fellowship Services" that week in the church; Dr. Cullom was asked to speak on Tuesday evening and chose as his text Philippians 4:19—"My God shall supply every need of yours according to his riches in glory in Christ Jesus." Dr. Cullom began:

> Paul's message to the Philippians may be said to be a personal testimony growing out of his own experience of God's all-sufficient grace and help in every time of need. This day (September 1) is an important anniversary with me. Just fifty years ago today I walked into the Wake Forest campus for the first time. . . . If you will allow me, I should like to make my message to you this evening to be a word of personal testimony growing out of the gracious dealings of God with me through these fifty years.

Dr. Cullom told of his staying six years at Wake Forest and four at

Louisville; he spoke of his return to Wake Forest in 1896 and his teaching for forty years.

> Suffice it to say that God's hand and help have been too manifest all through these years to allow any question whatever. Difficulties have arisen, of course. Perplexities and many occasions of misgiving have had to be met. It has been my privilege during these years to be with many of you in this church as you too have walked through trying experiences. You, in turn, have walked with and helped me in similar experiences . . . All of us have felt to say with Cardinal Newman many time: 'Keep, thou, my feet; I do not ask to see the distant scene. One step enough for me.' Never has our God failed any of us, nor will He do so.

After speaking of our physical, mental and moral needs, Dr. Cullom mentioned those needs which we experience in times of crises, when

> we are thrust suddenly into a situation when we do not know what to do, nor what can be done. Our backs are against the wall. Help can come alone from some super-human source. These crises come all through life; they come in the hour of death. It is God who can enable one to say in such an hour, "I know whom I believed, and am persuaded that he is able to keep that which I have committed unto him against that day." . . . We should not wait for the hour of crisis to come upon us before beginning to cultivate acquaintance with God. Otherwise, we may render ourselves incapable of recognizing and of using His help in the hour when we need Him most.

Dr. Cullom then declared that the measure of this supply is not to be found in what we deserve, not in our goodness, not in our works; "the measure is 'according to his riches in glory.'

> One step I see before me,
> 'Tis all I need to see,
> The light of heaven more brightly shines
> When earth's illusions flee;
> And sweetly through the silence came
> His loving "Follow me."
> So on I go, not knowing
> I would not if I might,
> I'd rather walk in the dark with God
> Than go alone in the light.
> I'd rather walk by faith with him
> Than go alone by sight. (*BR,* Sept. 16, 1936.)

On September 16th, Wake Forest College opened with nine hundred, forty-seven students; the student body met and voted to withdraw its request for supervised dances on the campus. Immediately the Executive Committee of the trustees accepted the withdrawal of the request; Secretary M. A. Huggins stated that with this action, "We ought to consider the matter closed," and Editor Farmer urged his fellow Baptists "to devote our energy to the great work of promoting all our denominational work." (*BR,* Sept. 23, 1936.) At the Baptist State Convention which met that November in Durham, the General Board reported "a spirit of harmony, cooperation and hopefulness among our people." (*BR,* Nov. 18, 1936.) Dr. G. W. Paschal remembered the lingering of bitterness over the dance issue; "the convention came near to firing the trustees" and some went so far as to say privately that they didn't want "to be around a man like Cullom." This was hard to bear; years later Dr. Cullom would remark, "It seems that the brethren have never felt the same toward me as they did before." Yet he remaind "steady" in his place and at his task. He had not sanctioned dancing; never had he danced, nor had he ever attended a dance. As a member of the Convention's Committee on Civic Righteousness, he was in accord with its condemnation of dancing; at the same time, he had to confess that until the young people gave up dancing it seemed a part of wisdom to seek to regulate it.

- 20 -

In January of 1937 Dr. Cullom wrote again of the need of a chapel building on the Wake Forest campus:

> In this day when secularism, cynicism, and other sinister influences are working constantly and persistently among us to neutralize and undermine the teaching of the home and the church, and to beget an attitude of indifference and even (in many places) of hostility to all that our Lord stands for in the world, it is surely time when all that our Christian faith stands for should be asserted and emphasized in every practicable way on the campus of a Christian school. The chapel is not all that we need, but it is one thing that we need and need very much. *(BR,* Jan. 27, 1937.)

In April, Dr. Cullom urged the trustees and friends of Wake Forest to help the department of religion to keep abreast of "the best that is going on in its particular field." Quoting President Hatcher of the University of Chicago as calling for a concept of education which would enable men and women to see life as a whole, Dr. Cullom asked: And what place shall the teaching of religion fill in this endeavor to lead men into the conception of life as a whole? Dr. Cullom saw "the inevitable mingling and commingling of the world's various and sometimes opposing cultures and civilizations" as another stimulus to a renewal and enlargement of the department of religion at Wake Forest.

> What went on in Europe and Western Asia in the time of the Renaissance is going on today on a world scale. As we seek to introduce men to this situation and help them to get ready to take their places in it, what place and what emphasis is the teaching of religion to have? If we pass on to think of how the world's intellectual and mechanical developments have out-stripped that of its moral; if we think of the awakening in the Far East as its vast hordes of people begin to seize and apply the marvels of physical science to industry, to education, to war, and to every aspect of life; when we think of the world's problems of race, of nationalism, of class conflict, or what may well prove to be the real Armageddon for this age, surely the importance of putting the Christian Spirit and motive into the various sections and phases of the complicated and difficult situation assumes proportions that might stagger all of us. *(BR,* April 21, 1937.)

In June. a class of one hundred and seventy graduated from Wake

Forest, and the Board of Trustees voted "to give some relief from hard toil to its aged professors." Editor Farmer wrote:

> Taking full effect in June, 1938, a retiring allowance will be provided for all members of the faculty who are more than seventy years of age. Mr. J. M. Broughton, reporting the action of the Board at the Alumni dinner, showed up this in such an attractive light that it would be hard to see how any faculty member should regret its application to himself. And yet, it can easily be seen that when such men as W. L. Poteat, Sledd, Cullom, Lynch, Gorrell, and Gulley yield their places to other and younger men the change will not be unimportant. The character of the college will not be quite the same. *(BR,* June 9, 1937.)

Dr. Cullom protested this ruling; it seemed arbitrary and lacking in consideration for persons involved. Dean Bryan recalls Dr. Cullom's coming to his office, very much upset and hurt by it. Later at a conference, Dr. Cullom stated that he was worth as much to the college at that time as he had ever been. The college had never paid Dr Cullom more than $3,300 a year, and that would be cut, upon his retirement, to $1,200. (Later it would be increased to $1,806.72.) Dr. Cullom had not stinted himself or his means in the work of helping young ministers prepare themselves for the service of God. At times he gave all the money he had and borrowed more to help them; in fear of being carried away to the point of mortgaging his home to help some needy student, he had put the deed to their home in his wife's name. With Mrs. Cullom's declining health, some of his friends were concerned how he was to meet his financial responsibilities; Dr. Paschal wrote President Kitchin asking that something be worked out to help one who had served the college and denomination so well and so long, but nothing was to come of it. Dr. Cullom did not labor the point; he expressed his disapproval of depriving the college of the abilities and richness of its senior professors and returned to his work. That summer he carried a heavy teaching load in the summer-school of the college and did his regular church work at Spring Hope.

In August, at the Southern Baptist Education Commission at Ridgecrest, Dr. Cullom delivered an address, "The Education that Is Needed in Today's World," which was so well received that it was published in the *Review and Expositor* (January, 1938) and again printed in a separate pamphlet by the Education Commission. In "this scholarly interpretation of Christian education," Dr. Cullom diagnosed the "present-day world" by noting six of its characteristics.

> 1. It is a world whose foundations have been ruthlessly torn away . . . 2. It is a world in which the elementary forces of life are contending for the mastery with a sharpness, with a bitterness, and with a determination that at once constitute this conflict one of the major battles of the ages . . . 3. It is a world that is shot through with secularism . . . 4. It is a world in which there is much of uncertainty and confusion as to the real purpose and the proper direction of life . . . 5. Today's world is a world that despises sham, has a supreme contempt for hypocrisy and that demands genuineness in every sphere of life. Several generations of constant gazing through the microscope and through the tele-

scope has produced a frame of mind in the peoples of the earth that
demands that men see clearly all that can be seen, and then that they
report accurately and honestly what they saw . . . 6. It is a world in which
hosts of serious minded people—old and young—are honestly and earnestly trying to discover or rediscover, as the case may be, some eternal
verity or verities, if there be such, that will challenge the best that is
in them for life, for death (if need be), and for eternity.

Dr. Cullom said our times call for the laying of foundations for "a
structure that shall be no less than the realization of that all-compre-
hensive ideal of Jesus which He characterized over and over again
as 'The Kingdom of God'." Dr. Cullom noted the education for today's
world must,

first of all, seek to tell the truth, the whole truth and nothing but the truth.
Few things can do more to create a cynical attitude toward life than for
people to awake to the fact that they have been misled by their teachers.
Such a discovery was bad enough when the teachers involved were igno-
rant because they had no opportunity to know better. If the lives of such
teachers had been characterized by sincerity, sympathy, open-mindedness,
and a desire to teach only truth, the later discovery of mistakes on their
part is not so serious. But for teachers who had an opportunity to know
better and failed to make use of such opportunity through prejudice,
through laziness, or through careless indifference, to mislead people as
to the real facts of life is to create in such people a reaction that, to say
the least, is liable to kill in them all real interest in the search for truth.
When, however, a teacher really knows better and deliberately leads his
followers astray from strict truth, he will sooner or later be despised by
those whom he has thus misled and be held in supreme contempt by
them. . . .

2. The world calls for an education which "touches and brings to
their highest capacity every part of every man, and at the same time
puts men into touch with all their fellow human beings in the richest
and most vital sense possible"; the world needs "an education that
fits people in capacity, in sympathy, in purpose to be citizens of God's
universe."

3. Today's world calls for an education that finds in each human
personality an ultimate and entirely sufficient end in itself.

4. Today's world needs an education which will help people to see
and appreciate the deep and rich meaning of life; the Incarnation,
the Death and the Resurrection of Jesus Christ have created for
people "possibilities that could never have been dreamed of otherwise."

5. Today's world calls for education that recognizes man's life in the
flesh and life in the spirit are not two separate and distinct lives, but
that they are really one; the Great Teacher treated people always as
living in the immediate presence of God and represented the privilege
of fellowship with the Eternal through faith as always a present and
perpetual opportunity held out to men.

6. The world needs an education that "is centered and grounded in
the risen and ever-living Christ." Some years ago Lloyd George was
quoted as saying that it was either "Christ or chaos" for the world, and
Jesus likened those who heeded his words unto a wise man who built his

house upon the rock. Surely any education that seeks to lay fresh
foundations for life must seek to ground itself upon the center of
moral gravity as set forth in the sermon on the Mount.

> When we think . . . of men in the past who have been creators of
> new civilizations, and of how these men found their inspiration, their
> power and their guidance in what they believed was the presence and
> help of the living Christ, we are brought to feel again that to-day's
> world needs very much just such men to relay its foundations in truth,
> in justice, in love. I have in mind here such men as Paul of Tarsus,
> Augustine of Hippo, Francis of Assisi, Martin Luther, John Wesley,
> and Walter Rauschenbusch. Where these men have touched the world
> it has taken a new start for good. And they would all subscribe most
> heartily to Paul's pregnant statement: "I have been crucified with Christ;
> and I no longer live, but Christ lives in me."

- 21 -

At the opening of Wake Forest College, Judge Hubert E. Olive
drew "a striking parallel between 1937 and 1914," and Archibald M.
McMillan described this 104th session of the college as "unique in
that six widely-known members of the faculty will be teaching for the
last time." Dr. Cullom did not change his pace; he taught as he had
for forty-one years. His classes were crowded as students realized that
this would be their last chance to study under him. He walked back
and forth from his home to the campus, and looked very much as he
had for years. The students still called him "Potty"; his glasses were
thick and he had to use a magnifying glass to help them. Mrs. Cullom
read for him at home, and Miss Georgia Godfrey did his typing.
Different students drove for him and helped with his papers.

On February 23rd, Editor Farmer reported that Dr. J. W. Lynch
was back in his classes after having suffered a heart attack in January;
four days later Editor James S. Farmer himself suffered a fatal attack.
On March 12th, Dr. W. L. Poteat had just finished "a light supper"
when the death angel called his name; he answered,

> "Adsum" (I am here), and went off with the heavenly messenger with
> all the readiness and cheerfulness that he ever showed when he was
> starting, bucket and net in hand, with a class of students to collect algae
> and other biological materials. (*BR*, March 16, 1938.)

Dr. Cullom grieved for these friends, but he kept at his tasks; on
March 13th he assisted in the ordination of Albert M. Simms at the
Tabernacle Baptist Church of Raleigh and helped plan for a Seminar
on Christianity at Wake Forest. In the latter part of March, President
Kitchin announced that Dr. O. T. Binkley had been elected "head of
the Wake Forest School of Religion." Dr. Cullom stayed at his teaching
and preaching; in Durham, he assisted in the ordination of R. T. Hower-
ton, II, and preached the ordination sermon for Henry E. Walden, Jr.,
at Rockingham.

On May 25, 1938, the *Biblical Recorder* had a picture of four
16

"distinguished members of the 'Graduating Class' "—the quartet of
Wake Forest College professors who would retire from active service at
the end of the academic year. At the last meeting of the ministerial
conference for the year, Bill Hicks of Raleigh made the motion that
the class be named "The Cullom Ministerial Conference," and every
student stood up. A beautiful engraved key was presented to their
retiring leader and friend. There were twenty-one ministerial graduates
in the class of one hundred, seventy-eight; the campus, with "its
well dressed lawns and flowering magnolias and other trees, was a
delight to the returning former students." The *Recorder* reported:

> Much interest was manifested in the retiring professors, who like run-
> ners in an ancient torch-race, are handing on the lamp of knowledge to
> others. Among these we count Dr. W. L. Poteat, so recently departed.
> We hardly knew how much we missed him till this time of commence-
> ment. He was not there, and all were conscious of it at every turn.
> It was fitting that there should have been a memorial service for him
> in the church on Sunday night.
> The other four, Dr. N. Y. Gulley, Dr. J. W. Lynch, Dr. W. R. Cullom,
> and Dr. B. F. Sledd, were recognized with much honor at the alumni
> meeting and heard with a spirit of affection which prevaded the entire
> assembled group. All realized, as they heard the farewell messages,
> that the college is now losing the active service of the men who have
> had no little part in promoting its development and gaining respect for
> the character of the training of its students.

Again Dr. Cullom was leaving the college. Some of the thoughts
which he had had when he came from the examination of the Board
of Education in 1886 must have come again. Something of the experience on that spring morning in 1892 when, upon graduating,
"mist" had come into his eyes, must have occurred again. But there
was more; the ruling of retirement seemed arbitrary. He was in good
health and mind and still could be of service to the college he loved.
He could not have failed to contrast, at least in his own mind, the
privilege and pleasure of teaching which had been afforded Dr. Taylor,
Dr. Royall and others in their old age with what the new ruling
would mean to him. Yet he would not let bitterness linger in his
heart. At that time, a good revival service was concluding at Spring
Hope; Dr. Cullom reviewed the book of lectures given at the Wake
Forest Seminar on Christianity and trusted that the Lord still had
work for him to do.

"Judge not the Play before the Play is done;
Her Plot has many changes; every day
Speaks a new scene; the last act crowns the play."

FRANCIS QUARLES

SEVENTH AGE

FRUITFUL IN RETIREMENT

1938-1962

Dr. Cullom loved Spring Hope. And Spring Hope loved Dr. Cullom. Mrs. A. T. May said, "He came into the hearts of us all"; Mrs. G. W. Bunn, Jr., felt like "we have always known and loved him." Agnes Brantley Brantley, who had known him as her pastor at Wakefield, felt "like he was a member" of her family; her husband said, "Dr. Cullom always brought happiness with him; he made us all feel good." Once when Mrs. Theo Easom remarked before her daughter that no one was perfect, Mary Helen replied, "O, yes, there is—Dr. Cullom." After a pause Mrs. Easom said, "Well, I suppose he is as near being perfect as anyone." Mrs. O. B. Baines remembers sitting on the porch with her husband one Sunday afternoon when Charles Cree Hunter, their five-year-old grandson, called out happily, "Yonder comes Dr. Cullom. When I grow up, I want to be a preacher just like him!"

P. E. Daniel recalls Dr. Cullom's saying, "A person shouldn't just like what he is doing; he should love it." Mrs. L. T. Bartholomew, who served as B.Y.P.U. president for nine years, tells: "We ate when Dr. Cullom was here; we had suppers for the choir members, for the Sunday school teachers and officers, for the graduating class of the public school, and we had 'a cup of tea' over in the pastor's study for nearly every Board and Committee meeting." When Mr. and Mrs. F. D. Bissette were building their new house, Dr. Cullom told them to build a room for him; upon its completion he came to use that room for six years. Often he found the mother reading Hurlburt's Bible Stories to Maxine and Ted; often she took him visiting in the community. Mrs. J. A. Tunnell was another one to take him visiting; in her Pontiac they toured the country—singing for the shut-ins, distributing religious tracts and fruit. Dr. Cullom's visits were short, and he made many of them in an afternoon; often his companion would be "worn out" while he was still going strong. In his anxiety to help others, he sometimes imposed on the generosity of those who wanted to help him. Once, for example, a good woman got out of bed to take him visiting; after about ten calls, she invited him to her house for supper. That was agreeable to him; then he suggested, "Just go in and fix something light and then we can keep right on with our visiting." And she did! M. E. Edwards first met Dr. Cullom at Mrs. Saunders' boardinghouse; he would say:

> Dr. Cullom is dear and close to us all. But I have to tease him about being a woman's man. When he comes to town, he telephones all the women and inquires of their health and family. And not once have I heard him call a man!

O. B. Moss, teacher of the Men's Bible Class, confesses that there were times when he differed with Dr. Cullom; "as a master of diplomacy, Dr. Cullom would postpone a decision until he could get the women behind him, and then they would put it over." Like all the rest, Mr. Moss loves Dr. Cullom; he describes him as "very appreciative, forgiving, patient, gentle and sweet—and stubborn for what he thought was right."

During the depression, there were times when the people had very little to give their pastor; but Dr. Cullom said nothing about it. Some of the people became ashamed and went around, soliciting what they owed him. R. L. Pitts remembers Dr. Cullom's talking of Hitler's coming to power and was troubled about the world conditions; "he saw further ahead than the rest of us." G. C. Lassiter recalls Dr. Cullom's asking him to introduce a missionary to the church; later he told Dr. Cullom that he had played ball before large crowds of people but never had been as scared as he was that Sunday morning. When Lenore Stone came to teach music in the Spring Hope school, "Red" Lassiter persuaded her to make it her home, and soon she took her place beside her husband in the church; she found Dr. Cullom spoke with authority and conviction and was very appreciative of the work of the choir. J. A. Morgan waited on Dr. Cullom in the barber shop; he also worked with him in the church and would testify: "He has the best understanding of human nature of any one I know; he can handle all kinds of situations and always manages to say the right thing at the right time."

When he became principal of the public schools of Spring Hope in 1938, M. V. Parrish was surprised to find Dr. Cullom was still pastor there; as a student at Wake Forest, he had come over to Spring Hope to sing in a quartet for Dr. Cullom. Mrs. Parrish appreciated Dr. Cullom's kind words of praise when something was well done; "there were also times when he expressed his disapproval, but he was kind then too." Dr. J. R. Vann and his fiance had taken Dr. Cullom to the dedication of the Duke Chapel; later Dr. Cullom went to Clayton to marry them. Although Lena Waller was not of his church, Dr. Cullom was among the first to come to see her when her father died; when she and Garland Morgan were married, she received "a wonderful letter" from him, as she did when they moved into their new house and when each of their children was born. Mrs. Morgan would say: "I was amazed at the time he had for everyone; his family must have sacrificed a great deal for the rest of us."

In the summer of 1938 Dr. Cullom wrote of the need of putting the petition "Thy Kingdom Come" into our plans as well as into our prayers; he presented the Rev. and Mrs. C. K. Djang, a cultured and charming young Chinese couple, to his congregation in Spring Hope. The Munich crisis came that fall. In an article, "The War to End War," Dr. Cullom quoted Dr. John B. Macbeath as saying that to end war we must engage in a greater war against evil, prejudice, rancour, bitterness, selfishness, and sin; he pleaded for the application of the teachings of Christ. To those who might say those teachings would not work in this hardboiled world, Dr. Cullom asked if the spirit of enmity and revenge had worked.

> As the Christmas season approaches and the song of the angels shall be heard afresh in all the earth, shall we not try, each in his own "little corner" to do what we can to bring in that spirit of "peace on earth, good will to men?" (*BR*, Dec. 14, 1938.)

- 2 -

In January, 1939, Dr. Cullom attended the North Carolina Council of Churches in Durham and heard Dr. Clark M. Eichelberger declare that history may say that in 1918 the world turned back to the Dark Ages. In an article, "Southern Baptists and the 'Religious Fascists'," Dr. Cullom expressed regret that the Commission of Social Service of the Southern Baptist Convention had not replied to the request of the Department of Research and Education of the Federal Council of Churches of Christ in America in the spirit in which the request was made. He thought the principle of "the competency of the individual soul under God" ought to "put Baptists in a position to exercise a patience and generosity in dealing with others that would make them a peculiar people." He asked if, by our aloofness, we were not in danger of sacrificing "an opportunity to bear testimony to 'the precious faith' that we hold to be so dear" and of losing "altogether that sense of fellowship with many who do not see exactly as we do but who in their heart of hearts do hold this 'like precious faith with ourselves'." (*BR*, March 22, 1939.) In a later article, Dr. Cullom told of changing from saying "I am a Baptist, *but* I love everybody" to saying "I am a Baptist; *therefore*, I love everyone." He testified that this change of one word had affected "in a most helpful way" his attitude toward other people. (*BR*, April 12, 1939.)

At the time when Hitler was taking possession of Czechoslovakia and when Mussolini was threatening Albania, Dr. Cullom wrote that it was not "the combined ravages of Hitler, Mussolini, Japan" which alarmed him; he believed the psalmist who exclaimed, "The kings of the earth counseled together against Jehovah . . . but he that sitteth in the heavens will have them in derision." Rather Dr. Cullom told of attending a social club of men where some of the deacons of the church were planning for some activity on Wednesday night without the slightest concern for the regular Wednesday night prayer-service; he wrote of having a class on being a Christian for boys and girls for an hour once a week and of having several mothers "forgetting it and taking their children off to some other place." When will we become alarmed at what is going on in our own hearts, homes, churches and communities? he asked. "Everything about us would suggest that there is no time to lose!" (*BR,* April 12, 1939.)

At the Baptist World Alliance in Atlanta, representatives of German Baptists reported that they were free "to preach the gospel and to organize churches without let or hindrance on the part of the Reich government." G. W. Paschal wrote: "It is much the same as it was in the New Testament times in the Roman Empire of Paul's day. . . . The Baptists of Germany are preaching the simple gospel of the New Testament; they are not trying to determine the policies of the Reich." (*BR,* Aug. 23, 1939.) But was this enough? Under the title "The Church in the Present World Crisis," Dr. Cullom shared (Aug. 30, 1939) with his *Recorder* friends this pertinent extract from Basil Matthews' *Through Tragedy to Triumph.*

> The State has, in many parts of the world, steadily, and since the Great War, rapidly elbowed its way into a control of every aspect of life. While the extension of educational and other services may be helpful, the conscious endeavor to mold all its citizens not only to external obedience but to inner conformity with its imposed pattern vitiates these benefits. This, if achieved, must spell death to the Christian church, for the very core of the kingdom of God is the association of persons free to attain to their highest development in a fellowship of love and justice with God and each other.
>
> There can therefore be no basis of international justice and law to regulate its action between nations unless each nation recognizes the sovereignty of the righteous will of God. The church in each nation, as the interpreter of this righteous will, must act perpetually as the conscience of the nation, recalling it continually to the will of God. . . . Living thus within all nations and able to see from within the needs of each, and yet in its universal character seeing them from the eternal standpoint and in a world perspective, the church is in a position of superlative opportunity and responsibility.

On August 26th, as he returned home from the Education Commission of the Southern Baptist Convention at Ridgecrest, Dr. Cullom was met in the yard by his daughter, Nancy, who told him that her mother had fallen; she had put her cane on a rug in the bathroom and it had slipped, throwing her against the bathtub and hurting her across the chest. When Dr. Cullom saw Mrs. Cullom, he found her bruised and sore from her fall but no bones had been broken. However, her weakened condition would keep her in bed for the remainder of her life. She remained cheerful and bright and continued to run her house and to read to her husband. And Dr. Cullom continued his writing; he told how much the conception of "a progressive revelation" had helped him in understanding the Bible and that he had often wished for someone to give this doctrine a faithful application to the central themes of the Bible. He wrote:

> When I had finished reading *A Guide to Understanding The Bible* by Dr. Harry Emerson Fosdick . . . I said to myself that my wish had at last been realized . . . I do not mean that any man should swallow all that Dr. Fosdick says. I always read a book as I eat fish—take the

meat and lay aside the bones. But Dr. Fosdick has given us in this volume the cream of his many years of painstaking, careful, and thorough study of the Bible. *(BR,* Sept. 20, 1939.)

On September 1, 1939, Adolph Hitler sent his troops across the Polish frontiers. America was uneasy, but President Roosevelt assured the people by radio that he would do everything possible to keep America out of the war. Dr. Cullom continued to express great concern over the world-situation; he was not unduly pessimistic, but he was a realist enough to know that Europe was undergoing a terrible ordeal and that America would not be spared. In Spring Hope, some of the people wanted a more popular appeal and said a change would do the church good; others argued that Dr. Cullom's sermons were always good and that everyone loved him. In September, Dr. Cullom presented his resignation, but the church declined to accept it; R. L. Pitts said he could no more vote against Dr. Cullom than he could against Jesus Christ.

While the Second World War raged on two continents and seven seas, Dr. Cullom wrote one of his finest articles. *(BR,* Nov. 1, 1939.) After describing the trying times through which the world was passing, Dr. Cullom stated that Christ has "an assuring message for us" in such an hour.

> For the past few generations people have been making such wonderful discoveries in the field of the natural sciences and have been so busy with the task of applying these discoveries to the business of everyday living, that they have well-nigh forgotten the fact that "every good gift and every perfect gift is from above. . . ." In the sudden enjoyment of the abundance of the gifts, men have forgotten the Giver. . . . There is nothing that this generation needs more than to be brought to understand and to feel that "man does not live by bread alone!" There is something in a human being that can never be satisfied with "things." He may take his substance, wander off into a far country, spend it with riotous living, and think forsooth that this is life. But soon or late (may it not be too late for the men and women of this generation) he becomes hungry and longs for his Father's home and fellowship. Ours is a generation that has become so absorbed in things as to forget God. Unless 1 am greatly mistaken there is a deep hunger of soul that is crying out for fellowship with the Eternal. This is the first aspect of the message of Jesus to our day. He would tell men that the fear of the Lord is the beginning of wisdom, and would remind them that God is near, knocking at the door and seeking to enter in and bring an assurance, a satisfaction, and such power to help and blessing as can come from no other source.

Christ would call for "a new evaluation of man" as the second phase of His word for us. Dr. Cullom recalled that in his early days he heard laborers on his father's farm spoken of as "hands"; this term was so common that no one suspected that there was any lack of respect in it, but when we shall come to see our fellowmen through the eyes of Jesus we shall think of them as brothers and not as "hands," or labor or cannon-fodder.

> The most elementary concept in the teaching of Jesus is that of the family. The Model Prayer begins with the words "Our Father." God is

thought of as a Father of all peoples, races and classes, and men and
women are thought of as brothers and sisters in this ideal home. To
bring all of this to a direct and happy realization would surely be one
of the pressing demands of Jesus on this generation.

Dr. Cullom understood the third demand in the word of Jesus to be
the union of religion and life; this would amount to a reversal of
our estimate and use of religion.

> The elementary habits and the essential institutions of religion have
> been crowded out until they have come to have scarcely any place in the
> daily routine of the general run of people. Prayer and worship, the Bible
> and the church, the sabbath day, and the family altar, the habit of wit-
> nessing, and the work of the kingdom of God have all come to be more
> or less (and I fear very much more than less) conspicuous for their
> absence. And all this, surely, is exactly the opposite of what Jesus
> would have among his people.

But Dr. Cullom found evidences of a change; he noted the crowds
who attended the Preaching Mission and the demand for books and
guides of devotional literature; he wrote of how men "who have a
really spiritual message" are sought after. These observations led to
the fourth aspect of Christ's word.

> Our Lord is saying to the people of this day, "Believe on me," for
> "I am the way, the truth, and the life." . . . When a man gets himself
> subjected to the eternal Christ, and especially to the Christ of Calvary,
> he finds for the first time his true self, the self that God intended him
> to be.

Dr. Cullom concluded his article with Isaiah's exhortation (Isaiah
55:1-3).

As Hitler sent (May 10, 1940) his mechanized legions on a
Blitzkrieg (lightning war) through the Netherlands, Luxembourg and
Belgium, America was "profoundly moved . . . from coast to coast"
with the realization that Hitler might conquer the allies. (*BR,* May 29,
1940.) Dr. Cullom shared in this concern, but he was far from
becoming panic-stricken. He noted Dr. E. Stanley Jones's contrast (*Along the Indian Road*) between "the dead empires with their
dead dictators" and the Kingdom of love with its living Lord; he
quoted Dr. Jones as saying: "When the years and centuries have
spoken against the hours they will proclaim the fitness of this Man
(Jesus) to rule—and no other." Dr. Cullom concluded, "Surely Christ
is abundantly adequate for all roads, for all centuries, and even for
the eternal ages, whatever they may hold in store for us." (*BR,* May 29,
1940.)

- 3 -

In June (1940), the Southern Baptist Convention met in Baltimore;
Dr. John Calvin Slemp, the new editor of the *Biblical Recorder,*
charged it was insensitive to the needs of a changing world.

> Hour after hour was given to reading and discussing printed reports . . . while the mechanized columns of the nazis were striking at the heart of France . . . No word was spoken about justice and right in international sharing as foundation principles of a lasting peace. In a time when, if ever, the moral and ethical principles of Jesus needed sounding from the housetop . . . the Convention was busy with other matters.

However, a committee was appointed to answer an appeal to American Baptists from the British Baptists for a loan of $250,000 with which to support their 407 foreign missionaries during the war; the committee recommended that Southern Baptists alone make "an outright gift" of $200,000 and undertook to raise it by July 21st. While this was in progress, Dr. Cullom wrote an article, "Secularism and the Kingdom of God," in which he stated that when Judah had failed in her high and sacred mission in the time of Jeremiah, God turned to the individual soul as the seat of his sanctuary and power; this was true again in the time of John the Baptist and of Jesus.

> It was this same great fact of God in the soul of the individual believer that was to revolutionize the world and bring in the immediate reign of God. As often as this truth has become obscured . . . some prophet has been raised up to reassert it in the name and in the spirit of his Master . . . And so, may it not be that the very secularism which is so rampant, and which is serving as an acid to undermine and destroy the hollow and meaningless forms that would put themselves in the place of this first-hand knowledge of God . . . may it not be that this very secularism is to be used of God to prepare the way for the restoration of that which has been the salvation of his people in the past, and which must constitute the saving salt of men and peoples to the end? . . . Over and over again institutions as such have failed in the task of planting the kingdom of God in the earth, and it has been necessary for God to take possession of and use individual men to usher in the new day and to call men back to the living way. May not this secularism prove to be the negative preparation for a new and first-hand knowledge of God? But what man, or what group of people will now become the channel for this new and fresh entrance of God into the hearts and lives of his people? (*(BR,* July 31, 1940.)

In August, Dr. Cullom attended an Ashram conducted by Dr. E. Stanley Jones, served as chairman for the annual meeting of Bible teachers and teachers of religious education in Southern Baptist Colleges, and wrote another major article, "Variety in Unity."

> That it is God's will that his people should be united in the great and vital things is clear from our Lord's great intercessory prayer (John 17:20-21) . . . That it is the Father's will, likewise, that there should be variety in this unity is equally clear . . . The botanists tell us that no two leaves in the forest are exactly alike. Certainly no two human beings have ever been found to be exactly alike . . . In the Bible we observe a variety that is equally as marked.

After citing Paul's description of the Christian Church as a human body, Dr. Cullom concluded that God wills "both unity and variety."

> Whatever unites people around the will and purpose of God is sound, and whatever tends to draw people away from this will and purpose is of the evil one and is to be avoided. Let us rejoice that our God has

a place and a task for all sorts and sizes of people. Only one type of person need fear rejection at the hand of the Lord of the harvest— namely, the person who persists in setting up and in trying to establish and perpetuate his own will instead of the Will of God.

Dr. Cullom reasoned that the knowledge of such variety and unity should make us more tolerant of those who differ with us.

It is easy for "mydoxy" to be thought of as orthodoxy and "yourdoxy" to be defined as heterodoxy . . . Most of us would do well to read often the metaphor about the "mote" and the "beam" (Matt. 7:3) and the parable of the unforgiving servant (Matt. 18:21-35). This does not imply by any means that one is to go on "any sort of an old way" and make no distinction between what is right and what is wrong. It is far from it. It means that all must stand on the same level before God and ask simply, humbly, and honestly as to what is God's will on every detail. The man who does this will be slow to sit in judgment against his fellow man. God is the Judge of us all. Each in his own place and to the measure of his own light and opportunity, therefore, must seek to find and follow the will of God.

The knowledge of God's will for unity and variety "will lead us to appreciate and even to learn from those who differ with us."

I never allow myself to read just one side of a question. Both my background and my temperament lead me to be a rather extreme conservative in my thinking and in my actions. As a rule, however, I have tried to hear or read what the liberal has to say before making up my mind, and *vice versa* as to the conservative. For example, I have read *The Christian Century* for a long time, but I have also read the *British Weekly* with equal care and consistency. For me the two papers supplement each other in a beautiful and helpful way. Such a habit does not tend to create conformity to routine, but, in my judgment, it does tend to broaden and enrich one's sympathies and outlook on life. Of course one may become unbalanced and one-sided in either direction. Paul's principle here, as is generally true, is the wise one, namely, "Examine all things, and hold fast to that which is good." But what is to be the touchstone or the plumb-line of what is good? Here, again, we are brought back to the matter of interpreting and applying the will of God. And how fortunate we are at this point that we have "in our own tongue wherein we were born" the Book whose keynote from Genesis to Revelation is that of helping people to see what is God's will on every question and issue of life!

Dr. Cullom concluded that where Christlikeness is maintained "there will certainly be unity; and where each one is trying honestly and faithfully in his own way to attain unto this standard, it is equally certain that there will be variety." (*BR,* Aug. 28, 1940.)

Often Dr. Cullom had told his students that we need some man to set forth a statement of the Christian thesis which would constitute a sort of summary of the best that had been thought and experienced in our times; when he finished reading Dr. Harris Franklin Rall's *Christianity: An Inquiry Into Its Nature and Truth,* Dr. Cullom thought this came nearer doing this than anything he read. (*BR,* April 2, 1941.) In an article, "Religion and Education" (*BR,* April 9, 1941), Dr. Cullom declared that the intent of the first amendment of the Constitution of the United States was to prevent the establishment of a state church, and not to separate *religion* from the state; however, Dr. Cullom noted, there has been "a steady and progressive elimination of religion from public education" until we are in danger of rearing a people who are progressively pagan in attitude, ideals and actions.

- 4 -

At the time when Adolph Hitler sent three million men across the Russian border, Dr. Cullom wrote "A Faith for the Present Darkness" (*BR,* July 9, 1941), in which he remarked that the armistice of November 11, 1918, had turned out to be "only an armistice" and wondered, when shall we be able to begin that task of real reconstruction that is to give us a better world in which to live?

> Our souls are made to cry out in the language of the martyrs in that early Christian persecution, "How long, O Master, the holy and true, dost thou not judge and avenge our blood on them that dwell on the earth?"

Yet Dr. Cullom believed that the world was undergoing "the removing of those things which are shaken, as of things that are made, that those things which cannot be shaken may remain." (Heb. 12:27.) In a later article, "Faith and Reality" (*BR,* August 6, 1941), Dr. Cullom declared that "the faith which meets the needs of men in this day" must be grounded in "the very nature of things in the universe of which we ourselves are a part." He called for a faith "that really believes God governs the world—all of it, the present as much as the future, the here and now as truly as the there and then." He lamented that some people, convinced that certain expressions in the Word of God are figures of speech, abolish the reality that undergirds such expressions, while others take the bold imagery of the Bible as fact rather than poetic imagery. He stated:

> We need to take the figure for what it means to say, use it accordingly, and pass on. The simple fact is that the real truth lying back of such figures of speech is infinitely more awful or more glorious as the case may be than any such figures could possibly be if taken literally.

When Jesus spoke to Nicodemus of the necessity of a first-hand contact with God, Nicodemus was so hardened and crystallized in his thinking that he would see nothing but physical facts.

> There was a day when God accommodated himself to the childhood of his people and dwelt in tents and handmade temples, but now the time has come when fellowship with him is . . . real in the person of the Eternal Son . . . Let us not be afraid of reality, but rather insist on it and seek it with all diligence and with all patience.

Dr. Cullom stated that the faith which we seek must show it is capable of practical application to the needs of our world.

As I recall my earliest impressions of such matters I thought that the main tenets of the Baptist faith were two: "immersion" for baptism and "close communion" in the administration of the Lord's Supper. In the same way I thought the main tenets of the Methodist Church were two: "sprinkling and pouring" for baptism and "falling from grace" as a sort of human privilege. Who can wonder that sixty years later our churches are so weak when it comes to thinking of the great verities of our holy faith? I am raising no objection here to the teaching of either group as to the practices mentioned. The point that I am insisting on is that we might believe all that either group taught as to these matters, or even all that both groups taught and yet be as poor as the traditional turkey of Job when it comes to "the weightier matters of the law, judgment, mercy and faith." It is all right for people to try honestly and faithfully to follow the teachings of the Bible in matters of form and letter; but it is also important and even more important that people should go back of the form and the letter to the underlying spirit and purpose of God in such form and letter. There is high authority for saying . . . "These ought ye to have done and not to leave the other undone."

In August, Dr. Cullom attended the Association of Southern Baptist Teachers of Bible and Religious Education at Ridgecrest and wrote "The Return to Religion and Common Sense" (*BR,* Aug. 27, 1941), in which he told the experience of Henry C. Link who grew away from the Christian teachings of his childhood home to find that as a psychiatrist he was suggesting to his patients the very principles of life which had been taught in his father's home and church. Dr. Cullom was convinced that when we get back to the most elementary and essential principles of life we shall find that Jesus Christ enunciated them in the Sermon on the Mount.

In Spring Hope, Dr. Cullom set goals for the church to attain; some argued that they were doing all that they could and grumbled that they could do no more. Others thought they needed a resident minister. Dr. Cullom was not very well and asked different leaders in the church if they thought it best for him to resign. In September, he again presented his resignation; the vote was close, and several of the ladies began to cry. The minutes state: "In September (1941) the church met in conference and voted to accept the resignation of the pastor, Dr. W. R. Cullom." (From the retirement policy which the church had taken out with the Relief and Annuity Board of the Southern Baptist Convention, Dr. Cullom was to receive $30.00 a month for the rest of his life.)

In his article "Faith and the Spirit of Inquiry" (*BR,* Oct. 15, 1941), Dr. Cullom stated that many are in the state of childhood—believing whatever they are told to believe. Such was the belief of Job's comforters who repeated the harsh conclusions of former generations, whereas Job persisted in his inquiry until he broke through these traditions and came into real fellowship with God. In God's words to Eliphaz (Job 42:7), Dr. Cullom saw "a sort of eternal verdict" pronounced against "this rigid, unquestioning attitude"; "the approval of God . . . rests upon those who, like Moses (Ex. 3:3-8), 'turn aside to see' and who dare to ask, 'Why'." This does not mean that each man is left to follow his own thought, for faith comes to regulate, limit and bring "one into subjection to a Higher Power," to which there is a witness within one's own spirit (Rom. 1:19) and the testimony of the universe about us (Rom. 1:20). He who is "the way, the truth and the life" came as "the light of life" to those who live in fellowship with the living God and who follow where His spirit leads. The message of Christian history might well be summed up in the statement of John Robinson to the departing Pilgrim fathers: "There is more light to break forth from God's Word." The world needs a faith which approaches life with an open mind, with a sincere purpose to find and follow truth wherever it may lead, with a courage that is willing to suffer rather than compromise, and with a strong conviction that such a course will ultimately be vindicated by Him who governs the universe itself.

In November, the Baptist State Convention at Asheville sent "a fraternal message" to Dr. Cullom, vice-president of the Convention, "who was prevented by illness from attending." Rev. J. Winston Pearce of Durham presented the report on Social Service and Civic Righteousness which stated that "War is not the will of God or the spirit of his Christ, He would have it otherwise. . . . We must all repent; we cannot and we must not bless this war." On Sunday, December 7th, "a day which will live in infamy," about three hundred and sixty Japanese planes bombed Pearl Harbor in Hawaii; the next day, the U. S. Congress declared war against Japan, and on December 11th, Germany and Italy declared war on the United States.

- 5 -

In January of 1942, Dr. Cullom experienced one of his life's greatest joys. Eugene Olive says that it was upon Dr. Cullom's initiative that there was organized at Wake Forest "the Quintet Club," composed of Dr. Olin T. Binkley, Dr. J. Allen Easley, Dr. Everett Gill, Rev. Eugene Olive and Dr. Cullom; this was "a sort of free and easy fellowship" wherein the great issues of the day were discussed. Dr. Cullom wrote:

> For several months I had not been able to meet with the club on account of a stubborn case of bronchitis. Knowing that I was practically free from this trouble, two members of the club came to my house and told me that if I was willing the club would hold a special meeting in the home of Dr. Gill on the evening of January 15 when some of my friends would join the members of the club in greeting me on the occasion of my seventy-fifth birthday. (*BR*, Feb. 25, 1942.)

When Dr. Cullom arrived at the Gill home, he was shown what he thought was a guest book; it was beautifully bound with the caption "Friends Salute You" inscribed in gold on it. As he looked inside, he found it was a book of letters from friends and former students, "expressing feelings of interest and love that were tender and beautiful" far beyond his power to describe. From college presidents, senators, governors, ministers, lawyers, physicians, teachers, colleagues, parishioners, came such praise that Dr. Cullom would later say if he did not know he was "only a sinner saved by grace," he would surely think he was *some*body.

J. Edward Allen, superintendent of Warren County Schools, attributed the happy state of Wake Forest in the affection of our North Carolina Baptists to Dr. Cullom and his "level-headed associates." Senator Josiah W. Bailey wrote:

> Dr. Cullom and I were in College together. He was the same fine man as a student as he has proved to be these fifty years of lofty living and high service. He carried himself at college with excellent poise. He attended diligently to his studies and to his duties. He offended no one. He seemed to have a faculty of pursuing the even tenor of his way, looking to the main objectives rather than to the incidents of his college life . . . he has kept the higher level as preacher, teacher, citizen, and friend. There has been given to few to live so noble a life and few indeed today who have made such contributions to their day and generation.

Sankey L. Blanton wrote of Dr. Cullom's "great contributions to the world," and Nathan C. Brooks, Jr., expressed appreciation of Dr. Cullom's "friendly counsel," and "the unmistakable integrity" of his Christian life. The Governor of North Carolina, the Honorable J. Melville Broughton, wrote:

> When a college student I learned to love and respect you; and during the thirty years since my graduation I have been associated with you in many delightful ways. Your life has been a benediction not only to me but to thousands of young men throughout North Carolina.

There was not time to read all the letters that evening in the Gill home; Dr. Cullom might have noted some of the names signed to others—Sherwood Eddy of New York, C. Sylvester Green (President of Coker College), W. W. Hamilton (President of the Southern Baptist Convention), Zeno Wall of Charlotte and many, many more. Other friends began arriving; Mr. and Mrs. E. B. Earnshaw, Mrs. R. E. Royall, Mrs. John G. Mills, Mrs. J. W. Lynch, Mr. and Mrs. S. W. Brewer were among the first to express their personal congratulations to Dr. Cullom. Before the evening was over, a hundred and ten special friends had called.

When Dr. Cullom was taken home, he sat by Mrs. Cullom's bed and shared some of the things said to him. Likely she read him more of the letters.

> All through the years, now fifty of them, I have from time to time been strengthened and encouraged in my own work by contacts with you and by my thought of you as a fellow-worker in our efforts to interpret and release the liberating mind of Christ for our generation. W. O. Carver.

R. Paul Caudill of Augusta wrote: "The noble example of your life as a scholar and Christian gentleman will be a benediction to the lives of your students as long as they shall live." Leslie H. Campbell, president of Campbell College, wrote: "Our denomination today has a safer, wiser leadership because of your guidance and counsel." Dean D. B. Bryan told of the twenty years in which Dr. Cullom had been "a source of constant encouragement and inspiration" to him; P. E. Burroughs dated his love for Dr. Cullom from "the days of our youth" and said there had been "a distinct overflow from your good strong life into my own poor heart." Oscar Creech of Ahoskie declared: "Perhaps more than any other man you have the right to say to me, as Paul said to Timothy, 'My Son'." From Pennsylvania, J. H. Franklin declared: "You have consistently stood at the bow of the boat looking for new lands ahead." From Tennessee, Walter N. Gilmore said: "Perhaps no man had had more to do with directing the course of my life . . . than you." From Missouri, H. I. Hester stated: "The very fact that so many of your students have gone out to occupy places of responsibility is an ample testimony to the great work you have done, and this is all the more significant because every one of these men honor, respect and love you." From Maine, Lowell Q. Haynes said Dr. Cullom had probably trained "more Baptist ministers and influenced more Baptist students than any other teacher in a Baptist college in the world" and that that teaching had been "sound, liberalizing in the best sense of the word, and gracious." The night must have been far spent when the Culloms had to lay aside the book.

The next morning the reading was resumed. Mrs. Cullom read from J. B. Hipps:

> I shall never forget your speaking to me about entering the ministry at the end of my junior year. Although I did not decide then, it was one of the influences which led to my decision. I have also valued very highly your letters to me in China, and the many contacts that I have had with you when home on furlough.

M. A. Huggins, General Secretary of the Baptist State Convention, wrote that Dr. Cullom had "every reason to feel proud" that he had been permitted "to make such a noteworthy contribution." Thurman D. Kitchin, President of Wake Forest College, wrote:

> You have set your impress upon the ministry to a degree that cannot be estimated. May I say that my affection and admiration for you have increased from year to year. Your calmness, your faith, your wisdom— these have influenced my life. What has impressed me most . . . is your understanding heart.

Hight C Moore, secretary of the Southern Baptist Convention, dated their "comradeship" from the eighties of the last century: "You have filled the days of your radiant career with abundant good deeds, and the Lord has crowned the years with his grace and goodness." L. B. Moseley stated:

17

> After being away from Wake Forest for fifteen years, and after spending nine years in one of the great educational centers of America, I am prepared to say that I have come in contact with no scholarship in religion which has been more helpful to me, no spirit which I felt was more Christ-like, no personality which crossed my path at a more crucial time and which left upon me the point of view which I still hold, than that of my honored and greatly loved teacher, Dr. W. R. Cullom. . . .
>
> P.S. Your judgment is not only good in religion. It is good in matters domestic! When you saw Kathryn you advised me to marry her as soon as I could make $150 per month. I did, one year later. That was *good* advice.

Wayne Oates wrote: "Your Christ-like walk of life as well as your wise counsel has been a guide for me in some very dark hours." Eugene Olive, pastor of the Wake Forest Baptist Church, turned back the pages of memory and underscored a few of the most impressive lines recorded there.

> You were my teacher of the Bible in the formative teen age days. You gave me then a wholesome picture of what the peer of all the books really is, and inspired me with the purpose of making a life-long study of its living truth. Your teaching was forceful because of what you were as much as for what you said. In my twenties I became pastor of a church to which you had ministered for more than a dozen years. There again I saw healthy fruitage of your teaching and preaching, of your living and ministering. In my thirties you officiated at my marriage because you had baptized and instructed and inspired to noble living the girl who in womanhood consented to be my wife. In my forties you allowed me to become your pastor, but the relationship has been one wherein you have appeared to me more like the shepherd and I as an adoring sheep.

J. M. Ormond of Duke University testified that his own life had been enriched by association with Dr. Cullom in "numerous experiences of common interest." J. Bailey Owen, president of Citizens Bank and Trust Co. of Henderson, wrote: "In my business dealings with you, extending over a span of fifty years or more, I have always found you to be a true Christian gentleman in every sense of the word."

Dr. G. W. Paschal wrote of their friendship through the years and of Dr. Cullom's contributions to the Baptists of North Carolina, and then concluded:

> Mrs. Paschal and I also want to express our deep appreciation of the sweetness and fortitude with which both you and Mrs. Cullom have borne declining physical strength and sometimes suffering. . . . Our hearts have been gladdened as we have talked of the Christian spirit both of you have manifested and still manifest.

Bishop W. W. Peele of the Methodist Church wrote: "Your influence has gone far beyond the bounds of your denomination and has made richer and stronger a large portion of the religious life of North Carolina." Bishop J. Kenneth Pfohl of the Moravian Church said:

> We would add also our appreciation of your noble Christian life and service . . . Personally, I shall always be grateful that through our North Carolina Council of Churches I came to know you and to witness

in your spirit and service that "mind which was in Christ Jesus" which gave us brotherhood and love and Kingdom-seeking and all that goes to make up the Christian Way of Life. I have been helped and cheered by you, yes, "refreshed" as was Paul by Philemon.

Dean Emeritus Elbert Russell of Duke University expressed appreciation of Dr. Cullom's great intellectual and spiritual contribution to religious liberalism in North Carolina: "Your love of truth and spirit of tolerance have been among the potent forces that make North Carolina stand out as a state of unusual intellectual progressiveness and religious seriousness." David H. Scanlon, pastor of the First Presbyterian Church of Durham, wrote: "Through all these years you have been a strong, dependable pillar in the religious forces of this state; . . . your wisdom, prudence and brotherly love have placed you in the front ranks of cooperative service among your brethren in Christ."

H. Shelton Smith of Duke University:

I have caught a glimpse more than once of your truly ecumenical Christian spirit. In all that you have done as a member of the North Carolina Council of Churches, you have made us feel that in your own heart you knew that the Church of Christ is one. To have achieved that faith in a period of time when so few have experienced the deeper unity of the church is indeed a badge of your truly prophetic spirit.

Bernard Washington Spilman wrote: "More than half a century of personal friendship has given you and all yours a large warm place in the inner circle of my best friends." Carl M. Townsend of Raleigh:

God only knows just how much you have influenced my thought and action. I was a lad sixteen years of age in the first few weeks of my freshman years at college, struggling with what proved to be a call to the Ministry, when I went to you one day for a conference. You enabled me to see more clearly the will of the Lord for my life . . . I have *so much* for which to thank you that I cannot express my gratitude in words, but I promise you I'll try to do my very best to express it in the high type of Christian living you inspired me to seek.

The reading continued all morning and afternoon, and yet there were more tributes. J. H. Gorrell wrote: "No man, in my judgment, has done more and better work in North Carolina as a Pastor and a Teacher than you." N. Y. Gulley believed "the seeds planted by you will grow and blossom in beauty to bless mankind and will reach full fruition in a bountiful harvest in the extension of the Kingdom of Christ on the earth, and to the glory of God."

Garland A. Hendricks of Knightdale wrote that some students may not have fully appreciated Dr. Cullom until later in life they realized how much they had been helped "by his genuine unselfishness, by his confidence in people, and by his sane interpretation of the Scriptures." J. Allen Easley recalled many happy hours with Dr. Cullom: "In all of our contacts I have felt the rich stimulus of your intellectual activity, the benediction of your strong yet gentle spirit, the depth of your sympathy, and the breadth of your outlook, and I am profoundly grateful." Mrs. J. Allen Easley recalled an impromptu lunch Mrs. Cullom had served them the day they had arrived in Wake Forest:

> When we came here, Mrs. Cullom was an active part of the community, and her opinion was sought and valued in both civic and church affairs. Her influence is felt today, though it goes out from her bedside.
> I have in my mind pictures of Mrs. Cullom going to walk with you in the afternoon, teaching her large Sunday School Class, or leading the W.M.S. meetings.
> Every Christmas I can see again the hall of the Culloms' house as it looked when the bags of the Relief Committee were being filled there. Many beautiful gifts have gone from your house to other doors, and their fragrance goes still.

Everett Gill wrote of the years he and Dr. Cullom shared as students in the Seminary and stated that although their fields of labor had been widely separated, yet their hearts had been "close together in brotherly love."

> It is a privilege and joy for me that in these more serene days of our lives I can be near you and take part in this coronation service of love and appreciation on the part of your world circle of friends and brethren. I am happy and honored to have a part in this festival of love.

J. Clyde Turner of Greensboro was grateful for the two years he had been in Dr. Cullom's classes where he had received "deep and lasting impressions which have lived with me through the years." Rufus W. Weaver, executive secretary of the District of Columbia Baptist Convention wrote: "Quietly, unostentatiously, but effectively you have maintained in a fair and liberal spirit your devotion to the Christian faith and by so doing, you have aided a multitude of young men in making the necessary adjustments between a traditional and often times prejudiced belief to a clear acceptance of the eternal truths that God has revealed in His Word and in His World." J. B. Weatherspoon of Louisville expressed his appreciation and "undying gratitude" for what he had received from Dr. Cullom in his early student days.

> With special appreciation do I remember the studies in the Life of Christ and the Epistles of Paul, and the special course in sermon construction given with such sympathy and patience. And besides, I recall gratefully some personal kindnesses of which you have no recollection, but which have proved to be decisive influences in the whole course of my ministry.

Kyle M. Yates of Louisville confessed he could "never begin to thank you adequately for the marvelous contribution you have made to my own life." Allen L. Young, principal of the Wake Forest Normal and Industrial School for Negroes, wrote:

> I consider it a privilege to be given opportunity to speak the sentiment of my group in recognition of your service and influence as they

have affected our community. The manner in which you have embraced every opportunity to give aid and encouragement to a less fortunate race than that of your own, has gone a long way in establishing and preserving a spirit of harmony and good will between the races at Wake Forest.

As one of his own teachers, John R. Sampey, recalled Cullom's address on Matthew T. Yates at the Seminary and commended him for "sending to us here in Louisville a large number of ministerial students who have done good work and have gone out into the active ministry in all parts of the world."

As Mrs. Cullom read on, did Dr. Cullom think of her reading to him in Louisville in the spring of 1896 when his life's work was ahead of him? God had been good to him to have used him in His service. E. C. Shoe of Taylorsville said time had played havoc with the history and geography books he had studied; many things are swept away, but some men outlast the flood.

> Yea, some live on both sides of the flood. . . . Many of us who sat in your classes think of you as a Growing Christian. That fact has caused some of us to grow in our love for the Truth, in appreciation for the beautiful, in faithfulness to the Lord and in the interest for His Kingdom. . . . I often think of the pleasant chats we had together as we went to our pulpits, you to Spring Hope and I to Harris Chapel. I well remember running out of gas one night. The roads were muddy and the rain was falling. You had just been telling me what you preached about that day: "Don't Worry." Well, we had a good chance to practice your sermon. Oh, the blessings that were mine to have this chance of knowing you better.

Frank K. Pool of Furman University knew Dr. Cullom well; he wrote:

> It is now almost forty years since you preached at the close of the Mount Moriah school. Your text was, "Let there be light." It was then that you first came into my life. I was only a small boy, but your message impressed me. It opened up new horizons that I have never been quite the same since that day. . . . As I think of what your life has been to so many persons and institutions it seems to me that the message of that school closing is prophetic and symbolic of your entire career. We are told that the path of the righteous is a shining light. I have known you in the school room as teacher, in the pulpit as preacher, in the home as comforter, in the press as interpreter, and in all these relations the problems of life have appeared nearer solution because of the light of your words and manner.

There were fifty other letters of the highest praise and appreciation. When the last of them was read, Dr. Cullom likely asked, "Fannie, are they talking about me? If there is any truth in all that they are saying, then here is an example of what the Lord can do with a poor man who loves Him." Very likely, he thanked his dear wife for the noble part she had played in making such a life possible—and together, they thanked God. This could have been a proper ending, but there was yet more—much more.

- 6 -

Dr. Cullom did not let this grand outpouring of appreciation deter him from continuing to do what he could in the Lord's Kingdom. He arose upon "a point of personal privilege" in the *Recorder* (Feb. 4, 1942) to thank the "dear friends" who had showered such "bouquets" upon him; then he turned back to his tasks. In an article, "Faith and God" (*BR,* Feb. 4, 1942), Dr. Cullom wrote of Mrs. Shelly's great story *Frankenstein* as containing a prophecy which "is almost infinitely more serious in its realization than its author could possibly have had in mind when she wrote it."

> And when we look beneath the surface of what is taking place today, is it not all the outcome of one thing—we have been building a civilization with God left out? In their pride of spirit, men have looked upon the work of their own hands and shouted to each other, "See what our hands have wrought."

Dr. Cullom pointed out that this was not the first generation that had tried to leave God out of its plans and performances: the generation of Noah tried it; the generations of Amos and Isaiah tried it.

> It is an awful day in the life of any people when they come to feel that the Governor of the Universe does not see them, that the sceptre of righteousness has slipped out of his hand and that all is going pell-mell into a confusion that is worse confounded. . . . If we are to be saved from such an experience it will have to come . . . through *faith and God* . . . Daniel Webster said, "The greatest thought that ever came into my mind was and is that of my personal responsibility to God." . . . Here is: (1) a definite recognition of God—"He that cometh to God must believe that he is"; (2) a recognition of the fact that there is a definite and mutual relationship between each individual soul and God—"he is a rewarder of them that diligently seek him"; (3) that this relationship is primary and takes precedence over all other relationship—absolutely nothing must be allowed to lead one to compromise in his personal obligation to God. The man who pitches his life and lives his life in harmony with this principle will have a regulator that influences in a vital way every detail of his life.

Dr. Cullom stated that until we can have some sort of world-wide arbiter to whom all nations and peoples may appeal and who is recognized by all people as Lord over all, there can be no permanent and satisfactory settlement of world issues.

In a second article on this theme, "Our Need of God" (*BR,* March 25, 1942), Dr. Cullom said the time has gone when groups of people could live to themselves. Someone has said that science has made the whole world one neighborhood; it remains for Christianity to make it a brotherhood; Dr. Cullom added "and the first step toward such a brotherhood . . . will be the recognition and the acknowledgment of the common lordship of the Maker and Ruler of the universe." Dr. Cullom quoted Augustine's heart-cry ("O God, thou has made us for thyself, and our hearts are restless until they rest in thee.") and the psalmist's longing ("As the hart panteth after the water brooks, so panteth my soul after thee, O God."). He cited the prodigal son's utterance ("I perish with hunger. I will rise and go to my father.") and declared, "Each individual soul needs this experience of personal fellowship with God—a fellowship that brings into the soul the assurance that wherever a man may be and whatever his circumstances may be, he is not alone." Dr. Cullom wrote of three young boys who decided they would discard God and give themselves to their own selfish and sensual desires; when one of the boys became desperately ill with pneumonia and cried out to his mother's God, the other two said, "Tom, old boy, hold on; don't give in like that." He looked into their faces with a yearning that came from the lowest depths and said, "Boys, what can I hold on to?" Dr. Cullom shared this experience:

> A little child some two or three years of age was lying in his little crib beside my bed. One night I discovered that the child for some reason was not sleeping, but said nothing to him. Finally he spoke and said, "Papa, are you awake?" I said, "Yes, son." The little fellow said, "Stretch out your hand." My hand at once went out from under the cover and towards the child. He took hold of the hand which was outstretched in the darkness, and in a moment was asleep with the assurance in his soul that his father was right there by his side. . . . Like the appetite for food and water, the soul's need of support, of companionship, of an intelligent apprehension of life's meaning, of assurance for the future is one of life's constants. Our Lord never uttered a word that touches upon a more universal need than when he said "Man shall not live by bread alone, but by every word that proceedeth out of the mouth of God."

In "A Post Script" (*BR,* April 15, 1942), Dr. Cullom quoted from Dr. J. A. Hadfield's *The Psychology of Power:*

> Speaking as a student of psychology who as such has no concern with theology, I am convinced that the Christian religion is one of the most valuable and potent influences that we possess for producing that harmony of peace of mind needed to bring health and power to a large portion of nervous patients. In such cases I have attempted to cure nervous patients with suggestions of quietness and confidence, but without success until I have linked these suggestions onto the faith in the power of God which is the substance of the Christian confidence and hope.

That spring, Dr. Cullom congratulated the students at Campbell College on "living in a time like this" and challenged them to have faith in God; "He is greater than anything or anybody He created." Into his household, he welcomed "Uncle Ed" Farmer who, since the death of his wife, had been alone in Louisville; his presence in the Cullom home was a special joy and comfort to Mrs. Cullom. Dr. Cullom added Dr. George Buttrick's *Prayer* to a list of books on prayer which he thought every minister should possess (Dr. Fosdick's *The Meaning of Prayer,* Dr. Heiler's *Prayer,* Dr. Alexander Whyte's *Lord, Teach Us to Pray*) and quoted some of Dr. Buttrick's thoughts to whet the appetite of the reader. (*BR,* April 15, 1942.) As the church in Spring Hope had not been able to secure a pastor, Dr. Cullom continued to serve; in May, Rev. Guy Moore of Lewiston helped him in a "successful revival." In an article, "Our Lost Generation," Dr. Cullom asked:

> Were you ever lost in a forest? I have had that experience. In my boyhood it was customary in our community to fence in the growing crops and leave the woods, meadows and swamps for free grazing for cattle, hogs and stock of all sorts. One of the chores assigned to me was to "go for the cows" in the late afternoon. I would go off into the woods where the cows ranged, listen for the "cow bell" until I had located them, and then drive them home in time for my mother to milk them before night. On one such occasion the cows had gone off into a strange, out-of-the-way place, and I failed to find them. . . . This failure seemed to beget within me a queer sense of confusion which grew more and more intense as I ran hither and thither trying to locate myself. In a little while every path, tree, rock, and everything else about me was as strange to me as if I had suddenly dropped into the midst of an African jungle. My confusion had become a state of panic, and my actions were such as might be expected of one in a state of frantic delirium. It seems to me even now that if darkness had overtaken me out in those woods I should have become thoroughly crazy. Fortunately at this point the "cow bell" was heard. In wending their way homeward the cows had come within hearing distance of me, and as soon as possible I found myself one in their slow and steady procession. So that, instead of my driving the cows home, they led me home!
>
> This personal experience from the days of my boyhood is recorded here as a sort of parable of much that is going on in the world today. . . . What is it to be lost? We used to think it meant being cast into the lake of fire and brimstone after death and the judgment. What did it mean in the experience of the boy referred to at the opening of this article? It meant that he was away from home, away from parents, brothers and sisters. He was so confused and upset that he had lost all sense of direction and had no idea as to how to get back home. And is not this the essential thing in being lost anywhere and at any time? There is a little evangelistic refrain which says, "Back to my Father and home . . . I will arise and go, back to my Father and home." And this refrain carries with it the essential point in being lost. It is separation from God. This was the trouble with Adam; it was the trouble with the prodigal son; it is the trouble with the people of the earth today. . . . To be separated from God is to be separated from the source of life, and to be separated from the source of life can bring only death. In case of the body, it brings physical death. In the case of the soul, the part of our make-up that links us in fellowship with God, it means moral death—that brings disintegration of the mind, the affections, the will. This is what Paul describes in Romans 1:21-23.

Three times Paul says in this chapter that God "gave them up." And when we note to what it was that he gave them up and the fatal and awful results of such giving up, we can see very clearly what Paul means by being lost.

> It is not something that is to come to people after death. It is something that takes possession of them here and now. To my way of thinking, Paul's description of what comes to people when they do not "like to retain God in their knowledge" is the ugliest passage in the Bible. He here speaks in no figurative language. He lifts the veil and lets us look into the very depths of the soul that is lost because of its separation from God.
>
> If one will apply what I have said to what is going on in the world today, I believe he will agree that he sees much to remind him that ours is indeed a "lost generation"—a generation that has separated itself

from God and is consequently floundering in its own folly and blindness. (*BR*, May 13, 1942.)

Dr. Cullom continued this discussion in a second article (*BR, July 1, 1942*), "What Must We Do to Be Saved?" He cited some examples of other "lost generations": the generation of Noah, the children of Israel on the way to the Promised Land, the Jews at the time of the Babylonian Captivity, the time of the fall of the Roman Empire, the experience of the Crusades, the French Revolution and so on. From the Garden of Eden to the present day, the human race has been subjected to catastrophes which come as the judgment of God on men and nations for their neglect of Him and for their consequent folly, degradation and corruption. "It is also apparent that God's ultimate purpose in each such experience was the mercy and salvation beyond the day of judgment." Dr. Cullom cited "the rich outlook that followed the flood as seen in the promise of salvation that was to come through Shem," the triumphal entry into the Promised Land after forty years wandering in the wilderness, the rich assurance given of God through Jeremiah which was to follow the captivity, and so on. Noting that the other catastrophes were limited in their territory and scope, Dr. Cullom said:

> The present experience covers the whole globe, touches every aspect of life, and is as violent as scientific invention and mechanization can make it. If a corresponding change for the better and richer blessing of God is to follow upon the close of the present conflict as compared with those referred to above, surely we can afford to be patient, to wait on God, and do our best. And it seems to me that there is every assurance that such will be the case. . . . In this critical hour many hearts are crying out with Simon Peter, "Lord to whom Shall We Go?" Someone points out the vast difference between the request of the prodigal son when he was leaving home, "Father, *give* me," and that which he made as he was returning, "Father, *make* me." The difference here pointed out is the difference between a soul that is lost and the same soul when it is saved. It is a question of attitude, of purpose, and of the life that grows out of such attitude and purpose.
>
> How can this change be brought about? In the case of the Philippian jailer, when the earthquake came, when the foundations of the prison were shaken, when the foundations of his own life were shattered, and when he cried from the depths of his soul "What must I do to be saved?" he was told to believe on the Lord Jesus Christ and he would be saved.

This believing on the Lord Jesus Christ enables one to come into vital fellowship with God. This is what changed the libertine Augustine into a great Christian and theologian, what changed the rich wayward Francis of Assisi into one of Christendom's "most saintly and fruitful Christians," what laid hold of the monk Martin Luther and led him to defy all the corruption of the Roman Church, what inflamed the heart of the formalist John Wesley to become "one of the most transforming and beneficent influences in the world." This is what happened to give Christendom its Robert Morrison, its Robert Moffatt, its David Livingstone—Grenfeld, Schweitzer, Kagawa, the Soongs, the Koos,

Muriel Lester, John R. Mott, Booker T. Washington, George Carver, Moody, George Adam Smith, Jane Addams, Florence Nightingale and "a host of others whose names and whose record of sacrifice and service are written in the Lamb's book of life." The secret of these is Christ, and "there is no other name . . . whereby we must be saved."

In June, Rev. A. L. Fulk began his pastorate at Spring Hope; Dr. Cullom spent a week at the Coats Baptist Church, teaching an adult department in the Daily Vacation Bible School and preaching at night. Mr. Owen Odum reported:

> This work captivated our people as nothing else has . . . I wish he could do more of this work in the churches over the state. His knowledge of the Bible, his sound judgment, his rich experience, and his great soul combine to make his work quite worth while. (*BR*, July 15, 1942.)

- 7 -

During the summer of 1942, it became necessary for someone to turn Mrs. Cullom in the bed; Mrs. B. P. Hinton of Spring Hope and others came to help at different times in the home. Mrs. Cullom did not suffer any pain but grew weaker and weaker; she was always cheerful. Dr. George C. Mackie, her physician, would remember she was "a very high class woman, very patient through a long disabling illness." Mrs. Willie Hall Gill, a fine Negro woman who had come as cook in the Cullom home in 1935 and who came to be loved as a member of the family, would discuss the meals with Mrs. Cullom each morning; she found Mrs. Cullom "very nice, kind and easy to please." Mrs. Cullom's bedroom was large with windows onto the front porch and a bay-window to the south; it was pleasant with flowers and with Mrs. Cullom's winsome personality.

Dr. Cullom continued to serve as he had opportunity. He praised Dores Robinson Sharp's biography of Walter Rauschenbusch and helped ordain Ernest P. Russell at the Corinth Baptist Church; he preached in North Wilkesboro and in Southern Pines. The *Recorder* of July 29th carried another of his fine articles, "Faith and Fear." From the first human being who hid himself from his Maker, fear has accompanied man, wrote Dr. Cullom; "this sense of fear is perhaps more general on earth today than ever before." Noting that fear "sooner or later will undermine the strongest constitution," he described four roots of this malady: (1) a sense of inferiority, (2) a sense of insecurity, (3) a consequent sense of uncertainty, (4) a sense of unfulfilled obligation, which is "perhaps the most disturbing and distressing of all." In an effort to relieve this fear, some give themselves over to liquor or dope; others resort to sensuous indulgences. Many try to overcome it by their own strength and say with Mr. Henley, "I am the Captain of my soul"—only to find the world is too much for them. Faith alone can cure this fear—not as a magic formula but as an assurance that "the Lord of hosts is with us." The fortitude and patience exemplified in the eleventh chapter of Hebrews "can come alone from a faith that links one to the eternal God"—a faith which is at once "the assurance of things hoped for, the conviction of things not seen."

In August, Dr. Cullom conducted a Communion service at the First Baptist Church in Raleigh and taught two study courses in the Wake Forest Church—the Book of Romans for adults and "Turning Points in the Life of Jesus" for Intermediates. In an article, "Keeping Up with God" (*BR,* Aug. 12, 1942), he recalled having heard Dr. R. T. Vann preach a sermon on Enoch in which he urged his hearers (1) to get into the way God is going, (2) to move in the same direction that God is going and (3) to keep up with God. Taking Dr. Vann's last point, Dr. Cullom stated that our God is at work on a progressive and forward-looking purpose; He is "really and truly moving on." Those who refuse to move with God in this purpose are left by the wayside—like the Judaizers in the New Testament Church, like the anti-missionary Baptists of a hundred years ago. Some try to go ahead of God; "young people find it hard to submit to the tedious discipline of waiting on God and be faithful to their better selves while they wait." Enoch walked *with* God; he knew God's way because he was a man of prayer who harkened to the voice of God and because he was

> a man who was in the habit of doing promptly and faithfully whatever God made known to him to be his will for him. An old man whom I used to hear pray in my boyhood always asked the Lord to give his people an "applying conscience." Enoch must have carried such a conscience with him.

On September 23rd the *Recorder* had another major article by Dr. Cullom, "Faith and Revelation," in which he stated that before there can be a revelation there must be (1) a personal revealer, (2) a personal receiver, and (3) a sufficient similarity between the two for mutual understanding. All of this is found in the statement "And God made man in his own image and after his own likeness"— which means that man was made with the power to think, to feel (in an emotional sense) and to choose; "this endowment gives to man a dignity, a glory, a possibility, a prospect possessed by none other of God's earthly creatures." This is also the basis for revelation; "God can and does speak to man, and man can and does answer back."

> In these two primary and basic facts we have the possibility of eternal fellowship with God, which, . . . means the possibility of immortality. The first of the possibilities (Mutual communication between Creator and creature) we see realized in Genesis 3, where God speaks to man and man answers back to him. From the Garden of Eden to the present day God and man have been communicating with each other "at sundry times and in divers manners."

Dr. Cullom stated that science in "the generation that lies just back of us" made man feel altogether sufficient in himself and left no place for revelation or even God; "but science is much more modest today . . . more humble and teachable."

> The prodigal world has wandered about in the "far country" until it has lost its way. It has fed on "husks" until its soul has become hungry. Is it ready to say, "I will arise and go to my Father?"

At the first indication of the prodigal world's return, the Father will come to meet that world and will speak to it "fresh and living words of grace and blessing." And how does God speak? In many ways— sometimes "where there is no speech." Dr. Cullom said:

> It was my privilege many years ago to be pastor of an old man whose wife was a deaf mute. . . . In visiting his humble home one day, I asked him to tell me how he courted his wife. . . . He said, "Me an' her always knowed each other." There was between them a touch of soul, a mutual response each to the other that was far deeper and much more meaningful than any language could express. It is well known to musicians that when two instruments are in the same room and are keyed to the same pitch, if you strike a key on one of them, the corresponding key on the other will sound at the same time. This figure of speech suggests an important factor in the matter of man in perfect accord with the spirit and character of God. To the extent that such harmony is perfect, revelation can be perfect; and to the extent that such harmony is broken and marred, to that extent will revelation be imperfect, neutralized, and even prevented.
>
> Of course there has been on earth only one perfect organ of revelation—the Word which was made flesh and dwelt among us. Of him and him alone could it be said that "the only begotten Son which is in the bosom of the Father—he hath declared him," or brought him out from behind the veil to show him to the world, so that in Jesus, and in him alone do we have the perfect revelation.

Faith's part is: (1) to listen, (2) to believe, (3) to appropriate, (4) to obey, and (5) to follow. God is moving on, and if faith is to be kept vital, responsive and growing, it must follow the way God is moving. God is trying to say some very important things; O, that his people would know!

That fall, Dr. Cullom preached wherever he was asked; he wrote "Our Tangled World," in which he called for repentance for "our share in sins of omission and commission" that had brought on "this catastrophe" and declared the cross of Christ is the only hope for our world — the cross where "Jew" and "Gentile" become "one new man" and which includes sharing "that which is behind of the afflictions of Christ." (*BR*, Sept. 30, 1942.) In another article Dr. Cullom gave three reasons why Baptists should join the North Carolina Council of Churches: (1) *We need it.*

> If Southern Baptists do not turn from their isolationism and recognize the day of internationalism, we are sunk. . . . If we persist in an attitude and habit of aloofness, I fear that a spirit of ugly suspicion, not to say Pharisaism, will be developed among us. We ourselves need the influence that should come to us from fellowship with the brethren of other faiths and practice.

(2) *They need us.* We, Baptists, are now many, with a fair share of intellectual ability and influence; our moral, spiritual, financial and cultural strength could be used more effectively for the glory of God through the Council than otherwise would be possible. (3) *The world needs us all;* no one religious group is adequate for the crisis through which the world is passing; "the combined resources of all the friends of our Lord, under his guidance and control, will be required even to make a respectable beginning in taking hold" of the tasks before us. We cannot afford to wait until the catastrophe is over; "to dally will be to bring on ourselves a guilt that will be hard for those who come after us to forgive." (*BR,* Oct. 21, 1942.)

On November 2nd (1943), as he was helping to lift Mrs. Cullom on her bed, Dr. Cullom was troubled with his back; later when he had Dr. Mackie to examine him, he was told that he had sprained his back. Sometime later he was upstairs "for something" and fell as he was going to the back room. It seems he fainted or, for some reason, lost consciousness. Nancy, Lawrence and Uncle Ed got him up and put him on the bed in Uncle Ed's room. There must have been some form of heart-failure; he was put on a derivative of digitalis, and pneumonia followed. The chills were so severe that Dr. Cullom caused the bed to shake. The physician prescribed one of the sulfa drugs and left word that Dr. Cullom must drink some liquid every two hours. He was so sick that often the nurses could not get him to drink and they would have to call Lawrence Harris, who would insist upon his drinking it.

By Christmas, Dr. Cullom was up again to the surprise of many; Lawrence Harris would say, "Dr. Cullom is physically a miracle." Dr. Mackie would say: "When it comes to human flesh, Dr. Cullom is tough and tops; he is very cooperative and does everything to the best of his ability." For Christmas the church at Spring Hope sent him a check; the Ladies Class presented a sweater, and Mrs. Ben Wood brought some of "the Lillian brand of sausage." There were hundreds of Christmas greetings, but there was no "peace on earth"—American troops were fighting in North Africa, and the Russians were counter-attacking at Stalingrad; the allied bombers had begun their raids on Germany, and the United States marines had landed on Guadalcanal.

- 8 -

The new editor of the *Biblical Recorder,* Dr. L. L. Carpenter, continued to use articles by his dear teacher, Dr. Cullom. In "Helpful Preaching" (*BR,* Feb. 17, 1943), Dr. Cullom stated that many of us judge preaching by the entertainment it brings or by the way it falls in line with our peculiar whims, prejudices or ideas; he suggested that his fellow-ministers check "the heart of what we are preaching." He

listed three marks of helpful preaching: (1) It should be saturated
with the evangel of God—the good news that God does really and
truly love men and this in spite of their sins, failures, mistakes, weak-
nesses and all the rest. (2) It should teach people the basic principles
of life. Dr. Cullom related that a woman at Irvington, Kentucky,
once told him: "Mr. Cullom, you never tell people to believe until
you have given them something to believe." Through the years he had
prayed to know "the truly essential things for life in time and eternity"
and to give faithful, loving expression to them in season and out of
season. (3) Preaching should have in it the note of encouragement
and of comfort, for "life" can separate people from God (Rom. 8:38).
Paul writes of the whole creation groaning and travailing in pain
together; does this not suggest a conception that is adequate for the
present world-situation and the prospect of "a new heaven and a new
earth" which shall be born out of these experiences? In such an assurance, we can "believe all things, hope all things, endure all things."

By April Dr. Cullom had recovered sufficiently for his physician to
advise him to proceed with the plan of having the cataract removed
from his left eye. The operation was successful, but the condition of
his heart did not permit the removal of the cataract from his right eye.
While he was in the hospital, he developed pneumonia and was again
very sick for several days.

Upon his return home, a friend came and read to him Lloyd C.
Douglas' *The Robe* ("a modern Ben Hur"). He urged his fellow-
ministers to hear Dr. Arthur Hewett at the Rural Church Institute at
Greensboro and wrote of "Wesley and Marx."

> Wesley believed human welfare was attainable only by faith in God
> and by the direction of all material powers toward the development of
> abundant spiritual life. Marx, contrawise, denying God, denied the
> existence of the spiritual life and excited the proletariat to world revolu-
> tion by bloody means. Wesley's crusade represented the epitome of
> spiritual power; Marx's crusade the epitome of material force. (*BR,*
> May 31, 1943.)

Dr. Cullom pointed out that this conflict has an ancient history (Cain
and Abel, Jacob and Esau) and stated that "the flesh" makes its immediate appeal and then is exhausted, whereas "the spirit" offers a
better and a more lasting way. (*BR,* Sept. 15, 1943.) In a later
article, "Today's Call for a Prophet," Dr. Cullom asked who will do
for our generation what Wesley did for his. Unless someone leads an
attack on present-day unbelief and materialism to a tearing down of
its strongholds, "we are heading for another period of the dark
ages" which will surpass the darkness of the former age as much as
the deadly and diabolical powers of today surpass those of the past.

> We are witnessing all over the earth the ravages of this awful
> juggernaut going forth destroying and to destroy. What can be done to
> head him off? At present we are trying to answer him in his own lan-
> guage. This seems to us the only thing to do. The language of physical

force is the only language that he can understand. We must, therefore, use this language until he is stopped. But while we are using force, and after force has said all that it can say, we must keep in mind that there is another language—the language of spirit, of conscience, of love, of grace of God, of Christ, of the gospel. This is the only language that can change the nature of this Frankenstein and convert his marvelous powers of destruction into equally marvelous and even more marvelous power of positive and constructive help and blessing in the earth. And unless I misread all that is going on in the earth today, the transformation that I am here alluding to is the most urgent and pressing need of our human race. Can it be brought to pass? If so, the greatest age of all history is ahead of us. If not, then alas! alas! (*BR,* Sept. 29, 1943.)

Dr. Cullom's writings were by no means confined to the pages of the *Recorder.* On August 20, 1942, a series of his articles, under the heading "Wayside Heroism," began appearing in the *Charity and Children,* a publication of the Baptist Orphanage. In these he "told on" ordinary people who faced poverty, illness, misfortunes with heroic faith; he found in them evidences of God's working in our world.

When we look about us today we are often tempted to fume that maybe the world is going to the "bow-wows." Not so. God is not only in his heavens; he is also in the earth and is as truly working in our midst in and through such people as Mrs. (Minnie Young) Middleton as he was when Browning sang his song of the happy spinning girl. Such people constitute the salt of the earth.

He wrote of Mrs. Janie Pritchard Duggan who, widowed early in life, had served as missionary in Mexico until rheumatism had forced her to return to Wake Forest; in her little house in President Poteat's yard, she read and wrote and taught with such radiance that it was a privilege to visit her. On November 18th, Dr. Cullom told of having called on Mrs. Cora Warren Denning of Dunn; when he reminded her of the morning she accepted Christ in the church service, Mrs. Denning corrected him:

Mr. Cullom, I did not accept Christ as my Saviour on the morning when I joined the church. It was done as I lay in my bed the night before. I heard you preach that night and went to bed to think about it after getting home. God loves me and has done everything that is necessary for my salvation in Jesus His Son; why should I not then accept Him as my Saviour and Lord right here and now. I do accept Him and will unite myself with His church at my first opportunity. The next morning when you opened the doors of the church, I went forward and did what I promised God that night before that I would do.

In an article on Miss Luetta Cash, Dr. Cullom stated that whereas the critical method of studying the Scriptures is important, necessary and useful for teachers and scholars, the devotional method which takes the Bible as God's eternal message to the souls and lives of men and tries to find and follow what He says is the method that most of us should follow.

People need to be told to do what Paul bade the Christians at Philippi to do—"work out (put into practice) your own salvation with fear and trembling, for it is God which worketh in you both to will and to do of his good pleasure" (Phil. 2:12-13). This is the rhythm that the world needs today—God working in and his people working out. It will be marvellous when God's children learn to work out into life what He works in the way of impulse, desire and purpose. *(Charity and Children,* Thomasville, North Carolina, Feb. 10, 1944.)

In a beautiful article on Tom Jeffries, "the head janitor" at Wake Forest for about a half century, Dr. Cullom wrote (March 2, 1944):

Much is being said on all sides today about race troubles. When men and women of all races shall learn to "fear God and keep his commandments" in the spirit of Tom Jeffries, and with such degree of faithfulness as did he, the race issue will be a thing of the past. Nor will there ever be a real and sure settlement of such issues until men shall bring themselves to stand side by side before God and face Him in the light of eternity.

Some people seem to think that there can be no such thing as heroism apart from the spectacular. Nothing could be further from our Lord's idea of the heroic. The real hero with Him was the man who was "faithful unto the end." After many years of association with Tom Jeffries, it is my deliberate judgement that he measure up to our Lord's ideal of a hero in a most worthy manner. I thank God for having known him and for the privilege of serving side by side with him in our respective tasks.

For *Christian Frontiers,* Dr. Cullom wrote "My Manifesto" which was mainly an account of his life; it contained this paragraph:

About twenty years ago or a little more the young ministers at Wake Forest requested me to speak to them on the matter of a Baptist minister in a given community in his relationship to his fellow ministers of other denominations. The three things that I said to those young men gathered in Wingate Memorial Hall on that day seem to me now to be thoroughly safe, sensible, sound and wise as guiding principles in just about all of the ministers relationships. These were my suggestions on that occasion: (1) be a gentleman; (2) be a Christian; (3) be a Baptist. And I urged those young men to take and follow my suggestions in the order named.

- 9 -

Mrs. Cullom continued to have weakening spells; someone had to be with her all the time. Friends continued to come and found that she had not lost her "mental vigor, nor her interest in human affairs, nor her happy disposition." G. W. Paschal visited her in February and remarked that he had seen her as a young bride and as an expectant mother and with a babe in her arms, but never before had he seen her so beautiful—there was something about her which "seemed almost divine." *(BR,* June 14, 1944.)

In March, Dr. Cullom had another seige of pneumonia and was unable to leave his bed to go to her. Dr. Mackie had explained to Dr. Cullom that pernicious anemia "moved in cycles"; Dr. Cullom would write:

Occasionally she would go down very low. The doctor would then shoot big doses of liver extract into her hips and she would come back and go on as well as usual for a while. In March, 1944, Mrs. Cullom went down into one of those valleys.

"Willie" remembers, "She got so low as not to pay us any mind." Dr. Cullom was in the room adjoining hers; of Thursday, March 30th, he recalls:

> Mrs. Cullom was very low, so much so that Dr. Mackie told me not to go into her room. About 11 oclock that morning Nancy's husband came in and told me she was gone.

On Friday afternoon, Dr. J. Allen Easley conducted a simple funeral service at the home; he read Deuteronomy 33:27; Psalm 23, John 14:1-3, 6, 15-16, 25-27; Romans 8:14-17, 23, 31-39. After a prayer he said:

> We are reminded today of that New Testament character, Dorcas by name, whom Luke described as "a woman full of good works and alms-deeds which she did." For more than forty-five years this community has been the beneficiary of the good works and almsdeeds of Mrs. W. R. Cullom.
>
> Mrs. Cullom was endowed by her Maker with a keen mind, with good judgment, with practical wisdom and with a generous heart. She had a personality marked by vigor and initiative and forthrightness.
>
> She entered with understanding and true helpfulness into the life and work of her husband, and she ministered to her children with unstinted devotion.
>
> . . . Her ministry in the church and community life and the strength of her personality were undergirded by her strong religious faith. God was a living reality for her and Jesus Christ her living master and friend. One of her favorite Scripture verses was, "The eternal God is thy dwelling-place and underneath are the everlasting arms." One of her favorite hymns was that hymn beginning, "We would see Jesus." The secret of her rich spirit lay in her deep conviction of the trust-worthiness of God and her deep desire to know better the Lord Jesus Christ and to serve Him more effectively. We join the host of those whose lives she has touched to rise up and call her blessed.

Her body was put beside that of her infant son in the cemetery beyond Gore practice field. Obituaries appeared in all the state papers, and expressions of sympathy and love came to Dr. Cullom from near and far. The local Wake Forest newspaper had editorials on her community activities—noting especially that she had been the first woman to serve on the school board. Grace Beacham Freeman, a neighbor and friend, wrote:

> I never saw her take one step,
> And yet I felt her spirit knew
> Cool wooded paths and quiet pools
> And where sweet honeysuckle grew.
> I think she sensed the springtime's coming
> And thrilled at the promise of white dogwood
> And sunshine caught in daffodils.
> Would she change it if she could—
> Her time for going? The first of Spring
> When new life stirs in every clod?
> I think she knew that when she waked
> This time, she'd walk through Spring with God.

Dr. Hubert Poteat came and read two hours a week for Dr. Cullom; another friend took him for rides around the campus, where he was

18

"deeply and happily impressed" by the spire of the new chapel. (*BR*, May 24, 1944.) He reviewed C. S. Lewis' *Christian Behaviour* and described the Rev. Albert G. Willcox as "easily one of the most potent and helpful factors that came into my early life." (*C. & C.*, August 31, 1944.)

In writing of Rev. Wade D. Bostick, one of his earliest students and an heroic missionary to China for thirty-one years, Dr. Cullom said: "The Christian spirit is the same the world over, and its power and blessing are as truly manifest in China as in America, in England, or in any other place where the name and saving power of Christ have been known and felt." (*C. & C.*, Nov. 23, 1944.) Upon reading Rackham Holt's *George Washington Carver*, he wrote of having heard Dr. Carver lecture in Raleigh several years before and described him as "one of the real heroes of this generation."

> The date of my birth was January 15, 1867. It will be seen, therefore, that the years of my life are practically coterminous with those of the freedom of the Negroes. I can say, moreover, that these years have been spent right in the midst of this race and people. I have worked in the cotton fields with them; I have seen them when they seemed to have absolutely no faith in themselves; no one about them seemed to have any faith in them or for them. . . . And yet in face of all this here stand before us Drs. Washington, Carver and Moton, along with a host of other Negro men and women just as capable and worthy. . . . No group in all the history of the human race has made such notable progress in the same length of time as the Negro race in America has made during the years since 1865.
>
> And how shall we account for this progress? . . . How did Dr. Carver do it . . . (1) he did not allow himself to go around grumbling about what he did not have; (2) nor did he allow himself to spend his time airing his grievances; and (3) he did not allow the spirit of resentment and retaliation to embitter his soul or to affect his conduct. . . . Dr. Carver may have been said to have been possessed of a positive spirit and that his life was one consistent persistent faithful expression of that spirit. Using the materials and the opportunities that God placed around him, he was never able to exhaust them. As he used what he found in this way these materials and opportunities multiplied after the manner of the loaves and fishes in the hands of the Master. (*C. & C.*, Jan. 25, 1945.)

With the war's ending in Europe and the prospect of victory in the Pacific, Dr. Cullom wrote:

> Soon millions of men in arms will begin to disband and turn their purposes to plans of construction and life. . . . Will God as he had been revealed to us in Christ be recognized and followed in the execution of the task ahead of us?

Remembering Ohajima ("my friend and fellow student in our Louisville Seminary fifty years ago"), Kagawa and many other "friends of our Lord in Japan," Dr. Cullom stated that "we should go slowly in making a universal condemnation of any nation."

> I have followed, by the help of friends, the progress of the war with fair consistency from day to day since September 3, 1939, and have uttered in my soul a hearty "amen" to the ultimatum sent to Japan

from Potsdam; I should like to see the real perpetrators of all this awful mischief punished; . . . as Christians I should like to see all who bear the name of Christ perpetuate and spread abroad as far as possible the spirit of Him who said as He hung on the cross, "Father, forgive them, for they know not what they do." I should like for us to exercise an intelligent conscience which is at the same time Christian. (*BR*, Aug. 29, 1945.)

- 10 -

Dr. Cullom continued to write of heroes he had known; he paid tribute to Dr. N. Y. Gulley who had died in the spring and saluted Lt. Opie Gray Edwards, Jr., who had been shot down over Hungary on December 12, 1944. He told of his last visit with Dr. Edwin McNeill Poteat who, when Dr. Cullom entered the hospital room about forty-eight hours before the end, laughed: "Cullom, I'm in the process of shedding my chrysalis." (*C. & C.*, Sept. 13, 1945.) He also wrote of Rev. Elias Dobson who had been so concerned about rectifying the wrong done the Indians that once when a woman turned down his proposal of marriage he asked, "Well, won't you give me a dollar for the poor Indian, then?" (*C. & C.*, Sept. 27, 1945.) In his "Wayside Heroism," Dr. Cullom gave some biographical bits such as in his fine article on Dr. William B. Royall (Oct. 18, 1945):

> On the night that he passed out from us to enter his eternal home, his oldest son, his foster daughter, and I stayed with him. There were no "chariots of fire," as in the case of Elijah, to "bear his soul away." He went quietly and simply to sleep as a tired child would lay its head upon its mother's breast to fall into forgetfulness and leave its worries behind.

In his article on Fred N. Day, the evangelist-jeweler of Winston-Salem, Dr. Cullom told that Dr. Henry Brown had challenged Mr. Day to witness as the early Christians had and that his father had urged him not to take any money for his preaching.

> Nor did he ever use a penny that was given in this way for his personal use, not even to pay his railroad fare. He would take an offering at the close of the meeting, but it was always turned over to the treasurer of the church where the offering was taken for some kingdom enterprise. It was during a meeting at Rolesville that he decided that he would give these offerings henceforth to some specific object. And what should that object be? Several were considered. At my suggestion he decided to use all the money that came to him from this source to help educate worthy and ambitious girls who could not otherwise get such an education. . . . He kept the names of all those who joined the church under his preaching. . . . The last time I spoke to him about this matter I think that there were between six thousand and seven thousand names in these little books. (C&C, Nov. 1, 1945.)

Dr. Cullom wrote of having had, on the fiftieth anniversary of his graduation, "a simple breakfast" at his house for as many members of his class as he could get together and of treasuring Dr. Sloan's last Christmas card, on which these words were written: "Affectionately yours from 1900 A.D. to all eternity."

In "a word for the Christmas season," Dr. Cullom thought of those who had lost loved ones and of those who were seeking God's will in "the unparalleled challenge of rebuilding a shattered world." He made these suggestions:

> (1) That we bring ourselves to realize deeply and strongly that our help must come from God; and that his resources are amply sufficient; (2) that we learn to wait on God in earnest prayer and in humble supplication until our souls shall be reinforced "from on high"; (3) that we see to it that no root of bitterness, no feeling of resentment, no suggestion of retaliation shall be allowed to find lodgment in our souls; (4) that we believe in God with such fervent earnestness that we shall not lose hope even for those who have tried to destroy all that we have considered most worth while in the world; (5) that while we wait and pray, we shall make sure that we respond promptly, heartily and faithfully as step by step God shall make known to us His will and purpose for us and for the world about us; (6) that we understand thoroughly that absolutely nothing short of this will be anything like a worthy or even an approximately adequate response to the approach of God in Christ which gave us our Christmas with all that it signifies to us. (*BR,* Dec. 19, 1945.)

That winter and spring, many churches had dinners for their returning veterans, and college enrollments began swelling with "G. I.'s." Many of these veterans called on Dr. Cullom who was interested in all of their experiences and observations. While he was concerned for the changes in them, they observed that his bay-window was gone and that he was thin and weak; he kept Mrs. Cullom's shawl draped over his shoulders and used the cane Dr. Taylor had left for him. Dr. Cullom's interest in the recruiting of ministers remained constant; he urged parents, pastors, teachers, assembly-leaders and professors to give attention to guiding young people into channels of Christian service. (*BR,* April 3, 1946.)

When the Baptist State Convention voted (July 30, 1946) to accept the ten-million-dollars offer from the Smith Reynolds Foundation for Wake Forest College, Dr. Cullom urged the college to remain true to the principal purpose of its founding, that "of furnishing to our churches an educated and capable ministry."

> While this purpose has been broadened and modified in many ways, the supreme purpose . . . has never been lost sight of. On the contrary, it has been cherished, nourished, and kept in mind and made to function in a great way through the years. . . . Wake Forest men have taken the place of leadership in every place that calls for strong, capable and good men. All this is not to say that the work of the college has been perfect by any means. Like everything else that is human, the college has had its limitations and short comings, but when we consider what it has had to do with, I believe that any sort of reasonable appraisal of its history and its work will make it plain that no money or life energy spent by North Carolina Baptists has produced a richer or more abundant harvest for good than what has been invested in Wake Forest College.

In November (1946) the Baptist State Convention in Asheville sent greetings to "a few of our outstanding leaders" among whom was

Dr. Cullom; the Convention approved a million-dollar-enlargement program for the Baptist Hospital and undertook to raise 1½ million dollars for Wake Forest. The Convention also unanimously adopted the nine-page report on Social Service and Civic Righteousness; later some of the messengers were shocked to read that the report included this statement: "Segregation of believers . . . into racial or class churches is a denial of the New Testament affirmative of the equality of all believers at the foot of the cross, and alien to the Spirit of Christ, the Head of the church." On the last day of the Convention, with about a third of the messengers present, the Convention voted 250 to 158 to delete this sentence from the report. This action was widely discussed. *The News and Observer,* a daily newspaper printed in Raleigh, stated that it is not necessary for all to go to the same school or to the same church but "it is essential to be helpful, kind, considerate and just." William M. Brooks of Mebane wrote that it had taken "some experiences" from New Guinea to Japan to make him see what is plainly written in the New Testament.

> After working with, eating with, sleeping next to, and putting up with a lot of discomfort with good and bad white boys, good and bad Negro boys, I am glad to say that if I am kept out of the kingdom of heaven it will not be on account of racial prejudice. (*BR,* Dec. 11, 1946.)

Dr. Louis S. Gaines of Fayetteville wrote that the report "should deal with the relationship where we come to grips with life, and it ought to be our confession of our sense of the burden of those judgments of the Word of God upon any and all of our practices which are short of being Christian." He declared that in the report we should expect to be challenged in our complacencies and provoked to spirited debate, but time should be allowed for careful presentation and discussion. "We must deal with difficult questions with the assurance that our Convention is trustworthy to deal with them with consecrated courage."

In his Christmas message for 1946, Dr. Cullom stated that "the mind of Christ" as expressed in Philippians 2:5-8 embraces: (1) his renunciation of all privilege that would in any way minister to self-consideration, (2) his voluntarily leaving his place of equality with the Father that he may take human form in being "born of a woman," (3) his experiencing the lowest possible depths of suffering and agony that he might be fitted to "bring many sons into glory." Over against this mind of Christ, we see a shattered world: more property lies in ruins, more of earth's fair youths lie in foreign soil, more of man's hopes have died than in any previous generation. And what can we do? "We can do all things through Christ who strengthens us." And how can we bring our need and God's grace together? This was answered when it was announced that "The Word was made flesh and dwelt among us." To make this potentiality a reality is *par excellence* the Christian problem of this age. And how can it be solved? We are called to follow him who is called "the Captain" or pioneer of our salvation (Heb. 2:10). It is told that when our Lord returned to heaven He was asked if He had made any provisions on earth for telling the good news. "Yes," said the Master, "I told Peter, James, John and the rest to tell others." "But, what if they should fail?" Confidently Jesus replied, "I'm depending on them." But some will say, "The task is so big and I am so small, and besides I need help myself; how can I help another?" Dr. Cullom then told of a man who, caught in a blizzard, was at the point of freezing when he came upon another man who was down in the snow.

> What should he do? Leave his fellow to die while he pressed on for safety? The decision was quickly reached, "If we perish, we'll perish together." As he began to help the one who was down, the blood began to course more freely through his own veins and soon both men were safe in a warm room. In saving another the man saved himself. And is not this a parable of just what we are thinking of here? (*BR*, Dec. 18, 1946.)

- 11 -

The Wake Forest College's newspaper, *Old Gold and Black,* honored Dr. Cullom on his eightieth birthday (Jan. 15, 1947), and the *Biblical Recorder* wrote of "the great service" which Dr. Cullom had rendered to Wake Forest College and to thousands of his students. But this service was not finished. He recommended that New Testament students "eat" Dr. E. F. Scott's *Man and Society in the New Testament* and described Dr. Willard Sperry's *Religion in America* as "an excellent guide in getting acquainted with the religious forces and groups in America"; he three-starred Arthur J. Gossip's *In the Secret Place of the Most High.* In an important article, "Christ and Race," he stated that no generation in the world's history had witnessed "a deeper or a more bitter exhibition of race prejudice than did the one in the midst of which our Lord lived his life in the flesh"; we should note how Jesus met this issue as a basis for our attitude and action. With regard to the prejudice against the Samaritans, Jesus, as far as practicable, ignored it and made "his appeal to something deeper and more fundamental" than the surface matter of race. He gave evidence that he *believed* in the Samaritans as having the divine impress upon them as had all other men and held the Samaritans up in a good light. Dr. Cullom stated if we cannot learn from Jesus in this, "we are very dull pupils."

> Every community has its own race issues. In one place it is the Jew; in some other place it is the Italian; in another place it is the Chinese or the Japanese; in another place it is the Negro. The last, of course, is the one we find ourselves involved with here in the South. What shall we do about it here? What shall *I* do about it?
> A good many years ago it began to dawn upon me that my Negro neighbors and friends had their ups and downs, their temptations and trials, their difficulties and their hardships, their short-comings and their failures, their afflictions and their sorrows, their aches and their anxieties, their mistakes and their misdeeds, their sins and their sufferings

just as all the rest of us have. . . . This conception has been growing on me for a good many years and has come to influence my attitude and my actions more and more apace. It has led me to cultivate an attitude of faith and of friendliness, and patience and forbearance, and sympathy and positive good will toward my Negro neighbors. Nor have I allowed myself to take it all out in mere thinking and feeling. It has been my purpose and in some measure my habit to express this attitude in as many, in as vital, in as practical, and in as helpful ways as possible. To specify here in any elaborate way would be out of place both from the standpoint of space and of taste. Suffice it to say that a little sack of fruit in the hour of sickness, a brief call in the time of sorrow, a little note following a death, a small offering in time of accident, fire or other calamity—any token of tender, sympathetic thought one will find will be appreciated in a way that must bring joy and blessing to the one so doing.

As a simple, concrete example in this connection may I mention an experience that grew out of my participation in the funeral of Tom Jeffries, "Doctor Tom" as the boys called him? There was nothing fulsome or extravagant in what I said on the occasion in question. I simply spoke such words of commendation and of appreciation as I felt were thoroughly fitting. It must have been three or four years after this service that one of my Negro friends told me that he had never believed that white people really loved Negroes until he heard me speak at Tom's funeral.

Dr. Cullom hoped that this "little piece of personal testimony" would help some one else to cultivate the attitude and to do the "simple little acts" of kindness that had been such sources of blessings to him. (*BR,* August 6, 1947.)

In an article, "Smiling in the Furnace," Dr. Cullom wrote: "Whenever I see the presence and the power of God's love and grace manifesting themselves about me, my first impulse is to tell somone—to tell everyone about it." He cited three such cases, the first of which was of Mrs. John G. Mills, Sr., who in spite of having to wear a steel brace had served as president of her Missionary Society and had carried sunshine and blessing to her neighbors and friends; on August 25th she fell and broke her hip, and yet messages came to Dr. Cullom from her hospital bed that were fraught with the spirit of one who was "smiling in the furnace." (2) After relating the death of Dr. Carl Townsend, Dr. Cullom told of going to the Townsend home during the morning of the day of the funeral.

> I hardly expected to see Mrs. Townsend, but she graciously came down to the living room to see me. We talked together for ten minutes or so. . . . I was honored—greatly honored—in having those few minutes with this great servant of the King, and especially so under those conditions. Mrs. Townsend entered the room smiling, held a smile on her face as we talked together, and left the room . . . with the same smile.

(3) After leaving Mrs. Townsend, Dr. Cullom was taken to see "Captain" and Mrs. Thomas Wright whom he had married almost fifty years before; "Captain" Wright had suffered two strokes and was as helpless as he was the day he was born. Yet as Mrs. Wright walked with Dr. Cullom to the car, she told him with a smile that "she was thoroughly happy" in what she was doing. Dr. Cullom concluded:

If these three cases are not as truly furnace cases as ever were those of Shadrach, Meshach and Abednego (Dan. 3), I must confess that I know nothing of what I am saying here. Moreover, if God is not as really and truly with the three friends in question as he ever was with the three young Hebrew slaves named by Daniel, then I'm all off again in my way of seeing things. It is comparatively easy for people to think of God as being present in the beginning of things; it is perhaps about as easy to believe that he will be present at the final windup of world; but to think of him as being really present in one's daily routine is not so easy. (*BR,* Sept. 17, 1947.)

- 12 -

In January, Arthur S. Gillespie wrote of China: "This land, after the eight years of horrible world war, and now in the throes of terrible civil war, is torn, changing and swirling like waves in a storm at sea." (*BR,* Jan. 28, 1948.) In March, Dr. Cullom wrote on Mahatma Gandhi and on Dr. O. C. S. Wallace; "Uncle Ed" Farmer read *The Last Days of Hitler* to him, and Rev. Lee Pridgen took him to Centerville for a Sunday School Rally of the Tar River Association. Dr. Cullom wrote that he was again able to go to church and to sit in the pulpit to preach (Matt. 5:1-2); "I love to preach and as long as I can do so I want to go on doing it."

This was good news to many of his friends and former students. Invitations soon came pouring in. On April 10, 1948, Mr. Eustace Norfleet, who was in college to complete the course of study he had begun as a fellow-student with Dr. Cullom in 1890-1892, took Dr. Cullom down to Wilmington where, like "the aged John, ripe in faith and love," he remained seated while he preached in the Baptist churches of Masonboro and Winter Park.

In the *Biblical Recorder* of April 21st, Dr. Cullom cited as examples of "light in darkness," (1) "the poignant sense of our need of God" which President Truman expressed in his recent address to the nation; (2) the series of articles in *The British Weekly* which define the real crisis today as "a crisis in values"; and (3) the example of a friend who took into her own home a woman who was sick and who had no place to go.

When I was a boy I read a book called *Mother, Home and Heaven.* One chapter in that book bore this heading: "Night Brings out the Stars." If the darkness that surrounds us today isn't bringing out the stars of hope, of faith, of love, of assurance, than I am greatly misled.

While I was preparing this article one of my best-loved friends—a layman—came in to see me and brought with him a copy of the March 15 issue of *Time.* From it he read to me the account of the conversion of Professor C. E. M. Joad of the University of London. . . . Of his rediscovered faith Joad says: "It affords me a light to live by in an ever-darkening world."

Dr. Cullom spent the first nine days of May at Gardner-Webb Junior College in Boiling Springs; on Sunday and on Wednesday evenings he preached in "the lovely church" there. He wrote (*BR,* June 2, 1948):

My messages in the college dealt with some of the fundamental things of our Christian faith. These messages were delivered in the college auditorium, and this auditorium is somewhat "high and lifted up." When I alighted from the car in front of the auditorium on Monday morning, a good strong chair was on the sidewalk. I was asked to sit in the chair, four strong men picked it up, and almost before I knew what was going on they had taken me up the flight of steps, and taken me down the aisle and deposited both chair and me on the rostrum! As they were bringing me up the steps, I remarked to my good-natured bearers that I was literally "the man borne up of four." One of them retorted that he hoped they would not have to "tear up the roof."

On May 17th, Dr. Cullom spoke at the Baptist Church in Dunn; he also called at the home of Major General William C. Lee who had served nobly in the development of the strategic Airborne Branch of the United States Army and who was very ill. Dr. Cullom wrote:

I had no idea that I could see him. His good wife soon returned to the living room with the pleasing announcement that both the physician and the nurse said I might see him for a "moment." . . . He was under the oxygen tent and gave me such a smile as only he could give. I called him "Willie," reminding him that such was the name by which his mother called him when I first knew him and her in 1895. Of course the "moment" was a tender one. (*C. & C.*, Aug. 12, 1948.)

On June 27th, Dr. Cullom was back for General Lee's funeral and was ushered in to the family for another tender moment; later he urged:

Give attention to the boys and girls; in them is locked up the future of everything and everybody. Willie Lee was ten when I first knew him; General William C. Lee was 53 when I last saw him. During the intervening 43 years much came to pass in him and through him. Did I do my best for him and with him while I had an opportunity during those impressionable years? This is a heart-searching question. Give attention to the boys and girls. (*C. & C.*, Aug. 19, 1948.)

On June 16th, Editor Carpenter visited Wake Forest and took time for "a short visit" with Dr. Cullom, which he described as "delightful and stimulating." He reported:

Dr. Cullom is enjoying better health these days, and although, as we say "advanced in years," he has the spirit of eternal youth. He is keenly interested in what is going on in our denomination and in the affairs of the world and has constructive and progressive ideas along the lines of building a better world. (*BR*, July 7, 1948.)

On July 28th, Mr. Ed Farmer was married to Mrs. Florence G. Lockhardt of Durham; Dr. Cullom missed his brother-in-law who had continued to live in the home since 1942, but he was also happy for him. He continued his "Wayside Heroism" in the *Charity and Children;* he wrote (Sept. 9, 1948) that he could not "tell on" all his heroes but these were written that we might know that the world had not gone altogether to the bad. Elijah was reminded that God had seven thousand who had not bowed a knee to Baal and Paul said, "Even so at this present time also there is a remnant according to the election of grace." (Rom. 11:5.)

> Even so again in this very year of our Lord 1948 is there a remnant . . . to be numbered by the hundreds of thousands and found in all parts of the world . . . who in quiet faithfulness, in simple loyalty and in diligent service in their daily routine, are living lives of faith and faithfulness as truly as did those who are named and referred to in that marvelous roll call of the faithful, the 11th chapter of Hebrew.

In writing of these, Dr. Cullom said he hoped to beget within his readers "the attitude and habit of watching for this sort of thing in the lives and habits of those among whom they move from day to day."

> These are great days in which to live. They are days of trial, of difficulty, and perplexity, of misgiving, of uncertainty, of anxiety and fear. Let us not become discouraged. The day in which the angels sang over the birth of the babe in Bethlehem was just such a day. May the one who ushered in the great dividing line between the old and the new dispensations be with us now and through these "wayside heroes" usher in an even greater day than any that the world has yet seen. If and when such a day comes it will have to come through God working in and through people. And it is the deepest conviction of my soul that it must come through God as revealed in the person and work of Jesus Christ His Son, our Saviour.

In August, a polio epidemic in the state caused many of the churches to cancel their meetings, but in September (20-24) Dr. Cullom was at Mars Hill Junior College to speak on "some of the fundamental things of our Christian faith." Betty Ferrell, a senior, found him "an inspiration at eighty."

> While at Mars Hill, Dr. Cullom stayed in Huffman Dormitory for girls. I helped prepare his breakfast each morning and carried it in to him. The mornings were filled with delightful chats. In particular his sense of humor was a joy to me. . . . Another phase of his life with which I was greatly impressed was that of a calm assuredness. Just to be in his presence was to feel relaxed and refreshed. The peace in his life certainly gave one the feeling that surely the spirit of Christ was living within him.
> Dr. Cullom also impressed me by his deep interest in and love for people. He possesses an unusual gift of remembering names. One morning I was presented with a copy of the pamphlet "My Manifesto." I received such a blessing from this that I asked him if he had written any books. He told me that he had not. He said that *people* are his epistles. People, all kinds of people, are Dr. Cullom's interest . . . Dr. Cullom is a very learned man and one who continues to learn. . . . He says that he wants a teacher with whom he will not be able to "catch up" and excel. He has found that teacher in Christ Jesus. *(BR,* Oct. 27, 1948.)

On the afternoon of September 26th, Dr. Cullom was in Spring Hope at the request of its pastor, Rev. Harold Hawkins, for a dedication service of his two children. After appropriate music and a lovely solo, Dr. Cullom explained that the early Baptists, in repudiating infant baptism, failed to emphasize the responsibility of parents to create and maintain a religious atmosphere about their children.

> Someone has said that "religion is caught rather than taught." I should say that it is both caught and taught . . . one may ask why have a

special service of dedicating children. The main thing is the feeling, the conviction, the purpose behind it. But would not the same reasoning apply to the marriage ceremony, to joining the church, to attending public worship and a thousand other similar things? The experiences of the ages show that life at its best calls for definite, positive, affirmative committal if we expect to get anywhere with it and make anything of it. *(C. & C.,* Oct. 7, 1948.)

- 13 -

In January of 1949, Dr. Cullom preached at Cypress Chapel in a special service honoring "Uncle Ruff" Collie, "the only Confederate soldier" he knew still in the flesh; he continued writing his "Wayside Heroism." In an article, "Mothers and Ministers," Dr. Cullom told that in his nearly fifty years of examining ministerial students on their call, "it came to be almost a refrain to hear these boys speak of their Christian homes, and more particularly of their mothers." After writing of Hannah and her son, Samuel, who at a time when "the word of the Lord was precious" was used of God to turn back the darkness and to inaugurate the era which brought to Israel the glorious days of King David, Dr. Cullom said:

> Many of us feel that the world is much in need of a sufficient number of Hannahs to give to this world of ours the Samuels that will usher in the day of fresh "seeing"—a vision that will enable people to distinguish between the things that differ and that will lead them to ally themselves with those things that are really worthy. *(BR,* May 4, 1949.)

On July 3rd, Dr. Cullom gave the charge to Gerald Weaver at his ordination at the Rolesville Baptist Church; on July 10th, he preached for Rev. Worth C. Grant in Weldon. In the *Biblical Recorder* of August 24th, he wrote:

> It has been and still is my earnest desire to continue to serve our Master and the work of his kingdom as long as he shall give me strength to do so. I am very grateful to be able to say that I am stronger now than I was two years ago. May this continue as long as I can serve!

In November, the Baptist State Convention met in Raleigh; on Wednesday afternoon the Convention moved to Wake Forest for the dedication of the new and beautiful chapel. Editor Carpenter reported:

> It was a beautiful autumn day, and the red brick colonial chapel stood clear and beautiful in the midst of the great old oak and magnolia trees on the campus. . . . The chapel seats 2,200 people, and it was just about filled to capacity. . . . The College Glee Club and College Choir sang under the direction of Thane McDonald. . . . The main address of the afternoon was by Dr. T. F. Adams on the theme "Christian Education." . . . The prayer of dedication was led by Dr. W. R. Cullom. *(BR,* Nov. 30, 1949.)

This was a great day for Dr. Cullom, for he was privileged to participate in the realization of a dream; but he turned homeward to write of the everyday heroes beside him—the Paschal twins, Mr. Eustace Norfleet, Dr. John Lake, the Moores of Mars Hill, Mrs. B. F. Sledd.

Arthur R. Gallimore wrote that "the venerable Dr. W. R. Cullom" was himself deserving to be included among the Wayside heroes:

> If you should go to his home on North Main Street, often known as Faculty Avenue, in Wake Forest, you will find the good doctor a gracious host, alert in mind and spirit, still "living in clover," as he likes to phrase it. . . . A visit to this radiant personality is a pilgrimage very worth while.
>
> This hero of the years is not confined to his home altogether, for not a week passes that he does not go out with some of his preacher boys. Old friends are constantly calling on him for his gracious presence at funerals, for no one can bring more helpful messages to those who are bereaved. Indeed, many who are young and alive to all that goes on in the world often turn to Dr. Cullom for counsel. No day in the life of this octogenarian is lost for doing good. *(BR,* Feb. 22, 1950.)

In the *Biblical Recorder* of June 3, 1950, Dr. Cullom wrote that "the true basis of immortality is to be found in personal fellowship with a personal and eternal God."

> Wordsworth speaks of heaven being about us in infancy I am saying on the best of authority, that heaven is about us always. I have been saying for some years that I have quit trying to go to heaven; I am trying rather to bring heaven unto me. To the extent that I can succeed in doing this, to that extent will immortality be a present reality, and the consciousness of it will become an ever-increasingly happy reality . . . (John 17:3) . . . When we think of the immediate presence of God about us, what a challenge there is as we hear his knock at the door (Rev. 3:20) to open the door more and more through every day and through all the days of our respective lives to let him in that he may "sup" with us and we with him. "Supping" suggests intimate, happy, meaningful fellowship—fellowship in spirit, in life, in service, and all that goes to make for larger, fuller, richer, and ever better personality world without end. And, so, we see what is the real basis of immortality and something of the nature of the immortality that has already begun and that is to go on developing and growing richer as we hear and hearken to the voice of God as he knocks continually at the door. Let us keep in mind, too, as Holman Hunt has suggested in his great painting, *The Light of the World,* that the bolt on that door is on the inside.

Dr. Cullom shared the general enthusiasm which greeted the announcement that Dr. Harold W. Tribble had been elected the new president of Wake Forest College; in "an open letter," he wrote of the great task of moving the College to its new home and of conserving all that is worthwhile from the past in such a way as to make the college fill its place in a rich and worthy way in the new day. He commended Dr. Tribble to God who "is able to do exceedingly above all that we ask or think." *(BR,* Aug. 26, 1950.)

In an article, "Reversing God's order in Salvation," Dr. Cullom cited four ways in which men have reversed the order of restoring their fellowship with God. (1) Men have tried to build from beneath; from the time of the tower of Babel to this, men have tried "to make us a name" in ten thousand different ways and with the same result—confusion, division, scattering, failure. (2) Many would make the nature of salvation consist mainly of negatives, but "salvation that comes from fellowship with Christ is positive, happy, and full of sunshine, and it grows more so with age and use." (3) Often we reverse God's order of salvation in the *"how, when,* and *where* our salvation begins and progresses." Often we will pray for this favor and that blessing and then conclude "and at last save us," as if the last thing to be thought of is that of being saved.

> This is sort of double reversal of God's order and plan; (a) in that it postpones first-hand fellowship with God until the flesh is left behind us; and (b) it makes this direct fellowship with God a matter of place rather than of spirit and life. I defy anyone to justify such an attitude from the New Testament. In a key passage (Jno. 17:3), our Lord says, "This *is* life eternal"—and not *will be* after we are dead.

(4) We speak of our "going *up* to heaven" when the New Jerusalem is described (Rev. 21:2) as "coming *down* from God out of heaven," and the seer heard a voice saying, "Behold, the tabernacle of God is with men." "To the extent and in the measure that men make their response to this approach of God in Christ, to that extent is his salvation a present reality." (*BR,* Sept. 30, 1950.)

In a second article, Dr. Cullom stated that he shudders at the attitude and example of many Christian workers in the important matter of evangelism; "if I understand the real 'burden' of evangelism, it is to be found in the earnest desire and the strong purpose to bring people into a first-hand knowledge of God." And yet much of our communication of the "light of life" is "merely in words that have been learned by rote, or from lips that utter them in a cold, heartless, formal, meaningless fashion." The early Christians were imbued with such an overwhelming sense of God's presence and power in their own souls as to send them forth with a compelling urgency to share their joy and blessing with all whom they could find. Dr. Cullom gave "a crude illustration" of his memorizing a "courting speech"; but when he fell in love with Frances Farmer, he needed no memorized speech to tell her about it.

> On the other hand, my heart was bubbling over and I could never get through my message. We lived together here in Wake Forest for forty-seven years. She left me for her eternal home on March 30, 1944. It seemed to me at that time that my message to her had just begun.
> Surely my message here is so clear that "he who runs may read." If we expect the world to harken to our gospel message, we must somehow catch afresh the experience of the early Christians and go forth everywhere proclaiming the word in its pristine glory and in its vital power. (*BR,* Oct. 7, 1950.)

In a third article, "Reversing God's Principles of Living," Dr. Cullom asked if there could be something left "behind" of the suffering of Christ as Paul suggests in Colossians 1:24. Dr. Cullom argued that suffering for righteousness has come right on down to Bunyan, to Judson, to Niemoller; and it will go right on until the kingdoms of this world shall become the Kingdom of our Lord.

What I am trying to insist on here is the challenging fact that the cross that stood on the "green hill far away" was not an isolated event. It was unique in that the person who "suffered and died" there was unique; but that same One calls upon each would-be follower of his to deny himself, take up his cross and follow him.

There is "a cross for everyone, and there is a cross for me"; it is only as we catch a vision of the meaning of Calvary, incarnate that vision and live it out in our daily routine that the suffering of Christ can move forward toward completion. (*BR,* Oct. 21, 1950.)

In "Christmas and God's Self-Disclosure," Dr. Cullom said that when Paul wrote of God's "having made known unto us the mystery of his will" (Ephesians 1:9) he meant that we would not know God's will at all except as God makes it known to us. And how has God revealed His Will to us?

One of the most fascinating themes of Bible study that I have tried to pursue was that of tracing what we may call the *Messianic Ideal* through the Old Testament. It was probably an outcome of this study that my definition of the Bible came, viz., "The Bible is the story of God's special and progressive revelation of himself, his will, and his purpose for mankind and for the universe about us, reaching its climax in the person and the work of Jesus Christ, our Saviour and Lord."

Our Lord recognized this method of progressive revelation as the Creator's ordinary method of procedure (Mark 4:28) and declared that he had come to fulfill or complete the law and prophets (Matt. 5:17). And was this not what the writer of "Hebrews" thought when he declared, "God, who at sundry time and in divers manners spake in time past unto the fathers by the prophets hath in these last days spoken to us by his Son." This gradual and progressive self-disclosure reached its climax in the coming of the eternal Word into our human flesh; the shadows, figures, suggestions of the Divine Presence are now left behind and "we are privileged to stand face to face with, and even enter into fellowship with divine Reality."

There is no higher or richer knowledge of God to have than that which has come to us in Christ. Our growth in the knowledge of this glorious God in Christ is the happy task set before us for time and for eternity. It begins now and never ends. What a challenge does Christmas bring to everyone in all the earth! Who can wonder that we like to sing—"Joy to the world! the Lord is come!" (*BR,* Dec. 16, 1950.)

- 14 -

Sometime after the first of the year (1951), Dr. Cullom was troubled by his bladder so that he had to stay in bed. As this trouble grew worse, his physician recommended surgery. Mrs. Sue Thomas Page visited him on his 84th birthday; later she wrote:

You were expecting to go for that serious operation. Suffering as you reclined on your bed, my dear husband asked you, "Why does God let a good man like you suffer so much?" I especially listened for, and was happily pleased, at your reply of: "More things are wrought by suffering than men ever dream of." I may not have the direct wording . . . but this is the meaning of what I remember as coming from one already undergoing great suffering at the time. I knew another Christian man, who suffering long, asked "What have I done that God sent this upon me?" I was disappointed in this his last testimony to me of God toward him. (Letter, April 18, 1952.)

Dr. Cullom was taken to the Mary Elizabeth Hospital in Raleigh where Dr. John Rhodes did the operation. For two weeks his condition was very serious, but again something of a miracle occurred. Upon his return home, he was confined to his bed for about six more weeks.

With the recovery of his physical strength, Dr. Cullom's spiritual appetite grew keen; on Sunday, March 15th, he turned on his radio at ten o'clock and heard three sermons before turning it off. Having had nothing read to him for a couple of months, he was delighted when, one day in April, Harold Hawkins dropped in and read for him an article in *The British Weekly*. In May, he had "a third rich experience"—that of resuming his devotional hour. (In addition to Bible-reading, he had been using *The Upper Room* (the Methodist devotional guide), *Open Windows* (Southern Baptist), *The Secret Place* (Northern Baptist), Frank E. Garbelin's *Looking Unto Him* and Daniel Russell's *Meditations for Men.*) He wrote:

> I sometimes say that it takes a good deal to help to keep me straight. But if I may lay bare a little secret of my inner soul, I would say that I should like to enlarge and enrich my soul while trying to find strength and help for keeping straight. . . . During the four months of my sickness my habit of going to these devotional books morning by morning has, of course, been interrupted. Having become strong enough to resume this habit two or three weeks ago, I am finding in it a joy and a blessing that makes me sorry for the Christian who fails to provide for himself or herself and to use what God is so graciously and so abundantly supplying for us. *(BR, June 2, 1951.)*

Thus renewed, Dr. Cullom wrote of many things. Of suicide, he said: "For a human being to cut short his life and compromise his Maker in all that is entrusted to him is super-tragedy." *(BR, July 14, 1951.)* He told of having been "with President Wait's Descendants" in their family reunion *(BR, July 21, 1951)* and declared that "the world's greatest need" was of lives "in which Christ is incarnate and through which he is made manifest to the world about us." *(BR, Aug. 18, 1951.)* He congratulated Chowan College upon choosing Rev. Oscar Creech as an associate to its president *(BR, Aug. 25, 1951)* and saw the opening of the new Southeastern Baptist Theological Seminary on the Wake Forest campus as an extension of the work he had begun fifty-five years before. *(BR, Sept. 29, 1951.)*

On September 13th, Dr. J. B. Hipps took Dr. Cullom to call on each member of the faculty. During his visit with Dr. Sydnor L. Stealey, president of the new seminary, Dr. Cullom remarked: "I hope that you and your colleagues will try to make Southeastern a little different from our other seminaries." Dr. Cullom recalls:

I don't think that I have ever had any one to give me a more searching look as Dr. Stealey looked into my face and said, "Dr. Cullom,
what do you mean by that?" And I proceeded to tell some of the things
I had in mind. . . . "I have been at Wake Forest longer than any other
man here. . . . If I know anything about what has come to pass on that
campus there has been developed there an attitude toward truth as
such that is not to be found in every place. Such men as C. E. Taylor,
L. R. Mills, William Bailey Royall, his father, William Royall and others
wanted to know the truth about life in its bearings, whether it pleases
or hurts. They wanted the *truth*. If the new seminary can catch that
and make it to continue here as a part—an essential part—of the seminary attitude, you will have accomplished a notable and noble achievement for this seminary and for Southern Baptists."

In a letter to Dr. Stealey the next day, Dr. Cullom explained that he
did not mean to make any unkind criticism of any person or any
institution, but he had noticed that quite a number of our men "have
turned away from our seminaries because they have failed to find there
what they felt was best suited to their needs." Dr. Cullom stated:
"Other things being equal, I believe it will be better for our men to be
trained in our own institutions where the atmosphere and surroundings tend to acquaint them with the history, the purposes and plans of
their own people." Therefore, he had been moved to make the
suggestion that Southeastern be "different." He explained further:

(1) I would have our new seminary seek to create in its students
attitudes rather than fill them with facts, dogmas, and *ipse dixit* methods
of dealing with human beings. (2) Someone has said that there are three
genders of people in the world—men, women and preachers. I would
have our seminary recognize only two genders, male and female, and
seek to put its students in a frame of mind and life to go out into the
world to deal with people accordingly. Matthew Arnold's purpose at
this point seems to me to contain a worthy suggestion, viz., "to see life
and see it whole." (3) A great educator said on one occasion that
education teaches people *how* to think; *propaganda* teaches people *what*
to think. I would have our new seminary do a great task in the work
of education rather than in that of propaganda.

In an article, "Job's Comforters (?) and Christian Reality," Dr.
Cullom wrote that while Job's soul was calling for a vital, first-hand
touch with its Maker, the "preachers" of his day were repeating their
intellectual formulas.

If I may say so, it seems to me that the conditions about us today
are very similar to those of Job's day. People have been fed with creeds,
confessions, and all sorts of intellectual formulas until their souls are
literally starving for "the living bread that came down from heaven."
. . . If religion is to be vital and meaningful in any age it must be nothing
short of a personal, first-hand fellowship with the living God. . . . In
Romans 10:6-10, the great Apostle tells us how such a fellowship is
to be effected. (*BR*, Sept. 22, 1951.)

In his review of E. F. Scott's *The Lord's Prayer* (*BR*, Oct. 27, 1951),
Dr. Cullom related having heard "this great New Testament scholar"
some thirty years before; he also testified:

My mother had me memorize the Lord's Prayer when I was a child. I am now an old man, but this prayer has grown fresher, more vital and more vitalizing to me through the passing years.

In October, Dr. Henry Walden took Dr. Cullom to see the new pastor at Spring Hope, James H. Blackmore, who had just returned from Scotland where he had completed his doctorate. As they sat together in the living room of the parsonage, Dr. Cullom turned to this former student and asked, "What's next, Jim; what will be your next project?" The young minister replied:

You, Dr. Cullom. Last winter when you were sick, I asked God to spare you until I could get your story. The people abroad have a distorted conception of what Americans are really like, and even our fellow-Americans have strange notions about Southern Baptists. I think your story will do good. In the course of your life-time, the world has changed vastly and is still changing; it will do us good to see how a man can so embody the Christian faith that he comes to have something in common with Christians of every age and every land—something "eternal," if that doesn't frighten you. We need the witness of that life.

Dr. Cullom didn't have much to say at that time; later he wrote that he was highly honored and would cooperate in any way he could.

On November 12th, Dr. Cullom started out for the 121st annual session of the Baptist State Convention in Asheville; but after several visits along the way and after helping to straighten out a tangled church situation, he feared he was taking a cold and decided to return home. He made the trip home by bus without any difficulty, and the cold did not amount to anything. With great interest, he read that at this Convention 1,831 registered messengers heard Dr. S. L. Stealey say he hoped to develop "consecration, studiousness and manliness" in his students at Southeastern and Dr. Harold W. Tribble declare, "We must be separated from the world and be dedicated to the truth."

There was sadness in the land that December; long lists of Americans who were held prisoners in North Korea were published, and General Matthew B. Ridgeway said that in all the long history of Asia there had never been a tragedy to equal that of Korea. Dr. Cullom shared this sorrow; yet he was thankful for his own improved health. He wrote (*BR,* Jan. 26, 1952) that during the Christmas holidays he had been "in clover": "dear Willie" had prepared good meals for him to enjoy, and friends had read for him such books as Elton Trueblood's *The Life We Prize* and Peter Marshall's *Mr. Jones, Meet the Master.* For his "heart," he was reading E. Stanley Jones's *How to Be a Transformed Person* along with two other devotional books and several periodicals.

Besides all these, there has come to me during these days literally a bushel of Christmas cards bringing hundreds of assurances of love and of

tender, loving thoughts. So overwhelmed was I in receiving and reading
these cards that I was made to think of our great Civil War Governor,
the inimitable Zeb Vance. At a reception in his home the people came
by and shook hands, and shook hands, and then shook hands some
more. One of the Governor's friends whispered to him, "Governor, it
looks to me that it would kill you." "It does almost kill me," said the
Governor, "but if they didn't do it, that would kill me."

- 15 -

In January of 1952, Dr. Cullom preached at Tillery and commended
the practice of the congregation's following the minister's reading of
the scriptures in their own Bibles, as he had seen done at old Saint
George's in Edinburgh in 1907. He also visited his old homeplace in
Halifax County; the kitchen was gone, but the big house was still
standing among the elm trees he had helped his father plant. Out by
the cemetery, he looked toward old Quankie Church as his companion
asked, "Do ghosts of yesteryears haunt you, Dr. Cullom?" "Not at
all; I did the best I could then and am willing to leave it with the
Lord now."

The next day was Dr. Cullom's 85th birthday; friends called throughout the day. At six o'clock, his daughter, Nancy, gave him a lovely
birthday dinner-party. All during the evening, there were phone calls
and callers; as the guests left, Dr. Cullom invited them back for his
100th birthday!

When word got around that a biography was in the making, Dr.
Cullom's pupils and parishioners began writing letters of what he had
meant to them. James M. Hester, retired Navy Chaplain in California,
wrote:

> I became acquainted with Dr. W. R. Cullom in the fall of 1913, when
> I entered Wake Forest College. . . . My relationship to him was similar
> to that of a father and son. He is . . . neither a fanatic, a faddist, nor
> a fatalist; and he has not been carried about with every wind of doc-
> trine. . . . He stays on the main track. He deals with eternal things.
> He is aware that one day with the Lord is as a thousand years and a
> thousand years as one day. Therefore, he has not overly concerned
> himself with such ideologies as communism, facism and nazism. He
> knows that these will pass into the recesses of forgetfulness; but that the
> Kingdom of Love will come and that Jesus will be Lord of lords and
> King of kings.

Mrs. Edith Davis Rogers of Tallahassee remembers Dr. Cullom when
he came to help the new church at Creedmoor.

> Our church, slow to grow, was in a very depressed state when we were
> advised to seek as minister, Dr. Cullom, who was looked upon as the
> trouble shooter for the ills of struggling country churches. His quiet,
> calm, deep spirituality was immediately felt, and it gave a great spiritual
> uplift to our handful of members. One of his first activities was to
> organize a Woman's Missionary Society and a Sunbeam Band. He gave
> us a vastly broadened vision as well upon the Christian's responsibilities
> beyond himself and his immediate community. In one or more sermons,
> he brought before us a realization of the Christian's duty to give the

tithe to the work of the Lord. It was the first time I'd ever heard a
minister mention tithing.

At the time, I was a young married woman living on a nearby farm.
Our daughter was an infant. One evening when Dr. Cullom and his wife
were spending the night with us and we were talking around the open
fire, I asked him how a farmer could know what his tithe was. He replied, "When a person gives his life to Christ, he gives his all. All he
has belongs to God."

And then, I suppose from my perplexed expression, he went on to
explain in substance thus: "Before making any expenditure, we can first
ask ourselves:—'Is this expense a necessity? Will it help us to serve
God better? How can we share what we have and the Gospel with
those who know not of Christ?'" Then to illustrate his meaning, he
added, "Here is your little daughter. Some day you will wish to give
her a Christian education that she may serve God better. In giving
her this education, you are serving the cause of God."

Carmen Rogers of the Florida State University stated that she grew up
amid her parents' "expressed appreciation" of Dr. Cullom; as she
observed him herself, she was amazed at "his remarkable physical
powers and his even more remarkable intellectual vigor."

While many men with similar responsibilities have worn themselves
out in more dramatic ways of doing things and in tensions which they
unquestionably regarded as proper Christian anxieties, Dr. Cullom has
moved calmly through the years with a strength seemingly inconsistent
with the strenuous routines of his life. We ponder why. The answer
seems to lie in his ability to follow better than many of us the fundamentals of God's regimen for the long and useful life. . . . He has not
doubted that in God's strength men are made whole. He has taken
literally God's Word that men should think on things that are true, just,
lovely, and of good report. In the flurries and confusions of daily living,
he has remembered the injunction: "Be still and know that I am God."
In the quietudes of contemplation, the human soul is best sustained.
Through spiritual composure, mind and body are most surely released
for their best activities. Not every man learns to practice these truths
in a lifetime, but Dr. Cullom had learned them uncommonly well. Here-
in, I believe, is his fountain of youth.

Dr. Cullom kept on doing what he could to promote the Kingdom
of God. At the Junior High School of Spring Hope he urged the young
people to adopt the six virtues of Philippians 4:8 as guideposts in
life's journey; he wrote that every Christian should "incarnate and
express in his daily routine the spirit and purpose of God as revealed
in Christ." The witnessing of every Christian, wherever he is, is the
method by which God used to overcome the opposition of the Roman
Empire; will anything short of this suffice to meet the church's
present opponent? (*BR,* April 5, 1952.) The week of April 1-8
was spent with Superintendent James H. Hayes in "Resthaven," the
new Baptist Home for the Aging at Winston-Salem; each evening of
June 21-26, he spoke on "Some of Life's Ultimates" at the Masonboro
Baptist Church of Wilmington; Rev. Gordon Weekley wrote:

It would be hard to overestimate the blessing which was ours in his
ministry with us these days. Despite the heat we have had, our people
attended the services in good numbers and sat most attentively at the
feet of this sage and prophet while he broke unto us the Bread of Life.
His manner is quiet but forceful; his logic is clear and penetrating; his

knowledge of the Bible is what one would expect of a man who has
taught it for nearly a half-century; his spirit of earnestness is contagious;
and the whole warp and woof of his message was punctuated most
delightfully with the mellowed sense of humor that only a saint of 85
years could have. (*BR*, July 26, 1952.)

In the *Recorder* of June 28th, Dr. Cullom quoted two paragraphs from
the *Christian Century*: the first, a request to the Ford Foundation from
the American Federation of Labor asking that body to finance a project
whose purpose would be the discovery of a religious faith that would
meet adequately the world situation; the second, a quotation of Dr.
Harry R. Rudin of Yale University:

> Whatever policy America adopts to meet the present crisis, great sacri-
> fices will be required. . . . It is not ours to choose whether sacrifices shall
> be made or not; our only choice is to select the objective for which our
> sacrifices are made—either to create a world favorable to human decency
> or to keep the old world of unsolved problems that will drive men into
> barbaric madness. We do well to ask who has the message of our salva-
> tion.

These caused Dr. Cullom to say, "let us evangelize the churches."

In August, Dr. Cullom reviewed J. N. Sanders' *The Foundations
of the Christian Faith* and visited the Tim Savages at the Cale-
donia Prison Farm. On September 9th, he gave the invocation at the
opening of the Southeastern Seminary and supplied the pulpit of
the First Baptist Church of Graham on September 14th. He warned
against "Sins of the Mind" and judged that there was no question in
all the field of religion that needed "honest, careful, prayerful, faithful
study" more than "the nature, the working and the effects of sin";
we cannot have "a real revival until such a study has been made."
(*BR*, Oct. 11, 1952.) In October, he spoke at the 100th anniversary
of the First Baptist Church of Monroe and was elected "pastor emeritus" for life by the Spring Hope Church. With great interest he read
the report of the Baptist State Convention's Committee on Social
Service and Civic Righteousness (*BR*, Oct. 25th), which noted the
progress being made in race relationships and urged that "our churches
continue to take the lead in the abolition of discrimination between
the races"; it condemned "colonialism as sinful" and urged support for
the United Nations as "the best available medium for the expression of
the conscience of mankind upon great ethical principles and the most
effective means of cooperation between the nations."

On November 10th, Dr. Cullom went to Winston-Salem for the
Baptist State Convention; he had to stop all along the way to see
"very good friends," but he heard a part of the pastors' program before
hurrying off to Spencer to speak at a prayer-meeting. "Downpours of
rain" did not dampen the ardor of 1,948 Baptists who gathered to
hear an encouraging report on the Nine-Year Program of Advance
and to hear the Rev. O. L. Sherrill, secretary of the General Baptist
Convention, report on the 300,000 Negro Baptists in North Carolina

and express their appreciation of the interest and cooperation given them. Dr. Cullom was recognized; he was especially pleased to see and hear Dr. R. Paul Caudill who embraced his dear old teacher and spoke of his great joy in seeing him still active and busy in the Lord's Kingdom. Dr. Cullom "skipped" one night of the convention and went out to Yadkin Valley to meet with some of his former pupils and friends.

As the Korean conflict continued, Dr. Cullom wrote of a group of college students who gathered for "a bull session"; everyone present believed in God but only one or two feebly confessed that He was anything of a present reality to them. Dr. Cullom was reminded of the words of the Samaritan woman at the well and declared that the Christian message is of God's disclosure of Himself in Jesus Christ—the Emmanuel experience. The coming of the Logos into our human flesh is nothing short of leading ("exegete") the Eternal God from behind the veil for any and all to see. "Raphael evidently caught the true significance in John's statement (Jno. 1:18) and put that significance on canvas in a marvelous way in his Sistine Madonna." Dr. Cullom related being startled at the Twentieth Century translation of John 1:5 "The light shined in the darkness and the darkness overcame it not." He went to his Greek lexicon and found that the new translation was "certainly correct."

> Moreover, when I looked about me in the world I saw the same conflict between truth and error, between right and wrong, between God and the prince of evil still going on. And I was very grateful for the statement that in this conflict, the "darkness overcame it not." Then when I read on a little further, I came on this statement: "But as many as received him, to them gave he power to become." Not simply power to do something; not simply power to be something; but power to *become* something. And what is that something? Wonder of wonders! Power to become sons of God!" Who would not rush to seize and to use such an opportunity? (*BR*, Dec. 6, 1952.)

Dr. Cullom wrote that the Christian thesis (John 12:23-26) is "entirely adequate for our present situation and for any situation that can arise." This can be demonstrated by any person or any group of persons that will put it to the test.

> It was Gilbert Chesterton, I believe, who said that the Christian religion had not been tried and failed: it had been tried, found to involve complete denial of self in the service of God and of one's fellowmen even unto death, and had been abandoned by men to do as they did in Isaiah's day, "turned every one into his own way" (Isa. 53:6) . . . The way is open on any day or at any moment that the human family is ready to follow Isaiah's prescription: "Let the wicked forsake his way, and the unrighteous his thoughts; and let him return unto the Lord and he will have mercy upon him; and to our God, for he will abundantly pardon." . . . But the risen and ever-present Christ—the real "Emmanuel"—goes even further . . . and says, "Behold I stand at the door and knock: if any man hear my voice, and open the door, I will come in unto him and will sup with him, and he with me." . . . The "Emmanuel" teaching and especially the "Emmanuel" experience assure me that this is and will forever be a *present* reality . . . His assurance,

moreover, is that as we go forth doing his bidding, he will be with us to the end.

May this Christmas season bring to our harassed and distressed world such a sense of the Emmanuel experience that the whole earth shall be able to sing . . . "Joy to the world! the Lord is come. . . ." (*BR*, Dec. 20, 1952.)

- 16 -

On January 15th (1953), the Spring Hope Church honored Dr. Cullom with a birthday banquet; at 86, his health was improved from former years so that he stood up to speak and spoke with a strong voice and good humor. He also shared in the funeral services for Mrs. Lelia McNeill Privette and attended the deacons' annual supper. In all this, he was with the Spring Hope pastor, and they shared all the thoughts of their hearts and lives. On January 28th, he wrote:

Dear Jim,
   Somehow when I am deeply stirred over Kingdom matters I find myself wanting to turn to you for conference. Would that I could "talk over" things with you to-night! Two experiences of today have served to make me feel deeply that I wish I could see you. (1) Today had been "Missionary Day" in the Southeastern Seminary. Dr. Bill Decker has been the speaker for the day. (2) My *Christian Century* . . . came today and I have read two stirring articles in it tonight. Both of them have to do with Asia—the report on the meeting of the International Committee and the article commenting on that report. Of course you will read these. May our God give you wisdom to think of them in the right way and then come over and tell me what you think. Dr. Decker referred to the Communists' threat as being the most serious since Islam came so near to crushing Christianity from the earth! I'm very tired tonight and hope I can go to sleep and feel brighter by the morning.

And the pastor in Spring Hope gave his dear teacher all the time he could; together they visited the churches he had served and called on scores of former parishioners. Dr. Cullom was like a schoolboy out of school; he thoroughly enjoyed being with people and seemed to gain strength from them. Whenever surprise was expressed at his endurance, Dr. Cullom replied, "I have the power to relax when not in action." Wherever they called, something like a spiritual Aurora Borealis took place; everybody became "super-charged" with delight and excitement. "Why, it's Dr. Cullom—O, John—Mary—Aunt Sue —come and see who has come!" And men and women rushed to embrace him. "Where, on earth, have you come from?" they would ask as if somehow they expected to hear him say he had come from heaven.

Dr. Cullom continued to mail hundreds of letters and cards; Rev. S. L. Morgan, who had retired in Wake Forest, wrote of this "Ministry of Kindness."

Most others ignore your little courtesy or kindness as too little to notice. He doesn't; he sends a postal. You do a signal deed of bravery that costs you blood—maybe friends. Likely he'll write a postal with one word—"Bravo!" Do you write something eminently sensible and worthwhile? Will *nobody* read it and say a word? He sends a postal with just two words, "Thank you!" and his initials. *(BR,* Jan. 31, 1953.)

That spring, Dr. Cullom heard Dr. Robert J. McCracken in a special series of services at Wake Forest and reviewed Harry Emerson Fosdick's *A Faith for Tough Times;* he spoke to a group of young mothers in Wake Forest on Canon Max Warren's articles on "the situation in today's world." As he concluded this discussion, one of the young women earnestly asked, "What can I do?" This "pertinent" question became the title of an article in which Dr. Cullom offered these suggestions:

> (1) If we would fit ourselves to make a contribution toward meeting and solving the world's present problems, let each of us give earnest and faithful attention to the task of growing and applying a strong, rich, wholesome personality. (2) The personality that is most Christlike in spirit, in attitude, in purpose, and in life is the one that will effect most in meeting and in solving today's problems and difficulties. (3) The simple secret of growing such a personality is the habit of cultivating daily intercourse and fellowship with the risen, the living, the omnipotent Christ. (4) To such personalities our Lord said, and so can we, "Ye are the salt of the earth; ye are the light of the world" (Matt. 5:13-14). And let us keep in mind that salt serves two purposes—it preserves, and it seasons. Light also serves two purposes—it illumines, and it guides. (5) With a sufficient number of such personalities surrendered and dedicated to the purpose of following our Lord's challenge to deny self, take up the cross and follow him (Mk. 8:34), no problem will be too complicated, nor any task too difficult in dealing with the present situation in the world or with any future situation that may arise. Such personalities can say, "I can do all things through him that strengthens me." *(BR,* June 6, 1953.)

In June, Dr. Cullom congratulated Dr. W. F. Powell upon his 40th anniversary as pastor of the First Baptist Church in Nashville, Tennessee; within a few days, he received this reply:

> Dear Dr. Cullom—No person on earth could have made me as happy by writing me a letter as you did. I would rather have those words from you than from any living man. You took time when enrolling a young country boy in college for a word to him personally. You remarked about the "W. F." in my name and called me "Wake Forest Powell." It stuck. My highest ambition has been to be worthy of it, and of you.

Also with this letter was an envelope upon which was written: "The least bit of a lot of love and appreciation from the unworthiest of all your boys." Fifty dollars was enclosed. This thoughtfulness on the part of Dr. Powell was secretive, but as it indicated something of the devotion of his former students, may we be forgiven for telling it. Also that he and others might know how greatly appreciated such "bits of love" were, may we be forgiven for sharing this bit of information as to how it was used: Dr. Cullom wrote:

> I went to Raleigh on Tuesday morning to hear the men at Meredith. When I came home, Nancy told me that the cashier of my bank had called to remind me that my account was overdrawn by $54.00. Next morning I gave her the money to deposit for me. So you can understand

as to how welcomed Dr. Powell's gracious gift was and is. (Letter, June 20, 1953.)

Dr. Cullom continued to help in gathering material for the biography by writing a sketch of biographical data and listing friends in Wake Forest who might help "tell on" him. September 22nd (1953) was a typical "biography-day." It began with a call on Mrs. R. L. Brewer —"You always expect the best of people, and we have to live up to it." Mr. Jesse Hollowell told that through the years Dr. Cullom had bought bags of fruit (ten or twelve at the time at 75 cents per bag) for the sick and shut-ins. Mrs. Ethel Carroll Squires recalled that in 1911, while attending her brother's graduation, she and her parents had been invited by Dr. and Mrs. Cullom for dinner.

> After the meal was over, I felt we had feasted in many ways. In 1912 I came back to Wake Forest as a bride, and Mrs. Cullom became one of my special friends. . . . I don't know whether or not he has a favorite hymn, but I always think of him when we sing "My Faith Looks Up to Thee."

Mrs. Alma Helm said that for a year she had read for Dr. Cullom— three mornings a week for an hour or two or three.

> He had great interest and great knowledge of modern trends in philosophy and religion. His mind was keen, and often he interrupted the reading to make a comment.

Mrs. Edith Taylor Earnshaw remembered that she was just a girl when she first knew Dr. Cullom; later she heard him speak to the Woman's Missionary Society, at the conclusion of which he began to sing "I've wandered far from home, but now I'm coming home." Mrs. Earnshaw also recalled:

> At one time we had a student in the college by the name of Crow. One night at the church, Dr. Cullom said, "Brother Pray, will you please Crow." That broke up the meeting.

Mr. Lincoln Robert Best, the Negro principal of the DuBois Public School since 1936, told of first meeting Dr. Cullom in the post office.

> He extended his hand, introduced himself, welcomed me to Wake Forest and expressed interest in our school and race; he hoped we would be happy here. In the years that have followed we have had him to speak to the faculty, in chapel and to preach our baccalaureate sermon. For the past 13 or 14 years he has sent *The Upper Room* to every member of our faculty, and these devotional booklets are used each morning in our classes. Dr. Cullom is a man of broad catholic spirit—deep and sincere. I have often discussed with him the racial attitude in town; he shows the progress that has been made. He knows whence we came and is interested in us; he has taken a personal interest in me. I've been to his home when he was sick; he has been to mine. He is always encouraging us and complimenting us for anything he thinks is praiseworthy. The students think highly of him because of what their parents have told about him. He has been very kind and a great encouragement; I value his friendship very much and regret his age and infirmity. We need him just now, and I don't see any one like him coming on to take his place.

Mrs. Betty Dent, an elderly Negro woman, welcomed Dr. Cullom into her home as "my friend for over 40 years" and told that through her husband's long illness (seven years), Dr. Cullom had come many, many times with bags of fruit to talk the scriptures, to sing, and to pray with him. Dr. J. B. Hipps told of being with Dr. Cullom in New York for three days—"sharing classes and talking about everything."

> From that time on, we have written frequently to each other. When I came home from China, I tried to see him. He often invited me to speak at Wake Forest, and I would spend the night in his home. In 1925, when I came to Asheville with my little boy, after the death of my wife, Dr. Cullom came to see me and visited with me and my father. Later he had me discuss world issues at the preachers school in Raleigh. In 1947 when I was back from China, Dr. Cullom and I had been talking for quite a while; I was afraid I was tiring him, and so about 9:30 I hinted that he might want to retire. "Retire?" he asked; "Do you think 11:30 will be too early." We shared our deepest thoughts and opinions in almost complete agreement. . . . I have never had a friend I've treasured more highly.

In October, Dr. W. O. Carver, "that grand old man of Louisville," gave three lectures at the new seminary on the Wake Forest campus; after his first one, he made his way to Dr. Cullom, and the two old friends embraced each other. Later at Dr. Cullom's home for lunch, the two talked of the old Seminary days and discussed the problems and challenges of the day; they agreed that such an experience was "heavenly" and looked forward to its being uninterrupted.

- 17 -

With great interest and sorrow, Dr. Cullom learned of the trouble in the North Rocky Mount Baptist Church. Under the leadership of its pastor, the Rev. Samuel H. W. Johnston, this church of 1,300 members had voted (241 to 144) to withdraw from the Baptist State Convention and the Southern Baptist Convention because of "modernism" in some of its institutions. The church split into two factions, each claiming the church's property. The contention was taken to court—the majority claimed that the property was theirs because they were the majority; the minority claimed that they, although a minority, were the *true* church.

To prove their charges that the Baptist State Convention had departed from the beliefs, practices and usages of the Missionary Baptists, the Johnston party cited the program of the annual Baptist Student Union Convention which included an address by Dr. Nels F. S. Ferré on worship; they read excerpts from his writings which they claimed raised questions of his belief in the virgin birth of Jesus. On the eve of the Baptist Student Union Convention, Dr. Ferré was notified that his address had been cancelled; the students protested vainly. When the Baptist State Convention met a few weeks later, a committee of seven was appointed to study the Baptist Student Department.

On December 30th, Superior Court Judge Malcolm Paul ruled that in the North Rocky Mount Baptist Church Case the plaintiffs (although a minority) represented the "true" congregation of the church and were entitled to possession of the property. The North Carolina Supreme Court sustained Judge Paul's ruling; Justice R. Hunt Parker stated:

> While it is true the membership of the North Rocky Mount Missionary Baptist Church is a self-governing unit a majority of its membership is supreme and entitled to control its church property only so long as the majority remains true to the fundamental faith, usages, customs, and practices of both factions before the dispute arose.

This decision, while saving "the structure of the missionary Baptist organization" (*BR,* Jan. 9, 1954), raised questions which were to trouble Baptist conscience for some time.

A case of bronchitis did not prevent Dr. Cullom from writing about the North Rocky Mount Case and of the Baptist Student Union. Characteristically, he did not mention the particulars; rather, in an article "Democracy Gone to Seed" (*BR,* Feb. 27, 1954), he told of having entered a country church when "a plain, godly countryman" was leading in prayer. As Dr. Cullom waited and felt the humble reverence of the man's soul, he thought that this was a rebuke to much that was going on in the name of religion. Noting the great reverence accorded God in holy Scripture, Dr. Cullom wrote: "I believe in democracy with all my soul, but real democracy places the holy God as the center of all life, keeps him there, and adjusts every detail of life to this elementary and fundamental fact."

For twelve hours, on March 30th, the General Board of the Baptist State Convention considered the report of the special committee appointed to investigate the Baptist Student Union; in "a clash between so-called 'liberals' and so-called 'conservatives'," the BSU state secretary and two of his associates were dismissed. To those who were "carrying on the current discussion about our young people," Dr. Cullom declared "too much of it is in a negative tone"; he thought the "positive and constructive" principle should be used by Christians at all times and under all circumstances—and to the Nth degree now "with nation rising up against nation, with class antagonizing class, with hatred and strife rampant in the earth, and with all the doubt, perplexity, confusion, misgiving and all the rest that we see in the earth about us." (*BR,* April 10, 1954.) He wrote that this trouble over the Baptist Student Union had "sprung up from the soil about us as naturally as the stalk of corn springs up from the grain that was planted" and told of a denominational leader's saying to a friend that a certain motion before the convention ought to be opposed, but if he should speak out against it he would "cut off his own head" (that is, he would hurt his own chances of advancement, etc.). Dr. Cullom said:

So long as we sow such seeds . . . just that long shall we continue to reap such harvests as the one of March 30. We have been dealing with a specific case here, but the real trouble goes much deeper than a mere current surface manifestation. *(BR,* May 8, 1954.)

In another article, Dr. Cullom told of having been asked by a young minister, while he was in Jerusalem in 1914, how he classified himself—"Modernist or Fundamentalist?" Dr. Cullom replied, "I do not like to be labeled; I am only an unworthy sinner saved by the mercy and grace of God in Christ, our Saviour and Lord." He told the young man that if he *had* to classify himself he would say he was a conservative with his face to the future. When asked to clarify this, Dr. Cullom explained, "With Harriet Beecher Stowe, I believe that 'Our God is marching on'."

I believe that any person who would walk in fellowship with God must get into the way that God is going by means of reconciliation in Christ, must move in the direction that God is moving, and must keep up with God, but not "run before him."

I told the young man then that according to my conception of the matter, this progressive experience begins when by faith we become reconciled to God in Christ and continues through Eternity. This carries with it, of course, the thought that the life we are now living is an essential part of our life eternal. *(BR,* June 19, 1954.)

Dr. Cullom developed this thought further in a little booklet, "The Fatal Division," which he had printed and circulated in May of 1954. Defining the "fatal division" as the distinction we make between time and eternity, Dr. Cullom told:

While visiting in the home of dear friends a year or two ago, I asked my hostess whether it had occurred to her that we are at this moment in eternity. With a look of astonishment on her face, she said, "No, Mr. Cullom, I never thought of such a thing." I said to her, "They tell me that the word 'Eternity' means that which has no beginning and end; if that be true why are we not as truly and as much in eternity just now as we shall be a thousand years from now?"

Dr. Cullom thought this revolutionary concept would change our entire lives when we understand and honestly accept it.

When I was a little boy, my mother would take me by her lap at night and have me say my little prayer before going to bed. I thought then and think now that God heard and answered that prayer. But how different is my concept of God now from what it was then! At that time I thought of God as seated upon a great white throne far, far beyond the sky. What appears to us as a solid blue dome is only the dust with the sun shining against it. When I became convinced that this was true, I said, "Where then is my God?" As has been my habit for many years, I then turned to Him who was manifest in the flesh. I have never looked to Him yet and had Him to fail me. I hear Him say, "He that hath seen me hath seen the Father . . . God is Spirit . . . He is not far from every one of us for in Him we live and move and have our being."

Jesus confirmed this definition (Lk. 4:21, Mk. 1:14-15, John 17:3); yet after His days in the flesh, the fellowship which He made possible changed from "an organism" into "an organization."

> The tie that binds an organism together is internal, vital and personal; the tie that binds an organization together is external and mechanical. . . . The New Testament organism was guided and directed by the Holy Spirit; the Christian organization, alas again, has all too often been guided and controlled by men whose dominating purpose was to carry forward their own personal plans and purposes rather than to develop and carry forward the interests and the needs of the body of the risen and ever-living Christ. The living organism spread itself by contagion and vital contacts, and by personal testimony; the Christian organization spread itself by human planning and by mechanical devices.

With this change, the concept of Jesus that time and eternity are one continuous whole also changed into a dull acceptance of our days in the flesh and the hope of a glorious transformation in the next. This is a *fatal* change because it tends to take the Christian movement from under the direct guidance of the Holy Spirit and leads to the secularization of our churches with its leaders seeking to manipulate an organization rather than to direct the growth of an organism. Dr. Cullom suggested: We believe that *now* is eternity, accept it as the basis of our living and adjust ourselves from a *credit* to a *cash* system. Too long and too strong has been our attitude of looking to the far-distant future for the reward of our faith; we have thought of death as the way to eternal life whereas the New Testament teaches that faith is the doorway to all that God holds in store for us, and this faith is a present reality.

> I recall my sermons of years ago on Amos 4:12, for example—"Prepare to meet thy God, O Israel." I tried to picture the kind of judgment that I looked for as a child when I would go upstairs and look out of the windows toward the East to see whether I could see the beginnings of the judgment fires. Do we not need to know and feel that each day is a judgment day and really counts in the life record?

The removal of "the division between time and eternity" will enable us to think of life as a unit, to enjoy our fellowship here and now, and to rejoice in the assurance that this fellowship will grow richer and more meaningful world without end. Of death, Dr. Cullom wrote:

> When I was a child an old man who made "coffins" lived near my paternal grandfather's home, and there seemed to be a peculiar sound to Mr. Ives's hammer when he was making a "coffin." When this sound was heard my grandmother would stop in her routine work and make the solemn comment, "Somebody's dead; Mr. Ives is making a coffin." Whereupon everybody in hearing automatically became possessed of a feeling of unspeakable solemnity.

Dr. Cullom stated that he had long changed from such a view and now believed that death has "its place along with all that goes on about us as a part of Nature's Laws, which are God's laws."

> There is nothing in death to fear or to dread. Nor is there any magic power in it to undo any of God's plans and processes. The main thing, therefore, is that we shall be in harmony with God and with his will for us and for the world about us. Nor again is it difficult to discover that Plan and Purpose: they are laid bare before us in that Word which became Flesh (John 1:14) in order that He might expose God to all

men (John 1:18). "In Him was life; and the life was the light of men" (John 1:4). This is the light that lighteth every man and every situation that man has to face, even death itself. So that He says to each of us, "Fear not, for I have overcome." In Him, therefore, we are "conquerors and more than conquerors. For neither death, nor life, nor any created thing shall be able to separate us from the love of God, which is in Christ Jesus our Lord." (Romans 8:37-39.)

Of the life that awaits us beyond the flesh, Dr. Cullom said:

(1) It will be a purposeful activity. The seer on Patmos describes this life under the picture of the New Jerusalem . . . and says: *"His servants shall serve him"* (Rev. 22:1-5). We are not told as to what this service will be, but why should he do when about him and about us one can see a thousand times more than he can do? It is amply sufficient for me that we are to *"serve him."* (2) It will be a life of perpetual growth and of endless progress. David Smith says in his comments on John 14:2 that many have thought that the word "mansions" means eternal abiding places. Not so, he insists: they were temporary abidings to use until we appropriate what God has for us in one of them, and then we move on to another. So that eternity will be one constant, never-ending exploration party. What a glorious concept is this! (3) It will be a life of ever increasingly happy fellowship. As I grow older, the experience of congenial, purposeful, happy fellowship comes to mean more and more to me. This fellowship will center in and around the things that are richest and most worthwhile. In his description of the New Jerusalem, the tabernacle of God is with men. God himself is there, and all are in happy fellowship with assurance that we are now the sons of God, that it does not yet appear what we shall be, but that we shall be like him, for we shall see him as he is (I John 3:2). How can one fail to look forward to the future with a joy that is truly unspeakable and full of glory?

Of the second coming of our Lord, the climax toward which "the whole creation moves"—Dr. Cullom stated:

I do not know enough about all this to discuss it as yet. I believe in it because the Book teaches it. . . . I am like Mr. Charles H. Spurgeon was about the prospect of our Lord's return. Someone had figured it all out to a nicety as to just when He would come, and announced that He would come on a certain day in April of that year. Mr. Spurgeon came to his pulpit in his great London Tabernacle on the first Sunday in the new year, mentioned the prediction in question, declared that he knew nothing at all about it, that our Lord had said He did not know the time, but "when He comes," said Mr. Spurgeon, "I shall be very happy to see Him." With that, this great man of God proceeded with his service of worship.

In view of all this, Dr. Cullom urged:

(1) that every Christian in all the world begin to practice the consciousness of the presence of God at the moment and on the spot of reading this sentence; (2) that he begin and cultivate the habit of thinking of himself as a messenger from God to every other human being in all the earth; (3) that he think of himself as more than a mere messenger, but even as a real helper in doing God's service in the present hour; (4) that he take Paul's statement in I Corinthians 3:9 and our Lord's statement in John 17:18 as being just as applicable to us just now as they were to the first Christians; (5) that he disregard all distinctions of race, of color, of social status—absolutely every distinction—in the application of these principles; (6) that he begin to think of himself as being in heaven just now and to act accordingly.

Dr. Cullom concluded by stating that if the acceptance and application of these principles do not make life a new and an increasingly happy experience, he would surrender to any penalty anyone may wish to lay upon him.

- 18 -

On May 17, 1954, the Supreme Court of the United States declared segregation in all public schools unconstitutional; this was a reversal of the famous case of Plessy *versus* Ferguson (1896) which had given the basis for the separate-but-equal doctrine upon which segregation had been legally maintained. Editor Carpenter, who had studied under Dr. Cullom, reported, "The decision was unanimous and almost inevitable in the light of Christian truth, the claims of democracy, and the demands of the world situation." (*BR,* May 29, 1954.) John L. Coley, who revered Dr. Cullom as a beloved teacher, declared that the decision of the Supreme Court should awaken every Christian in the land; "We know that the gospel in its very essence outlaws segregation in every way, shape, and form." (*BR,* May 29, 1954.) T. Lacy Williams, a Baptist attorney in Raleigh, called for patience and tolerance as "two virtues which we should nurture in the months and years ahead" and declared if we who love the Bible would follow its precepts it might well be that we would come to thank God that our Supreme Court is "a city of Refuge for the oppressed." (*BR,* June 5, 1954.) Stating that we ought to support and steady our leaders when their "hands are pointed heavenward in a just and righteous cause," Dr. Cullom wrote:

> (1) If there has ever been a time in which our leaders needed reinforcements from their constituency that time is right now. (2) We have leaders who, in spite of the nauseating McCarthy affair, seem to me to be trying to lead us in the right way. (3) Let us not grumble and complain, but help.

At the Southern Baptist Convention at St. Louis that June, 10,962 messengers heard Dr. A. C. Miller read the report of the Christian Life Commission on race-relation:

> In the light of the recent decision handed down by the Supreme Court of our nation declaring segregation of the races to be unconstitutional, and in view of the position of this convention in adhering to the basic moral principles of our religion as they apply to race relations, we recommend:
> 1. That we recognize the fact that this Supreme Court decision is in harmony with the constitutional guarantee of equal freedom to all citizens, and with the Christian principles of equal justice and love for all men.
> 2. That we commend the Supreme Court for deferring the application of the principle both as to time and procedure until the nation shall have had time to work out methods by which transition from the present practice may be effected.
> 3. That we urge our people and all Christians to conduct themselves in this period of adjustment in the spirit of Christ; that we pray that God may guide us in our thinking and our attitudes to the end that we may

help and not hinder the progress of justice and brotherly love; that we may exercise patience and good will in the discussions that must take place, and give a good testimony to the meaning of Christian faith and discipleship.

4. That we express our belief in the public school system for our nation as one of the greatest factors in American history for the maintenance of democracy and our common culture, and we express the hope that in the working out of necessary adjustments, its place in our educational program shall not be impaired.

5. That we urge Christian statesmen and leaders in our churches to use their leadership in positive thought and planning to the end that this crisis in our national history shall not be made the occasion for new and bitter prejudices, but a movement toward a united nation embodying and proclaiming a democracy that will commend freedom to all peoples.

Mr. W. M. Nevins (81 years old) of Lexington spoke against this report; "I believe in emancipation and equality for the Negroes, but not amalgamation of the races." A man from Albuquerque declared that the decision of the Supreme Court had been "a political decision"; "the Negroes need opportunity, but we must not mix the races." Then Dr. J. B. Weatherspoon, formerly Dr. Cullom's pupil, arose and said,

> We are faced with a realistic situation, and we are not going to shut our eyes to the future. We, Baptists, have always faced up to the tough issues. We have over our heads the banner "Forward with Jesus Christ." Our only question is, what is the most Christian thing to do. If we vote down these recommendations we are saying to the people of the United States, count Southern Baptists out on the issue of equal justice for all. I do not believe that we want to say that.

The Convention gave him a long and loud applause; the question was called for, and over 9,000 messengers stood in favor of the Christian Life Commission's recommendation, with only 50 opposing them. *The Christian Century* stated that in this action Southern Baptists did more than any other group in the country to carry the public toward accepting the Supreme Court's ruling against segregation. Mr. Henry Belk, editor of the *Goldsboro News-Argus,* knew that the convention's action, as fine as it was, would not be the last word; he wrote that the churches would fight it out on a thousand fronts, "but in the end there will be advance." (*BR,* June 26, 1954.)

Dr. Cullom stayed at the tasks he could do to help make this advance possible. He commended "most heartily" Grace Noll Crowell's *Moments of Devotion* and John Bailey's *Diary of Private Prayers* and, in July, spent another week in the Masonboro community. In August, he was at Goldsboro; the *News-Argus* reported his preaching-schedule would keep him "jumping about the state" for several weeks. Wherever he went he sought out such shut-ins as Janie Belle Blackmore of Warsaw and Annie Swinson of Bear Marsh. But he kept writing of the race problem. In the *Recorder* of August 7, 1954, he shared, from E. Stanley Jones's *Growing Spiritually,* the testimony of a white woman who was to speak to a Negro audience.

As I stood up, I paused a moment . . . and saw Jesus . . . and heard him say, "Mary, you were called to witness, not to speak. Look full in my face and tell them what you see." And the message just spoke itself, without any notes, or any effort on my part. When I had finished, one of the sisters came up and took me in her arms and kissed me on the cheek. It was so tender and soul-searching I thought I would never want to wash that cheek again. . . . At that moment there wasn't any question of color or race; it was just one child of God loving another. . . . And it came to me that this is the perfect solution of the so-called race-problem; being one in Him.

That fall, Dr. Cullom attended a meeting where Negroes and white people sat down together and talked of the recent decision of the Supreme Court. Dr. Cullom wrote:

This decision was inevitable, but it has thrust upon our Southern people a matter that calls for all the wisdom, all the patience, all the plain common sense, and all the spirit of Christ that we can command. Without speaking further about the conference of last evening, I have a little story to relate:

A Negro man stepped on a bus recently to find that all the seats for Negroes were filled. A white man sat alone in a seat just in front of the Negroes. This gentleman invited the standing Negro to share his seat with him. The conductor came back at once and told the Negro that he was trespassing and would have to move. Without a word, the Negro got up and stood. When he did, the white man in question arose and stood with the Negro until one of them reached his destination.

Four comments: (1) An old saying says, "Action speaks louder than words." This surely is sufficient. (2) Our Lord says something about going the second mile; this white man was acting in the spirit of his Master. (3) The people of our Southland, not to speak of other parts of the earth, are having an opportunity to cultivate and show the spirit of Jesus in a way today that should challenge the best that is in us. (4) I repeat and would emphasize my heading: "A story that tells much and suggests more." *(BR,* Sept. 11, 1954.)

At 88, Dr. Cullom attended the birthday banquet at Spring Hope, made a tape-recording for the 120th anniversary of the Rolesville Baptist Church, reviewed *The Prayers of Peter Marshall,* wrote of the needs of the Baptist Home for the Aging and commended Miss Dixie Bryan for having served as a helper and companion to Mrs. J. A. Tunnell. He asked "how to get the work of 48 hours into a day of 24" and urged his friends to use their time wisely. *(BR,* Jan. 15, 1955.) In March, he participated in the funeral services of "the gentle, unassuming, faithful Arthur Gallimore" and in April was taken by Dr. G. G. Grubbs to Duke University to hear Mr. Arthur Hallam Tennyson III, tell of his great-grandfather. April brought the establishment of the W. R. Cullom Student Aid Loan Fund at Southeastern Baptist Theological Seminary. It came about in this way. In speaking at the Western Roanoke Baptist Union at Momeyer, Rev. Ben Fisher told of the trials many a young seminarian was enduring in an effort to prepare himself to answer God's call to preach; he related his own experience.

I came to Wake Forest in September of 1933 with a desire for an education, an old worn Bible, and $7.50. As a ministerial student, I knew the college would give me my tuition, but I had to find ways of paying for a place to stay and my meals. The first place I asked for employment I found it, and I felt I was in. With great joy I went to register at the college. After standing in line a long time, I reached the bursar and was told that the matriculation fees would be $32.00— and I had only $7.50. . . . My world crashed around me. What would I do? I went into the library and sat down; there was nothing to do but to try to get home. But I just sat there for awhile, when I became aware that someone had come before me. When I looked up, there stood a short, bald-headed man with a bay-window; he was smiling. "It's a mighty pretty day for such a long face as you have; what's the trouble, young man?" As I told him, he took out his pen and on a scrap piece of paper wrote something, and told me to go back and get in line. "When you reach the bursar again, give him this." And he gave me the piece of paper, upon which was written: "Enroll Mr. Fisher and look to me for his matriculation fees—W. R. Cullom." And I stood up, thanked the professor, and raced back to the line.

When Mr. Fisher told this before the Union meeting in Momeyer, Mr. S. V. T. Chamblee asked that a special offering be taken for the needy students at Southeastern Seminary; Mr. Henry Jones, a prominent farmer, proposed the establishment of a permanent fund honoring Dr. Cullom; he said,

For a long time it has been my desire to do something for Southeastern Seminary and for Dr. Cullom. Dr. Cullom has had a wonderful influence in my part of the state, and I know that he made it possible for many a young man to get an education.

Mr. Jones wrote a check for $700 and gave it to Mr. Fisher—who took it to the man who once had befriended him. That piece of paper gave the professor as much joy as his note had given to the student twenty-two years before. As others learned of this, they sent in their contributions; in commenting upon the letter and gift of Mrs. Lena Jones of Wendell, Dr. Cullom said he doubted if there were "any part of Christian service that counts more in real Kingdom service and growth than that of helping to produce a strong, capable, rich leadership in it and for it." He wrote: "Personally, I am greatly honored and am also greatly delighted with the establishment and the development of this Fund." (*BR,* May 21, 1955.)

At the Southern Baptist Convention in Miami, Dr. Casper C. Warren of Charlotte was elected president of eight million Baptists; this brought special joy to his former pastor and teacher. Also Dr. Cullom was delighted over the success of the special schools for ministers such as the ones at Mars Hill, Meredith and at Hendersonville. Another "pleasing experience" came during the commencement program at Wake Forest when, at the Alumni Luncheon on May 30th, he was given such an ovation that he was "unable to speak." He found pleasure in visiting the old Spring Hill Church at Wagram and in participating in the centennial celebration at Cypress Chapel. His stay

(June 26-29) at Brookford with Rev. W. C. Laney and his interracial church was especially delightful:

> My special mission there was to preach each evening for four days and to conduct five conferences looking toward the enrichment of personal life, the clearer understanding of the scriptures, and the better equipment for living in the world as servants of the King. In the conferences the majority of my group was Negroes; in the preaching services the majority was white people. . . . When you saw Brother Laney darting around the cook room, washing dishes, waiting on the table and such like, you might have thought that he was a *Brother Lawrence;* when you had personal fellowship with him, you were sure that he was a duplicate of Brother Lawrence in the *Practice of the Presence of God.* . . . They say they mean to have me again, I say to them, "Barkis is willin'!" *(BR,* Sept. 17, 1955.)

In July, Dr. Cullom preached at Cherry Point and spoke to the pastor's conference at Maysville; in August, Mrs. I. T. Valentine of Nashville took him to the "Camp Further Out" at Kanuga Lake, and in September, he gave the opening address at Wingate College.

In an article, "A Sane Word on a Delicate Matter," Dr. Cullom said that people outside of the South "can have no conception of the depth and the power of the feeling that lies just under the surface in both races" with regard to the matter of desegregation of the races in the public schools of the country.

> One of the best informed men in America told me 30 years ago that there should be only one school in each community, and that white people and Negroes should all go to the same school. I told him that his plan would come in time, but that our people were not ready for it then. Nor are they ready for it to be thrust upon them suddenly now, and especially are they not ready to have it forced upon them.
>
> Some years ago a Negro deacon was driving Dr. John A. Hutton of London to a conference at Massanetta Springs, Virginia. The two men talked over many things in a heart-to-heart way. Finally, the deacon said this: "Mr. Hutton, the good Lord has a way of bringing things around after a while if you'll just give him time." That Negro deacon was speaking good sense. His words might well have come from the wise men of Israel.
>
> In the *News and Observer* for Monday, September 19, another Negro spoke wise words on this question of segregation. If I caught the heart of what Dr. Taylor was saying, it was this: Let a small group from each race meet regularly, talk this matter over in a frank but sympathetic way, and let these lead in the matter of applying the decision of the Court to the schools about us, and give them reasonable time in which to do it. In my opinion Dr. Taylor is right, and a careful attention to his suggestion may save our land a lot of trouble in the future that is just ahead of us, and at the same time make the issue one of positive and constructive progress and blessing to all concerned. *(BR,* Oct. 15, 1955.)

At the Baptist State Convention in Asheville that November, the Committee of 21 recommended that "we request the Trustees of the institutions of our Convention to give careful study to their responsibility and opportunity to open doors of knowledge and service to qualified applicants regardless of race." Mr. H. V. Scarborough of Raleigh declared that desegregation would disrupt every school district and every church in eastern North Carolina and "bring anarchy to our part of the state." Rev. Donald Morris, a Silver Star and Purple Heart veteran of World War II, pleaded: "We should act like Christians on this matter. Those who harbor Civil War ideas on this principle are on the wrong track." When the resolution was voted on, 816 stood up favoring its adoption, with 285 opposing it. (*BR*, Nov. 26, 1955.) Recognizing that the complex problems of race relations cannot be solved by "federal compulsion alone," the Committee on Social Service and Civic Righteousness stated:

> The enduring solutions will be thought out and wrought out in morally productive communities by men and women of faith and wisdom who look at human relations in the perspective of the sovereignty of God, who earnestly believe in the Christian way of life and in the values of democracy, and who keep themselves in the long, slow path of understanding and reconciliation. (*BR*, Nov. 5, 1955.)

The year ended with the white and Negro ministerial associations of Greensboro merging into one fellowship. (*BR*, Dec. 24, 1955.)

- 19 -

Dr. Cullom wrote of being "overwhelmed" by cards, gifts and other expressions of "special and loving attention" given him at Christmas and his birthday. But he did not slacken his pace one bit. On New Year's night at Rolesville, he told the story of his life which Rev. S. L. Morgan described as "his testimony of God's power and readiness to guide and use any life dedicated to him." In Charlotte, he spoke at the Providence Baptist Church on "Sixty-Nine Years in the Ministry" and in the *Recorder* wrote of the advancement of the Negro people in America; he described the prominence of many of the Negro leaders as marking "well-doing in a marvelous way" and warned against extremists who would lead into "a wild fanaticism that can bring nothing but tragic chaos to all concerned." (*BR*, Jan. 14, 1956.) In February, he wrote of a profitable "second reading" of E. Stanley Jones's *Abundant Living* and urged a good offering for the Baptist Homes for the Aging; he thought Peter's description of his generation as "this untoward generation" as expressive of ours and wished he could go into all the world and call people to turn their attention to what is really wholesome and to what will really make a better world. (*BR*, Feb. 25, 1956.)

In the meantime, there had been considerable agitation against President Tribble of Wake Forest. Dr. Cullom was troubled; he had not seen much of Dr. Tribble, but he was greatly concerned for him and for the college. One morning he was rather startled when Dr. Tribble called him and asked if he might come to see him. Dr. Cullom told him he would be welcomed to come any time and wondered what advice to give him. After a few courtesies, Dr. Tribble reminded

Dr. Cullom that this commencement would be the last on the old campus and said, "We would like to honor some of our old professors; Dr. Hubert Poteat has consented to give the commencement address, and we would like for you to preach the baccalaureate sermon." Taken completely by surprise, Dr. Cullom assured him he would be glad to do his best.

Alumni from near and far gathered at Wake Forest for the last commencement of the dear old college on its old campus; many, like the Honorable James F. Hoge of New York City, returned to take a sentimental walk on the campus and to sit awhile with their old Bible teacher. Some of Dr. Cullom's students and friends were a little anxious for him in fulfilling the responsibility of the hour. On Sunday evening, May 20th, every available seat was filled in the large and stately chapel long before the appointed hour. At the proper time in the service, Dr. Cullom was brought to the pulpit and after the microphone was adjusted, he began in a clear strong voice. After congratulating the 320 seniors, he said:

> This occasion is really the *Commencement* occasion in your respective lives. I shall never forget the first time that I heard the word "commencement." I was a barefoot boy in Halifax County. A neighbor boy across the road had a sister who was graduating at the college in Murfreesboro. This boy told me that some of his family were going down to "Commencement." Innocently I said to him, "No, David; this is the close of school, not its commencement." How innocent, I repeat, I was! I have learned . . . that there are many commencements.

Taking his text from Ecclesiastes 12:13 and John 1:18, Dr. Cullom spoke of "the preacher" and his experiments and stated that the wise man of Ecclesiastes came to this conclusion: "Fear God, and keep his commandments; for this is the *whole* of man." Dr. Cullom reasoned that some might think he had omitted a word, but he reminded them that the word *duty* is not in the Hebrew and had been added by someone who thought it was needed, as is shown by its being in italics.

> The real meaning of this conclusion is that whatever else a man may have or how much he may have, he is not complete until he takes God into his life—"Fear God and keep his commandments, for this is the whole of man"—this is the rounding out of man into completion. And what is it to fear God? . . . It means that a person comes to recognize God as the essential thing in life; he comes to reverence God, and so to possess a humble, consciously dependent spirit, feels the need of and seeks the help of God in the prosecution of his daily routine. He feels deeply the need of God's counsel, guidance and help. Hence the habit of prayer is born into daily habits of thought and action. . . . Then the last statement follows as naturally as . . . water flows down the hill— he will "keep his commandments" and obey them. . . . Without devotion to God and his commandments, man will find life little more than a treadmill business without any real meaning.

There was a time when man dimly understood God—the days of the "urim" and "thummim," but we now live in the day of "reality" when

God's presence is made known unto us by the coming of Christ Jesus. "As many as receive him, to them gave he power to become the sons of God, even to them that believe on his name." Dr. Cullom then reminded his vast audience:

> No one is expected to take it all in at once. We are expected only to appropriate what is at hand at the present moment, and as we do this the next moment will bring more, and the next moment yet more and since God is infinite there can be no such thing as exhausting the supply.

He brought his sermon to a close by stating that in bringing ourselves to face up to life at its highest and best, we come to the conclusion that to take God into one's life and to live in fellowship with him is the highest life of which we are capable.

> Fellowship with God in Christ is a progressive experience leading to larger, richer and better experiences through the eternal ages that are ahead of us. We hear him say to all and each of us: "Behold, I stand at the door and knock. . . ." There is a little poem that I love to repeat . . .
>
> > I'd rather walk in the dark with God,
> > Than go alone in the light.
> > I'd rather walk by faith with him
> > Than go alone by sight.

The organ began playing the recessional hymn, and hundreds of voices began singing "Lead On, O King Eternal; the Day of March Has Come."

Already the trek had begun; truck after truck moved the equipment of the 122-year-old college 110 miles west to Winston-Salem. The Seminary, which took over the old campus, placed a marker honoring the old professors of the college and began tearing down the front of the old library building to make it more modern. And Dr. Cullom turned to other tasks. He wrote of having been at Quankie on the first Sunday in May; the church had moved from its old site and had a "beautiful, well-arranged brick building with a full-time pastor and the foundation laid for a new parsonage." He preached at Tillery and Scotland Neck and attended the Meredith School of Christian Studies. He reported having gone, on the evening of May 1st, to the Ministerial Class at Wake Forest and told of having been given a package which later he found to contain three books. He wrote:

> It then began to dawn upon me that I had met with this group for the last time except as I may go to Winston-Salem as a special visitor. The shock and the feeling of bereavement continues to grow on me. My fellowship with these young preachers has been one of the greatest joys and blessings of my life. They will have my love, my prayers, and my best wishes to the end of the journey. (*BR*, June 23, 1956.)

He commended Margaret Truman upon the story of her life and wrote appreciations of Dr. George Washington Paschal and of Mrs. Lula Purnell Hollingsworth. In July, he attended Dr. E. Stanley Jones's

Ashram at Bridgewater, Virginia, and preached at Buie's Creek Baptist Church; in August, he was with Rev. W. C. Laney in the Brookfield Baptist Church for "a few days of special evangelistic services."

Amid the racial tensions throughout the nation, Dr. Cullom appealed for "the Christian Spirit"; he became cautious.

> I do not think we are ready for mixing the white and Negro races in our public schools. There is a background in this matter that no one can understand who has not experienced it. And it is hard for me to state clearly just what I mean. . . . I am sure of four things: (1) That what we are trying to effect cannot be done by legal fiat: it must come from the inside; (2) that it cannot be forced: it must come from a voluntary leading of God's Spirit; (3) that it cannot be brought to pass overnight: it will have to come gradually as all of us apprehend and adjust ourselves to reality; (4) that it is going to call for the exercise of all the patience, all the common sense, and all the practical wisdom that we can find and use. (*BR*, Aug. 11, 1956.)

Dr. Cullom wrote of having spent eleven days in a church where he spoke on Paul's letters; during the last days of the meeting the pastor said he was having difficulty in deciding as to whether God had sent a revival or a judgment. Since what was involved in this statement applied to the condition of Christendom as such, Dr. Cullom hoped that it would cause many to do some thinking on it. Then this unique and pathetic "post script" is added:

> As I lay on my bed sleeping during the night following the writing of the above I had a dream in which I saw the world in such chaos and confusion as to beggar description. I got up at three o'clock, took my pen and paper to write three comments:
> (1) It is said that Nero fiddled while Rome burned. Are not God's people in the world today doing worse than fiddling with their gone-to-seed machinery and organization? Are we not fiddling while the world about us is literally falling to pieces?
> (2) It sems to me that I hear an ancient cry saying: "To your tents, O Israel"! Shall we not modify this old cry by saying "To your knees, O people of God!"?
> (3) For a long time I have been saying that there are two hymns that should be much in use: I would underscore this call today: (1) "Lead on, O King Eternal"; (2) "Jesus, Saviour, Pilot Me." (*BR*, Sept. 15, 1956.)

Like many others, Rev. Bruce H. Price of Newport News, Virginia, made a pilgrimage to Wake Forest to see Dr. Cullom; he reported:

> A colored maid came to the door, and without asking my name or business, invited me to follow her to the study of the retired college professor, who has not retired from supplying pulpits and writing a multitude of articles each month on various subjects for leading religious publications across the nation.
> Coming to meet me with a large smile and outstretched hand, he assumed that I was one of his students in years past. "Let me have a good look at you," was his greeting. Making myself known and telling him that we had not met before did not change the warmth of his personality and friendly attitude. I felt as if one of the prophets had walked out of the Old Testament to greet me. (*BR*, Oct. 21, 1956.)

That winter Dr. Cullom conducted a week of evangelistic services in the Baptist Church in Marshall; he spoke three times in the public schools and twice at Mars Hill College. He preached in Spring Hope and shared in the funeral service of Mrs. N. B. Weldon of Warren Plains; he read of the dedication of the new $20,000,000 Wake Forest College buildings and campus at Winston-Salem and wrote of the need of self-respect in politics. He wrote of "salvation as fact and as process" (*BR*, Dec. 1, 1956) and at Christmas received 626 greetings —Ricky Harris, his grandson, counted them!

- 20 -

On the occasion of his 90th birthday, Dr. Cullom was saluted by Editor Carpenter as "the dean among American teachers and preachers, greatly beloved by thousands of people far and wide"; the Spring Hope Church had its annual birthday banquet, and the Rolesville Church observed "a W. R. Cullom Day" during which they contributed $500 to the Cullom Student Loan Fund. On February 1st, another $500 was given to this fund by Mr. John Matthews of Spring Hope; Dr. Cullom replied,

> My major interest has been in training the man in the pulpit. If he is right, I feel other things will be rightened. There is only one place more strategic—the parent, and the preacher can help there too.

In an article, "Let Me Give Thanks," Dr. Cullom likened himself to Mr. John Pullen who, when asked by Rev. O. L. Stringfield to pray for him and his efforts to raise money for a college for women, replied:

> I can't do it, String. I don't have time to ask God for anything; all my time is spent in thanking God for what He has already done for me. (*BR*, Feb. 16, 1957.)

Dr. Cullom was also anxious to continue serving God. He appealed to the lawmakers of North Carolina to back up the law-enforcers by passing a law to withdraw a driver's license for speeding or driving under the influence of liquor. (*BR*, Jan. 12, 1957.) He dreamed of restoring the old Calvin Jones residence, of moving the granite arch to North Main Street and of making a memorial park of the old athletic field. (*BR*, Jan. 19, 1957.) He recommended Dr. E. Stanley Jones's *Mastery*, wrote of the need of a home for the aging in Eastern North Carolina and described Miss Evelyn Hendricks (stricken with arthritis for twenty-eight of her forty-one years) as "one of the most remarkable women" he had ever known.

That spring, the Southeastern Seminary at Wake Forest announced that it would accept qualified Negro students in the fall, and Congressman Brooks Hays of Arkansas was elected president of the Southern Baptist Convention. But the big issue among North Carolina Baptists that spring and summer was the old question of "supervised dancing" on Baptist campuses. The trustees of Wake Forest and Meredith voted to permit such dances; the chorus of protests and resolutions sounded like "the second stanza of the same song."

Sunday, August 4th, was something of "a W. R. Cullom Day" at the Wake Forest Baptist Church. In the absence of Pastor Ben S. Lynes, Dr. Cullom filled the pulpit for both morning and evening services; Editor Carpenter reported that "the honored and beloved preacher" took his text from Isaiah 55:2 and declared: "It is tragic if we do not have a purpose in life." The parable of the Rich Fool was cited as example of a man who had missed life; the life of Dwight L. Moody was used as an example of a man who lived with a purpose. Dr. Carpenter was impressed by the sermon and the preacher; he wrote:

> In trying to explain the youthful vigor and outlook of a man more than 90 years of age there are at least three things that I can say about Dr. Cullom: (1) He has always appreciated the good and lovely things about people, his community, and life in general. (2) He has spent much time in thought and study along the lines of richer and better living. (3) He has always maintained an active interest in what is going on in the world, including the spread of the gospel at home and abroad.
>
> He is wide-awake, alert, and interested in life and beauty wherever he finds them. He has an inquiring mind and always has plenty to do. There are yet a thousand times more interesting things to do than he has been able to get around to, even in a long life, he says. It is amazing to find a man old in years but still so vigorous and youthful in his interests and outlook. (*BR,* August 24, 1957.)

Dr. Carpenter thought the quotation from John Donne on the church bulletin summed up the philosophy of Dr. Cullom: "I count all that part of my life lost which I spent not in communion with God, or in doing good."

At the time of the Little Rock school dispute, Dr. Cullom wrote of having heard Dr. E. Stanley Jones say that we were trying to handle mature questions in a very immature way and urged "every minister —white and colored—every teacher, indeed, every person who is charged with the responsibility of leading people in any way" to read Dr. W. D. Weatherford's *American Churches and the Negro"* at once. (*BR,* Sept. 21, 1957.) In the meantime, the debate on having supervised dancing on Baptist campuses had been continued, and at a rather stormy session in November "the largest number of messengers ever gathered at a North Carolina Baptist State Convention" reaffirmed the Convention's action of 1937 which prohibited social dancing at Baptist colleges.

On Thursday morning (November 21st), the last day of the convention, the Wake Forest student body was in chapel when an alarm-clock went off; many of the students rose and went outside where some of them jitter-bugged to the delight of reporters and photographers. That was the year the Russians put up their first "Sputnik"!

Dr. Cullom was saddened by all these things. He urged that we turn "from quibbling to thoughts, feelings and actions that will be positive, constructive, and useful in the making of a better world." At times he was tempted to say more, but a cold had weakened him, and some personal matters troubled him. Once when the Spring Hope pastor called, he was told that Dr. Cullom had been hurt by someone's saying that he imposed on his friends. Dr. Cullom was on the phone at that time. When he finished his conversation, his face was flushed, and it was obvious he was upset. Back in his room, he told about the incident and was soon laughing about something else and planning a trip to Spring Hope.

On another occasion, it was not as easy; he closed the door and spoke confidentially of another matter which was quite serious. Of this matter, no one was able to help. But the pastor of Spring Hope did what he could; on Dec. 17th, he came over to spend the day as Dr. Cullom chose. Dr. Cullom asked that the book of letters, "Friends Salute You," be read to him. And this was done. It took all day, with his adding comments. He remembered Senator Josiah W. Bailey had been "sorta loud" as a student; "when he saw a young woman walking across the campus, he would call out 'angel on campus'." J. H. Franklin roomed "just across the hall from me in York Hall"; it was through him that Dr. Cullom had been invited to attend the conference held for the laymen's report on missions. Dr. Cullom told that W. R. Bradshaw spoke so loud when he was speaking in the Euzelian Literary Society that he was heard all over the campus and the fellows outside would holler: "Go to it, Bradshaw." When Dr. Carver's letter was read, the Spring Hope pastor spoke of once receiving from Dr. Carver a card on which this dear man had written: "W. R. Cullom comes as near fulfilling the righteous man of the first Psalm as any one I know." Dr. Cullom replied, "That was kind of him. Jim, if any of this is true, it is not I—but God who is doing it. I have only loved Him, and He has been pleased to use me."

- 21 -

For the Spring Hope Church's annual banquet on his 91st birthday, Dr. Cullom was "in perfect mood and at his best"; among the 511 birthday greetings he received, there was one from President Eisenhower. The week end of February 9th ("one of the happiest of my life") was spent at Mills Home; Dr. Cullom stayed in the home of Mr. and Mrs. Roger Williams, preached in the Mills Home Baptist Church and at the Park Street Church, toured the grounds of the orphanage with Superintendent Reed and visited such friends as the Marse Grants. (*BR,* March 1, 1958.) On March 13th, Mr. and Mrs. William Oliver Smith took Dr. Cullom to Winston-Salem for the formal presentation of the Charles Lee Smith Library. Dr. Cullom reported:

President Tribble, of course, was Master of Ceremonies and he did it with grace, charm, and success. The presentation of the library of

7000 volumes took place in Wait Chapel. The son, William Oliver
Smith, made the presentation speech; President Tribble spoke the word
of acceptance; Robert Humber of Greenville made the main address
of the day. Following this we moved to the library where the books
were to be seen and where portraits of the two Smith brothers, Charles
Lee and Oliver, were unveiled. . . . After this, we moved to the Mag-
nolia dining room where we ate a sumptuous and delicious lunch . . .
I sat at the table with Dr. and Mrs. E. I. Olive. . . . Wednesday night
was spent in the home of Dr. and Mrs. Easley. . . . Both Mrs. Easley
and Mrs. Olive drove me around and showed me the campus, the college
buildings, and the homes of the faculty. The campus is beautiful now,
but give it five years more and it will be the realization of a happy
dream. (*BR,* April 5, 1958.)

That summer, Dr. Cullom read of the dismissal of thirteen professors
from the Seminary in Louisville, but he wrote of a lighter matter:

In warm weather I sit on my front porch a good deal, and my porch
is only a few steps from U.S. Highway No. 1. Of course, I watch the
cars as they pass and repass before me. The beauty of these cars makes
me think of a dear old friend of my boyhood days. He was speaking
of how women could serve the Lord. One way for them to do so, he
said, was to wear pretty hats to church on Sunday, saying that as he
sat in church the Sunday before he couldn't see the preacher because
of a large hat on the head of the lady who sat in front of him. But, he
said, she had on a pretty hat and that he enjoyed the service in a double
way—hearing the sermon and looking at the hat. As I watch the cars
pass in front of me I don't know that . . . their owners are serving the
Lord in a special way by their beauty, but they certainly make a real
contribution to the pleasure of one man who sits and watches them.
(*BR,* Aug. 16, 1958.)

In September, Rev. John R. Link of Warrenton wrote of having been
privileged "to spend a week with one of the greatest and most unusual
men" he had ever known; he wrote that, at ninety-one, Dr. Cullom's
interest was "as keen as that of a teen-ager, his memory as good as
that of a junior, and his reasoning ability as good as that of a philoso-
pher." (*BR,* Sept. 24, 1958.)

That fall an error was corrected. In every account that he had told
of establishing the chair of Bible at Wake Forest College, Dr. Cullom
had expressed his appreciation of Dr. James B. Shearer's letter and suggestions, but Dr. Cullom was under the impression that Dr. Shearer's
classes on the Bible at Davidson had been voluntary. However, the
*Catalogue of the Officers and Students of Davidson College for the
48th Collegiate Year, ending June 18, 1885,* lists four courses in Bible;
this Presbyterian College had been teaching Bible as a part of its curriculum for eleven years before Dr. Cullom initiated Bible study as a
part of the Wake Forest College curriculum. Dr. Cullom was now old
and heavy-hearted and had taken pride in speaking of his pioneering
work; when he was informed of this finding, he looked aghast and said,
"Then, I have been wrong; Dr. Shearer was the pioneer." "We do not
need to argue over who was first," replied Jim Blackmore; "you've hoed
your row honestly and can leave to others to debate these technicalities."
And Dr. Cullom relaxed in a smile.

Friends continued to send information for the biography. Mrs. Ruby Averitt MacDonell of Raleigh wrote that when she first met Dr. Cullom, she was "struck with his serenity."

> Only the very good, with a boundless love for their fellow man, leave that feeling of peace with one. . . . His joy of living, and his keen interest in so many worthwhile things—his giving of himself to all who called on him—these things keep his spirit youthful and his mind alert. (July 6, 1953.)

Cecil McGee Perry of Ridgecrest regarded "the Saint" as "one of the greatest teachers" he had ever known and told that he had learned Hebrew from him that never was mentioned in the classes in the Louisville Seminary. Rev. W. H. Lewis of Denton wrote of his boundless energy:

> For example, one Sunday, I picked him up at his home about 8:30 a.m. He was going to a church quite some distance beyond Rocky Mount and on the way there he stopped to visit in the homes of two of his old friends. Upon arriving at the church he taught the Sunday School lesson, preached during the worship hour. We went to a lovely home for dinner and in the afternoon he visited. In the evening he attended Training Union and conducted the evening service and later while on the way home stopped again to visit in several homes. This did not happen once but many times.

H. I. Hester of William Jewell College recalled: "Always he was a genuine friend who took his students into his confidence and who opened up the world of learning for them." Virginia Gorrell Hall recalled personal courtesies and kindnesses:

> One time I got left in Raleigh overnight, and being quite young I went to the Cullom home (they were living in Raleigh then) and there I received a warm welcome and spent the night with them. . . . I also remember one very cold day Dr. and Mrs. Cullom had the Gorrell family to dinner during the Christmas holidays. What good food, and what a warm fire, and what a feeling of friendship and congeniality of spirits.
>
> Later on, when my only brother died—(he was 14 years old and had always been well and strong. A burst appendix and he was gone)—Dr. Cullom would come almost every night and pray with Mother and Father, and he helped them bear this sorrow.

P. L. Elliott, president of Gardner-Webb College, gave this testimony:

> One who becomes the gospel he preaches or the truth he imparts is really the preacher and the teacher. He was not afraid of truth because he had the truth within him to test the truth he found. He had an open mind, the winnowing type and therefore could discriminate between the real and the apparent. He understood immature boys and knew how to help them grow into the same type of understanding. These things were not so real to me when I was in his classes forty years ago, but through a greater maturity I have come to look on him as one of God's great statesmen. (Letter, Oct. 3, 1958.)

Hoyt Blackwell, president of Mars Hill College, wrote:

> When I entered Wake Forest College as a student, I needed friendship, encouragement, and efficient and sympathetic Christian teachers. I

found all of this in Dr. Cullom. Being a very timid person, I kept
silent in dormitory, on campus, and especially in the classroom. I was
therefore greatly surprised when Dr. Cullom asked me to drive his
Ford Coupe for him. . . . This recognition and evidence of confidence
strengthened my limited belief that I could do something and be somebody. . . . (Letter, Oct. 25, 1958.)

In September, Dr. Cullom was invited to Birmingham, Alabama,
to share in honoring Rev. T. Sloane Guy upon his retirement. Dr.
Cullom flew to Asheville where he spent several days visiting Mrs.
J. Fred Severance whom he had known as a nine-year-old girl in
Middleburg. He told a reporter:

It is wonderful to have lived for almost 92 years and to have seen so
many changes. A horse and buggy took me to the church where I
preached my first sermon, but I'll go by plane to Birmingham tomorrow
to preach.

On Sunday evening, September 21st, in the First Baptist Church of
Birmingham, Dr. Cullom spoke of his association with Rev. T. Sloane
Guy and described him as "a super pastor." Dr. Cullom was back in
North Carolina for the 50th anniversary of the Calypso Baptist Church
and for the homecoming at Middleburg. On October 23rd, Dr. Cullom
went to Warrenton for the second day of the Tar River Association
which had grown so large that it was dividing. As the southern part
of the association was keeping the old name, the Rev. John Link of
Warrenton moved that the northern association be named "the W. R.
Cullom Association." After several speeches favoring this name, the
motion was carried. Dr. Cullom was escorted into the auditorium; he
was deeply moved.

Another honor came on October 30th when the Raleigh Association
voted to dedicate its 1958 Minutes to him—and then, another tender
moment at the Baptist State Convention in Durham, Nov. 12th,
when Dr. Cullom was escorted to the pulpit and honored by the Convention for his long service. In thanking the messengers, Dr. Cullom
said, "I can say, in the words of the Psalmist, 'Surely goodness and
mercy *have* followed me all the days of my life,' and now I look
forward to 'dwelling in the house of the Lord forever'."

But there was sorrow for Dr. Cullom that December—a sorrow
which caused him to break and to sob as seldom he had ever done;
amid his tears, he asked, "Jim, is not God of the earthquake the
same as the God of the sunrise?" Perhaps a simple statement from
the *Recorder* will suffice:

Mrs. Nancy Cullom Harris, Wake Forest postmistress, was found dead
in bed Monday, December 8, after complaining of feeling ill the night
before. Before she was appointed postmaster about six years ago, she
was assistant librarian at Wake Forest College before it moved to
Winston-Salem. She was the wife of Assistant District Attorney Lawrence Harris and daughter of Dr. W. R. Cullom, well-known Baptist
minister and retired professor of Bible at Wake Forest College.
    In addition to her husband and father, she is survived by two sons,

Lawrence Harris, Jr., a senior at N. C. State College, and Richard Cullom Harris of the home; two sisters, Mrs. Fant Kelly of Spencer and and Mrs. C. C. Pearson of Wake Forest; one brother, Ed Cullom of Raleigh; and several nieces and nephews.

Funeral services were held at 2:00 p.m. December 10 at the Wake Forest Baptist Church by Dr. Ben Lynes, pastor, and Dr. J. Allen Easley of Winston-Salem, and burial was in the Wake Forest cemetery. *(BR,* Dec. 20, 1958.)

- 22 -

At his birthday banquet in Spring Hope, Dr. Cullom was "delighted" and "delightful." In April, he commended the Committee of 25 for its report on "the cooperative work" of Baptists in North Carolina and warned against losing "the personal touch" in our institutions and programs. With great interest, he followed the special session of the Baptist State Convention in Raleigh, May 5-6, when Dr. Douglas M. Branch of Rocky Mount, a former pupil, was elected to succeed Dr. M. A. Huggins as General Secretary of the Convention. He was "thrilled" by the Pastor's Annual Conference at the Seminary in Wake Forest; it recalled "the vision" which he had had in 1896 of having a special season of study each year for the pastors of the state. In August he wrote that today's greatest need was a renewed "fear of the Lord" — not in the childish fear of thunder and lightning, but as "the conscious and abiding sense of God's presence, his control, his powerful guidance of all that goes on everywhere and of adjusting oneself to all of this in the assurance of success and blessing in so far as we do so."

The questioning for the biography stimulated Dr. Cullom's own efforts to record his early experiences; during the summer of 1959 he wrote and circulated papers on such topics as "My First Job," "A Teacher for Forty-two Years." In his paper, "God's Call to Special Service," Dr. Cullom wrote:

Many people have been worried, more or less, because their call to special work did not come to them as it came to Moses, Paul, or to someone else. I freely confess that I am one of those people. For a long time as a young man I was worried quite a bit because my call came in a quiet way with no striking vision, no startling shake-up, or anything of that kind. I believe the reading of A. B. Bruce's *The Training of the Twelve* helped me at this point as much as anything could. I saw then more clearly and definitely than I had seen before that each of the Apostles was possessed of his own personality and surrendered that personality to God as it was and went forward from that surrender to obey whatever direction that God might give him. Nor were all these directions given at one time, but from time to time and from place to place as each occasion might demand. I am now 92½ years of age, and am just as dependent on God for direction and help as I was when I was 20 years of age.

And he wrote of other matters. He picked the Gospel of John as his favorite book of the Bible, the Psalms his second, with Paul's Letter to the Romans as a close third; he described the prologue to John's Gospel (John 1:1-18) as "the greatest section in the greatest book" and gave John 3:16 first place as the favorite verse, with Deuteronomy 33:27 as his second favorite. In a paper, "For Jesus' Sake," Dr. Cullom said:

> Most of us close our prayers with this or a similar phrase. The question has pressed itself upon me recently when I use the phrase: Do I really mean it? Down deep in my soul, am I wishing and asking for these blessings in order that my Lord's interest in the universe may be promoted, or am I really wishing for my own personal interests to be prospered? When I have pressed this question on my conscience I have been compelled to confess that the best that I can say for myself is that I am confused. Take the question of health, for example. When I pray that I may be strong and vigorous in body, am I desiring these blessings for my own comfort and use, or am I wishing them that I may use them in promoting the interests and work of our Lord's Kingdom? And so with every blessing for which I ask.

Dr. Cullom borrowed Dr. Elton Trueblood's term "cut-root civilization" to explain the "wilt" which we are experiencing in our homes, churches and schools; he warned that unless a change is accomplished the future of our civilization looks dark.

> But I think I hear someone say, "Who would believe that Brother Cullom would allow himself to become so pessimistic?" With deep and bitter regret I confess to the charge, and wish so deeply and as sincerely as any one that it were otherwise. I believe, however, that any one who will look squarely at the world's present condition, will have to say that this description is as realistic as it is pessimistic.

In a further word, he asked: What place does Bible-reading, prayer, hymn-singing, and such exercises have in the average home?

> I think I hear someone say, "I don't have time for the cultivation of religion." But each one has all the time there is, and one of the most important things in life that I can think of is that of thinking and planning as to the use of time. God should have His place in ever hour of the day, but special time should be given to the cultivation of religion. Nor can we hope to see a religious revolution until men and women give thought and time to it. People think and talk of what is really on their hearts, and no one knows this better than do the children in the home. Nor shall we see the situation changed until people put a new estimate on religion and regulate their lives accordingly.

What will the school do for the child in view of our world's desperate need of the fear of the Lord and of the spirit of Jesus Christ?

> The most important factor at this point is the teacher. The personality, the outlook, the attitude to life of the teacher means more in molding the life of his or her pupils than all their academic training. And this statement is not meant to discredit academic training. My purpose is to emphasize the supreme importance of the teacher's purpose in living. Pupils may forget facts and figures, but they can never forget their teacher.

Dr. Cullom rejoiced to note the way our country churches are moving up to full-time service and wished he could see a corresponding deepening and enriching of the spiritual life about us.

I believe that people talk about what is uppermost in their hearts. If this be true, who would claim that the chief topic of conversation is religion when people meet in their homes, in their community gatherings, on the highways, and in their general contacts? . . . In my opinion the greatest need in our churches today is that of the deepening and the enriching of religious life. . . . Why can't our regular church services produce something of the spirit of Dr. E. Stanley Jones's Ashrams or the C. F. O. meetings.

Dr. Cullom pointed out that at the time when the churches in England had "grown cold and formal" Susanna Wesley took time to take aside each of her nineteen children and talked to them about God and prayed with them; thus she helped prepare Charles and John Wesley for the great experiences which led to the transformation of English life.

It seems to me that with a few Susanna Wesleys in our present crisis, we shall soon see a revolution of spiritual life and Godliness amongst us that will stir men and nations in their depths. Whenever there is such a movement of spirit toward God and the pursuit of His will and purpose for the human race, we shall see communism and all such movements swept from the earth, and the reign of God in Christ take their place to the glory of God and to the blessing of men.

To those who asked what they as individuals could do, Dr. Cullom gave three exhortations:

(1) That as our Lord's followers we strive more earnestly and faithfully to incarnate and exhibit the spirit and attitude of Jesus in every position, in every sphere, and in every relationship in which we find ourselves; (2) that we try earnestly to make our fellowship with Jesus so strong, so vital and so contagious that all whom we shall touch shall take knowledge of us that "we have been with Jesus and have learned of Him"; (3) that when we assemble for fellowship, for counsel, for worship we go out from such meetings to apply to our everyday routine the inspiration and principles gathered therein.

In August, Dr. Cullom preached in the Rosemary Baptist Church of Roanoke Rapids; he remembered that this city was on the same spot from which he as a boy had hauled cords of wood while staying at his Uncle Jim's. He attended the mid-week prayer service at the Hayes-Barton Baptist Church of Raleigh, where his son was deacon, and heard Mrs. Carl Townsend speak. He was also a guest in the Holly Springs Baptist Church in Iredell County and shared in honoring the Rev. J. N. Binkley who had been pastor of this church for forty-six years. Through the kindness of Pastor Lynes and his good wife, he was "privileged to share in the great convocation" at Campbell College the evening of September 10th. He thought the reading of J. B. Phillips' *Is God at Home* would help any reader to have a more vital "grip on eternal things" and judged that in *This Jesus,* Dr. Eric G. Frost had "given to our generation a book that is really needed." In October, he was pleased to learn that Mr. J. Marse Grant was elected new editor of the *Recorder,* and at the first session

of the "W. R. Cullom Association" he was pleased to hear the Rev.
W. W. Finlator of Raleigh say:

> I should like first of all to congratulate your program committee . . .
> for choosing alcoholism, church-state separation, labor-management and
> race relations as the matters to be discussed before this first session of
> the W. R. Cullom Baptist Association at the Christian Life hour. It
> was a forthright decision and one in keeping with the sensitive social
> conscience of the honored and beloved gentleman for whom your Associa-
> tion has been named, and I shall try to deal with the assignment in the
> spirit it was given me. *(BR,* Nov. 7, 1959.)

Dr. Cullom was also present at Concord Church in Granville County
when "a new brick sanctuary" was dedicated; later he wrote:

> Like every other place in North Carolina, the Concord Church has
> been completely transformed since I was its pastor many years ago.
> When Pastor Daylon Green issued his call to worship and the choir sang
> its response, one might imagine himself in one of the great churches
> of Richmond or Philadelphia. Nothing in present day life pleases me
> more than to note the marvelous improvement in the life and work of
> our country churches.

On November 16th, Dr. Cullom paid a visit to his dentist; Dr.
J. E. Swindell of Raleigh reported he found a wisdom-tooth which his
last X-rays had not shown. The pastor of Spring Hope teased: "Dr.
Cullom, I have often heard that when you cut your wisdom teeth,
you've lived half of your life." The ninety-two-year-old man laughed,
"Well, I have no objection to staying around for the second half."

- 23 -

Dr. Cullom began 1960 with writing of "a dear woman" who was
trying to care for an invalid husband and needed an occasional visit
from her pastor; he found it difficult to understand how a pastor could
stand by and see such people linger and wait in a lonesome way and
fail to minister to them. *(BR,* Jan. 9, 1960.) On January 15th, the
Spring Hope Church had its annual birthday banquet for Dr. Cullom
(93), and on January 16th, Dr. Cullom's children held "an open
house" for over 200 "friends and admirers," among whom were some
Negro friends who were just as cordially received as any who came.
Dr. Cullom commended Pastor Lynes of Wake Forest and Pastor
Jones of Rolesville for having classes in church membership and
stated that if he were going back over the 73 years of his ministry, he
should certainly use this good custom. *(BR,* Jan. 23, 1960.)

On March 14th, when the Spring Hope pastor came to the Cullom
home, "Willie" (Mrs. Gill) told him that Dr. Cullom had not been
doing well at all, that he had fallen the day before and hurt his leg.
Dr. Cullom was still sleeping, but she insisted that the pastor go in
and call him. Dr. Cullom told that he had gone to his wardrobe to

get a cough-drop when his muscles seemed to have given way and he had crumpled to the floor.

> This is the second time this has happened. I was here by myself; Rickie had been in but was out at that time. I reckon, I was on the floor for twenty minutes. Finally I managed to work myself to a chair and to pull up onto the bed. Nothing was broken, but my left knee is swollen.

The pastor said, "Be sure to use Mrs. Cullom's old remedy (camphor and kerosene oil)." "I have already, and it's better," Dr. Cullom replied. Mr. Don Johnson came in to see him and to tell that "Don Junior" had called the night before and asked to be remembered to him.

In that same March, many were troubled over the "sit-in" demonstration by some Shaw University (Negro Baptist) students against lunch-counter segregation in downtown Raleigh. Dr. Cullom was quick to repeat his suggestion of each community's having a standing committee of Negroes and white people, "whose function should be to meet regularly, talk the situation over calmly and sympathetically, and advise the schools, the churches, the restaurants, and all places where this matter has to be met." (*BR*, March 12, 1960.) Nor was Dr. Cullom the only minister who could not remain silent; fifty-seven ministers of Raleigh described the issue of discriminatory service at lunch counters as "only a symbol of the many problems which need to be faced openly and frankly" and in accord with our Christian faith.

In April, Dr. Cullom recommended Thomas R. Kelly's *Testament of Devotion* as "an earnest effort" to call Christians back to the deeper realities, which he feared were being neglected as our churches seem more and more concerned with organization and statistics. Dr. and Mrs. John M. Lewis of Raleigh took him to the Pastor's Conference at Wake Forest College in Winston-Salem where he thought he gained "more in one day" than he could have gained in a week of reading at home. Many helped him with his reading—Mrs. Wallace Rogers, Mrs. John Wayland, Mrs. Bob Winston and many more; for several years, Mrs. Emily Becton came at 8:30 each morning to read the Bible and his devotional booklets. With the help of these, Dr. Cullom was able to follow the meeting of the Southern Baptist Convention in Miami, which Editor Grant likened unto "a big, teen-age boy outgrowing his clothes year by year, and, at times it is about as immature and awkward." Editor Grant wrote:

> Until Southern Baptists take steps to achieve more depth in all that they do, we are not going to make the impact on America and the world that a denomination of nearly 10 million members should be making.
> Establishment of more departments and programs will not bring about this sorely-needed depth. In fact, we have been fooling ourselves in thinking that this was the way to achieve depth. We make a grave error

when we assume that the "institution" is the reason for the church's existence. *(BR,* June 4, 1960.)

Mr. Lawrence Harris married again and continued to live in the house with Dr. Cullom so that Dr. Cullom might stay in his own home. As he had before Nancy's death, Dr. Cullom continued to pay the fuel-bill, the taxes and insurance on the house and to give $15.00 a week for household expense; Mr. Harris took care of the rest. This was mutually acceptable, and Mr. Harris continued to honor and to care for Dr. Cullom as he had through the years. In July, Dr. Cullom complained of a soreness on the left side of his face and confessed he was "no 'count." Disorder in the Congo made him concerned for Gerald Weaver who was one of the few missionaries to remain in Leopoldville. With great interest he read Senator John F. Kennedy's declaration, as the Democratic nominee for the presidency of the United States, that his religious affiliation was not relevant to the performance of the duties of the presidency: "My decisions on every public policy will be my own—as an American, a Democrat and a free man." Dr. Cullom followed the campaign closely and anxiously; he read all he could, discussed it with close friends, prayed. Then, he voted and waited for the verdict of his fellow Americans. North Carolina, where Baptists are in the majority, voted against a Baptist for governor and for a Roman Catholic for president. Terry Sanford had appealed for progress in racial understanding and relations; John F. Kennedy, in the words of James Reston of the *New York Times,* had "appealed to the loyalty of the Catholics and the conscience of the Protestants." *(BR,* Nov. 19, 1960.) When the announcement of the election was made, Dr. Cullom prayed for "our new governor and our new president."

Dr. Cullom had not been idle during the fall of 1960; he had spoken at the 75th anniversary of the Baptist Church in Dunn, and of the reports on the Advance Program for Colleges and Christian Life, he had written:

(1) Probably no one can open just one eye on what is going on about us in today's world without feeling, and feeling deeply, that we are in the midst of the world's greatest and most tragic crisis; (2) There is not a moment to lose in taking hold of and doing what each of us can do toward finding and following God's purpose and will for him in such an hour. *(BR,* Nov. 12, 1960.)

He had been encouraged by the reports of the Convention and was led to believe that "our people are returning to more vital things." *(BR,* Nov. 10, 1960.) He had heard Dr. Baker James Cauthen speak in the Seminary Chapel at Wake Forest and had visited friends in Warsaw.

On December 13th, the Spring Hope pastor had lunch with Dr. Cullom; it was cold (20°), and Dr. Cullom said the cold was "piercing" him like he had never remembered its doing before. As the two ate mushroom broth, cinnamon toast, apple sauce and coffee, they talked of the election, Castro, the renovation of the Spring Hope Church and the Carlyle Powells' being invited by the Nigerian government to its independence ceremonies. The two stayed at the table and chatted quite a while; finally the pastor said he would have to return to the library and his research in the *Biblical Recorder*. As he accompanied him to the door, Dr. Cullom said, "Jim, I wish you could stay all afternoon with me." The pastor replied, "I could—if you hadn't written so well and done so much; you have filled many pages in the *Recorder* alone, and it is all good." Dr. Cullom laughed: "I have been right busy; haven't I?"

- 24 -

Dr. Cullom was in Spring Hope for the Student Night Program on January 1st, 1961; he was back the next day to participate in a funeral. On January 9th, the pastor at Spring Hope had lunch again with him and spoke of the plans for the birthday banquet; Dr. Cullom told of having been at Sulphur Springs the Sunday before and having spoken on Paul's farewell words, which were translated in the new translation (RSV), "I have fought *the* good fight" instead of "a good fight." Dr. Cullom accepted the pastor's invitation to go with him to see Mrs. Theo. Easom; as they called at Hollowell's for some fruit, he said, "I wish I could do this more often."

On February 19th, Dr. Cullom attended the morning worship service in Spring Hope at which time the law-enforcing officers were honored; he commended this service to other pastors in an effort to develop a "sympathetic and intelligent appreciation of these officers and their place and work in the community." (*BR,* March 11, 1961.) A letter in the *News and Observer* of March 28th disturbed him; Mrs. Mabel Lilly wrote that she, her husband, and children had been travelling on the highway when they stopped "at a public house on the road" to refresh themselves with a little ice cream and milk shake, but they were told by the proprietor that he "served only white people." Dr. Cullom wrote: "Of course, this treatment was bitterly resented. Who would not have resented it?" He stated that the race issue had had "a long and chequered history"; he called for "patience, good-will and forbearance on both sides" and again suggested each community to have a capable committee to advise "what steps to take" in solving these problems. (*BR,* April 15, 1961.)

In June, Dr. Cullom commended Dr. A. C. Reid's *Christ and Human Values* for containing "just the message" for which these critical times call (*BR,* June 10, 1961) and, despite a fall from his chair, was able to preach in Spring Hope on July 16th. Speaking on Isaiah 55, he described the human hungers and how men seek life in many ways. Speaking of his own devotional habits, he said:

Early in each day, I turn aside to talk with the Lord and ask Him to help me give to every person I meet that day some good thing of His spirit. As the day progresses, I remember this and seek to use every opportunity, however meager, to impart something of God to every one I contact. When the day is over, I turn back to the Lord and think of what I've given away.

On July 17, 1961, Dr. Cullom went to Spencer for a visit with Elizabeth (Mrs. Fant Kelly). She and Mr. Kelly had a daughter who lived within a few blocks of them and who had two young girls (6 and 7). As an example of "God's Guarantee against Staleness," Dr. Cullom wrote:

Circumstances brought it about that I saw quite a bit of these two great-grandchildren during my few days stay in Spencer. Over and over during these days I was taken back to the early days of my life and was permitted to live those days over again. In this way, I was permitted to review my youth, as it were, and to experience again some of the thrills that were mine 50, 60, 70, 80, and even 90 years ago. Nor is this the only modern experience that has shown to me God's goodness in so arranging life for us that it can never, never grow stale, but is renewed and made fresh over and over day by day. (*Spring Hope Enterprise,* August 3, 1961.)

In August and September, Dr. Cullom continued to have "weakening spells"; he was taken to the new Wake Memorial Hospital in Raleigh. It seemed that there was a general weakening of his whole body. After a week in the hospital he returned home. In the *Recorder* of October 7th, Dr. Cullom addressed this letter to all his friends:

Three weeks have passed since I came home from the hospital and my strength has not yet returned to its normal state. In a week or two more, however, I hope to write a letter to you myself, but I felt that I must let you know at once as to how I appreciate your expressions of love and kindness, and beg you to do the same for your other friends who need your love and sympathy as I did. Blessings on all and each of you always. (*BR,* Oct. 7, 1961.)

In the fall (1961), the Spring Hope pastor resigned his church to give his full time to completing the Cullom biography; Dr. Cullom knew the power of the written word and wrote of the need of publications which will give people an honest statement of God's will for them and which will cry aloud for clean ideals, wholesome pastimes, righteous living.

I say that our day calls loudly and strongly for a revival of the fear of God on all sides and for a paper that will advocate these principles with courage, with boldness, and with unfailing persistence. (*BR,* Oct. 28, 1961.)

Dr. Cullom wrote of the vows of marriage and of church as "the sacred, the most important, the most binding, and the most fruitful"; he urged that husband and wife be united in the same church and build their lives around the same ideals and purposes. (*BR,* Nov. 4, 1961.) He was pleased to read that at the Baptist State Convention in Greensboro, Rev. W. A. Honeycutt, a former pupil, had stated that, as ministers, "we have been commissioned to bear the truth" and that Secretary Douglas M. Branch, a former pupil, had defined "the greatest need of North Carolina Baptists" as "a stirring of our consciences . . . to a sense of mission and sacrifice." Dr. Cullom was also pleased that the 1,600 messengers "overwhelmingly adopted" the Christian Life Committee's recommendation that "the Convention urge our churches again to seek God's will concerning our responsibility and opportunity to open the doors of worship, service, and fellowship to all Christians regardless of race."

- 25 -

On January 15, 1962—his 95th birthday—Dr. Cullom was found seated in his rocking chair, talking with his granddaughter, Virginia Chilton Pearson. Outside the rain was taking away the snow, but it was not spring. Dr. Cullom told that the birthday supper at Spring Hope had been postponed because of the weather. Of world problems, he said the outlook was serious, but he was not gloomy; he knew that God still reigns, and yet he feared that the average Christian attended church, heard a sermon and then went home without another thought about what it's all about.

> We'll never get anywhere that way. We've got to live our faith. We've got to get out and tell people what it means to us. This witnessing was the main feature of early Christianity, and we've got to return to it.

In a letter to the *Recorder* (Jan. 20, 1962), Dr. Cullom wished that "we ministers might form the habit of giving more personal testimony in our preaching."

> In the New Testament pages every man that spoke gave his personal testimony. I believe we should go back to that habit and follow it faithfully always.

After two postponements, the Spring Hope dinner was held on January 31st; Rev. John A. Bracey, the new pastor, was master of ceremonies. Dr. Cullom was not "up to par." When he rose to speak, he informed Mr. Bracey that he might be the pastor but he wanted him to know that *he* was pastor-emeritus. He turned to the pastor's wife. "Now, what is your name?" "Wilhelmina," the lovely lady replied. "What?" asked the old man. "Wilhelmina," she repeated. "Well," he commented; "I once had a cook by that name. She borrowed five dollars from me and that was the last I ever saw of her." The pastor's wife was quick: "You lend me five dollars, and I'll pay you back." Everyone laughed in relief. Dr. Cullom was among friends who made allowance for him, but it grieved them to see him "somewhat childish." Dr. Cullom recovered himself to welcome the Braceys to Spring Hope and to wish them happiness and success in the pastorate there; he thanked the church for its continued kindness to him and urged it to be faithful unto the Lord.

On February 6th, Dr. Cullom was seated in the hall at the phone, when he became aware that someone was standing by him; he told his party that he had company and would have to hang up. Then to his visitor, he said: "Jim, my dear boy, I am certainly glad to see you; it seems like it has been a month of Sundays since you were here last." When apologies were made for interrupting his phone conversation, Dr. Cullom said it was Mr. S. L. Morgan who was reading to him. "Mr. Morgan is a good reader. In all that he has read to me, I don't think he has mispronounced a single word. We've just finished re-reading Norman Vincent Peale's *The Power of Positive Thinking* and now we are reading *Archibald the Arctic.*" When reference was made to the biography, Dr. Cullom said, "I have enjoyed life. I've worked hard all through the years, and I've stayed busy since retiring. And I want to keep on serving the Lord. He's been good to me."

On February 27th, Dr. Cullom admitted he had not been very well; "it seems like I just can't get my strength back." He had been hesitant to leave his room—even during Colonel John Glenn's orbital flight; "Ricky" (his grandson) and others had kept him informed as it progressed, but he wanted to know more about it. When he was told the full story, Dr. Cullom exclaimed, "Why, Jim, that's wonderful. This is the beginning of wonderful things, and aren't we glad to have a fine young man like Colonel Glenn to pioneer in this?"

In a paper, "Needed: A Teaching and a Testifying Evangelism," which he wrote in February (1962), Dr. Cullom stated that it seemed

> but little short of sacrilegious for people to get together, make out the blue prints for a revival to begin on Sunday or Monday night, to close on Friday night and lay it before the Lord for Him to ratify and "make good." It reminds me of the remark of a friend of mine about young Samuel: when the Lord called to the child, Samuel said, "Speak, Lord, for thy servant heareth." But we say, "Hear, Lord, for thy servant speaketh." . . . The greatest need of our world today is that of a thorough return to God and an unconditional dedication of all that we have or hope to have to His complete control.

On March 9th, an automobile pulled up in front of the Cullom residence on "Faculty Avenue." A man got out into the falling snow; he pulled his hat down and took a little boy out of the car and hurried toward the house. He did not bother to knock, but, opening the door, he went in and put his son down. In the living room, on his right, he saw Raphael's Sistine Madonna over the mantel and ushered his son down the hall to the room on the left. Dr. Cullom was seated in his rocking chair. Recognizing the voice of his visitor, he tried to get up and then resigning himself, he offered his hand. As they talked, he stumbled over names of close associates and kept referring to Larry (his grandson) as Edward. Yet he wanted to give something to the little boy. "I don't have any candy or fruit, but, Jim, look in the wardrobe and give John a copy of my 'Manifesto'; it's a little ahead of him right now, but in a little while he'll be able to handle it."

On March 15th, Dr. Cullom was dressed in his "Sunday best" and confessed he was going to see a lady. When asked who was the lucky woman, he replied, "I'm the lucky one. I'm going to see Agar Morgan's mother; she's been visiting the Morgans for awhile, and Agar is sending someone to take me to see her." While waiting, reference was made to completing the biography. Dr. Cullom said: "You know, Jim, it occurred to me the other day that in your story something of my life will continue after I'm gone from the human scene. I do hope it will do good and will serve our Lord, as I have tried to do."

"That certainly is my prayer," replied his visitor and the conversation turned to Dr. Cullom's proposed visit in Warsaw. Dr. Cullom was pleased with the plans, but he added: "I have some dear friends in Calypso that I would like to visit, and do you suppose we could go on down to Wilmington to see our friends there?"

On his table, piled high with papers and periodicals, was a letter from his daughter, Elizabeth. When inquiry was made of her, Dr. Cullom replied, "She's coming Easter. Edward is planning to have all of us at his house on Easter Monday. Edward came over for me Saturday and took me to his church Sunday; Virginia Chilton had us for dinner."

"Will Sarah be able to go Easter Monday?" (She had fallen on the ice back in the winter and had broken her hip.)

"Yes, she is hoping to; she is much better."

At that time, Mrs. Turner, the wife of the Episcopal minister, called to take Dr. Cullom to the Morgan's. As they were leaving the house, Dr. Cullom asked if they might go by Mr. Hollowell's for some fruit.

- 26 -

On Wednesday, April 11, 1962, Dr. Cullom woke at his usual time of 6:30. He arose and dressed; after shaving, he changed his day-calendar on the back of his door and sat down at his table to write a letter. At 7:30, "Willie" called him to breakfast. Putting down his pen, he got his silver-topped cane and the towel he used for a bib and went to the kitchen. At 8:30, Mrs. Becton came to read the Bible and his devotional booklets. After she left, he sat alone and quiet for awhile. And then he went over to his single iron-framed bed and lay down. After a short nap, he got up. As he fumbled toward his rocker, he thought of the letter he had written. He must get it out to the mailbox for the mailman. Again with Dr. Taylor's cane, he walked slowly through the hall and opened the front door. As he stepped out on the walk, he felt weak and faint. He was going to fall!

In the kitchen, "Willie" became aware that cool air was blowing through the house. She went through the dining room into the front hall. Seeing the front door open, she looked into Dr. Cullom's room. His light was left on, but his chair was empty; he was gone! She hurried to the front of the house and out the opened door, calling —"Dr. Cullom, Dr. Cullom."

This was not the end, although it might have been. "Willie" found him sitting on the ground. He was not greatly hurt, but he could not get up. As she bent over him, he said, "Willie, I'm going to have to give you my letter to mail."

There would be other days and more letters, but the ending had begun. And there was a little of "second childishness" in it; Dr. Cullom followed Shakespeare's line of human failing—his teeth had been extracted; the sight in his right eye had long been gone, and the sight in his left eye was dim; his appetite was poor.

But, however fine an observer of human drama was the Bard of Stratford on Avon, he missed it when he wrote of "oblivion" and "sans everything." At least, he did in the story of W. R. Cullom of Wake Forest. For, that door Dr. Cullom left ajar on that spring morning of April 11th was an accurate symbol of his death. The body fails and the mind falters—but the spirit of a man who has walked with God goes out, in death, to be with that Friend for new adventures, closer fellowship, and greater service. The seven ages of a man are but his acts upon the terrestial stage; the play goes on.

EPILOGUE

Dr. Cullom suffered no great discomfort from his fall of April 11th (1962). Two days later, seated in his big rocker with his tie on the outside of his collar, he told of the fall and said he had quit taking the mail out to the mailbox. He was interested in the publisher's evaluation of his biography and told of having spent the preceding week end with his son, Edward. He referred to Mr. S. L. Morgan's reading to him over the phone but could not recall the name of "the man in the presidency."

On April 16th, he said he felt weak and chilled and wrote: "I am staying in my room until the weather is warmer." To a friend he confessed (April 23rd) that he was "no 'count" and asked: "Jim, do you see any difference in my mind?" His friend replied, "Your insight is as good as ever, but you are getting like the rest of us in not being able to call names and in forgetting dates." This seemed to have reassured him.

A week later he shared a letter from Oscar J. Sikes, a lawyer in Albemarle:

> I recently read your statement in the *Charity and Children* entitled "Mottoes." . . . I like to read anything that you write and when I see your name to an article in the papers I invariably read it. I often think of your brothers, Jim and Joe. To me, personally, I don't think I have ever contacted two more lovable personalities.

On June 14th, Dr. Cullom mailed four one-page articles to his friends and to the newspapers. In "The Kingdom's Challenge to Men," he wrote:

> What would you think of me if you heard me stand before a congregation and appeal to them to surrender one tenth of themselves to Christ? You would be shocked, of course. No, a thousand times! I appeal to men to give all that they are to Christ.
> The first call of Jesus is that a man deny himself. And this does not mean cutting off a little part of himself. It means to put self out of sight in surrender to Him who gave himself for us. And the challenge of the Kingdom is for all that a man has, himself included.
> To me, this is the New Testament doctrine of giving. So that when a man accepts the Kingdom Challenge, he is no longer his own man; he is henceforth a steward of God in the use of his time, of his possessions, of his influence, and of all that he controls.

In "Christianity Then and Christianity Now," Dr. Cullom asked if our Lord should walk among us today as He did in the days of the apostles, would He recognize Christianity as the religion that he left on the earth when he was "taken up from them"? Dr. Cullom thought the main difference between the two was to be found in the matter of *personal testimony*.

> Our Lord said to his disciples as he sent them out, *"Ye shall be witnesses"* (Acts 1:8). If you will follow these disciples in their ministry, you will find that a large part of this preaching was personal testimony.
> When did you hear a conversation between two Christians that gave a personal testimony? In my judgment, this principal difference between

the two sections of Christianity in question is to be found right here at this point in this one thing. Until our Christian people shall return to the "then" method, we shall go on limping and crawling instead of marching in triumph against the world about us.

In a half-page article, "Heaven: Place or Character," Dr. Cullom told that he had come to think of heaven as "being *what* a person is rather than *where* he is." (Lk. 17:21)

> I think of heaven as being wherever a person is who thinks as God thinks, feels as God feels, chooses as God chooses. The same is true of hell. The person who thinks, feels, and chooses in a manner that is the opposite to the way God thinks, feels, and chooses, is already in hell wherever his neighbors may be.

Also Dr. Cullom wrote of Miss Gertrude Allen Abernathy who after spending some time as a missionary in China has spent the latter part of her life in the State Hospital; her ministry in the hospital was comparable to that on the foreign mission field. Upon receipt of a card, telling that "Gertie had had a heart attack following a fall, which took her to her eternal home," Dr. Cullom wrote: "I'm sure the change is a blessing to her."

In a second mailing of short articles which he sent out on June 21st, Dr. Cullom described the home as "Earth's Greatest Institution" and cited the Hendricks home in Nash County as a good example. He spoke of a daughter in this home who had suffered with arthritis for many years and of the loving care which had been given her; he wrote of a son who had been in his classes at Wake Forest and who now is an honored teacher in a Seminary; he wrote of the other four sons who are fulfilling "their respective places" as fine Christian citizens. Such a home is "the greatest of earth's institutions" and such a family is fulfilling God's purpose and is blessing the world.

In a second paper, "The First Christians and the Holy Spirit," Dr. Cullom lamented the great, "consuming" emphasis placed upon organization in our church life.

> Organization is needed, but until we can bring the note of personal testimony, our religion will continue to be a formal matter, and be wholly lacking in that element that has in it the spirit of life.
> I wish I knew the Holy Spirit more intimately, and hope my friends will join me in prayer that all of us may come to know him better and be used of Him in making our religion vital and vitalizing.

Dr. Cullom entitled his third article "How to Begin" and stated that the Bible plainly tells us that "the fear of the Lord is the beginning of wisdom." This "fear" is what a son shows his father in respecting, loving and honoring him.

> To the degree that God, our Father, is higher, holier, and more removed from us in nature, to that extent should our reverence for Him, our respect for Him, and our love for Him be greater, more filial, and more trusting, and abundant in spirit than is true of our earthly father. . . . This is what the Book declares to be the beginning of wisdom. . . . May

we open our minds and hearts to receive it and go forth to show and exercise it in all our relationships.

In his fourth paper, "How and Where," Dr. Cullom wrote that without the fear of God, "a man is like a ship on the high seas without a rudder."

> This "fear of God" should appear in a man's home, in his business, when he travels the highway. Nor should he allow himself to make a parade of it. . . . Each person should walk humbly before God, telling before the world in all sincerity and honesty, this guiding star shines for itself. In so doing, he will reap the largest possible reward, and at the same time make the largest possible contribution toward the blessing of his fellows.

In a short article, which appeared in *Charity and Children* of June 28, 1962, Dr. Cullom asked, "Who is My Neighbor?" and said the lawyer of Luke 10:25-37 had had no trouble in recognizing the one who had showed mercy. Dr. Cullom concluded: "It seems to me that any of us could preach a sermon on those five words that came from our Lord's lips when he told that lawyer, 'Go thou and do likewise'."

Dr. Cullom spent the week end of June 29-July 1 (1962) with the Blackmores in Warsaw. He was tired from the trip, but "not overly so." After eating a good supper, a chair was placed in front of the television, and he enjoyed "International Showtime," a circus program, with Julia Ann and John.

Saturday was a rainy day. After breakfast and a short nap, Dr. Cullom brought out copies of the January issue of *The Princeton Seminary Bulletin* (Vol. LV, Number 2). "Jim, there are many good articles in here," he began; "but there is one by Donald Macleod on 'The Creative Preacher' which I should like for you to read and discuss with me." This was readily and joyfully done, with the two heartily agreeing with the words they read:

> Every contemporary gathering of Christian leaders shares a common concern: the church is in need of renewal. And more than a few possess the growing and healthy conviction that renewal can come only by the Word of God. This does not imply, however, an urge to return to bibliolatry or to a sterile biblicism, but to, what Visser 't Hooft has called, "the dynamic situation in which the Holy Spirit opens up the Bible anew." The church cannot renew itself, but "if it allows the word of God to do its creative work, there is always hope for its renewal."
> . . . But who will bring this "clear Word of God to the world"? We need, what Douglas Webster has called, "an instrument releasing the power of the Holy Ghost." The Word of God is destined to do its creative work, but it requires a preacher who is himself creative and who is able to interpret it to the world.

To be creative, Dr. Macleod stated, the preacher must (1) establish his own identity, (2) preserve the integrity of his message, and (3) interpret the response of the worshiping congregation. Dr. Macleod described the creative preacher with his church as "the living organic community who serves as co-workers with their Sovereign Lord in his plan for the redemption of the world."

When the reading was completed, Dr. Cullom said, "It seems to me Dr. Macleod is saying something that is very important for us to hear. I have several other copies which I want you to give to your ministerial friends." And Dr. Cullom himself had opportunity to give copies to two Baptist ministers who came to see him: the Rev. D. E. Parkerson of Warsaw and the Rev. Milton Boone of Mount Olive. Also he left a copy with Mr. and Mrs. Carlyle Powell, retired missionaries to Nigeria. On Sunday he attended church service in Warsaw and when called upon to lead in prayer spoke with a clear voice and tender emotion.

But Dr. Cullom was failing. He was pale and weak. At times he seemed quite confused and welcomed any help which reassured him. He was with loved ones and what might have been embarrassing in other circumstances was passed over with little notice. Upon his return home, Dr. Cullom wrote:

My dear Friends,   July 2
    You probably found my   [sic] in my room at your
house. Please wrap it securely and mail it to me. Use the inclosed
[a check for ten dollars] to purchase gas and oil at your convenience.
Thank you again for all your kindnesses to me. Come to see me if you
come this way.
                                              Cordially yours,
                                              W. R. CULLOM.

(What he could not remember he had left was his razor. It was found in the pocket of the bathrobe he had used.)

In August, Dr. Cullom went to Hamilton to visit the new home for the Aging; when he returned home he was so confused that "Willie" (Mrs. Gill) said he hardly knew where he was.

On September 27th Dr. Cullom entertained Mrs. Emily Becton and her sister for lunch. He was dressed in his best suit and looked much better than he had for some time. He was in good spirit and seemed to have enjoyed having company.

On October 17th, Dr. Cullom wrote that he was "in better plight" than he had been, that he had missed only one of the evangelistic services which Rev. Charles Howard was conducting at Rolesville. As he was feeling much better than he had, the pastor of the Rolesville church took him visiting. Rev. Crate Jones tells that at one place the lady of the house came out to the car; she was dressed in shorts. Later as the two ministers resumed their travel, Dr. Cullom asked: "Crate, what do you think of women wearing shorts?" Mr. Jones hesitated. Dr. Cullom continued, "I suppose it is all right, but I don't care to have that much of my anatomy showing."

At another time, Dr. Cullom's pastor, the Rev. Ben Lynes, came to take Dr. Cullom visiting. As he was helping Dr. Cullom into a low-built car, Dr. Cullom said:

I have seen many changes in automobile design in my time. And
most of the changes have been good, but here is one I think the designers
will discover is bad, and they will change it.

On October 31st, Dr. Cullom spoke in the Campbell College chapel; in his talk he wandered and rambled about and, at times, seemed to have lost his way completely. But President Leslie H. Campbell had prepared the students, and they listened patiently because of what he had been. After the service, President Campbell took his dear teacher to see his mother who would be ninety-seven years old on November 2nd. Dr. Cullom congratulated her upon the forthcoming dedication of the James A. Campbell Memorial Administration Building in honor of her late husband and his dear friend. (See *BR*, Nov. 17, 1962, for a picture of the two.)

On November 13th, Dr. Cullom attended the morning session of the Baptist State Convention in Raleigh. He was recognized and honored by the Convention; he told a news reporter that the controversy over Wake Forest College (which centered around the publication of a book, *The Education of Jonathan Beam*) should be "dropped" before it reached the floor of the Convention and hoped that a committee could work out the difficulty. (*News and Observer,* Nov. 14, 1962.) On the way home from Raleigh, Dr. Cullom said: "I am sure of God's power and victory, but I can't help being pessimistic about man's part in the world's outlook."

In many of his letters during December of 1962, Dr. Cullom included a mimeographed copy of E. H. Emmons' poem, "Pathways."

> When the evenin' shades is fallin'
> At the close of the day,
> An' I'm jest a sittin' round
> A passing of the time away,
> There's a thought that comes to cheer me
> If I'm feelin' kind o' blue—
> Sort o' little prayer o' gratitude
> For crossin' paths with you.

On January 15, 1963, the First Baptist Church of Spring Hope had its annual birthday banquet for Dr. Cullom; he was 96. He seemed to have enjoyed the evening, although he was quite feeble and was awkward in calling people's names.

Later, in the spring (April 30th), Dr. Cullom said he had no appetite whatsoever and "just felt no good." On May 11th he was dressed to go "somewhere"; he thought Edward was coming by to take him to Winston-Salem. "No, Dr. Cullom," replied Jim Blackmore; "you are to come with me for a few days."

Jane, Lawrence Harris' second wife, told that Dr. Cullom had not been eating anything and was very feeble and confused. But he was "game" to go; soon he was seated in the car and on the way. Several times he asked how much farther would he have to go. After reaching his destination, he ate a good supper of pancakes; he and Mr. Howard Blackmore (a bachelor of 85 years of age) kept the household in laughter as the two talked of courtship and marriage. Dr. Cullom slept well;

only once did he wake up during the night. Sunday morning he attended Sunday school and church services in the Sharon Baptist Church of Chinquapin. After a turkey dinner with the Robert Blackmores of Warsaw, Dr. Cullom talked and laughed and sang as Marina and Jane Blackmore played the piano. Then after a nap, he was ready to return to the Sharon Church for Training Union and the evening service. He got to bed a little after ten and, again, slept well. After a hearty breakfast, Monday morning, May 13th, he returned to Wake Forest. The journey back did not seem so far; he talked lively. There was some confusion.

"Jim, I should know; but is your dear mother still living?"

"Yes, Dr. Cullom, we went to see her on Saturday, and she was with us yesterday at Robert's. It is my father who died a few years back."

"O, yes, I remember now. . . . And Jim, who is Ruth's husband?" he asked.

"You mean, her parents; their name is Lillick. They are in Iowa. I am Ruth's husband."

"O, yes; wasn't that foolish of me to ask that?"

"It was only the slip of a word."

After his visit to Warsaw, Dr. Cullom's appetite and interest improved; for two weeks he was "brighter in every way." Then he began to slip backward.

On Friday night, June 14th (1963), Ed Cullom wrote:

> I put father in the new Wake Forest Hospital today at Dr. Mackie's suggestion. He is real weak and run down and sick enough to need hospital care. Has been right in bed all week. I don't believe he is critically ill, but will be unless something can be done to pick him up.

Elizabeth came, but he seemed hardly to notice her. One evening when Lawrence Harris asked if he wanted a banana before he left, Dr. Cullom replied: "Yes, but not here. The people are beginning to come in for the service."

On June 25th, he was rational, except to call Jim Blackmore "beautiful." He was delighted to have parts of John Baillie's *Christian Devotions* read to him; he dozed and seemed asleep until a word was mispronounced and he raised up to correct it. He was interested to learn the news and expressed great concern over the racial tension. In the afternoon, he was not clear; he apologized for being in bed and tried to get up.

His general condition improved some. On July 23rd, Ed Cullom wrote:

> Father is sitting up more and eating better, so has gained a little strength. He is trying mighty hard to get well enough to go home, but is not unhappy out there. He dictated a short story on Dr. Clyde Turner and I hope the RECORDER will use it. He gets mixed up in his thinking but generally it is better than a month ago.

By August 5th, Dr. Cullom was "clear and bright." He asked about the publication of his biography, told that he had thought it wise to put his business affairs in Edward's hand and talked of many things and people.

Then this tender question: "Jim, how is the Kingdom work?" When Dr. Cullom's dinner was brought in, he told his guest to go to the kitchen and tell them to fix something for him. His guest reasoned that Dr. Cullom thought he was at home and so went on his way without inquiring about getting a meal in the hospital. In a few days he received a letter someone had written for Dr. Cullom in which Dr. Cullom expressed his disappointment that his friend had not done as he had asked.

In the hospital, Dr. Cullom had many callers; nurses, doctors and attendants humored and pampered him, and he enjoyed all the attention they gave him. On September 2nd, he was moved from the hospital to the Wake Forest Rest Home which was next door on South Allen Street in Wake Forest. Dr. Mackie described his condition as a general weakening due to arterial sclerosis; he would need nursing care for the remainder of his life.

Dr. Cullom was satisfied to go to the Rest Home; he had rather be at home, but he adjusted himself to his new environment. He told Edward to sell the house and wrote to inquire of his insurance. Every morning attendants in the home got him up into a chair beside his bed. Friends continued to call upon him, and he thought it would be a good idea to get a guestbook so he could keep up with them. Some were hurt that he did not recognize them and did not ask of relatives and friends as he had. But he was always happy to have them come.

On October 17th, he was asleep when Jim Blackmore walked up to his bed. But he awoke at the touch upon his folded hands.

"Dr. Cullom, this is Jim Blackmore."

"Yes, Jim, my boy; it's good to see you. Let me get up."

"No, Dr. Cullom; it's late and soon they'll be bringing in your supper, but I could not let this day end without sharing some of it with you. You know, Dr. Binkley was inaugurated today as the Seminary's second president."

"Good. Binkley is a top man; he'll make a good president."

"He has asked that some of the flowers be sent here for you, and I have brought the prayer Dr. Stealey offered at the inauguration. Would you like for me to read it to you?"

"I don't know anything I would like better to hear. Please do."

And his friend began reading:

> Eternal God, Creator: Thou Source of life and grace and love; Father of our Lord and Savior, Jesus Christ, and of all who through Him are reconciled unto Thee, we thank Thee that in following the leadership of Thy Spirit we are given wisdom to set apart days in time like this inauguration day and thus are made more aware of eternity. We thank Thee for the kindred souls that are met to bless this Seminary in this significant hour of its history. . . .

Dr. Cullom dozed back to sleep; his friend continued the reading until it was finished. Then he sat silently by the bed for a while. When it was time for him to go, he again touched Dr. Cullom's hands.

"Dr. Cullom, I must go now. Shall we have our prayer together?"

"Yes, please."

The friend placed his face near to that of Dr. Cullom and spoke softly into his ear.

When the prayer was finished, the aged saint kissed the younger man on the cheek. "Thank you, Jim, for coming. Thank you for everything you have done."

"Thank you for sharing so much with me, Dr. Cullom. May God bless you and keep you."

Dr. Cullom was asleep almost before his friend left the room.

The sleep deepened; that Thursday night when Dr. Mackie roused him, Dr. Cullom murmured: "I won't be here—" and dropped back into unconsciousness.

By seven o'clock the next morning he was in a coma. The family was notified, and Dr. Mackie had Dr. Cullom moved back to the hospital.

As the nurses were changing him, one of them remarked: "We are glad to have you back. Do you know where you are?"

Dr. Cullom put forth a great effort to say, "Why, I'm back home."

These were his last words. His breathing became shorter and shallower; the kidneys ceased functioning.

Saturday (October 19th) his children stood around his bed; Elizabeth called to him: "Papa, Papa, this is Elizabeth; if you hear me, squeeze my hand."

Feebly his fingers closed for a moment around hers and then relaxed.

All day Saturday he weakened until it seemed that he could not last through the night. In those twilight hours, did Tennyson's lines flow through his mind as they had come so often upon his lips:

> . . . such a tide as moving seems asleep,
> Too full for sound and foam,
> When that which drew from out the bounding deep
> Turns again home.

Dr. Mackie, his beloved physician and friend, stayed on through the midnight hours. The heartbeat grew faint and the pulse feeble. Dr. Mackie was to say: "Like the light in an old gas lamp or lantern, his life burned lower and lower."

One o'clock. Two o'clock. Three o'clock. Three-thirty. Three-thirty-three—as it began to dawn toward the Sabbath morning (October 20th), there was a pause; then, "the whole of weary life at last stood still."

. . . And the light went out.

ages 10 and older.

WHAT BOYS WANT TO KN
ABOUT GIRLS
The former editor of thr
magazines for teenager
with wit, wisdom and c
of questions most of
today's boys about gi
ese. For ages 12-18

WHAT GIRLS WA
ABOUT BOYS
This book an
hundred questi
most frequent
of DATEBOO
girls to b
derstandi
facts wi
YOR CO
MAN
A d
techni
glim
13

story about a little boy who is given
Christmas. For all things—a live camel for
—of all things—a live camel for
Christmas. For all ages.

THE ILLUSTRATED BOOK ABOUT
EUROPE. $4.95.
This book is jampacked with interesting facts and breathtaking illus-
trations. The author covers such
interest areas as ancient history,
statistics on population, climate, principal cities, famous landmarks, major
products and industries of every country in Europe and the British Isles,
including those countries behind the
Iron Curtain. For ages 10-16.

THE ILLUSTRATED BOOK ABOUT
THE FAR EAST. $4.95.
An exotic tour through China, Mon-
golia, Tibet, Korea, Japan, Formosa,
est College, and the Philippine Islands for young
readers 10-16.

THE ILLUSTRATED BOOK ABOUT
SOUTH AMERICA including Mexico and Central America. $4.95.
Absorbing facts and color pictures
guide the reader through the modern
cities and primitive forests of our
neighbor continent. For ages 10-16.

ILLUSTRATED JUNIOR LIBRARY
Popular Edition $1.95
Superb value. Good quality cloth
bindings; handsome full-color jackets.
5½"x8 1/4"

Regular Edition $2.75
Distinguished boxed edition. Full-
color pictures on the sturdy cloth
bindings are matched by those on
the handsome, protective slip cases.
6⅛" x 9¼".

volumes—in a decorative slip case—
is one of the most charming gift
ideas of the season. For ages 3-7.

MY BOOK ABOUT GOD'S WORLD
                          $1.95
Two, three and four line verses
selected directly from the Authorized
King James Version of The Bible,
tell the story of the Creation simply
and beautifully. For pre-school age.

THE NIGHT BEFORE CHRISTMAS
                          $1.95
Clement C. Moore's beloved Christmas classic illustrated in full-color by
the brilliant artist, Gyo Fujikawa.
For all ages.

101 SCIENCE EXPERIMENTS $3.95
A book of science projects cover-
ing air, magnets, electricity, water,
sound, light, simple machines, heat,
chemistry and plants.